CONVENIENCE AND FAST FOOD HANDBOOK

other AVI books

CONVENIENCE AND FAST FOOD HANDBOOK

by MARVIN EDWARD THORNER, Ch.E.
Consultant in Chemical Engineering and Food
Technology
Specializing in the Food Service Industry
Lecturer, The Culinary Institute of America
Hyde Park, New York

WESTPORT, CONNECTICUT
THE AVI PUBLISHING COMPANY, INC.
1973

Preface

Modern man, especially in the highly mechanized and industrialized parts of the Western world, can be compared to a machine, specifically, the automobile. We drive our autos into a service station when it needs fuel, and usually adjacent to the area is a human fueling depot or so-called fast-food establishment. We rush in, fuel our bodies with food and beverages, generally prepared in advance and for the most part served from mechanized equipment. The fueling operations for both man and machine are quick, efficient, and stereotyped. Although the sequence of events may seem a bit exaggerated, the American public as well as residents of a number of European countries, such as Italy, England, Denmark, Sweden and Germany are experiencing and being subjected to this mode of fast food service.

The question usually asked is whether fast food service and its counterpart, convenience foods, are an outgrowth or a development of our times, which computerize and automate our lives. A possible answer is that both these components are a symptomatic outgrowth, and their rapid development is the curative agent necessary to cope with the situation. To further understand this trend we need only look at a number of acute problems facing the food service industry, such as labor shortages, dwindling profits, and demands by the public that fast food service be provided. All these have created the atmosphere and momentum to move ahead in this field.

As this book is being written, about 80% of the food establishments in the United States use some form of convenience foods and automated service (Hertzson 1970). Even those restaurants that are classified as havens for the gourmet are employing some form of these services. There is no doubt that the percentage of eating establishments at all levels will continue to multiply, so that complete menus will be based on this concept.

At the present time the food service industry is in a dilemma. Operators are confused and perplexed. They are faced with conflicting principles and ideas. Convenience foods covering a wide range of items are being offered. New companies are being formed that manufacture and merchandise these items. New equipment covering the entire spectrum of the food service operation is becoming available. Research grants have been allocated to universities for the purpose of exploring advanced techniques in this new facet of the industry. Items such as microwave and convection ovens, although not of recent origin, are being sold in overwhelming numbers. When they are installed the results are not up to expectations, so that a state of confusion exists and problems are compounded.

It is the aim of this book to weld together the numerous facets of this new and exciting concept of food preparation and automated service, and to answer the many questions plaguing those in the field or about to enter it.

The latest technological developments are explained and reduced to practical values. Quality control and purchasing methods are stressed. These can be used as a guide for product improvement and increased profits. Since there are few governmental regulations on grading of convenience frozen or prepared foods, except for the inclusion of additives and percentages of meat in various selected items, operators and purchasing agents must of necessity chart their own course of values.

It should be pointed out that this book is not meant to be a cookbook or menu planner, as there are numerous publications of this type on the market. Basically, it is a primer on the use of equipment and its effects on foods, handling, and preservation. Commissary techniques are explored and bridged to modern concepts of computerized operation. Each section is treated as a separate entity but meshed to the entire food service operation.

The author wishes to acknowledge with gratitude the assistance given by Dr. Martin S. Peterson, former editor of *Food Technology* and presently with the U.S. Army Natick Laboratories, for his critical reading and evaluation of the manuscript; and to Dr. Robert V. Decareau, Publisher and Editor, *Microwave Energy Application Newsletter*, Amherst, N.H., for his professional help in bringing into practical focus the material concerning microwave cookery.

In addition, we take this opportunity to thank the many industrial companies and individuals for their technical aid, photographs, and other illustrative material used in this book.

Leroi Folsom, Culinary Institute of America, Hyde Park, N.Y.
William Fraser, Friendly Ice Cream Corp., Wilbraham, Mass.
Richard C. Funk, National Frozen Food Association, Inc., Hershey, Penna.
Alfred Goldsmid, Culinary Institute of America, Hyde Park, N.Y.
S. L. Greenspan, Designs for Dining, Inc., New York, N.Y.
M. Kaplan, Cecilware Corp., Long Island City, N.Y.
Frank Kelly, G.A. Cinney Company, Cohoes, N.Y.
C. K. Litman, President, Koch Refrigerators, Inc., Kansas City, Kan.
Yvonne McKinney (Mrs.), Brooklyn, N.Y.
Marshall W. Neale, American Spice Trade Association, New York, N.Y.
John J. O'Neil, Vice President, AVI Publishing Co., Westport, Conn.
Mac Rosen, Idle Wild Farm, Pomfret Center, Conn.
Judy Russ (Mrs.)
Don Sanders, M. W. Houck, Inc., Bronxville, N.Y.
Bruce Smith, Editor, *Food Service*, Chicago, Ill.
Robert Sohngen, Litton Industries Inc., New York, N.Y.
Lynne Thorner (Miss), Art Director, Famous Music Corp., New York, N.Y.
Donald K. Tressler, President, AVI Publishing Co., Westport, Conn.
E. W. Williams, Publisher, *Quick Frozen Foods*, New York, N.Y.

AMF Incorporated, New York, N.Y.
Artech Corp., Falls Church, Va.
Automation Service Techniques, Inc., Bridgeport, Conn.
Ballantyne of Omaha, Inc., Omaha, Neb.
Bally Case and Cooler, Inc., Bally, Penna.
Colonial Beef Company, Philadelphia, Penna.
Columware, Inc., Lynwood, Calif.
Crescent Metal Products, Inc., Cleveland, Ohio
Dell Food Specialties Company, Inc., Beloit, Wis.
Duke Manufacturing Co., St. Louis, Mo.
Gulf States Paper, Tuscaloosa, Ala.
Henny Penny Corp., Eaton, Ohio
Hobart Manufacturing Co., Troy, Ohio
Hollymatic Corp., Park Forest, Ill.
Market Forget Co., Everett, Mass.
Micro-Aire Corp., Hackensack, N.J.
National Canners Association, Washington, D.C.
National Cash Register Company, Dayton, Ohio
National Hospital Foods, Inc., Northfield, Ill.
Pelouze Scale Co., Evanston, Ill.
Qualheim, Inc., Racine, Wis.
Raytheon Company, Waltham, Mass.
Sage Laboratories, Inc., Natick, Mass.
Sani-Serv, Indianapolis, Ind.
South Bend Range Corp., South Bend, Ind.
The Bastian-Blessing Co., Chicago, Ill.
The Coca-Cola Company, Atlanta, Ga.
The Cooper Thermometer Company, Middlefield, Conn.
The Procter & Gamble Co., Winton Hill Technical Center, Cincinnati, Ohio
Union Steel Products Co., Albion, Mich.
United Service Equipment Co., Knoxville, Tenn.

MARVIN EDWARD THORNER

April 1972

Contents

CHAPTER 1

History and Concepts

Prior to World War I, E. M. Forster wrote a book entitled "The Machine Stops." He vividly described the collapse of a totally automated civilization. He pointed out that his imaginary world suffered from a loss of all contact with basic human aspirations and became completely uniform. The population, as he described it, was fed on synthetic foods and was supplied with synthetic air. People were completely subjected and became subservient to everything the machine produced. Efficiency became a habit and the people thrived, until one day the machine collapsed by malfunctioning and produced tasteless food, noxious air, and total darkness. This signalled the end of the machine society, and its people died.

A more recent book "Future Shock," by Alvin Toffler, discussed change and the extreme rapidity with which it is presently taking place. The main question posed in this book is whether man is reaching the outer limits of human adaptability to the stresses and strains imposed by dramatic and uncontrolled changes.

Both these books, although written years apart, can be applied to the present state of the food service industry and the thoughts and projections that are running through the minds of many operators.

A Revolution in Foods and Services

The word revolution generally refers to a sudden and dramatic upheaval or sharp change in direction. If we apply this definition to the character of the public feeding industry we can then bring into focus the situation as it exists today.

The industrial revolution of the 19th Century did not occur overnight; many decades passed before the machine was readily accepted. Machines became "co-workers" of man, without supplanting him, as so many feared at that time. A parallel exists with the present transition of the food service industry. However, what is not presently known is the point or stage of this transition that we are now entering.

Because of the complexities of fast-food service, high cost of equipment, the confusion that surrounds convenience foods, and the use of mechanized kitchens and serving facilities, it is the opinion of many in the industry that the changes are too rapid and the results may be disastrous. Those who share this belief, do so as a normal reaction to a revolutionary environment, since time and education are needed to reach the goal of this new food service concept.

AUTOMATED AND FAST FOOD SERVICE

Automation can be defined as a self-activating operation or control of a process, equipment, or system, and is the totality of mechanical and electronic techniques and equipment used to achieve such operation or control.

Fast is defined as acting, moving, or capable of moving quickly, swift, and accomplished in relatively little time: it is expeditious, which combines the senses of rapidity and efficiency.

Both these terms are being applied by food service personnel to describe the modern concept of these food services. For the purposes of this book they are treated as separate entities, since each system has a different approach.

HISTORICAL BACKGROUND

Automated and convenience food services are not entirely new, nor can they be considered an outgrowth of our modern age of technology. As was pointed out in the Preface, a number of factors that exist at the present have created the atmosphere for their acceptance on a broader scale than was possible in the past. Modern techniques of preservation, freezing and packaging, coupled with novel modes of service and new concepts and developments of equipment have helped accelerate the pace within the public food service industry.

Since the beginning of time, nature has provided man with edibles that can be consumed without prior preparation, in the form of nuts, fruits, some vegetables and varieties of marine life. The preservation of a number of foods dates back to Biblical times; preservation by salting, smoking, cheese and bread making have been traced back some 4,000 years. During the latter part of the 18th Century, techniques were discovered for preserving fruits and vegetables by crude methods of canning and bottling. Nicolas Appert, a French confectioner, in 1795, while working in a simple kitchen, observed that food heated in sealed containers was preserved if the container was not reopened or the seal did not leak. Some thirty years later, Appert had developed formulas for processing some fifty different canned foods. In the 1820's canning plants appeared in the United States in Boston and New York. By 1840, canneries were in operation throughout America.

With the advent of canning a variety of preserved prepared foods in every conceivable category became available. A complete line of fruits, vegetables, meats, gravies, macaroni and spaghetti mixtures, fish, condiments, jams, pickles, salads, soup and a myriad of other items too numerous to list were offered to the consumer. During World War I advancements in packaging and preservation methods continued as a means of feeding our armies in Europe. Other major strides in the field were recorded during World War II. The period from 1941 to 1946 signalled not only a dramatic need for prepared packaged foods, but also a concerted effort for the development of fast food-serving techniques and assembly line production commissaries.

The armed services together with their industrial counterpart required prepared foods and quick methods of service. The prerequisites were foods that were palatable and that required a minimum of labor to prepare. Due to labor shortages industrial food establishments were forced to develop make-shift fast food-serving devices. Food vending machines of all types were introduced to ease the critically short labor market and central commissaries were established to mass-produce food. These were centrally located so that they could supply their output to a number of plants within a small radius.

During the post-war period refinements were made in the crude methods introduced from 1941 to 1946. The frozen food industry exhibited wide gains and became a major source of freshly prepared and precooked edibles. Many food concoctions appeared and entire menus were built around them. In addition automation became more sophisticated as new equipment was designed to handle the precooked foods. The vending industry mushroomed as a result of new machines incorporating electronic components that achieved a high degree of automation.

The Birdseye Era

The "father of frozen foods," Clarence Birdseye, in his Gloucester, Mass. laboratories, experimented with a wide range of prepared products, beginning in 1923. In this research he was assisted by Dr. Donald K. Tressler, Clifford F. Evers, Bertha E. Nettleton, Lucy Kimball, James Powers, Stuart MacDonald, Karl B. Norton and Gerald A. Fitzgerald. The results of the work of these pioneers revolutionized the eating habits of the Western world, since this was the beginning of the "convenience food" age.

In 1930 Birdseye began to market frozen vegetables, fruits, meats, and fish in the New England area under his trade name. His ideas were considered premature, and the program did not meet with popular appeal. In addition, the primitive state of distribution, poor freezing control, scarcity of suitable storage facilities, and the economic severity of the depression had a deterrent effect on his program. World War II rescued the infant frozen food industry and it began to flourish. Frozen orange juice concentrate made its appearance in 1945 and became an immediate success. Other frozen items followed, as it now seemed that the public was ready to accept them.

The Age of Convenience Foods

From its humble beginning in the Birdseye laboratories, the age of convenience foods, featuring pre-prepared frozen entrees, started a meteoric rise during 1950. French-fried potatoes spearheaded the surge in the popularity of prepared frozen foods. Sales were mainly in retail stores, but as labor costs continued to rise, the food service industry realized the economies of this product and commenced to use it. Other items soon followed. C. A. Swanson and Sons, Omaha, Neb., introduced Chicken Pot Pie and Chicken a la King. The latter was first prepared and marketed by Birdseye. These were followed by complete dinners packaged on aluminum trays. During 1958 Swanson merchandised these dinners under the "T.V." trade name. The original concept underlying this idea was to meet the television craze sweeping the country and to help feed those viewers who were "glued" to their sets.

During the early part of the last decade the plastics industry developed film that served a dual purpose. Not only did the film protect the contents of the package, but enabled the entire package to be placed in boiling water for heating. The advent of the boilable pouch led to many other novel types of packaging materials and disposable products, including aluminum containers, tab-pull cans, new light-weight steel cans, paper and foil combinations, flexible laminated films and plastic containers.

With advances in packaging and methods of freezing, nearly every conceivable food item appeared on the market. Networks of freezer facilities and storage areas were constructed to accommodate the needs of the frozen food industry. Specially designed trucks and freight cars were constructed to move the vast amounts of frozen food products. The food service industry, because of economic factors and the growth of fast food systems, realized the merits of convenience items, so that service facilities were designed and planned to take advantage of their use. Equipment manufacturers and frozen food processors pooled their resources in the form of research grants to foster methods of handling and reconstituting prepared frozen items properly and efficiently. These efforts brought about the development of microwave and convection ovens, high-speed steam cookers, infrared ovens, automatic deep fryers, char-broilers, thawing refrigerators and new concepts of freezer design.

Development of Fast Food Service

Since prehistoric times the human being, primarily because of his animal instinct has for the most part devoured his food in a ravenous manner. Throughout history the mass of the population ate rapidly and gave little thought to their food. Only on rare occasions, such as religious festivals, did man actually relax while eating. Royalty, the educated and others in the higher social order, consumed their food in an easy and slow manner. Wars, social unrest, revolutions and problems resulting from abnormal acts of nature, such as storms, famine and earthquakes, are the factors chiefly responsible for the inherent rapid eating habits of mankind.

Gradual Changes in Eating Habits.—Modern modes of eating, with the use of utensils and dishes, are of recent origin, dating back about 400 years. The knife, ladle and spoon were the only eating utensils employed by Western man until the 12th Century. The knife or dagger was basically used to cut a chunk of food, which was then held by the hand and devoured. The two-prong fork was introduced in 1100 by the wife of a Venetian nobleman. However, it wasn't until the 16th Century that the four prong fork was widely used in combination with a table knife and spoon. The first fork to appear in America was introduced in Massachusetts in 1630. Towards the end of the 17th Century, tableware such as dishes, serving bowls and other items for the table were generally introduced.

Emergence of Public Feeding.—Concurrent with changes in eating habits was the emergence of public feeding establishments known as taverns, which were built adjacent to or within the confines of an inn. Travellers staying at an inn were fed in the tavern. Local citizens would visit the tavern, not to eat, but to listen to the travellers' narratives of far away places. Soon provisions were made to cater to the demands of the local citizenry, as well as the transient guests. However it wasn't the tavern but the coffee house that became the forerunner of the restaurant.

In 1645 the first coffee house to appear in Europe was opened in Venice. Venetian traders, returning from the Middle East, where the coffee house had become a way of life, prevailed upon local businessmen to open similar shops. The early coffee house was a gathering place for the elite and nobility. The only item sold was coffee. Within fifty years, coffee houses spread throughout Europe. By 1700 there were more than 2000 of them in London alone. As competition increased, so did their forms of merchandising, in order to keep and attract customers. Additional food items were made available, such as desserts and exotic coffee concoctions. The decor also underwent a change from drab bare walls and tables to decorative interiors that became more alluring. Table service was increased, the menu enlarged, and an atmosphere of congeniality prevailed. By 1725 many coffee houses lost their identity and became full-fledged eating places. The term restaurant was not used at that time. It is derived from the French *restaurer*, which means to "restore," and was first used in Paris in 1865.

Although coffee houses were established in America at about the same time, they never became popular. The tavern and ale house met the success in America that the coffee house realized in England. The tavern attracted people from all walks of life and was the forerunner of the eating places opened after the Civil War. In 1827 the Swiss Delmonico family opened the first of ten fine restaurants; however, these establishments did not enjoy popular appeal until many years later.

The Post-Civil War Period.—The period after the Civil War, generally referred to as the reconstruction era, was the start of the modern food service industry. Posh and elegant service restaurants began to emerge in many of the larger cities of the United States. These eating places were frequented by the rich, and many were gathering places for society; but it was not until the latter part of the last century that places catering to the general public were opened. These were small restaurants, operated by families; often they became the haunts of clientele linked by ethnic ties. Immigrants flocking to this country used these small restaurants as gathering places and hospitality centers for meetings with old friends and relatives. The movement of these eating places, such as Chinese and Italian, to other parts of a locality was done either to meet consumer demands or to follow a particular ethnic relocation.

This period also saw the growth and development of the self-service and counter-type eating place.

Fast Food Service in the Drug Store.—About 1850 drug stores began to sell carbonated water. The pharmacist at that time generated carbon dioxide gas and produced sparkling water. This beverage met with instant popularity. In order to create added interest, flavors were incorporated in the carbonated water. As time progressed, separate areas of the drug store were set aside to sell these carbonated drinks. This eventually led to the development of the soda fountain. The inclusion of ice cream, desserts, sandwiches and other quick-service foods soon followed. The counter and stand-up type of eating place apart from the drug store began to flourish at the turn of the century.

The Saloon and the Self-Service Restaurant.—The saloon of the post Civil War era is considered to be the birthplace of the self-service food establishment. Saloons during this period expanded dramatically. Many became the hub of society for the middle and working classes. Their expansion was so rapid, that in the larger cities two or three could be found at many street intersections. Competition was fierce and attractions for the consumer were many. Customers were lured by free food and entertainment. These merchandising gimmicks were given gratis with the purchase of a nickle mug of beer or shot of whiskey. The food was set up in separate areas, usually on counters. The customers helped themselves to as much food as they desired. The usual fare consisted of cold meats, cheeses, hot stews, pickles, hard boiled eggs, bread and rolls. The sandwich era also had its commercial origin at about the same time. The customer found it convenient to place the meat and cheese between the bread, fold the bread and hold it in one hand, which freed the other hand for the beer mug.

The self-service and stand-up methods of food service started as an offshoot of saloons situated in business areas. Food was displayed on counters; customers would help themselves, and paid for whatever they ate after they finished eating. In the early days there were no checks, as the transaction was based solely on the honor system. One of the first of these shops was opened in New York City in 1885, and was known as the Exchange Buffet.

The year 1885 is considered to be the beginning of the mass fast food service industry. The growth of these eating places was phenomenal. The public liked the idea of the fast service and being able to see the various displays of food and dessert. As time went on, styles and methods of self-service changed.

Various Types of Public Feeding.—After 1900 the food service industry progressed at an accelerated pace. The development was orderly, however, and centered around two primary methods of operation: namely, service and self-service restaurants. Service restaurants accounted for all establishments where the food was brought to the guests, whereas self-service required that the guests obtain their food from a table or counter. Each facility was a complete self-sustained production unit. Many had their own bakeries and butcheries.

Until 1946 few changes from these basic concepts occurred. From 1946 to the present time ideas in public feeding changed dramatically, so that many installations in existence consisted of a composite of the two fundamental types of service. The changes in scope and complexities of the industry can best be illustrated by comparing the operations of various forms of self-service facilities.

In-the-Line or Linear Self-Service.—The customer in this type of service selects his food from a departmentalized counter. All the food is on display for selection according to category, such as desserts, salads, and meats and vegetables at the steam table. The customer takes a tray at the beginning of the line and after the selections are made, the items are checked and paid for at the end of the counter. The customer is then free to sit at any location of the dining room he chooses.

Spot Self-Service.—A check is given to the customer as he enters the store. The customer proceeds to the food display counter, makes a selection, and the charge for the food is immediately tallied on the check by a counter employee. When the customer is finished he presents the check to the cashier for payment. This type of service is faster, since the customer does not have to pass along the entire counter but proceeds to the station serving his needs.

"Call" Self-Service.—The customer goes directly to the counter and places his order with a counter employee, who then relays the request to the kitchen. The customer makes his selection from a visible menu board hung behind the counter. The kitchen prepares the order and notifies the counter employee when it is ready. Desserts, beverages and salads are usually on display. The customer may be required to pay for his food as it is received or is given a check and pays on the way out of the store. Many fast food operations have adopted this method. Roadside eateries, such as those featuring roast beef sandwiches, hamburgers, or fried chicken, are examples.

In-the-Line Table Service.—The customer selects his food as previously described under in-the-line self-service. However, when the end of the counter is reached and the food is checked, a waiter or waitress takes the tray to the table. Usually beverages and desserts are served at the table. This type of semi-self-service is popular in the southern section of the United States. Buffet service usually follows this system.

Vending-Hot Entrée Service.—This combination of services is found in a number of industrial or institutional feeding operations. Vending machines are available that dispense beverages, desserts, sandwiches, or salads. However, a hot or steam table is set up to provide two or three featured entrées. The Horn and Hardart Automat chain of restaurants, based in New York City, introduced this type of combination service prior to World War I. However, the original concept emanated from Germany.

CONCEPTS OF FAST FOOD OPERATIONS

In the past a fast food operation generally denoted: (1) any facility centered around a short-order counter, where the customer sat on a stool or remained standing. Typical of these operations were the drug store soda fountain, luncheonette or snack bar; (2) self-service, such as the cafeteria or buffet. However, the use of the term "fast food," when applied to segments of today's public feeding industry, takes on a much broader meaning and covers a wide range of installations.

Fast food service based on current concepts falls into three basic categories: (1) utilization of time-saving equipment; (2) utilization of labor-saving equipment; (3) utilization of self-service devices or methods to reduce labor overhead.

When we apply these concepts to fast food service we find that facilities with or without table service can meet these requirements. Combinations of both are encountered, such as drive-ins, where personnel are needed to wait on those customers in their cars; in addition many drive-ins provide counter or cafeteria areas. Diners are another example of both counter and table service.

The utilization of time-saving equipment encompasses for the most part those developments of recent origin, such as the microwave oven and postmix beverage dispensers. Examples of labor-saving equipment are ware washers, automatic potato peelers and automatic coffee brewers. The utilization of self-service devices or methods to reduce labor overhead include vending machines, cafeteria systems and buffet tables.

Examples of Facilities Employing Fast Food Systems

airline catering	drive-ins	mobile catering
banquet catering	home catering	office catering
buffet service	hospital & college feeding	schools & college feeding
cafeterias	in-plant feeding	take-out counter service
diners	military feeding	vending

In addition, many establishments that are classified as conventional service restaurants are using some form of fast food methods and devices.

Automated Food Systems

When we attempt to apply a specific definition of automation to some of the present modes of fast food service we find that it does not adequately describe the actual operation. The only segment of the industry that might possibly fall into an automated "push-button" classification would be vending, yet even this form of feeding hasn't reached the ultimate goal of full automation. The feasibility of total automation may never become a reality, although many facets of food service procedures and methods of operation are heading in that direction.

Automatic food service is based on computerized systems. These systems rely on electronic data processing, and they can be adapted to monitor nearly every operation within a food establishment. Computerized controls are flexible so that systems can be fabricated to meet the needs of most situations, both large and small. The cost of these devices may be prohibitive for a single unit operation. However, small units are being developed for them.

Installations Using Automated Food Systems.—Successful applications of automated systems have been developed for hospitals, schools, universities, drive-ins, chain and franchise organizations. Hospitals, such as the Providence in Washington, D.C., pioneered a patient-feeding program based on computer control. Although not considered a feeding establishment, the Sara Lee bakery

Courtesy AMF Incorporated

FIG. 1.1. AN EXAMPLE OF AUTOMATION THAT PRINTS A CUSTOMER'S CHECK, KEEPS AN AUDIT TAPE, CALCULATES AND PRINTS THE TOTAL CHECK, GIVES INSTANT INVENTORY, AND MAINTAINS EMPLOYEES' RECORDS

in Deerpark, Illinois, was one of the first in its field to install a fully computerized manufacturing facility.

The following are examples of computerized applications within the food establishment:

(1) Collates customer's orders
(2) Prints customer's bill (see Fig. 1.1)
(3) Assembles orders
(4) Stock and purchasing control
(5) Bookkeeping and accounting control
(6) Payroll
(7) Quality control
(8) Menu and nutritional control
(9) Control of automatic cooking devices

NCR ELECTRA BAR

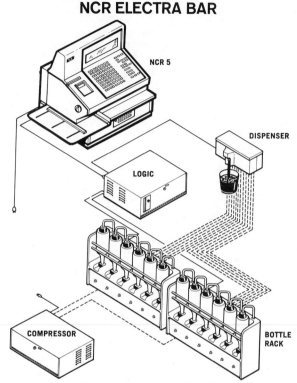

Courtesy The National Cash Register Company

FIG. 1.2. PRESSING ONE KEY POURS, PRICES, PRINTS A GUEST CHECK, RINGS UP AND CONTROLS BAR INVENTORIES WITH THE NCR ELECTRA-BAR SYSTEM

(10) Cash flow, profit and loss statement for any period of the day

(11) Recalls and tallies volume of sales for any given day and will show the effects of weather on sales for a quick forecast

(12) Liquor service, dispensing and serving (see Fig. 1.2)

THE FAST FOOD PREPARATION CENTER

The fast or automated food facility, where the entire activity is based solely on convenience and convenient production, is sometimes referred to as the "kitchenless" restaurant. To use the expression kitchenless is a fallacy, since fully complemented or conventional kitchens and those for the fast food operation are both necessary centers for the preparation and portioning of food. The conventional kitchen is equipped for the complete cooking process, so that a variety of raw or semi-processed foods can be prepared, portioned, and served. Fast foods, for the most part, employ pre-prepared items that also require preparation, garnishing, and portioning. However, the differences between the two are the techniques and equipment involved. If we interpret both concepts within the framework of preparation centers, we can then evolve a better understanding of the basic requirements for proper fast food handling. This concept will aid in the production of acceptable, high quality, and palatable edibles.

Straight-line Production Systems

Fast food preparation is conducive to simple straight-line production. The design and layout of efficient preparation systems are feasible. Efficient production lines were rarely achieved with conventional kitchens. Within the conventional facility the many steps needed to prepare a variety of foods necessitated the re-use, overlap, and back-tracking of equipment, so that effective systems could not be generated without duplicating costly devices, as well as increasing kitchen areas beyond their economic capabilities.

Mobility is a unique advantage of many items of equipment used for the preparation of fast foods. Dollies or wheels are provided so that changes in location can be made in order to meet changes in production. The added advantage of mobility makes for increased flexibility, enabling a number of desirable and efficient systems to be worked out.

The fundamental straight-line concept starts with receipt of raw materials at one end of the plant and shipment of finished goods at the other end. Between the two are raw storage areas, manufacturing and the finished storage adjacent to the shipping. This subject is discussed in detail in Chapter 2.

Essentials of the Preparation Center

The preparation center for a systematized and departmentalized fast food installation revolves around seven prime operating sections or areas. Regardless of the size of the facility or the volume of food, the primary requisites remain the same. It should also be noted that each prime area has subsections appended to it in order to effectively increase productivity and efficiency.

(1) Storage Areas
    Receiving and quality control
    Freezer and "cooler" facilities
    Dry storage
    Thawing sections
(2) Product Assembly Area
(3) Production Areas
    Ovens, e.g. microwave, convection;
    Grills, broilers, fryers and griddles
(4) Garnishing, Portioning Areas
    Holding units
    Garnishing tables plus spice, condiment storage center
(5) Serving Area
    Finished order assembly

Dessert service
Beverage preparation
(6) Ware Washing and Storage
(7) Sanitation Control Center

PRE-PREPARED FOODS

"Soggy," "tasteless," "lacks consistency," "washed-out look," and "what will our customers think," are reasons given by food service operators when asked about their attitude or experiences with pre-prepared foods. On the other hand, those organizations that have embarked on a pre-prepared food program cite the following positive views as to why they have proved successful:

(1) Service has improved; added flexibility resulted.
(2) Food costs have been reduced by waste reduction, less shrinkage, easier inventory and portion control.
(3) Sales have increased since more time and effort are spent on merchandising and customer relations.
(4) Foods and beverages are more uniform after we have mastered the art of their preparation and handling.
(5) Sanitation chores have been reduced.
(6) Reliance on skilled chefs and cooks has diminished.
(7) Overall efficiency and employee morale have improved.
(8) Increase in menu versatility, especially by the addition of nationality foods.

Although the foregoing list exhibits many advantages of pre-prepared foods, two other factors are considered responsible for this dramatic shift from conventional cooking. The demands by the younger generation and young couples have created a major market for quick service and a stereotyped menu. The second reason is that this form of service is a direct outgrowth of our technological society.

What Are Pre-Prepared Foods?

Pre-prepared foods of all categories cover a countless number of items. The exact number of these products is unknown because of the overwhelming introduction of new items.

It is difficult to specify an exact definition of the edibles that fall into this category. Basically a pre-prepared food is one that can be served with little or no preliminary preparation, other than heating or cooling to increase palatability. Smith (1971) has suggested the following terminology: (1) the raw-to-ready scale, (2) readiness values, (3) patron-ready, and (4) value-added foods. Definitions of these terms can be found in Chapter 8, Efficiency Foods.

Pre-prepared foods include many foods and food forms, i.e., fabricated and engineered foods, intermediate moisture foods, dehydrated foods (freeze-dried, natural and artificially dried), bakery products, canned foods, fermented, pickled and cured items, natural foods, pre-prepared frozen foods, convenient foods, and sugar-concentrated items.

Convenience foods are pre-prepared frozen products. These form one segment of a vast industry. The basic categories of convenience foods are: vegetables, fruits, juices, ades, beverages, seafood, meat, poultry, pot pies, soups, specialty entrées, desserts, bread, rolls, snacks, and appetizers.

Pre-Cooked Frozen Meats

In a recent survey taken by *Quick Frozen Foods* it was revealed that the annual growth of pre-cooked frozen meats will exceed 20% a year. This survey did not include poultry products. It did include pre-cooked hamburger patties, cooked meatballs, entrées, meat slices in gravy, corned beef, roast beef, pastrami, shish-kabob, spare ribs, pre-fabricated and pre-cooked veal patties and scores of other items including main courses or entrées.

Pre-cooked hamburgers or charbroiled and specialty burgers are the front runners because of the following advantages: there is almost no further shrinkage and the end-user knows the final size; they are easily heated and do not require grilling, or they may be thawed and eaten as is. Volume feeding establishments, such as sports arenas and schools, were found to be using these products in large quantities. Pre-cooked meatballs are a major item. They form the base for many dishes like spaghetti, soup, and pizzas. Pre-cooked meat slices enjoy excellent sales, and are versatile in that they may be used as the starting point for many dishes (see Chapter 9).

BIBLIOGRAPHY

ANON. 1967. Today's Coffeehouse. The Coffee Brewing Center, New York.
ANON. 1969. Food Service Seasoning Guide. American Spice Trade Association, New York.
ANON. 1970. The Ingredients of ARA Services. ARA Communications Dept., Philadelphia, Pa.
HERTZSON, D. 1970. Frozen foods. Metropolitan Restaurant News 7, No. 7, 29–30.
JENSEN, L. B. 1953. Man's Foods. Garrard Press, Champaign, Ill.
LEMOINE, F. K. 1970. Profile of a Restaurant Organization. The Culinary Institute of America, Inc., New Haven, Conn.
MARTIN, S. 1971. Precooked frozen meats growing at better than 20% annually. Quick Frozen Foods 34, No. 3, 41–45.
RIETZ, C. A., and WANDERSTOCK, J. J. 1965. A Guide to the Selection, Combination, and Cooking of Foods, Vols. 1 and 2. Avi Publishing Co., Westport, Conn.
SIMON, A. L. 1952. A Concise Encyclopedia of Gastronomy. Harcourt, Brace and Co., New York.
SMITH, B. 1971. A new language for today's systems implementation. Food Service 33, No. 6, 8.
SPRITZLER, M. 1971. The manual service line. Vend 25, No. 5, 99–102.
STOKES, J. W. 1969. Food Service in Industry and Institutions. Wm. C. Brown Co., Dubuque, Iowa.

The Fast Food Preparation Center

CHAPTER 2

Preparation Systems

The word "system" is highly regarded by the general public as portraying some kind of mechanical or automated operation and is looked upon with awe. When applied to the conventional food service establishment, a system is usually thought of as something that belongs elsewhere and is not conducive to the preparation of food and its ultimate service to the customer.

Basically food service systems are divided into three groups: computerized or automated, semi-automated, and manual. Any device or method that will form a smooth-flowing, workable bridge between another device or method so as to increase efficiency and productivity is classified as a system. In this regard, a device can be a machine, a work table, a directional sign, a set of instructions, a flow plan or any other item that will lead to greater productivity and reduction in costs.

It is interesting to note the dictionary definition of a system as being a group of interacting, interrelated or interdependent elements forming, or regarded as forming, a collective unit. The definition also refers to a functionally related group of elements, such as a group of interacting mechanical or electrical components. The fast food preparation center is best described by the latter part of the definition.

Systems can be categorized as "organizing" tools, which are used to complete a task efficiently. Systems are aids to management, but do not take its place. They should assist in increasing service without increasing overhead. The success of any system depends on the attitude of employees and their confidence in it. Generally, management's goal in adopting a system is to eliminate unproductive work by combining, rearranging, and simplifying existing procedures, or by introducing new ones. Many small systems may be required to form a full working entity.

Conventional versus the Fast Food Kitchen

Conventional cookery requires numerous operations, types and sizes of equipment, and a host of raw materials. These are converted to a variety of finished products, one step at a time. Regardless of the size of the establishment or the

14

volume of food needed for peak demands, the various preparation and cooking chores are practically identical.

Fast food preparation is adaptable to the so-called assembly line production technique. Systems can be created to control operational flow at any station by simply adding to or subtracting from the numbers of production units in the line. In addition, piecemeal handling, which is so costly for the conventional operation, is sharply reduced.

Size and Shape of the Preparation Center

It is not within the scope of this book to discuss or plan a specific food preparation center. The size and type of a feeding facility have a major bearing on any final layout. The fundamental aspects considered necessary for a systematized fast food preparation operation are, however, discussed.

Since we are dealing with systems that lend themselves to orderly procedures, a sequence of operational steps can be developed that is highly efficient. By following this scheme it is possible to equate this procedure with that of a typical manufacturing plant. Although food service personnel would probably not be pleased with this comparison, we must bear in mind that the successful and efficient modern manufacturing operation is a composite of the basic principles of work simplification and smooth materials flow.

FIG. 2.1. BASIC LINE FLOW PLANT PRODUCTION LAYOUT

Figure 2.1 shows a basic plant layout that generates an efficient and simplified production flow. Figure 2.2 shows a similar flow plan adapted to a fast food preparation center.

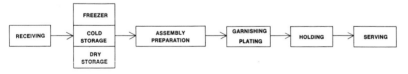

FIG. 2.2. BASIC FLOW PLAN FOR A FAST FOOD PREPARATION CENTER

A major advantage of fast food preparation is its flexibility. Although adequate space is of prime importance, the area does not have to conform to any specific shape, such as a square or rectangle. Portable or movable equipment can be purchased so that a variety of flow arrangements can be worked out to yield maximum efficiency. Use of modular units of equipment, work tables and storage cabinets has aided in promoting effective flow patterns.

Examples of Production Layouts

Any effective arrangement that is suited to the preparation space, so that the flow of work is facilitated without bottlenecks, should be considered. Although this procedure may seem loose-fitting, a tailor-made flow scheme is far better than one that is rigidly designed and poorly suited to the operation.

Conventional kitchens usually follow three operational patterns: (1) straight-line, (2) parallel, and (3) decentralized. Because of the wide flexibility engendered from fast food preparation centers it is found that the following examples of productive patterns may be achieved:

(1) Straight-line	(5) U-shaped
(2) Parallel	(6) H-shaped
(3) Square	(7) T-shaped
(4) S-shaped	(8) B-shaped

Figure 2.3 shows the layout of these patterns. It should be noted that without exception each arrangement produces a forward flow pattern without backtracking or overlapping. Although aisles and walk through areas are not shown, breaks in the pattern can be made without disturbing the overall scheme.

Space Requirements

Space requirements for the fast food preparation center will average 25 to 40% less than its conventional counterpart. The amount of kitchen space to dining room area for the conventional counterpart may range from 40 to 100%. These percentages include all storage areas, production areas, ware washing and waste disposal sections, and employee dressing rooms.

Time-worn ideas pertaining to space needs of the conventional kitchen should be discarded when considering the confines of a fast food preparation center. For example, a range and oven may take up 40 sq ft of space, while one microwave oven will need less than 4 sq ft and a convection oven about 9 sq ft.

A preliminary space estimate can be calculated based on the type of service, namely, cafeteria, table, take-out, counter, banquet, hospital or industrial; the number of items listed on the menu; frequency of service; number of meals served during peak periods; and turn-over of table space. Included in the basic estimate are the total floor space required for receiving, all storage, assembly, preparation, plating and serving, ware washing, waste disposal and employee dressing rooms. The actual job of preparing the estimate necessitates working backwards from service to receiving. Once determination of the number of items to be served, frequency of service, and peak load has been made, a relationship can be established showing the needs of the production area in terms of the number and capacity of the equipment. Next to be considered is the space to be allocated to food assembly, garnishing, plating, beverages, desserts, and service. The number of sinks, all storage facilities, ware washing and refuse disposal areas and receiving space are also determined.

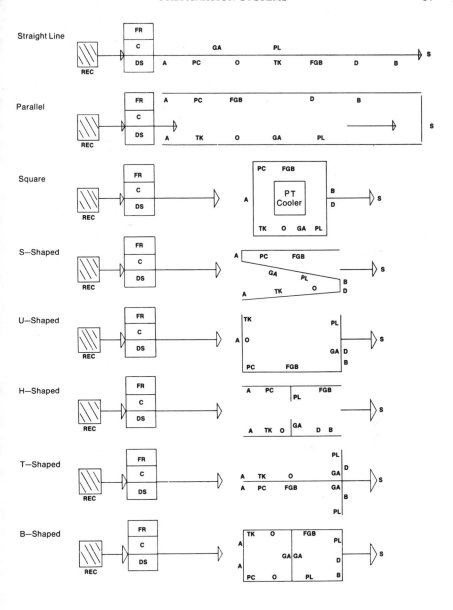

Key To Symbols

A—Assembly
O—Ovens (Microwave, Convection)
PC—Pressure Steam Cooker
FGB—Deep Fryer, Griddle, Broiler
TK—Trunion Kettle

D—Dessert
B—Beverage
S—Serving
Ga—Garnishing
Pl—Plating

C—Cooler
DS—Dry Storage
Fr—Freezer
Rec—Receiving

FIG. 2.3. EXAMPLES OF FAST FOOD PRODUCTION PATTERNS

Operational and production flow patterns require intensive study in order to reduce future problems to a minimum. Installations designed from scratch should receive several intensive studies before equipment location plans are finalized. It is considered a wise investment to employ the services of a facilities designer to ensure the effective workability of the preparation center. Once a prototype has been established for multiple-unit organizations, subsequent designs should follow identical patterns with possible minor changes. Two or three flow plans should be kept available to accommodate various shapes that may be encountered. In the event that an existing operation is to be remodeled or altered, consultation with an expert in the field is mandatory. In either case floor plans can be used to good advantage. Employing scaled down models of all equipment will make the job easier to visualize. These models can be placed in various positions until the most efficient production flow is determined.

The following items should be given added attention so that production snags will be avoided:

(1) Freezer and cooler storage components, considered to be the hub of a fast food preparation center, if not adequately provided for, will create serious bottlenecks. Frequency of food deliveries must be evaluated. Will deliveries be made twice a week, once a week, or once a month? How will adverse weather conditions affect the delivery situation? Another condition that requires study is the number of featured items on the menu, and the rotation period of the entrées. Portion size should also be given consideration. Frequent delivery means that storage requirements can be reduced. However, in any event, when the storage capacity is ascertained, a safety factor of at least 25% for additional area should be considered for future expansion and an increase in business. Dry storage space should be evaluated in the same manner.

(2) It is considered good practice to increase the size of the total preparation area by 25% for future expansion.

(3) Sufficient work space (elbow room) for employees, predicated on peak demands, should be given careful scrutiny. This one factor, if not properly planned, will contribute to low employee morale and a resulting loss in productivity.

(4) Combined with (3) is the need for sufficient aisle space and a flow pattern that will eliminate cross traffic. Sufficient aisle space is a paramount feature where carts or other movable equipment will be used. If a cart is 3 ft wide, aisle space should be provided that is at least 4 ft, so that an employee is not disturbed by the passing cart.

(5) Sufficient counter space adjacent to all equipment is necessary so that ample room is available for plating, garnishing and assembly.

(6) Sufficient slop or utility sinks, conveniently located, will save time and reduce unnecessary walking. Movable sinks, mounted on wheels, are useful. (See Fig. 2.4). Provisions must be made for them, such as quick-attach drain pipes or open drainage troughs. Hot and cold water feeds can be provided by hose or quick-attach pipe assemblies.

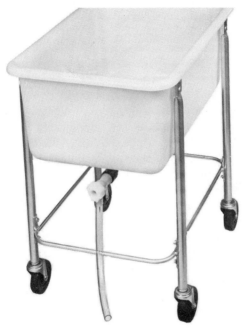

Courtesy Union Steel Products Company

FIG. 2.4. POLY PORTABLE TANK OR SOAK SINK

(7) Ample illumination, adequate ventilation and colorful wall decor should be incorporated in the original design. All these elements will increase and sustain a high level of employee morale, which is directly related to an increase in productivity.

HUMAN ELEMENT, THE KEY TO PRODUCTIVITY

No matter how automatic or systematized a program appears, the key to its continued success is the personnel who operate it. Simplicity in itself is not enough to bring about a smooth-flowing operation. Historical references are numerous and explicit on the subject of assembly line production failures that were caused by "exhausted" or bored labor. Costs per man hour may have been substantially reduced at the onset of a highly organized fast and convenience food operation. As time progressed, noticeable decreases in production were registered, together with an apparent disregard for basic preparation instructions. This situation resulted in unpalatable food, poor service, and loss of business.

The underlying reasons for these events are explained by the application of a field of study called human engineering. Although this term may seem awesome, it came into being to describe problems that arise when man is confronted with technological advancements.

One of the major problems emanating from the machine age concerned man's role as the so-called weak link in mechanized production. Investigation of this problem started about 1885. During the early part of this century the Gilbreths, pioneers in the field of industrial engineering, realized that man and machine could become more closely aligned as effective partners. Motion studies were contrived and evaluations made that determined which individuals are best suited for a particular type job. The motion picture camera was used for testing purposes, and thus formed the basis for the term "motion studies."

The importance of this field was not realized until the involvement of the United States in World War II. During the early stages of the war, it was discovered that the full potential of operating modern weapons and equipment was not being realized. Psychologists and engineers teamed together to investigate the specifics of this momentous problem. The results of these investigations had a marked impact on future machine design. Equipment had to be altered or planned to fit the natural operating characteristics of the human being.

A new, diverse and self-sufficient field of endeavor emerged that helped to pave the way to solving many of man's behavioral characteristics when exposed to machines or systems. The combined efforts of physicians, psychologists, physiologists, and biologists were responsible for many notable achievements in this field. Prosthetic devices or artificial limbs, designed and manufactured to parallel those of the human body, were one of many important contributions from this joint effort. Dr. Allen Russek, M.D. of the Institute of Rehabilitation Medicine, New York, headed a team of scientists who were successful in developing limbs for war veterans, simulating actual body motion. Thousands of limbless veterans were thus able to return to an active and productive life.

Human Engineering in the Food Service Industry

Basically human engineering is that endeavor which seeks to match human beings with modern machines so that their combined output will be comfortable, safe, and more efficient (Abt 1951). In addition it was found that environmental problems of heat, noise, lighting, humidity, and objectionable odors were all related to behavioral attitudes. If any of these factors are below standard, a tendency toward errors, sloppy work, fatigue, and imaginary illnesses is generated. The overall effect is a marked reduction in performance, quality, and profits.

Successful fast and automated food systems require that management attune its outlook towards dual teamwork. This concept will provide the means of achieving an efficient, flawless system of labor teamed with labor, and labor teamed with equipment and material. One of the advantages of fast food systems is that they can be operated without highly skilled employees. This ideal situation can be accomplished only by forming all preparation employees into a cohesive working group, so that if an employee leaves or is sick, a replacement will be able to take over his chores without intensive training. This approach is helpful in alleviating the evils of high labor turnover.

Recognizing the Problem.—The food service industry, for the most part, is a volatile type of business. Many installations are seasonal in nature, most have peak demand periods, and all require instantaneous service. The concepts embodied in this book de-emphasize the art of culinary creativity, and substitute for it repetition, stereotyped production, and service. Creativity of another sort comes into play in garnishing and plating techniques, and the use of new kinds of equipment. Management, in looking for methods of coping with the volatile aspects of this business, is adopting systems because they provide the means of rendering efficient service with the prospects of higher profits. However, unless employees and management are oriented into one entity in order to understand the goals of the operation and the benefits of a proposed system, success will not be attained.

This facet is of prime importance where changes are contemplated from conventional food service methods. Employees, in these cases, must be shown all the benefits of a change-over, such as easier planning, scheduling, less physical work, better working conditions, faster and more efficient service.

If a system does not meet its anticipated goal, a thorough investigation should be instituted by management to locate the causes, so that remedial action can be taken. Many of the causes, once recognized, may be minor, and immediate action to correct them can be a simple matter. Other causes may necessitate major physical alterations. A list of causes that bear investigation follows:

(1) Poor working conditions.
(2) Poor employer–employee relations.
(3) Poor employee–employee relations.
(4) Lack of team work.
(5) Snags in production.
(6) Lack of adequate and simplified instructions.
(7) Not enough equipment.
(8) Poor safety procedures.
(9) Poor sanitation procedures.
(10) Unnecessary movement of materials.
(11) Ineffective use of work space and equipment.
(12) Poor and ineffective communication.
(13) Out of stock or inventory conditions, resulting in frequent menu changes.
(14) Frequent breakdown of equipment, lack of preventive maintenance.
(15) Equipment too complicated to operate.
(16) Equipment controls are inaccessible or too difficult to manipulate.
(17) Equipment poorly displayed or deployed.

Correcting the Problem.—Many of the factors listed above are attributed to environmental conditions within the food preparation center. All will affect the behavioral attitude of the employee. By applying the principles of human engineering, a solution to these problems is possible. Throughout its long history, a large percentage of the food service industry has been guilty of not providing adequate physical surroundings for kitchen employees. Excessive heat, humidity, poor ventilation, poor lighting, and other "dungeonlike" conditions prevailed. Today's labor force will not tolerate substandard working conditions. In addition, fast food and automated service systems will not succeed if they exist.

The "Tired" Employee.—The tired employee will contribute to production snags and breaches in safety practices. Tiredness may not be the result of off-the-premise activities or physical strain. Exhaustion or fatigue will occur from mental upset as a result of the job assignment and uncomfortable environmental conditions. The following remedial actions will tend to decrease mental fatigue: (1) improve illumination; (2) reduce disturbing noise; (3) maintain comfortable physical conditions, e.g., temperature, humidity, and proper ventilation; (4) provide sufficient instructions and communication; (5) equalize the work load; (6) reduce boredom by allowing employees to interchange jobs within their respective departments.

Illumination.—Poor and improper lighting are major factors that affect production efficiency and quality. It is of paramount importance to ensure good illumination at all levels within the preparation center. This is especially necessary where the use of equipment, such as microwave ovens, is dependent on correct control settings to process the food within a specific cooking time. Proper lighting will reduce fatigue, help maintain a steady output, reduce errors, and increase safe working conditions.

Effective illumination should provide uniform lighting over the entire preparation center, including storage rooms, freezer and cooler areas, without shadows and high contrasting characteristics. Because of the importance of this subject, a lighting engineer should be engaged to plan and supervise the installation with respect to fixtures best suited for the facility and their proper location. The effect of light on the human body and a person's mental attitude (Fig. 2.5 and Fig. 2.6) shows the results of good industrial illumination on plant operation.

These illustrations help to stress the relationship of lighting on the efficiency aspects of the human body. Eye-strain, visual discomfort, distraction, annoyance, and lack of concentration, all of which are related to the studies of human engineering, are an outgrowth of poor illumination. Illumination engineering is a composite science comprising physics, physiology and psychology; its object is to produce and control light radiation for the purpose of creating better visual conditions.

Noise Discomforts.—Undue and abnormally high levels of noise will contribute to human physical and mental discomfort. Under these conditions productivity will become erratic, accidents will result, and hearing may become impaired. Certain noises, such as intermittent, high pitched or shrill, are considered to cause the most annoyance. Noise levels are measured in units called decibels. Moderate noise of 50 to 60 decibels can be tolerated, whereas levels of 80 to 90 decibels are in the uncomfortable range. Table 2.1 illustrates those noise levels that are considered acceptable. The ill effects of unwanted noise on the physical

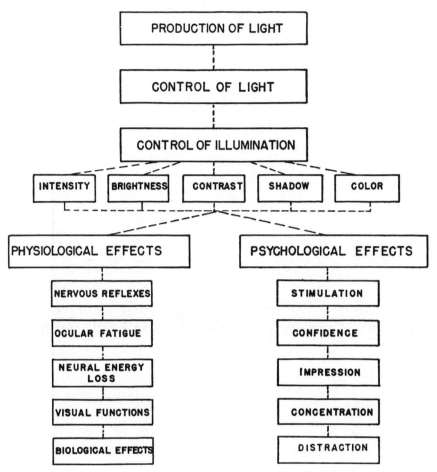

Courtesy *The New York Academy of Sciences*

FIG. 2.5. EFFECT OF LIGHT ON THE HUMAN BODY AND MENTAL ATTITUDE

TABLE 2.1

ACCEPTABLE NOISE LEVELS

Type of Space	Sound Level (Decibels)
Hospitals, conference rooms	30–35
Hotels, motels	35–40
Offices	40–45
Restaurants	45–50

Source: Kazarian 1969.

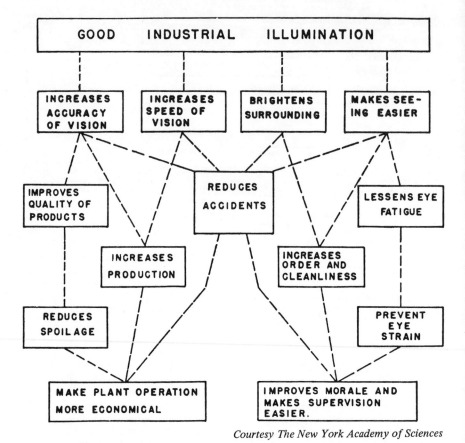

Courtesy The New York Academy of Sciences

FIG. 2.6. THE RESULTS OF GOOD ILLUMINATION ON PLANT OPERATION

well-being of a person were considered important enough for the Congress to enact legislation to help protect workers against increasing dangers from background and impact noise. In 1969 an addendum (Federal Register May 20, 1969) to the Walsh-Healey Act was passed for the worker's protection.

Annoying sounds and noises are controllable. If they emanate from the street, measures should be taken to provide insulating barriers. Lubrication, as a part of protective maintenance procedures, should be applied to wheels, hinges, and other moving parts. Equipment used in fast food preparation centers, for the most part, will operate without adding to the total noise level. If possible, ware washing and waste disposal rooms should be isolated by constructing enclosures around them. Acoustical ceilings, walls and floors are ideal materials to absorb and muffle noise.

Low background music, which has been used by industry for several decades, should be considered as a means of sustaining efficiency. The total absence of noise is considered to be objectionable. Employees working within a noiseless room will tend to react to these conditions by operating more slowly.

Decor and Color Planning.—Dismal, dark and drab interiors tend to create a depressing atmosphere. These cheerless decors have an adverse effect on an employee's morale and fatigue factors. Colors, if properly applied, render the working areas more appealing, aid production, and help to decrease accidents. Color schemes are useful indicators to departmentalize open areas, and to emphasize production flow. Table 2.2 is a useful guide in determining the functional applications of color. Color can also be used on pipes, controls and switches.

TABLE 2.2

FUNCTIONAL USES AND ASSOCIATIONS OF COLOR

Sensation Desired or Association	Best Colors to Use
Attention getting	red, orange, yellow
Warmth	orange, red
Coolness	blue, green, violet
Spaciousness	white, light blue
Closeness	dk. brown, dk. green, dk. blue
Heaviness	black, dark brown
Lightness	white, ivory, cream
Largeness	yellow, white, red
Smallness	black, dark brown
Action or movement	red, orange, yellow
Idleness	white, light blue, light gray
Distress	orange, red, black
Comfort	blue, green, yellow
Contrast	use complementary or warm-cool color combinations.

Source: Kazarian 1969.

Targeting controls with color is a simple method of ensuring safety and reducing errors. The painting of pipes and conduits provides an easy method of tracing leaks and locating sites where other repairs may be needed.

Temperature Comfort Factor.—It is common knowledge that temperature changes combined with humidity play an important role in an employee's moods and physical activities. If the day is hot and humid, he will normally take it easier and find some means to "cool-off." If he is chilly, or is in a draft, the natural tendency is to get more comfortable. If comfort is not obtained, he will become agitated, annoyed and distracted. These symptoms will affect his efficiency and overall performance. Age, sex, clothing worn and type of job are all related to the degree of discomfort and resulting work output.

During the summer 70° F is considered acceptable, while 68° F is deemed comfortable for the winter. Table 2.3 shows the effects of temperature on a person's well-being and performance. The relative humidity, if too high or too

TABLE 2.3

EFFECTS OF EFFECTIVE TEMPERATURE ON WELL-BEING
AND PERFORMANCE OF HUMANS

Effective Temperature F°	Effects
Below 55	Physical stiffness of extremities, increased accidents.
55–65	Discomfort, morale problems, period of adjustment needed.
65–73	Optimum working conditions.
73–80	Discomfort, morale problems, labor turnover.
80–90	Reduced physical and mental output, increased errors and accidents.
90–100	Marked reduction in work capacity, circulatory strain.
100–110	Tolerable for very short periods of times.

Source: Kazarian 1969.

low, will change a comfortable feeling to that of annoyance. During the last decade the United States Weather Service adopted a means of reporting a person's comfort area by the use of the Comfort Index. This Index is a measure of the prevailing temperature and relative humidity.

Designing for Employees' Comfort.—Until recently, if anyone suggested that a kitchen should be made comfortable for employees, the idea would have met stiff resistance. Today, however, these suggestions are taken very seriously as underlying factors for cutting overhead and increasing efficiency.

Are the ceilings too low so that labor feels entrapped? Are the workbenches adequately designed, so that an employee doesn't have to bend or stretch; and if seats are provided, are they comfortable, at the correct height, and with good back rests? These are only a few problems that may arise from poorly designed working areas and work spaces. It is worth the time and effort to analyze these factors, since poorly designed areas will affect the employee's attitude and lead to unproductive work habits.

Improving the Work Area and Working Habits.—The work area should provide ample room without undue stretching or reaching. The following are average dimensions and must be taken into consideration if a person is to perform his chores in a comfortable, fatigue-easing manner:

(1) Average reaching height is 72 in.
(2) Average stooping height is 28 in.
(3) Average close surface reach is 16 to 18 in.
(4) Average maximum extended reach is 29 in.

Between the work surface and the bend of the worker's elbow, 4 to 6 in. of space should be provided. Adjustments in height of the worker's immediate work area can be accomplished by using a 2-in. wooden chop board, which is placed across a metal pan. By using pans of various heights, the height of the work surface can be adjusted to the comfort of the employee.

Improving work habits is possible, as shown by the following examples:

(1) When cutting or dicing food, place a cutting board across a 12 X 20-in. pan or in an 18 X 26-in. pan so that the food will drop into the pan; or place a container on a stool at the end of the work table to catch the food as it is pushed into the container.

(2) All food and utensils needed for a required job should be collected and available before starting the operation.

(3) Plans should be formulated to give one or several people the responsibility of replenishing food and utensils to those whose job requires them to remain in a fixed position, such as on an assembly line.

(4) Workers should be trained to use both hands for certain jobs. The use of both hands will reduce fatigue. For example, put lettuce on two salad plates at a time; place two biscuits on the baking pan; when pre-plating, one hand positions the dish while the other dips the food; when making sandwiches, one hand positions the bread and moves the filled sandwiches, while the other hand spreads the filling.

(5) Save time and energy by using the correct tool, such as a knife specifically designed for the job to be done. Use a French knife and a cutting board when slicing or chopping foods by hand. Use a slicing knife to slice meat. Utility knives may be used for coring vegetables, peeling, etc. Keep all work tools in good condition. This one rule will provide for continued efficiency and reduce accidents. Knives should always be kept sharp. Knife handles should be repaired if broken.

(6) Weigh all ingredients in a recipe to assure accurate measurements.

(7) Where scales are not available, use only calibrated metal measuring cups and/or spoons for measuring ingredients.

(8) Use scoops for filling muffin tins, measuring sandwich fillings, serving mashed potatoes, or rice. To assure standardized portions, keep records of the scoops used. Store them according to size. Scoop size refers to number of servings yielded per quart, whereas ladle size refers to number of ounces each one will hold.

(9) Handy waste receptacles can be made by attaching a large paper or plastic bag to the work table. These can be made to stick to the work table by means of freezer tape.

Industrial Engineering Enters the Food Service Field.—During the past 30 years the application of industrial engineering has produced notable results by increasing manufacturing output many fold. During this period the food service industry was neglected either because of apathy on the part of management, or because the profit structure was deemed sufficient. The need for applying the principles of industrial engineering to the food service field is more apparent now than at any time in the past. This is especially true with the establishment of fast and automated food systems.

The efforts of Professor Edward A. Kazarian in utilizing the concepts of industrial engineering for the feeding industry is considered a breakthrough towards standardization and effective procedural systems. In his book "Work Analysis and Design for Hotels, Restaurants and Institutions," a comprehensive and detailed discussion of the subject and its applications have been developed. This book provides management with a tool to solve productivity problems and and to create efficient systems.

BIBLIOGRAPHY

ANON. 1969. Koch food service bulletin, No. 644. Koch Refrigerators, Inc., Kansas City, Kansas.
ABT, L. E. 1951. Human Engineering. Annals of the New York Academy of Sciences, New York.
ANTIL, F. H. 1970. Training Handbook. Volume Feeding Mgt. *35*, No. 3, 19–26.
BRODNER, J., CARLSON, H. M., and MASCHAL, H. T. 1962. Profitable Food and Beverage Operation. Ahrens Publishing Co., New York.
COFFMAN, J. P. 1968. Introduction to Professional Food Service. Written for The Culinary Institute of America. Institutions Magazine, Publishers, Chicago, Ill.
COPSON, D. A. 1962. Microwave Heating. Avi Publishing Co., Westport, Conn.
KAZARIAN, E. A. 1969. Work Analysis and Design for Hotels, Restaurants and Institutions. Avi Publishing Co., Westport, Conn.
RYAN, J. P. 1970. Design Considerations in Commissary Planning. Vend *24*, No. 4, 22–26.
WARNAKA, G. E. 1970. Is anyone listening? Industrial Res. *12*, No. 10, 21–23.

CHAPTER 3

Storage Areas

Storage facilities for a fast food, convenience-oriented operation are of major importance when considered from the standpoint of the overall scope of the program. This factor assumes further significance when the amount of refrigerated space required to ensure a smooth-running system is determined. Location of storage areas is another item that must be carefully analyzed so that production bottlenecks are avoided. In Chapter 2, it was pointed out that freezer and cooler facilities must be located in an advantageous position so that a workable forward moving system is achieved. In each of the illustrations shown in Fig. 2.3, storage facilities are the focal point for each scheme.

Storage areas fall into four categories, namely: (1) receiving, (2) refrigerated, (3) dry, and (4) refuse. Supplemental or adjunct components consisting of small satellite units to facilitate localized production are also necessary. For example, under-the-counter coolers, dry food and nonfood cabinets, trash and garbage receptacles should be planned or added as required.

Following are the sub-divisions of the four categories of storage areas:

(1) Receiving station
   (a) Loading and unloading dock
   (b) Quality control and/or receiving office
   (d) Interior distribution area
(2) Refrigerated storage
   (a) Freezers
   (b) Coolers
   (c) Thawing units

   This category also includes such units as walk-in refrigerators (coolers and freezers), reach-ins, roll-in cabinets, pass-through refrigerators and upright moveable units.

(3) Dry storage
   (a) Food storage for canned, dry and bottled items.
   (b) Nonfood storage for linen, janitorial supplies, and locker and dressing rooms.
(4) Refuse
   (a) Main refuse collection center containing compactors
   (b) Sub-stations, trash cans and bins

THE RECEIVING STATION

Statistics gathered over the years reveal that poor receiving procedures have the following results: pilferage; accepting underweight merchandise; contamination; and spoilage due to mishandling and merchandise that was received but did not meet specifications. These factors in combination or individually have contributed to severe losses and many business failures.

When measurements are made to determine which step in a feeding operation is the most important, the usual answer is that all are of the same magnitude and equally necessary for a team-oriented, profitable system. However, it is not unusual to find that receiving activities in numerous establishments are loosely knit, and the chores of this important function are relegated to menial labor, without proper supervision and final inspection.

A tightly controlled, highly organized receiving activity is a prerequisite of a successful fast food and convenience service organization. Unlike the receiving function of a conventional operation, convenience foods require quick handling, exacting quality control procedures, and trained personnel possessing good judgment and experienced in interpreting specifications, coding and temperature measurements.

Essential Components and Procedures of the Receiving Area

The receiving area should consist of a covered all-weather loading dock, sufficient interior space to dispel bottlenecks, quality control and/or record office, scales of various sizes, movable bins and other mechanical equipment needed to transport the merchandise to the various storage areas in an orderly, rapid manner.

Unloading Dock and Distribution Area.—The loading or unloading dock or platform should be of sufficient height to accommodate the average truck and 8 to 10 ft in depth. Magnesium dock board runways are useful if a truck is too high for the platform, as these are easily lifted into position. The platform should be at least two truck widths wide. The platform requires a sturdy roof with a 3-ft minimum all-around overhang, so that bad weather does not interfere with unloading. Guard rails and steps are a necessary safety feature. Rubber bumpers should be provided so that a truck does not fracture the face of the platform. Both the platform and interior distribution areas should be of sanitary construction and provided with water drains and hose outlets.

The interior or distribution area should be separated from the loading platform by heavy-duty, double-hung, free-swinging metal doors. Each door should be at least 4 ft wide, and equipped with rubber bumpers and safety wired glass windows for sight safety. Since space allocations are usually a problem, the distribution area should be large enough to assure ease of movement and freedom from jamming or crowding of the incoming merchandise.

Within the interior area, provisions must be made for scales. Scales are manufactured in many shapes and sizes (Fig. 3.1). They are made to rest on the floor, built into the floor or set on a bench. Scales are also marketed to record and print weights. In addition to large scales, it is advisable to equip the quality control office with a small 10-lb capacity check weigher, provided with an under

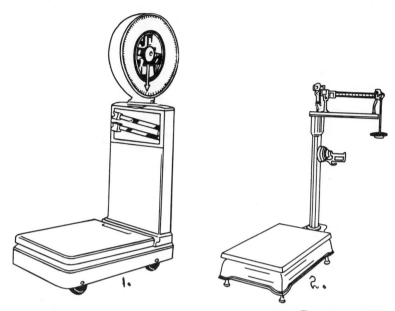

From Anon. (1965)

FIG. 3.1. NO. 1 SHOWS A FLOOR MODEL AUTOMATIC INDICATING-TYPE
SCALE; NO. 2 SHOWS A FLOOR MODEL BEAM-TYPE SCALE

and over tolerance indicator. These small units are ideal to check-weigh small packages of convenience foods.

Mechanical and Mobile Moving Devices.—Mechanical equipment such as conveyors, fork-lift trucks, hand trucks, dollies, bins, movable shelves, and trolleys are a necessary adjunct to a swiftly moving receiving station (Fig. 3.2).

Depending on the location and the distance of the receiving station from the storage areas, rollers or belt conveyors may be practical. If storage facilities are located in the basement, a reversible belt conveyor is a necessity. Volume of merchandise handled, ceiling height, floor loading capacity, and the size of the area to be served are factors that determine the feasibility of using fork-lift trucks. Storage incorporated into central commissaries is ideal for fork-lift, palletized mobility.

Record Keeping.—The practice of maintaining receiving records varies from one organization to another. Record keeping is important, especially for frozen foods and canned goods. Regardless of the variations in record keeping, certain fundamentals are necessary. Methods of recording data are sometimes found to be highly personalized and irrelevant to the operation. Those companies that maintain computerized controls will require recording systems suited to the needs of the programming methods.

Specifically, receiving records should list the following data: name of pur-

Unassembled skid.   Assembled skid.

From Anon. (1965)

FIG. 3.2. EXAMPLES OF MECHANICAL EQUIPMENT

veyor, date and time of receipt of goods, description of the item and brand name. When frozen foods are received, condition and temperature of the re-frigerated truck should be noted, as well as the temperature of the food. Cross checking the purchase order for quantity, weight, specifications, size of item, pack date code, as well as results of a visual examination for defects and damage are also required, and must be made a permanent part of the record. These are necessary for future reference, so that referral to them can be made in cases of contamination or unforseen spoilage attributed to the vendor.

Receiving Procedures.—The following procedures apply to frozen foods and other perishable items.

(1) Arrival of deliveries must be anticipated. Appointments should be made well in advance. Freezer and cooler space should be made available prior to ar-rival of merchandise. Assure stock rotation by moving aside or marking present inventory. Employ the "first-in, first-out" procedure (FIFO).

(2) Mechanical moving equipment should be clean and ready for use.

(3) When the truck arrives, the interior temperature should be noted. Products must not be accepted if their temperature is above $0°F$.

(4) Unloading must be accomplished quickly to minimize exposure to exterior temperatures.

(5) If frozen foods are received with product temperatures in excess of $0°F$, notification should be made to the manager or others in authority, so that quick disposition of the shipment can be made.

(6) Separation of the merchandise or quality checks should not be made on the platform or in interior distribution areas. Merchandise must be moved into the freezer space immediately, where segregation can begin.

(7) Weighing and counting should be done as rapidly as possible to avoid temperature increases.

(8) Segregation within the freezer should begin immediately. Lost time is costly, so that orderly storage by commodity groups is essential, to save extra labor and reduce handling. Inventory control will also be made easier. Cold weather clothing should be made available for employees since a great deal of time may have to be spent in the freezer or cooler during the receiving period.

(9) Labels and case markings should always be visible. This will save time when stock has to be removed to the preparation center.

DETERMINING STORAGE SPACE NEEDS

Many theories and methods have been explored over the years to calculate the amount of storage space required for a food service operation. None of these were practical because of the number of factors that had to be established relating to space needs. With the advent of total convenience food service, conventional theories had to be changed to accommodate the increased importance of freezer space.

Although there are no specific "rule-of-thumb" formulas to follow, one idea that has persisted equates refrigerator needs with the number of meals served. This formula provides 1 cu ft of refrigerated space per person per meal. However, this method has its limitations: luxury restaurants may require more space, whereas schools and short menu establishments need less.

The following basic factors enter into the calculations of storage space requirements: type of menu, number of items on the menu, anticipated volume, future expansion and frequency of deliveries (urban vs rural locations). Another item is the cost reductions given by purveyors if deliveries are less frequent.

In addition to the above, ideas must be postulated concerning the rapidly expanding convenience food market. Introduction of new items is being stepped up; the market is becoming saturated with new and novel food concoctions. This puts a burden on existing storage space. In addition, purveyors will periodically feature a special, run a sale, or reduce prices on volume purchases. To take advantage of these offerings, storage space must be available to receive and properly store this merchandise.

REFRIGERATED STORAGE

Refrigerated storage for a fast, convenience food service operation is a major link in the overall production system. Because of the prominent role that refrigerated facilities play in coupling the preparation center into a unified, smooth-running entity, a great deal of time and effort should be spent in planning and selecting the equipment. A thorough investigation of the advantages and disadvantages of available units and systems is necessary when selecting these facilities. A slow and painstaking approach will tend to eliminate future time-consuming problems resulting from inadequate refrigerated space and poor locations. Failure to solve them can snarl a smooth-flowing system. In addition, the investment for refrigeration required to meet the needs of the modest establishment is sizable; and although many units are mobile and flexible, once they are installed, the chance of changing their location to improve production is remote.

Refrigerated storage falls into three general categories: (1) freezers, (2) coolers, and (3) thawing units. Freezers and coolers are available in many sizes, from small under-the-counter types to massive, self-contained structures. Thawing equipment, the newest addition to refrigerated storage, is an outgrowth of the increased use of convenience foods. These specialty coolers can be adapted from conventional equipment or purchased as separate units. Combination units are available that incorporate freezers and coolers into one entity. The freezer may be placed inside the cooler or located adjacent to it.

Definitions of Refrigerated Storage

Storage Freezers.—These are low-temperature range units that will maintain an even, steady temperature of $0°F$ maximum, and not lower than $-10°F$.

Processing Freezers.—These facilities are used to perform the actual freezing of food at temperatures of $-20°F$ or below. They are specialty units, not generally used as storage freezers.

Coolers.—These are medium-temperature range storage units that hold the temperature at a mean of $38°F$, with a minimum of $32°F$ and maximum of $48°F$. Coolers are used for thawing frozen foods, storing meat at $33–38°F$; storing dairy products at $38–40°F$; and storing vegetables and fruit at $44–48°F$.

Thawers.—These are specially designed to maintain a steady even temperature of $40°F$, regardless of room temperature or product load. Reverse-cycle refrigeration is employed, so that the refrigerant is used for both cooling and heating.

Criteria for the Selection of Refrigerated Equipment

The refrigerated equipment field is broad and diverse. New developments and designs are introduced yearly, so that a complex picture faces the trade. Attempting to evaluate the advantages and disadvantages offered by the manufacturer can become a monumental task. Since refrigerated equipment is expensive and once installed is rarely changed, expert advice should be obtained from a refrigeration engineer or restaurant consultant.

Regardless of the manufacturer or design, there are a number of basic characteristics and general specifications that should be incorporated into refrigeration to meet the demands of a successful operation.

(1) Walk-in equipment should be easily assembled or reassembled to any size, shape, or configuration. Those with prefabricated or modular panels are advisable so that the unit can be enlarged at any time.

(2) Operating costs should be evaluated. These costs become part of the fixed overhead.

(3) Operating controls should be accessible and easy to use.

(4) Interior space should be at maximum, with no obstructions.

(5) Ease of sanitation for both the exterior and interior should be a feature. Units should be sealed against vermin.

(6) Safety features, such as excellent lighting, non-slip floors, a safety lock so that the door can be opened from the interior, sealed explosionproof motors, and waterproof electrical fittings should be included.

(7) Conformance with all governmental health standards and those of the National Sanitation Foundation (NSF) should be a basic requirement.

(8) Proper moisture balance should be easy to maintain.

(9) Guarantees and the reputation of the manufacturer should be evaluated. Ease of service and availability of spare parts deserve consideration.

(10) Insulation must be efficient. This subject is discussed later in the chapter.

(11) Interior storage facilities must be versatile so that various modular equipment, adjustable shelving, mobile cabinets and other accessories can be accommodated.

(12) An effective alarm system should be installed. This should include a high and low temperature signal alarm with visible flashing lights.

(13) Sturdy, reliable thermometers or recording devices should be installed to indicate the average air temperature of the interior (Fig. 3.3). Safeguards should also be installed that ensure the accuracy of the thermometers.

(14) Defrosting devices should be considered, either automatic or manually activated.

(15) Doors should be wide enough to allow the passage of mobile trucks and cabinets. Consideration must be given to the direction the door will open, either left, right, or sideways. Doors should have tight seals and heavy-duty, corrosion-resistant hardware.

(16) The floor level of walk-ins should be even with the outer floor.

(17) The length of time the equipment will maintain its temperature, in case of a prolonged power failure or a malfunction of the mechanical system must be known.

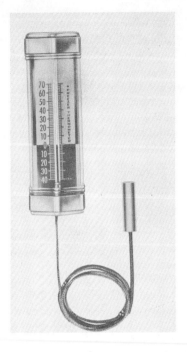 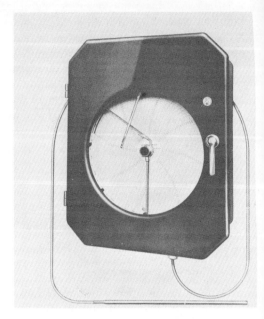

From Anon. (1965)

FIG. 3.3. REMOTE-READING THERMOMETER IS SHOWN AT LEFT; SINGLE-PEN RE-
CORDING THERMOMETER IS SHOWN AT RIGHT

(18) An evaluation of the cooling capacity of the refrigerator must be determined. Factors for this evaluation include ambient temperatures, the number of
times the doors will be opened in a given period, incoming product temperatures,
load and type of product that will be stored. Adequate cooling capacity will
provide refrigeration under extreme conditions of outside temperature and
humidity.

Standards and Regulations

Refrigeration must conform to local, state and federal health regulations. The
U.S. Department of Agriculture, National Sanitation Foundation, and the Frozen
Food Coordinating Committee have promulgated regulations and codes of practice for refrigerator design, safety and sanitation standards and the proper
methods of handling and storing frozen products.

Metals of Construction.—Stainless steel and specially treated aluminum are
widely used for refrigerated construction. Both are easily cleaned, resistant to
corrosion, and durable. Galvanized sheet iron is also employed for the exterior
section of walk-ins. This material is the least expensive. White or colored
enamel that is baked on the steel is used for reach-ins to a great extent. Various
durable plastics, colored to fit the decor of the establishment, are gaining in
popularity.

Insulation.—Insulation is regarded as one of the major components from the standpoint of refrigerator efficiency. Careful consideration should be given to the type of insulating material used. For example, operating costs and moisture balance are directly related to insulation. Insulation should be flame-retardant, rodentproof, impervious to moisture absorption, possess strength and rigidity without excessive weight, should not sag or mat, and should provide maximum efficiency with the thinnest possible walls, to conserve outer and inner space.

Polystyrene blocks or slabs, glass fiber, polyurethane blocks or slabs, and polyurethane foam or froth are insulating materials in common use. Urethane materials have an advantage over other insulators because they combine all the properties required of efficient insulation.

Insulation is rated by its thermal conductivity, or "K" factor. The lower the "K" factor the more efficient the material. Urethane has a low factor rating compared to other materials. For example the "K" factor of urethane is 0.11; glass fiber, 0.24; polystyrene, 0.23; and cork, 0.28. These figures show that urethane has more than twice the insulating value of the other materials. In other words, 4-in. thick urethane is equivalent to 8 in. of the other insulators.

Floors of walk-in or roll-in style refrigerators require properly installed insulation. This area is usually neglected, resulting in a reduction of cooling efficiency and higher operating costs. Several methods are employed to insulate floors. The material is poured between metal sheets in one method; in another, slabs are used which are then covered with metal or concrete coated with tile.

Assembly, Disassembly and Expansion of Walk-ins.—A novel advantage of modern walk-in coolers or freezers is that they are designed for versatile assembly, disassembly, or expansion. Vollrath, for example, provides modular panels of 2 ft and 4 ft increments. These panels are attached by "speed-loc" assemblies. Each panel is locked together to form a rigid bond. The unit is erected by placing the floor sections in position and leveling. Other sections follow until the front is reached and then the door is hung into place. Disassembly to increase size or for relocation can be performed with ease by unlocking each panel (Fig. 3.4).

Door and Entrance Design.—A wide range of door designs is available that meet all operating requirements. These include hinged and sliding entrance doors and hinged access doors. The location of doors and the direction in which they open is important to a smooth-flowing production system. Doors should be located where they will provide the most convenient access, and permit maximum utilization of the interior storage area. This applies to all styles of refrigeration.

Hinged doors are available in both right-hand and left-hand swings. Sliding doors are made to slide either to the right or left, or in bi-parting or split construction. Sliding doors can be equipped with motors so that they open mechanically. A convenient device for opening doors when the hands are full is a foot treadle; applying light toe pressure on the treadle will spring the door open. Locks should be easily opened by finger-tip touch. Magnetic gaskets if used will provide absolutely air-tight seals. Interior safety releases should be provided on all locks installed on walk-in and roll-in refrigerators.

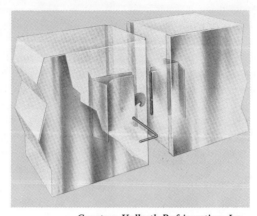

Courtesy Vollrath Refrigeration, Inc.
FIG. 3.4. "SPEED-LOC" AND HEX WRENCH, A QUICK, EASY
WAY TO ASSEMBLE A WALK-IN

All doors must be fully insulated and tight-fitting; otherwise air leakage will add to operating costs and require more frequent defrosting.

Many entrances have heater wires built around the openings. They are concealed behind the metal edge of the jamb and installed on all four sides of the door. These heating wires are thermostatically controlled and provide moderate heat to prevent condensation and frost formation on door edges.

Glass display doors are available in hinged or sliding types. These doors are usually glazed with sealed multiple glass units. Heating devices are built into them to eliminate condensation.

Self-contained and Remote Refrigeration Systems.—Self-contained refrigerated systems are the most popular, since they have many important advantages, such as simplified installation, improved efficiency, fewer service problems and cost economy. Systems are provided for both side-wall mounting and top mounting. These units are all factory-assembled and include condensers, blower coils, and all necessary controls; they are hermetically sealed, fully connected, and ready to operate after electrical and drain connections are made.

Remote refrigeration is sometimes recommended to reduce noise or heat arising from the condensing unit, or if the area is so hot that cooling efficiency will be impaired. Remote systems can be more costly to install and maintain. Installations are usually made by a refrigeration contractor who supplies all necessary valves, controls, switches, wiring, tubing and other accessories.

Modular and Mobile Interiors.—Modular and mobile storage interiors form a necessary part of a systematized operation. Orderly methods of storage for a convenience food establishment must incorporate versatile devices to aid the production flow. These take the form of modular shelves and mobile units. Regardless of the size of the refrigerator under consideration, an intensive study should be undertaken to assure that the interior storage arrangements will fit the needs of the operation.

Shelves are constructed from galvanized or stainless steel. The latter has a higher initial cost, but for ease of cleaning and positive corrosion resistance, the higher cost is offset over the long run. All interior accessories should conform to NSF standards. Raised-front shelf edges are recommended since they keep products from slipping off, and can also be used for affixing labels.

A choice of shelf depths is available to accommodate various pan sizes, i.e., lengths of 36, 48, 60, and 72 inches. Louvers cut into shelves to provide maximum air circulation are necessary; these should be at least 1 inch wide. Shelves are also manufactured from heavy-duty wire which provides maximum openings for air circulation. Shelf support posts should be slotted at 2-in increments to allow for easy adjustment. When determining shelf depth, a knowledge of all package dimensions involved will provide useful data in selecting this equipment. In addition, ample space will be needed for products that have to be stored in original cartons. The size of the carton will determine the space between the shelves and the number of tiers for each selection.

For added versatility, stationary shelf units should be provided with caster housing inserts, so that mobility can be achieved by installing casters on the bottom of the support posts. Casters should be heavy-duty, ball-bearing with neoprene tires, and a wheel diameter of at least 5 in. Two casters should be stationary and the other two of a swivel design with brakes and locking devices. Where mobile units are used, a minimum space of 6 in. per side must be allowed for ease of movement along the aisles of the refrigerator.

Reach-in models require versatile shelving equipment. These should be adjustable and easily removable for sanitation. Mobile storage facilities are available that include trays and pan slides, roll-out shelves and drawers. These are useful accessories that aid smooth-flowing work procedures.

Refrigerator Design to Suit Operational Needs

Modern refrigerators are designed and styled to meet many specific preservation and operational requirements of a food service establishment. They must be selected for a specific purpose that will form an integral part of the flow plan. Sinks, ranges, ovens and other equipment are purchased to perform definite functions. Refrigerators must be selected on the same basis, so that they will "go to work" for the operation. It should also be kept in mind that refrigeration is a continuous function, working 24 hr a day, every day of the year; thus reliability and utilization are major considerations.

The two refrigerator styles in common use are the walk-in and reach-in. Both styles are available as coolers, freezers and combination dual-temperature units (Fig. 3.5). Walk-in types follow the box construction for the most part. The reach-in, or "work-horse" of the food service field, is manufactured in a variety of styles and sizes, with many accessories available to facilitate production, ease of handling and space-saving.

Courtesy Bally Case and Cooler, Inc.

FIG. 3.5. ILLUSTRATED ABOVE IS AN 8 FT X 16 FT X 8 FT 6 IN. BALLY WALK-IN WITH A LOW TEMPERATURE (0°F) COMPARTMENT ON THE LEFT AND A NORMAL TEMPERATURE (35°F) COMPARTMENT ON THE RIGHT

Walk-in Refrigerators.—Walk-in refrigerators possess many advantages for convenience food operations. They are:

(1) Adequate storage facilities to meet any contingency.

(2) Storage for a large variety of foods.

(3) Quantity purchases can be made so that lower food costs will result.

(4) Frequency of deliveries can be reduced, which will decrease handling and labor costs.

(5) Expansion can be effected to meet demands for additional storage space.

(6) They can be used for temporary and quick storage upon receipt of merchandise. This will tend to reduce spoilage and thawing problems. Foods can be checked, inventoried and removed to final storage, all from within the walk-in area.

(7) They provide the means for quick visible inventory checks, since most items, if properly stored and stocked, will be readily seen.

Reach-in Refrigeration.—Reach-in refrigeration has been designed to fit a specific need within a system. Since styling is varied, reach-ins are more than just storage boxes. They have been designed for complete utilization as adjunct members in the production system. The following are a number of reach-in models in current use: under-the-counter, pass-through, mobile or portable, display cabinets, compartment boxes, back-bar units, and standard upright models.

Reach-ins are manufactured in sizes ranging from household units to models of about 90 cu ft capacity. The upright cabinets are generally 6 ft tall, 3 ft deep and in various widths. They are equipped with single, double or multiple doors. The pass-through models, for example, have doors on both front and rear, and are used for storage between preparation and service areas. Pass-through refrigerators save labor and eliminate interference by providing access of two working areas simultaneously. These units become the focal point in a modern fast food preparation center. Various layouts are possible, so that a straight line production system can flow through the refrigerator on to the preparation section.

Another example of an in-line production refrigerator is the under-the-counter drawer unit, placed below the counter or under equipment. It provides instant, on-the-spot storage. These units can be placed below fryers, griddles and salad preparation sections.

Portion Control Refrigeration Systems.—Convenience food systems involve the use of equipment that will facilitate product movement. Refrigerated storage design has kept abreast of these advanced concepts, and many novel and efficient models are being manufactured to meet the needs of this segment of the program.

Storage systems have been devised that simulate the orderly filing of office records and letters. These devices are known as "file-type" storage receptacles; they employ modular containers and pans. Equipment and accompanying accessories permit stacking and storage of all sizes of pans in layers on adjustable sliding devices. They are designed so that the bottom of one container will not press on the food of the container under it. Other advantages include provisions for labeling each tier with the name of the food and the date; removal of food without the necessity of disturbing other pans; and optimum use of refrigerated space.

Odd-sized pans can also be stored in an orderly fashion by adjusting the height of the slider. The one-half, one-third, one-fourth and other small size or fractional pans can be stored without danger of their tipping or getting lost in the rear. In fact, any pan size can be conveniently stored in portion control refrigerator systems.

Figure 3.6 shows the interior of a portion control refrigerator system. The main features are orderly and compact storage, and instant accessibility for all standard full size and fractional size pans and trays. Accessories are available that will convert standard refrigerator units to the needs of a portion control system, and are interchangeable from one cabinet to another.

An interesting development for convenience food refrigerated systems is the mobile floor rack dolly and assembly, that holds many tiers of trays. This accessory makes it possible to load or remove the entire contents of a refrigerator section, and transport it to or from the walk-in freezer and cooler to the preparation center reach-in storage unit (Fig. 3.7). Pass-through refrigerators can be used to advantage with this system. The mobile dolly is pushed into place on one side, and the products removed on the other side when needed.

Courtesy Stouffer Food Division of Litton Industries, Inc.

FIG. 3.6. INTERIOR OF A PORTION CONTROL REFRIGERATOR SYSTEM

Thawing Refrigerators

Thawing refrigerators (Fig. 3.8) are a valuable asset for a convenience food preparation system. They can be purchased in combination units. Their primary function is the rapid and uniform thawing of frozen foods. When there is no thawing to be done, the cabinets operate as standard medium temperature range refrigerators.

Courtesy Koch Refrigerators, Inc.

FIG. 3.7. ILLUSTRATED ABOVE ARE KOCH TWO AND THREE SECTION SERIES E ROLL-IN, ROLL-THROUGH MODELS

Courtesy Koch Refrigerators, Inc.

FIG. 3.8. ILLUSTRATED ABOVE IS A KOCH SAFE-T-THAW RE-
FRIGERATOR SYSTEM

Frozen foods require proper thawing. This operation has been and continues to be a major problem for the proper preparation of convenience foods. Waste, spoilage and texture changes are attributed to poor thawing practices. Rapid thawing, uneven thawing and thawing of certain mixtures during heating, will result in changes in flavor and texture, increase shrinkage, and cause discoloration. Prolonged thawing may also result in microbiological spoilage.

The thawing unit shown in Fig. 3.8 is a dual-temperature refrigerator. It provides mild heat to bring the refrigerator temperature to 40°F when frozen products are placed in it. After the mild heat has adequately thawed the frozen food, an automatic thermostatic control returns the system to normal operation. The thawing action usually takes about 12 hr and is ideal for use during the night, while the food service operation is closed. When business resumes, the properly thawed foods can be portioned for service. Thawing can be done at any time during the day or night, since the pans can be marked and labeled with the date and time that the product was initially stored. As items are withdrawn, the shelves can be replenished with fresh stock removed from the central freezer. If a pass-through cabinet is used, products can be pushed forward when space becomes available and fresh stock placed behind them and held until properly thawed.

Maintenance and Service

It was previously stressed that refrigeration within a convenience food service establishment is the focal point or heart of the system. Because of this impqrtant role, preventive maintenance and a working knowledge of the entire refrigeration system are necessary to eliminate breakdown. Problems of this nature are not only costly in terms of food waste, but a loss of business results if the operation has to close for an extended period until refrigeration is restored.

Cleaning and Sanitation.—Preventive maintenance starts with a strong program encompassing cleaning and sanitation. Dirt is a menace to food and beverages and is also the enemy of the mechanical parts of equipment. Cleaning and sanitation are made easier if the equipment is fabricated from materials that are designed to reduce these chores to a minimum. In this respect, the National Sanitation Foundation has led in the development of designs for easy sanitation so that every part that comes in contact with, or could come in contact with food is readily accessible and can be properly cleaned.

Refrigerator interiors should be washed weekly. This does not mean a casual wiping with a cloth, but removal of all shelving, trays and sliders. Each part should then be soaked in a mild cleaning agent, such as baking soda, rinsed, and sanitized with an approved solution. Exteriors require wiping as often as necessary to keep them spotless. Lemon oil will help prevent finger marks on stainless steel. Spills must be wiped up immediately, this includes drippings on the door frame and around the enclosure surfaces. Drains should be periodically flushed and cleaned. Door and other access panel hardware should be checked, adjusted and oiled once every three months. Door gaskets require frequent inspections to check for air leakage.

The refrigerator condensing unit should be shut off and cleaned. Brushing or vacuum cleaning is necessary at regular intervals, depending on the amount of dirt and dust. The entire unit should receive a complete visual inspection to determine if operating performance is up to standard. Thermometers should be checked for accuracy; this can be done by using another thermometer to check the reading of the instrument built into the cabinet. A record book or log must be kept for each unit. Each time an inspection is performed, or a temperature checked, the results should be entered in the book. In addition, when a repair is made, or an inspection performed by a service company, the observations and type of repair should be logged and retained for a permanent history of each refrigerator.

Defrost Problems.—Most normal temperature equipment is automatically defrosted and needs little attention, except to be sure that it is being done according to the specified cycle. Low-temperature equipment must be defrosted periodically. Automatic defrosters should be checked monthly to see that the mechanism is in proper functioning order. Manual defrosting will depend on use and climatic conditions. Ice on the cooling coils lessens the efficiency of the cooling system. By adhering to a regular schedule, problems of reduced cooling efficiency can be eliminated.

Service Checks.—A major drawback is the lack of qualified refrigerator mechanics. When a problem develops, it requires immediate attention, so that a reliable service company must be retained, preferably on a 24-hr basis. Many multi-unit organizations have their own staff of mechanics on 24-hr duty. In either case, should a unit fail, several things can be investigated that may correct the situation.

(1) Make certain the unit is connected to an electrical supply of the proper voltage and that the correct fuse is placed in the circuit. Many units require a time delay fuse. If the motor is connected by means of an electrical plug-in cord, check it to make certain that contact is being made.

(2) Check the circuit to make sure there are not so many pieces of equipment on the same line that low voltage conditions result. Voltage readings should be taken at the unit terminals while the unit is running, not at the fuse box.

(3) Check the cabinet to be sure it is level. It is almost impossible to seal the doors with a cabinet that is not level.

(4) Check the gasket seal. A loose door seal will allow entry of moisture into the cabinet, which will plug the fin coils or cover the refrigerator plates with frost and prevent proper cooling. Adjustment of door hardware, such as hinges and locks, may tend to correct a poor seal, unless the gasket is worn and needs changing. Check the seal by using a piece of paper or a dollar bill to determine if the seal is tight. Shut the door with the paper in place, grip it and pull forward. A tight seal will make it almost impossible to remove.

(5) Normal-temperature or cooling cabinets should defrost each cycle. If ice is accumulating, see if the control setting is high enough to give a coil temperature of about 40°F on each off cycle. Note the wording "coil temperature." Some units have the thermostat bulb set for the air temperature. In this case, a cut-in or temperature setting above 40°F may be required to assure defrosting. Find the thermometer bulb and see whether it operates on coil or air temperature before resetting. In either case, a cut-in temperature of below 40°F may cause trouble.

If the coil is heavily iced, be sure that all the ice is removed from the entire coil. The face of the coil may be clean while the back or bottom is still blocked with ice. This ice residue will again cause a frozen coil even with proper defrost cycles.

(6) Frozen food storage equipment is defrosted by using a time clock combined with either electric heat or a hot gas defrost method. The first item to check for this system, after the door was examined for leaks, is the time clock. Operate the clock mechanism and check the heaters or solenoid valves for proper function.

(7) A non-operating fan motor or a fan operating during the defrost cycle will cause problems.

(8) Other checks of a more technical nature should cover the inspections of relay and capacitors.

(9) Walk-ins should only be used for master storage. It is not advisable to work out of them. They should be opened infrequently. This procedure will reduce the number of times required for defrosting and will also save operating cost.

DRY STORAGE TECHNIQUES

Dry Storage Demands Exacting Procedures

Proper dry storage controls for the warehousing of semiperishable products are as important as those for frozen and perishable foods. Possibly because of more publicity, training or the knowledge that spoilage is likely to occur, frozen foods are generally handled with greater care than semiperishables. Food service personnel usually lose sight of the need for proper storage techniques when handling canned products and other food items that do not require refrigeration. Dry storage areas in a large percentage of food establishments are a "catch-all" for old equipment, junk and a variety of material that should either be discarded or put elsewhere. Many dry storage areas are in the boiler room, in damp cellars, or spaces that have hot water or steam pipes running through them, or are in the compressor room. These conditions will result in damaged, spoiled or unpalatable foods.

The following techniques should be followed to assure that foods kept in dry storage will not deteriorate:

(1) Dry storage areas must be maintained at high levels of cleanness, should be vermin- and rodent-proof, and should be constructed of materials that can be easily washed.

(2) Dry storage areas should be well planned. Shelving should be adequate and flexible. The entrance should be wide enough to allow passage of hand trucks and dollies. Aisles should also be wide enough to allow passage of mobile equipment and freedom of movement when loading or unloading. Ample space will help in inventory control and stock rotation.

(3) Dry storage areas must be well ventilated and protected from drastic temperature changes. Measures must be taken to guard against freezing temperatures or temperatures exceeding 70°F.

(4) Dry storage areas should be provided with good lighting, so that labels and cartons can be readily identified. Sunlight should be blocked to avoid deterioration from this source.

(5) Dry storage areas must be dry. This includes moisture from sweating pipes, high humidity and dampness due to wet walls or seepage. Items such as cereals, coffee, tea, hot chocolate powder and powdered creaming agents must

be protected from abnormally high moisture conditions that could result in mold formation.

(6) Dry storage areas should be located in the vicinity of refrigerated components, so that the composite forms one operating entity in the production system.

(7) Dry storage areas should have sufficient height and space between shelves. Space should also be provided to pile full cartons or to permit the use of pallets.

(8) Dry storage areas should not be a "catch-all" storage assembly warehouse. Items such as cleaning materials, soaps, paper goods (unless they are used for food preparation), and linens should be placed in separate storage places.

(9) Provisions should be made to contain and place apart odor producing items such as spices. Odors emanating from this source could contaminate such foods as dried beans, coffee and cereal.

Storage Control of Semiperishable Foods

Practically every food item that is put into dry storage will deteriorate, break down, or spoil. Stock movement must be monitored. It is important to maintain the "first in, first out" procedure with dry stores as with refrigerated items.

Supermarket Techniques.—One method that will tend to prevent deterioration is the supermarket display technique. All cases should be marked, separated into categories and dated. The date should denote the arrival day. Codes on cans and packages should be understandable, so that some idea as to when the item was packed can be gained. Goods stacked on shelves should be uniformly stored. Each can or box should be stamped with the date of delivery.

Handling of Canned Foods.—If canned foods are subjected to prolonged storage and temperature extremes, deterioration will become a possibility. High temperatures, for example, will accelerate the action of acids present in some foods. This action may in turn produce pinholes in the metal and darken the interior of the can. Fruit juices, especially citrus products, will develop off-flavors. High temperatures may induce changes in the texture of some foods. Emulsions may be destroyed, although this defect is more likely to occur with freezing temperatures. Mayonnaise, mustard and salad dressing fall into this category.

Canned foods should not be kept over six months even though they may be stored under ideal conditions. It is difficult to determine the length of time foods have been canned prior to delivery even with a knowledge of the coding data. It is for this reason that excess stock should be avoided. The advantage of purchasing large quantities to save money must be weighed against the possibility of spoilage. Other factors to consider with quantity purchases are the amounts of money tied up and the storage space required.

The ideal holding temperature for semiperishables is 60°F. The higher the temperature, the greater the chance of deterioration. For example, at 100°F the overall average shelf life will be reduced by two-thirds. Although 70°F is recommended for dry storage areas, the life of many foods can be extended at lower temperatures.

Several thermometers should be installed in various locations within the storage area, one hung near the ceiling and another midway from the ceiling to the floor. If air circulation is maintained, temperatures should be the same throughout the area. However, for safety insurance, especially during the summer months, temperatures within the entire area should be taken into consideration. Windows facing the sun should be shielded or blocked to avoid deterioration from the sun's rays.

HANDLING FROZEN FOODS

The quality of frozen foods changes with time and temperature of storage. Once frozen foods have deteriorated or have lost their original quality characteristics, it is unlikely that they can be restored to their original state by refreezing.

The techniques of handling frozen foods so that they retain their quality must be mastered. This is a prerequisite of the success of the entire program. It isn't an easy matter to train personnel to handle, store and control products efficiently. Usually those people assigned to these tasks are of marginal quality and in a menial classification, so that the results of their work follow the same pattern.

The first step in meeting the goal of a well organized frozen foods storage operation is to assign to one person the responsibility of running or directing it. In many establishments this assignment does not require full time; nevertheless, the functions of this department must be carried out by one person. He must be responsible for ordering, or advising the purchasing agent when the merchandise is low. His chores include stocking, rotating and the care and cleaning of all food storage facilities, including those satellite units located in the production and serving areas. In addition, he should become familiar with the operating aspects of the equipment, so that if mechanical problems arise he will be able to appraise the situation and call upon authorized repairmen to correct it. This is not a menial job, since it requires a person who is alert, efficient and of good judgement. A certain amount of training must be given the individual, so that he develops a thorough understanding of the reasons underlying proper frozen food storage control. This person should also be given the authority to direct those people who may be assigned to help him if the work load requires it.

Training and Management "Follow-Up"

Management cannot assume a haphazard attitude toward the training program. After an individual has been indoctrinated into the technical aspects of a position, he must be made to realize the importance of his work. If he is encouraged and motivated along these lines, success will be forthcoming. The importance of his department in relationship to the overall operation and to his co-workers should also be emphasized.

Management then has the added responsibility of following up and evaluating his work by periodic checks and inspections to determine if the job is being properly performed. This step is especially significant during the early stages of employment, so that corrective measures can be taken immediately.

Deterioration Is Not Reversible

One of the cardinal rules for proper handling of frozen foods is to maintain the product temperature at $0°F$ or lower. A $10°F$ rise in the temperature of the food can more than double the rate of spoilage. The higher the temperature, the faster the deterioration. Many people are of the opinion that if the food remains in a solid state it is acceptable. Unfortunately, this misconception has dire consequences with regard to quality deterioration. If, for example, a product is allowed to reach a temperature of $25°F$ (the solid state for most foods) for just one day, the resulting lower quality would be equivalent to one or more years of freezer storage. Once damage has occurred it cannot be reversed by giving the food proper storage treatment.

Effects of Intermittent Thawing

Repeated freezing and thawing during storage is detrimental to the quality of frozen foods. As little as a $5°F$ fluctuation in freezer storage temperature above and below the zero mark can be damaging to many foods. Above $10°F$ thawing intensifies the concentration effect. Upon refreezing, water melted from small ice crystals tends to bathe unmelted crystals, causing them to grow in size and form large clusters. This condition can cause physical damage to cellular structure of the food by rupturing and separating the cells. Solid food from living tissues, such as meat, fish, fruit and vegetables is of cellular structure containing delicate cell walls and cell membranes. Within and between the cells is water. Upon initial freezing, this water solidifies and increases in volume by 10%. However, the increased volume does not affect the cellular structure. Intermittent thawing has an adverse effect on frozen emulsions such as butter, ice cream, puddings and pie fillings.

AFDOUS Code Requirements

A significant development relevant to the proper control, handling and storage of frozen foods occurred when a code of standards or practices was formulated and issued on June 22, 1961. These guidelines were developed by the Association of Food and Drug Officials of the United States.

This code is not an official Federal regulation, but it has been adopted by the frozen food industry as a basis for good handling and storage practices. Since its inception, a number of states have incorporated various features of the code into law. Those states with regulatory handling requirements are: Arkansas,

Connecticut, Florida, Georgia, Illinois, Massachusetts, Maryland, Oregon and Pennsylvania. Because of the important and increasing role of frozen foods on the domestic and public feeding levels, full regulatory measures are now being taken by the Federal government and by other states and local agencies.

The code defines *internal product temperature* as the equilibrated product temperature of frozen foods. Temperature provisions of Section B, paragraph 1, are as follows:

(a) All frozen food shall be held at an air temperature of $0°F$ or lower except for defrost cycles, loading and unloading, or for other temporary conditions beyond the immediate control of the person or company under whose care or supervision the frozen food is held; provided that only those frozen foods destined for repackaging in smaller units may be defrosted for such purposes in accordance with good sanitary precautions.

(b) The internal product temperature of frozen food shall be maintained at $0°F$ or lower except when the product is subjected to the above mentioned conditions; then the internal product temperature shall not exceed $10°F$, and such product shall be returned to $0°F$ as quickly as possible.

(1) Internal product temperature for any case of frozen food shall be determined in accordance with the following procedure.

(a) Only when an accurate determination of internal product temperature fails without sacrifice of packaged frozen food shall representative packages or units be opened to allow for inserting the sensing element for temperature measurement to the approximate center of the packages in question.

(2) Internal product temperature of consumer packages of frozen food shall be determined in accordance with the following procedure:

(a) Open the top of the case and remove two corner packages.

(b) With an ice pick or similar tool punch a hole in the case from the inside. Do not use the stem of the thermometer.

(c) This hole is positioned so that, when the thermometer stem is inserted from the outside, it fits snugly between packages.

(d) Insert the thermometer stem about 3 in. Replace the two packages. Close the case and place a couple of other cases on top to assure good contact on the sensing portion of the thermometer stem.

(e) After 5 min read the temperature.

(3) Thermometers or other temperature-measuring devices shall have an accuracy of $±2°F$.

In addition the code contains provisions for sanitation conditions of equipment, buildings and grounds.

Temperature-measuring Techniques

The proper taking of temperature readings requires experience, patience, an understanding of the reasons for obtaining the data, and a knowledge of the product. In Chapter 7, Quality Control, a section is devoted to thermometers and their correct use.

Technical Service Bulletin No. 7 dated May 15, 1969 "Frozen Food Temperatures: Their Meaning and Measurement," should be obtained as a guide for this purpose. This useful information is issued by the National Association of Frozen Food Packers, Washington, D.C. The bulletin outlines in detail correct methods for taking product temperature, describes appropriate equipment for the proper care and handling of frozen foods.

Receiving and Storage Guidelines

(1) Be ready to receive the merchandise and know what is being delivered. Have storage space available for immediate unloading.

(2) Unload the products quickly and move them directly into the freezer.

(3) Follow the instructions for taking temperatures of the incoming food, and make a record of the data.

(4) Segregate the merchandise and stow it in its proper location.

(5) Inspect cartons for damage. Use appropriate sealing tape to repair broken cases or packages. Proper packaging is mandatory for sustaining the original quality. Packaging materials should be moisture and vaporproof to prevent dehydration, discoloration, odor absorption, loss of flavor and oxidation.

(6) Cases and packages should be stacked so that the labels or marks are visible. Additional marking may be necessary to supplement worn or torn labels.

(7) When loading or unloading the freezer, push carts all the way inside and work within the unit. This practice will help to maintain proper freezer temperatures and reduce the entry of moisture.

(8) Keep freezer absolutely clean, neat and sanitary. Don't allow junk, old cartons and other debris to accumulate. Remove and discard damaged food.

(9) Rotate the stock. Know the code or packing date and receiving date. Combine rotation procedures with the stacking operation.

(10) When stacking shelves with small items, use dividers between different products to avoid mixing items. This scheme will save space and make inventory taking easier.

(11) When stacking satellite units or thawing boxes, make a list of items beforehand so that trips inside the freezer can be minimized.

(12) Record all box temperatures every four hours. Report any unusual developments.

(13) Display case type freezers are being used to promote expediency in the preparation area. These are open-top freezers, similar in design to those used

in supermarkets. They expedite the production flow since the items can readily be seen and removed by personnel without stooping. A disadvantage is the need to defrost these open units frequently.

(14) If temporary power failures occur, do not open refrigerators or attempt to move the food. Depending on insulation, ambient temperatures and degree of tightness of the door seals, temperatures should hold for 18 to 24 hr.

Stability of Foods Under Frozen Storage

Stability of precooked and other forms of food continues to be a major area for research and development. The amount of investigation that has taken place during the last two decades has provided the industry with a great deal of information for proper methods of storage, handling and the optimum length of time foods can be held in a freezer without affecting the quality. The following will serve to illustrate the importance of stock rotation and proper temperature.

(1) Some doughs and batters, frankfurters, white sauces and thickened wheat flour-based gravies do not hold up under ordinary freezer storage $(0-10°F)$.

(2) White sauce thickened with waxy rice flour will remain stable for 3 yr at $-10°F$, 1 yr at $0°F$, 2 mo between -0 to $+10°F$, and 3 wk at $+10°F$.

(3) Soups, bread and most meat entrées hold their original quality remarkably well if the products are properly packaged and stored at $0°F$ or below.

(4) Methods of packaging have an effect on foods stored in freezers.

(a) Solid packed foods last longer since less surface is exposed.

(b) Meats covered with gravies and sauce will retain their original quality for long periods of time.

(c) Vegetables packed in liquid will be preserved for long periods.

(d) Foods packed in a nitrogen atmosphere plus a tight vapor- and moisture-proof paper will be protected against oxidative deterioration.

Foods Having Short Storage Life.—Although many precooked frozen foods and baked goods will remain in excellent condition for 6 mo or longer, a few products have a short storage life (2 wk to 2 mo). The following is a partial list of such foods (Tressler, Van Arsdel, Copley, 1968):

Product	Maximum Storage Life at $0°F$
bacon, Canadian	2 wk
batter, gingerbread	3-4 mo
batter, muffin	2 wk
batter, spice	1-2 mo
biscuit, baking powder	1-2 mo
bologna, sliced	2 wk
cake, sponge, egg yolk	2 mo
cake, spice	2 mo
dough, roll	1-2 mo
frankfurters	2 wk

Product	Maximum Storage Life at 0°F
gravy	2 wk
ham, sliced	2 wk
poultry giblets	2 mo
poultry livers	2 mo
sauce, white (wheat flour base)	2 wk
sausage	2 mo

Foods Having Medium Storage Life.—Foods which have a storage life of medium duration as listed below (Tressler, Van Arsdel, Copley, 1968) will remain in good condition for 6 to 8 mo at 0°F or lower. Storage stability is predicated on the formulation, methods of preparation and packaging. The optimum storage life of any food is dependent on many ideal conditions. Therefore, the following list is merely intended as a guide. Rotation and good freezer control should be applied to all products regardless.

chicken, fried	meat loaf
crab	pies, chicken
fish, fatty	pies, fruit, unbaked
fruit, purees	pies, meat
ham, baked, whole	potatoes, French-fried
lobster	soups
meals on a tray	shrimp
meat balls	turkey

Foods Having Long Storage Stability.—Foods of high storage stability should remain in good condition for 12 months or more at 0°F. These products are solid-packed stews, bread, rolls and waffles. A representative list follows (Tressler, Van Arsdel and Copley, 1968):

applesauce	chicken a la king
apples, baked	cookies
bread	fish, lean
bread (rolls)	peanuts
blackberries	pecans
blueberries	plums
cake, fruit	stew, beef
candies	stew, veal
cherries	waffles
chicken, creamed (waxy rice flour-based)	

Product Mishandling Indicating Devices

Product mishandling indicating devices are being introduced to show whether or not an item has been subjected to prolonged abuse at temperatures of 0°F or higher.   Many of these devices have had serious drawbacks.   Some were too expensive to place on each package or master carton. Others could not differentiate between a brief, relatively harmless rise in temperature and a damaging one. Another drawback was the large size so that they could not be fitted on a package.

Recently an indicating device has been developed that has eliminated the major drawbacks; it is claimed to be able to fulfill all the requirements of a useful temperature-warning unit.   These mechanisms are called "irreversible warm-up indicators" and are suitable for use with all forms of frozen foods (Fig. 3.9).

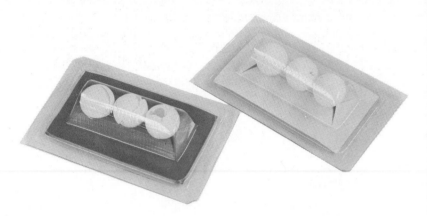

Courtesy Artech Corp.

FIG. 3.9. SHOWN ABOVE ARE TWO IWI® IRREVERSIBLE WARMUP INDICA-TORS; LEFT ARE THE CAPSULES BEFORE DEFROSTING AND RIGHT AFTER DEFROSTING

The following capabilities are claimed:

(1) It is activated only by freezing at very low temperatures.

(2) It can be manufactured to trigger only when excessive temperature has been prolonged for an unsafe period.

(3) It is small and will fit almost any frozen food package or carton (Fig. 3.10).

(4) It is inexpensive.

(5) All materials and chemicals used in the unit are nontoxic and FDA-approved.

(6) The action is irreversible.

(7) The device can be "tailor-made" with melting points to suit the product it monitors.   For example, it can be set for 3°F, 12°F, 32°F, or any other temperature.

Monitoring Mishandling Abuses.—Indicating devices are useful to pinpoint mishandling at any time during transit or transfer.   For example, when a trucker

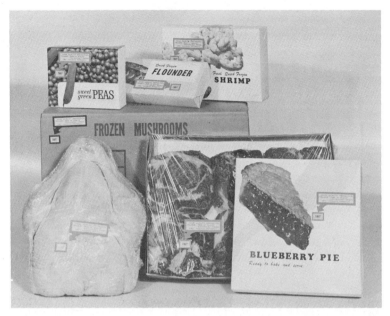

Courtesy Artech Corp.

FIG. 3.10. IWI® INDICATOR CAPSULES WHICH FIT ON MOST FROZEN
FOOD PACKAGES OR CARTONS

receives merchandise from a packer, he is requested to sign a statement that the indicators are normal. When he delivers the products to the final destination, the receiver checks the indicator, and if normal, he signs the receipt showing that the shipment was in good condition on arrival.

BIBLIOGRAPHY

ANON. 1964. A to Zero of Refrigeration. General Motors, Detroit, Mich.
ANON. 1965. Food Storage Guide for Schools and Institutions. Bulletin PA-103. Consumer and Marketing Service, U.S. Department of Agriculture, Washington, D.C.
ANON. 1970A. Code of recommended practices for the handling of frozen food. Frozen Food Coordinating Committee. Washington, D.C.
ANON. 1970B. Bally sectional prefab walk-in coolers and freezers. Bally Case and Cooler, Inc., Bally, Penna.
ANON. 1970C. Freezing activates temperature device which warns of product mishandling. Quick Frozen Foods *33*, No. 8, 43–47.
BARTLETT, R. D. 1970. Servicing Food Service Refrigerator. Koch Refrigerators, Inc., Kansas City, Kansas.
BROOKS, C. 1970. How to select refrigerator equipment. Vend *24*, No. 4, 31–33.
DESROSIER, N. W. 1970. The Technology of Food Preservation, 3rd Edition. Avi Publishing Co., Westport, Conn.
DULANY, R. O. 1967. Development of the frozen food industry in the United States. National Association of Frozen Food Packers, Washington, D.C.
GASCOIGNE, C. E. 1971. Frozen food, standards and regulations. Food Technol. *25*, 522–526.

HAYES, K. M. and BARROW, D. B. 1958. Frozen Food Leaflet R-5. University of Massachusetts, Amherst, Mass.

LITMAN, C. K. 1970. How to determine commercial refrigerator capacity. Koch Refrigerators, Inc., Kansas City, Kansas.

LITMAN, C. K. 1971A. Making refrigeration work for you. Bull. 1196. Koch Refrigerators, Inc., Kansas City, Kansas.

LITMAN, C. K. 1971B. Refrigeration for Convenience Food. Cornell Hotel and Restaurant Administration Quarterly *12,* No. 1, 64–69.

TRESSLER, D. K., VAN ARSDEL, W. B. and COPLEY, M. J. 1968. Freezing Preservation of Foods, 4th Edition, Vol. 4. Avi Publishing Co., Westport, Conn.

CHAPTER 4

The Production Area

The production area of a fast food, convenience-oriented feeding establishment must be designed and equipped for maximum productivity and mobility. The production facilities should be constructed in a minimum amount of space without crowding. Management personnel who have been trained in conventional or traditional modes of restaurant operations often view the preparation facilities of a fast food organization as being "kitchenless." As the tenets of this field are explored and developed, it will become apparent that fast food and convenience preparation centers are far from being "kitchenless." These areas retain all the characteristics of a kitchen, but instead of traditional equipment, they contain new forms of food-preparing devices which enhance production by generating a systematized and efficient flow of activities.

Instead of the kettles, ranges, ovens, power meat saws, choppers, mixers and a variety of pots, pans and utensils usually found in traditional facilities, items such as microwave, infrared, and convection ovens are used to cope with the handling and preparation of convenient and convenience foods. Personnel accustomed to the conventional type of kitchen describe the array of new equipment as highly sophisticated and specialized. These ideas deserve merit, since the traditional kitchen must be fully equipped and adapted to perform many preparations and cooking procedures, from the uncooked ingredients through the many steps required for preparing the finished product. In the fast preparation center, only a few specific units of equipment are necessary for production, since a major portion of the food preparation is performed elsewhere.

Problems of Equipment Availability

Since we are dealing with a relatively new field of food preparation, the problem arises as to which heating device or other form of equipment will be best suited for a given operation. At the present time a great deal of controversy exists regarding the most logical approach to this pressing question. Developments within the equipment industry are moving ahead rapidly. As new ideas are formulated and new models fabricated, older modes of preparation become obsolete, even though the latter may be of recent origin. This situation has resulted in a fragmented equipment industry with little progress towards standardization.

In this chapter, solutions to these problems are developed, since it is now realized that no one piece of equipment can perform all the chores required within a fast food preparation center. Some foods require dry heat, whereas others call for a moist, hot temperature atmosphere. A convection oven may be suited for high volume production, while the same food, served as an individual entrée, can be efficiently prepared in a microwave oven.

In light of these problems, food service personnel must acquaint themselves with the limitations, advantages and specifications of all equipment that is presently available for fast food service. In addition, the proper approach to the selection of equipment is predicated on the type of service, the extent of the menu, and the availability of space.

Guidelines for the Selection of Equipment

When consideration is given to the task of selecting production equipment, the job will become easier and be performed in greater depth if some way is available to compare the merits of one manufacturer with that of another. As a starting point, the following guidelines have been developed for this purpose:

(1) Will the equipment function properly without frequent breakdowns?

(2) Does the equipment need constant adjustment?

(3) Is the equipment designed within the physical limitations of the employee?

(4) Will the entire production system cease to function if one piece of equipment is out of order, so that two may need to be purchased?

(5) Are the methods and procedures designated for the equipment easily understood by the employee?

(6) Are the methods and procedures efficient and practical?

(7) Are the preparation processes completed at the proper time?

(8) Will the equipment perform the functions that it is intended for?

(9) Can the equipment be easily cleaned and sanitized?

(10) Is the equipment the correct size for the operation?

(11) Is the equipment necessary or will it duplicate existing units?

(12) Can performance and reliability be checked with other users?

(13) Is the equipment too costly, so that labor savings, if any, will be offset by the money invested in it?

(14) Is the equipment safe, or does it pose operational hazards?

(15) Can the equipment be installed economically, without incurring undue installation expenses?

(16) Is the equipment movable or mobile so that it can be relocated in conformance with prevailing or future production flow schemes?

(17) Does the equipment carry a manufacturer's guarantee or warranty? For what length of time? Does it cover labor and parts? Are the manufacturer's service people in your area? Are parts easily obtained?

The Kitchen of Tomorrow—Today

At a recent hotel and restaurant convention, a dramatic exhibit was displayed depicting the kitchen of tomorrow—today. It was complete in every detail and well defined. This exhibit demonstrated a kitchen that provided all the advanced concepts of a fast food convenience preparation center. Figure 4.1 shows the layout of this kitchen. It was designed by Philip Golden in association with Designs for Dining, Inc.

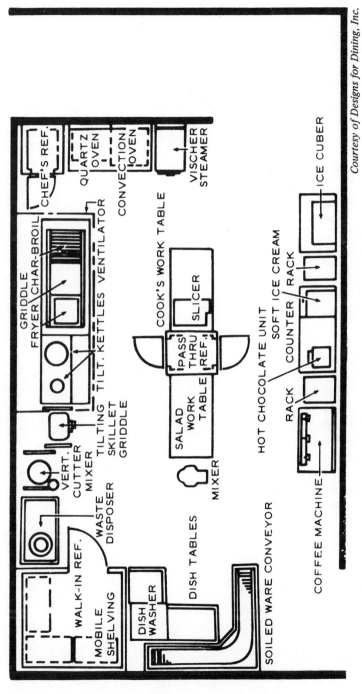

Courtesy of Designs for Dining, Inc.

FIG. 4.1. THE KITCHENS OF TOMORROW—TODAY

The basic features portrayed each section as a complete working entity, yet close enough to one another so that a positive, systematic and efficient work flow was possible.

CATEGORIES OF FOOD COOKING OPERATIONS

Before any measure of success can be achieved in this field, an understanding of the fundamental cooking operations involved in the preparation and production of food must be developed. The following list provides the basic cooking categories and selected examples of each (Copson 1962):

Frying
   (1) deep-fat frying: fish, potatoes, chicken, onions
   (2) pan frying: minute steak
   (3) sautéing: onion
   (4) braising: beef

Roasting
   (1) oven roasting: beef
   (2) barbecuing: chicken

Broiling
   (1) oven broiling: beef
   (2) pan broiling: pork chops
   (3) searing: stew meat, steak

Boiling
   (1) brewing: coffee, tea
   (2) parboiling: ham
   (3) scalding: milk
   (4) simmering: pot roast
   (5) steaming: clams
   (6) double boiling: pie filling, sauce
   (7) stewing: beef, lamb
   (8) blanching: vegetables
   (9) boiling: vegetables
  (10) braising: beef

Baking
   (1) oven baking: pies, cakes, bread, rolls
   (2) oven baking: foamy egg products, soufflés

Thawing

Heating
   (1) precooked foods

Cooling
   (1) desserts, puddings

These cooking operations, with the exceptions of thawing and cooling, are all adaptable to the latest types of heating equipment characteristic of a fast food preparation center. Examples are steamers, deep fryers, microwave, convection and infrared ovens, skillets, broilers and trunnion kettles. The function and application of each type of equipment and its respective cooking category are discussed in this chapter.

DEFINITIONS OF SPECIFIC UNIT FOOD OPERATIONS

Dry Heat Cooking.—Dry heat cooking methods are roasting, broiling and pan broiling. This method produces maximum flavor with less tenderness than most heat cookery is able to do. Dry and intense heat solidifies proteins. This affects the texture by increasing the chewiness. An advantage of dry heating is the formation of an appealing crust which is flavorful, has popular acceptance and helps to retain the juices.

Moist Heat Cooking.—Moist heat cooking contributes to tenderness. The collagenous or fibrous albuminoid constituent of bone, cartilage and connective tissue, in combination with heat and water, change from a chewy textured substance to a tender gelatin. Braising, stewing and pressure cooking are methods of moist heat cooking.

Braising.—Braising is done in a covered utensil in a small amount of liquid. The moist heat gelatinizes the connective tissues, renders a distinctive flavor and a tender product. Pot roast, swiss steak, fricassee are examples of braised foods. Braising is similar to pan frying except that a cover is used, and a small amount of water is added.

Broiling.—Broiling is another form of dry heat cooking. During broiling, surface protein coagulates, juices are retained, fats melt and are absorbed by the lean meat, increasing juiciness, emitting an appetizing aroma and distinctive flavor. Successful broiling is obtained under intense heat. Charcoal or ceramic coals produce the desired heat, but do not contribute characteristic taste or flavor.

Frying.—Frying, such as pan frying, deep-fat preparation and sautéing, are dry heat processes performed in a fat medium. Frying produces an appealing flavorful crust. There are two basic methods, pan and deep fat frying.

Pan frying is the method usually used in the home. A pan or iron skillet are the utensils employed. The latter will produce the best results, as it heats evenly and the heat retention is excellent.

Deep-fat frying is performed in a deep well, equipped with a basket and an automatic temperature control or thermostat. The well must be of sufficient depth so that the fat will more than cover the food. This subject is discussed in detail in Chapter 6.

Pan Broiling.—Pan broiling is a variation of broiling. This method employs the heat of conduction rather than convection or radiation. Pan broiling is usually performed in a heavy, cast-iron skillet. Cuts of meat such as club or minute steak are prepared by this method. Griddle type of equipment, providing that the heat can be controlled and is intense, will give desirable results. Crusts are created in a short time without overcooking the center.

Roasting.—Roasting is a dry heat process. The best results are obtained at low temperatures (325–350°F) under controlled conditions, such as a reliable oven fitted with an accurate temperature-regulating device. Roasting performed under these favorable conditions will produce a product of uniform doneness, with less shrinkage, more flavor and juiciness. Texture will also improve, providing more tenderness.

Sautéing.—Sautéing is similar to pan frying. Small tender pieces of meat are used which must be frequently turned during the quick heating process. Thin slices of veal or veal scallopine are prepared by this method and then garnished with a special blend of sauces and herbs.

Searing.—Searing is a form of dry-heat cooking that produces an appealing crust with a desirable brown color. Searing is performed as a first step prior to microwave heating. Chicken, steaks and chops are foods that are seared.

Stewing.—Stewing is a category of moist-heat cooking that results in a breakdown of the connective tissues. The product is fully covered with a liquid. A properly cooked stew is tender, juicy, will not fall apart, and is not stringy.

CLASSIFICATION OF HEATING EQUIPMENT

Equipment used for heating food is classified in five primary categories, which are based on their heating principles, such as hot air, water immersion, steam, infrared radiation, and microwave radiation (Co and Livingston, 1969). Each type performs a specific heating function. Preparation stemming from a menu composed of a number of selected entrées and other adjunct foods may require more than one specific type of heating device. There are currently available multipurpose units such as a combination convection-microwave oven unit. However, at present, combination devices are not in general use.

Heating equipment is primarily built to reheat precooked frozen foods. The broad spectrum of convenience foods necessitates various kinds of heating which will not affect their quality. Quality factors that will be destroyed by improper heating are color, flavor and texture.

Hot-air or Convection Ovens

Hot-air heating devices are commonly referred to as convection ovens. Heating involves the principle of thermal circulation or currents. Effective heating is obtained by applying the heat near the bottom of the cavity. By employing mechanically driven agitators, like a fan, the heat is distributed rapidly and uniformly. These ovens may be heated by gas or electricity.

Convection ovens have assumed a major role in food service establishments. They are ideal for mass volume feeding production, as well as for small to medium size establishments.

Advantages.—The heated air, which is circulated by a fan, makes uniform contact with the product, replacing the cold layer around it with the flowing hot air. The heat-transfer process is speeded up so that foods are more rapidly processed than in traditional deck ovens. The uniformly heated circulating air also eliminates hot or cold areas, and the food does not have to be turned during the operation. This advantage increases uniformity and overall doneness. Other advantages are: shrinkage is reduced; 25 to 35% less installation space is required than for conventional units; fuel cost is reduced, since convection ovens operate at lower temperatures; versatility is achieved, as this equipment is ideally suited to heat most foods; the operating temperatures are safe for plastic pouches or trays, though the processing time may vary with the packaging material used; foods packed in foil or metal containers may also be heated with safety. Although convection ovens are slower than microwave or infrared ovens, their larger capacity results in a greater mass output.

Accessories and Features.—Convection ovens are made in various sizes, from smaller counter top units to large roll-in ovens. Interior designs are flexible, so that a wide latitude is available to fit them into a number of systematic plans. This equipment will roast, bake, defrost, reheat, reconstitute, and brown.

Models are available that operate as two ovens, each with its own controls. By removing a divider the oven can be converted into a single heating chamber. Roll-in type ovens highly suitable for mass production will accommodate tiers of baskets. Interlocking baskets are stacked on a specially designed cart. The loaded cart is placed in front of the oven and locked into position, and the baskets containing the unheated food are then rolled into the oven.

Many useful operating controls are installed, such as timers, alarm buzzers, thermostats and signal lights. Some ovens are equipped with steam-injection systems to regulate the moisture content within the chamber. This provision is excellent for baked products. Other features are: cooling blower, self-cleaning interiors, and adjustable legs.

Operating Guide.—Regardless of the make or model, experimentation should be performed in order to solve special cooking situations and to learn about the features and operating characteristics of the oven. For example, Table 4.1 shows the time-temperature relationship for various foods prepared in a Market Forge gas convection oven, model M2500. Figure 4.2 is an exterior view of this equipment. The preparation data shown in Table 4.1 should be used as a guide, since the time and temperature will vary with the oven load, portion size, food texture, initial temperature of the food, oven insulation, moisture content of the food, and other mechanical characteristics of the unit.

The following procedures are common to convection ovens:

(1) Never overload an oven or increase heating temperatures to force cooking.

(2) Foods should be uniformly spaced on each shelf, allowing sufficient space between items for positive air circulation.

(3) Preheating is essential. Don't load an oven until the preheating temperature has been reached. Preheating temperatures should be set at about 50°F higher than the final cooking temperature. This method will reduce the temper-

TABLE 4.1

EXAMPLE OF CONVECTION OVEN HEATING INFORMATION

Food Item	Pan Size In.	Recommended No. of Shelves[1]	Temp. °F	Heating Time Min
Bread				
Rolls, white	18 × 26 × 1	3	350	12–15
Bread, white	1 lb loaf	3	350	23–27
French bread	18 × 26 × 1	4	350	20–25
Hot-cross buns	18 × 26 × 1	3	350	12–15
Desserts				
Brownies	18 × 26 × 1	5	350	25–30
Gingerbread	18 × 26 × 1	5	325	20–25
Pies, fruit	8	3	400	35–40
Pies, meringue	8	3	400	5–8
Cake, yellow	18 × 26 × 1	5	350	20–25
Cake, chocolate	18 × 26 × 1	5	350	18–22
Cake, banana	18 × 26 × 1	5	325	20–25
Coffee cake	18 × 26 × 1	3	400	12–15
Pastry squares	18 × 26 × 1	3	400	35–40
Meats, Fish, Miscellaneous				
Meatloaf	12 × 20 × 2½	3	325	60–75
Sausages	18 × 26 × 1	5	375	30–35
Hamburg patties	18 × 26 × 1	9	400	9–12
Turkey, fresh	12 × 20 × 2½	2	300	150–210
Roast beef[2]	12 × 20 × 2½	2	300	150–210
Haddock fillets	18 × 26 × 1	5	350	10–15
Baked macaroni & cheese	12 × 20 × 2½	3	325	25–30
Grilled cheese sandwich	18 × 26 × 1	3	400	10–12
Sirloin steaks	18 × 26 × 1	5	400	10–12

[1] The information provided by this table is for a Market Forge convection oven Model 2500 and 2600. There are nine tracks on the sidewalls of the oven. Five shelves are standard equipment. The correct location of shelves is important for satisfactory results. The tracks are numbered from the top down.

1 Shelf	Track 9	4 Shelves	Tracks 2, 4, 6 and 8
2 Shelves	Tracks 4 and 9	5 Shelves	Tracks 1, 3, 5, 7, 9
3 Shelves	Tracks 3, 6, and 9		

[2] Special racks are recommended for roast beef.
Source: Anon. 1970G.

ature drop when the door is opened for loading. When the oven is loaded the thermostat can then be adjusted for the desired cooking temperature.

(4) If the convection oven is not equipped with automatic steam or water injection, then a pan of water may have to be placed in the oven to maintain an even moisture balance. This is advisable for such foods as meat roasts, fish, poultry and baked goods.

(5) Thermostats and timers should be checked monthly, or when a problem arises with faulty preparation which can be traced to the oven operation. When

Courtesy of Market Forge

FIG. 4.2. GAS CONVECTION OVEN—MODEL M2500 OF INTE-
RIOR DIMENSIONS 27 IN. WIDE BY 24 IN. DEEP BY 20 3/4 IN.
HIGH

checking the thermostat for accuracy use a thermocouple or some reliable oven thermometer (see Chapter 7). Manufacturers usually provide calibration procedures which should be followed for this purpose. Timers should be checked against a reliable stop watch.

Some Results of Improper Oven Operation.—(1) Uneven degree of doneness: oven may be overloaded; oven may have a faulty fan; or food items are placed too close together so that the hot air does not circulate evenly. (2) Underdone food, which may be caused by low heating temperatures. (3) Excessive shrinkage, which may be due to low heating temperatures and long time cycle. (4) Exterior of food may be done or brown and its interior is undercooked; temperature may be too high or food is crowded. Oven load should be reduced and temperature and time may have to be changed.

Water Immersion Heating Devices

Water immersion heating devices are primarily used for the heating of pouch-packed convenience frozen foods. The water temperature is maintained at about 200°F. Individual portions are placed on racks and immersed in hot water for 3 to 10 min. Heating time is predicated on the type and weight of the food. This equipment is considered a specialty item in that it can only be used for pouch-packed heating. Boiled-egg immersion cookers have been in use for many years: the egg is put into a perforated metal cup attached to a chain connected to a timer; the egg and cup are dipped in the hot water and held in position until withdrawn by a mechanism attached to the timer.

Small and medium size operations, featuring pouch-packed entrées and vegetables, have found this type of equipment useful, since it is small enough to fit into a production system without a major installation.

Steam Cookers

Steam cookers are an excellent means of preparing a variety of convenience foods. They heat the food rapidly, and are available in many sizes. Steam cookers are classified into two groups: static and dynamic. They are further subdivided into high pressure (15 psi) or low pressure (5 psi) units, and may operate on either gas, electricity or direct steam.

Steam cookers classified as "static" employ low-pressure steam and are slow heating, especially with thick frozen foods. Dynamic steamers are faster, since the food is exposed to a continuous flow of fresh steam.

This equipment is excellent for heating frozen vegetables, sauce type entrées, and pouch-packed foods. Various modifications are available that will brown breaded frozen products. Foil-trayed items can be heated in several models that prevent moisture from condensing on the lids.

Steam-jacketed kettles have been used for many years, and are generally employed in traditional high-volume kitchens. Their capacity ranges from 5 to 100 gal. They operate on the double-boiler principle, in that heat is transmitted indirectly to the food under preparation. With some improvisations, steam-jacketed kettles can be adapted for the heating of pouch-packed foods. If racked properly, other prepackaged foods can also be heated in them.

Infrared Ovens

Infrared ovens derive their heat from quartz plates installed at the top, or top and bottom of the chamber, generating temperatures of between 650–750°F. Because of these high temperatures, infrared ovens are self-cleaning. Infrared rays are transmitted from the quartz plates to the food. Preparation is effective and can be accomplished with a minimum of scorching. Infrared heat is "long wave" and deep-penetrating, whereas ordinary heat is mostly "short wave" without penetrating ability.

Infrared ovens have not proved popular, even though they are versatile and quick-heating. They are capable of heating multiple portions of frozen or refrigerated entrées in a short time. For example, twelve 4 oz fresh-frozen lobster tails can be prepared in 6 min; or 5 lb of frozen prepared vegetables in 14 min. A 1-in. thick steak will require 2 min per side to reach medium doneness.

Preparation time varies in proportion to the thickness and density of the food product. A sauce-type food about 1 in. thick may require 14 min to prepare from the frozen state, while the same item 2 in. thick will need 22 min.

Browning, if not desired, is controllable, by removing the food from the oven after one half of the heating time has passed. It is then covered with foil and replaced in the oven for the remaining half of the cycle. Infrared heating has a tenderizing effect on meat, such as steaks and chops. Special care should be exercised with these foods. Venting is necessary, and caution is required to avoid grease accumulations.

Foods packed in plastic containers cannot be processed in the standard plate-type oven. They can be cooked in ovens that are provided with pulsed heating in combination with refrigeration. These units tend to reduce surface scorching.

Infrared ovens are manufactured in various models. There are two oven groupings, static and dynamic. The static group is available in 110- or 220-volt models, with or without doors. The dynamic group is in combination with pulsed radiation, refrigeration, freezing, and convection heating. The static group has a capacity from one entrée to a full-size steam-table pan. Dynamic ovens have been developed for volume production of from 100 to 150 portions.

Microwave Ovens

Microwave cookery combines a number of advantages that have been conducive to its phenomenal growth. Among these outstanding features are faster and more efficient work flow patterns, optimum efficiency of personnel, reduction of waste, positive food cost controls, faster customer service, rapid heating, and the possibility of adding new and exotic foods to the menu without the need of highly skilled chefs. In addition, if the food is handled and heated properly, its original flavor, appearance and nutritional values will be retained.

The disadvantages of microwave preparation are important, and must be remembered if problems of poor quality arise. Not all prepared frozen foods can be processed by this method. Items that are breaded will lose their crispness, because the steam generated within the food causes sogginess on the surface. A lack of uniform energy distribution within the oven cavity contributes to uneven heating and an inconsistent degree of doneness. Improper thawing results in inconsistency if the core is frozen while the outer portion is soft. Items packed in metallic containers cannot undergo microwave heating unless certain conditions are met. Foods of different texture and weight require a change in the heating time, since the processing period (cycle) is almost in direct proportion to weight. Ordinary thickened sauces may not heat properly. Some plastic materials cannot be used as dishes, since they may absorb the microwave heat and emit objectionable odors.

This method of heating makes use of time, instead of the conventional time-temperature exposure to heat. Microwaves are generated by a magnetron tube and directed into the oven cavity. The food in the chamber absorbs this energy, which is then converted to heat. The heat is produced by the friction of the fast-moving molecules.

Presently there are available three basic types of microwave ovens: (1) 110-volt, single magnetron; (2) 220-volt, single magnetron; (3) 220-volt, two magnetrons with high and low power selectors. In addition, combination units are manufactured that combine microwave with infrared browning units, and microwave with convection preparation. For high-volume use, conveyorized continuous operating devices are obtainable. See Chapter 5 for further details on microwave cookery.

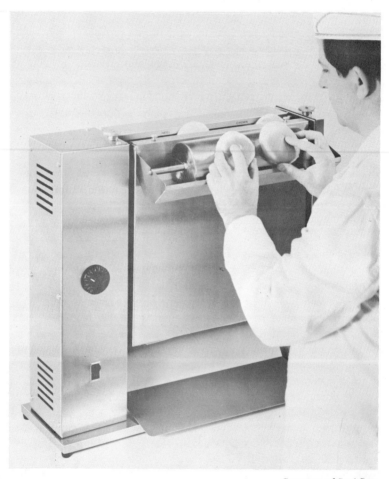

Courtesy of Sani-Serv

FIG. 4.3. HIGH VOLUME TOASTER

Toasters

Bread toasters are considered to be traditional equipment that has been in general use for decades. However, fast food establishments are finding them useful for heating certain forms of convenience foods.

Two designs are available: (1) the battery or "pop-up" type; (2) continuous or conveyor unit. The former is a familiar piece of household kitchen equipment. Battery toasters of various sizes, holding up to eight slices of bread per setting, are in common use within feeding establishments. The conveyor or continuous toaster consists of a flexible vertical moving metal belt. The product is placed on a cleat and is slowly moved upward, facing the heating elements. The upward movement toasts one side of the product. As the product descends, the opposite side is exposed to the heat source and toasted. These units are operated by gas or electricity.

The wide use of toasters within fast food operations is primarily due to the availability of a number of items which can be easily prepared by this method. Products such as frozen tarts, small pies, waffles, canapes wrapped in a flaky crust, pastries and muffins are ideally prepared in the toaster. Large-volume toasters are suited for high-speed heating of hamburger rolls. These are usually placed adjacent to the griddle. Figure 4.3 shows a high-volume toaster capable of producing 700 complete buns an hour. A roller and reservoir is shown at the top that conveniently butters the roll before it is placed in the toaster.

SHORT-ORDER PREPARATION EQUIPMENT

Short-order cookery is an old art and is no doubt the forerunner of today's fast food preparation systems. Some form of short-order production is found in nearly all public eating places in the United States. Vast multiunit companies, such as McDonald, White Tower, and Kentucky Fried Chicken, base their entire operation on short orders. In addition, restaurants established on fast food concepts usually contain short-order cooking equipment to enhance and round out a menu.

The following is a list of short-order cooking equipment and examples of food prepared in each group:

(1) Deep fat fryers
   French-fried potatoes
   fried seafoods
   onion rings
   meat cutlets
   some vegetables (eggplant)
   fried chicken
(2) Griddles
   eggs
   potato cakes and "home fries"

sausages
meat patties
ham, bacon
steaks (minute, club)
hamburgers
frankfurters
sandwiches
(3) Tilting Griddle Skillets
onions
sauces
Chinese food
fish products
pork
pork products
braised meat
chicken
(4) Broilers
lamb chops and patties
pork products: ham, bacon, sausage
beef products: steak, patties, tenderloin
chicken halves
seafood: fish, lobster, shrimp

Deep Fat Frying

Frying is done by two methods: (1) in a pan or on a flat surface using a small amount of fat or shortening; (2) by immersion of the food in a bath of hot liquid fat, oil, or shortening. The latter is known as deep-fat frying.

Deep-fat frying is the most widely employed method of frying, since the finished food is enjoyed by an overwhelming segment of the public. The popularity of deep-fat fried foods in restaurants stems from the appealing taste and aroma rarely achieved in the home. Deep frying is economical. Waste and spoilage are low because nearly all deep-fried products are cooked to order.

Modern deep-fry equipment has been a boon to this method of cooking. Many fryers are automatically operated and possess reliable temperature controls. They are easy to keep clean and to operate.

A detailed discussion of this subject can be found in Chapter 6.

Griddles

Griddles are considered the "indispensable" equipment, as they continue to fill an expanded role in fast food service concepts. About 70% of all types of food service installations have one or more griddles. Aside from this useful cooking role, griddles are appealing to the eye and have a favorable effect on the customer. Because of this, griddles are installed within view of the customer wherever possible.

Courtesy of Cecilware Corporation

FIG. 4.4. HIGH SPEED ELECTRIC GRIDDLE

Griddles are flat metal surfaces heated from underneath by gas or electric (Fig. 4.4). Their dimensions vary from small flat surfaces measuring 2 ft square to large 15 sq ft units. The small or light-duty griddle has a capacity for about 500 ¼-lb hamburgers per hour. The large or heavy-duty griddle will prepare up to 2500 ¼-lb hamburgers per hour.

Griddles are manufactured for permanent installation or as mobile units. Mobile griddles can be used in various preparation areas depending on the food being prepared. Optimum productivity results from mobility, especially during peak period volume. Automatic griddles are available. These consist of a revolving flat surface on which the food is placed, heated on one side, and flipped over so that the opposite side can be prepared. A metal guide or knife pushes the finished food off into a warming container. Automatic griddles are used for continuous high-volume hamburger production.

When selecting a griddle the following factors should be considered:

(1) type of heating source;
(2) capacity or volume per hour;
(3) comparison of labor-saving features;
(4) space requirements;
(5) ease of cleaning;
(6) reliability of temperature-control device;
(7) will the operation be enhanced by the use of a small mobile unit plus a small permanently installed griddle?

Broilers

Broiling is one of the most important methods of food preparation in commercial establishments and the home. The popularity of broiled foods stems from the pioneer days. Broilers in the shape of salamanders were incorporated into the earliest domestic stoves. With the spread of diet fads, broiled foods of all kinds have increased during the past decade.

Broiling is a combination of intense heat and a dry atmosphere. The intense heat is directed to the product's surface which browns and seals the exterior. This action eliminates dehydration and prevents the formation of a soft stew-like texture. The distinct and popular flavor of broiled foods is the result of the coagulation of protein which occurs at high temperatures. Thick portions of food are not suitable for broiling because of a tendency to produce an uneven degree of doneness. The outer surface of the product appears to be properly heated, leaving the center portions raw to rare. Broiling is adaptable to such items as chops, steaks, fish slices, poultry, some vegetables and casseroles.

Broilers are built in many shapes and sizes. Models are available that operate on either gas or electricity. In addition to conventional broiling equipment, specialty units such as char-broilers have gained a substantial following within the wide spectrum of the food service industry. Basic broiler designs encompass the conventional single-unit, combination griddle and broiler, salamander, char-broiler or grill, the rotisserie and vertical broiler. The vertical model consists of two upright heating surfaces and a vertical double grate that holds the food in a clamp during preparation.

Broilers can also be purchased that contain radiant infrared ceramic or Nichrome mesh elements. Infrared waves are long and penetrating. The rapid broiling operation is flameless and smoke-free. Cooking temperatures are reached in seconds and the heat is sustained at peak efficiency during heavy use. High productivity is generated per square foot of heating area because of the rapid and efficient heating. For example, a 1-in. thick steak will reach a rare degree of doneness in 4 min, allowing 2 min of heating per side; for medium doneness the time is 2½ min per side and for well doneness 3 to 3½ min per side (Fig. 4.5).

Grills

The use of the word *grill* for griddle by food service personnel has created a misunderstanding and loss of identification for this type of equipment. In England, grilling on a grill is similar to broiling. In the United States the process of grilling is different, as it is performed on equipment constructed for a specific purpose. The term char-grille is, however, interchangable with char-broiler, as both describe identical cooking methods.

A grill is a heating unit consisting of two flat heating surfaces. The food, usually a sandwich, is placed on the lower surface. The height of the upper heating plate is adjustable so that it can be positioned to meet the top side of the food. Grills are similar to waffle irons in that the upper heating jaw can be lowered to rest on the product or the flange of the lower section.

Grills are not widely used, since their main cooking function is for heating sandwiches. However, thin slices of meat, bacon or ham can also be prepared in

Courtesy of South Bend Range Corp.

FIG. 4.5. SOUTH BEND "MAGIC RAY" INFRARED BROILER

this type of equipment. But the cooking functions of grills can be efficiently performed on griddles by merely placing a metal weight on top of the food.

Char-Broilers

A novelty or specialty appliance that has had a remarkable growth during the past decade is the char-broiler or char-grille. A reason given for this phenomenal success is the popular appeal of the "char" or charcoal flavor that results, which is reminiscent of the outdoor barbecue. It has been clearly established that charcoal is not needed to produce the desirable authentic "char" flavor. The characteristic taste is derived when the food is seared by the high-intensity heat. During the searing process the fat drips on ceramic briquettes that produces a heavy vapor or smoke which is absorbed by the food. Char-broilers are generally used to cook steaks, chops, and some fish. As with the griddle, the consumer also enjoys observing char-broil cooking, and he will also find the aroma appealing if it is not too overpowering.

There is a wide range of char-broilers on the market. Important features to consider when purchasing this type of equipment are: (1) they should have fast pre-heating and re-heating features; (2) each grate section should be independently controlled so that operating costs can be monitored according to the volume; (3) safeguards are necessary to prevent overcooked food, that is, by the installation of accurate temperature controls; (4) construction should be simple to facilitate cleaning; (5) heating should be uniform to prevent occurrence of hot areas; (6) drip pans should be provided to collect grease, some manufacturers recommending that water be poured into the drip pan and maintained at predetermined levels; (7) heating elements should be built below the removable grates as a source of radiant heat and to permit flame control; (8) movable or lift-type heating elements should be positioned directly below and between the removable grates to supply radiation heat from the elements and heat of conduction stored in the grates; (9) a desirable feature that produces contact searing is from the heat generated within electrified grates; (10) leveling devices or adjustable legs are important for maximum performance.

Operating the Char-Broiler.—Char-broilers, if cleaned and operated properly, will provide long, trouble-free service. It is important that the instructions supplied by the manufacturer be followed.

Although it is impossible to pin-point instructions for all models, general guidelines can be applied to all char-broil equipment. The following cleaning procedures should be performed daily: (1) Always use a non-abrasive cleaner. Wipe all stainless steel surfaces with the cleaner applied to a damp, lint-free cloth. Wipe with a soft dry towel or absorbent paper toweling. (2) Clean all other exterior parts with a mild, warm detergent solution. Rinse and allow to dry. This operation will prevent build-up of grease and charred grease residues. (3) Remove grates and wash with mild detergent solution and rinse with warm water. Hard grease and carbon can be removed with a stiff-bristle brush; never use steel wool or abrasives. (4) Remove drip pans and, after emptying the contents, wash with detergent solution and rinse. Replace in grille and add water to recommended level. If equipment has baffles, these should also be removed and cleaned. (5) Remove all debris from heating elements. (6) When the cleaning of all parts is completed and they are correctly replaced, turn the heat on and allow the temperature to reach 400°F. Apply a thin film of cooking oil to prevent sticking. Allow the oil to settle for about 5 min, and wipe off the excess. (7) If charcoal briquettes are used, a vacuum cleaner will lessen the chore of removing ashes and dust. All encrusted grease accumulated in the firebox should be removed with a scraper. Where ceramic briquettes are used, all grease deposits and other foreign matter should be removed.

It is advisable to check the downdraft or updraft ventilators for grease accumulations. In addition, baffles and other parts that may be magnets for grease should be cleaned to prevent fire.

When the char-broiler is not in use, either shut off the power supply or turn

Courtesy of Ballantyne Instrument and Electronics, Inc.

FIG. 4.6. AUTOMATIC PRESSURE FRYER

down the temperature. Always preheat for optimum performance and never salt foods during broiling, as this will tend to corrode the heating elements.

Pressure Fryers

Pressure fryers are high-speed, specialty cooking equipment primarily employed to mass-produce fried chicken. They are also used to cook potatoes, meat, fish and certain vegetables. The average pressure fryer is capable of cooking about 100 lb of food per hour. Depending on the type of food, the average cooking time is about 6 to 8 min per charge.

Pressure fryers are completely sealed during the cooking operation. Pressure is generated by the vapor in the form of steam emitted from the food during heating. Portions must be fairly uniform, otherwise the finished product will vary in texture and consistency. In addition, the weight of the portions should be nearly uniform, not exceeding a tolerance of ±2 oz.

Figure 4.6 shows an automatic basket-lift pressure fryer. This unit features instant pressurization. Operating controls are simple, reducing the need for skilled employees. Its capacity is 60 pieces of 2¼-lb disjointed chicken per 8-min cycle. The food is placed in a basket, after which the machine is activated by pressing a button. When the top closes, pressure builds up immediately. As soon as the cooking cycle is completed, the pressure is released and the top

Courtesy of Henny Penny Corporation

FIG. 4.7. BREADING MACHINE FOR VOLUME PRODUCTION

opens, releasing the basket. Oil, fat or shortening are used as the frying agents. These must be preheated to 325°F prior to preparation. Timers are provided which can be set at any desired cooking cycle. Pressure gauges are visible; depending on the model, they should register 12 to 14 psi during the cooking cycle.

Coating or breading machines are useful accessories. These are perforated cylinders that are rotated with the product and breading material (Fig. 4.7).

The following is a list of recommended cooking cycles for various food products that are suitable for pressure frying.

Product	Cycle (min)
chicken	8
chops	5
French fries	4
breaded veal cutlet	5
shrimp	4
oysters	2
trout	7
lobster tails	4
scallops	2
corn-on-cob	4
onion rings	3
cauliflower	3
Brussel sprouts	1
apples	5

Tilting Skillets

Tilting skillets (Fig. 4.8) are useful cooking devices finding favor in fast food preparation centers. This equipment has a wide range of cooking applications, such as stewing, simmering, pan frying, braising, and sautéing. The operation is rapid and the results uniform. Tilting skillets can actually perform the work of a range, griddle, small kettle, fry pan and moist operating oven. Models are available that operate on either gas or electricity. They are easy to clean and sanitize because of their accessible polished stainless-steel cooking surfaces. The skillet shown in Fig. 4.8 is 36 in. wide and 33 in. deep. The steel pan body is 32 in. wide, 24 in. deep and 7 in. high, and has a 23-gal capacity. Skillets are provided with stainless-steel balanced lids that give easy accessibility for loading, unloading and cleaning.

Controls consist of a main power switch, signal light to indicate when the power is on, and a thermostat with a temperature range from 100 to 450°F.

The skillet pan is capable of tilting 90° under positive control by turning a crank. A removable pan support locks the pan in place when in the tilt position,

Courtesy of Market Forge

FIG. 4.8. TILTING SKILLET

holding it about 2 in. from the pouring lip, thereby eliminating splashing. Pan supports are available to hold pans of various sizes, such as 12 by 20 in., 12 by 18 in., or 10 by 16 in.

The following cooking temperatures are suggested; preheating is necessary for satisfactory results:

Simmering, 200°F (maximum to avoid boiling)
Sautéing, 225 to 275°F
Searing, 300 to 350°F
Frying, 325 to 375°F
Grilling, 350 to 425°F

Operating Factors.—Frozen vegetables can be cooked in a tilting skillet by leaving them undisturbed in the original serving pan. After heating they can be transferred to a holding cabinet or serving station. The loss of moisture is held to a minimum by the cover, which helps to reduce evaporation; it has a lip located at the back edge which collects and directs the condensation back into the skillet. Two different products can be prepared at the same time by putting two pans into the skillet and heating them simultaneously.

Breakfast foods can be prepared in volume for mass feeding, including sausage, bacon, pancakes, fried eggs, scrambled eggs and French toast.

It is important to portion the meat uniformly, so that all pieces are of equal thickness and have the same weight. Potting meat or corned beef, for example, require uniformity; otherwise the degree of doneness will vary.

Tilting skillets are excellent for storage or holding. This function is performed by placing water in the skillet, setting the thermostat to 175–180°F and then immersing the panned food in the hot water.

Labor Savings and Sanitation.—Tilting skillets have the advantage of reducing labor. Heavy lifting and transferring of foods from one pan to another and pot washing are greatly reduced. The skillet's interior should be cleaned with a mild detergent solution. If residues are difficult to remove, they should be soaked free with the cleaning solution. The wash water, waste and scraps are easily removed by tilting the skillet and catching the material in a bucket. Several rinses with warm water are necessary, followed by sanitizing with an approved solution. The cover should not be neglected. All crevices, grooves, condensate and pouring lips must be cleaned. After cleaning, the cover should be left in an upright position so that the air can circulate freely over all the cooking surfaces. The exterior should be wiped with a damp cloth, followed by sanitizing.

Table 4.2 shows suggested operating data, such as food quantities, temperature settings, number of portions that can be prepared for each cycle and the number of cycles per hour of cooking time.

Steam Cookers

Cookers that use steam as a source of heating energy comprise an important segment of the food service equipment industry. Steam cooking has been used commercially for about 40 years. Pressurized cookers were among the first of the fast food unit operations. The designs, capacities and capabilities of steam cookers cover a wide range. Equipment is available that is small enough to prepare a single food portion or large enough to accommodate mass volume production. Steam cooking equipment categories are: steam kettles, high-speed compression steam cookers, compartment steamers and counter-top superheated wet and dry steamers.

Modern steam-cooking equipment is adaptable to many kinds of preparation, e.g., basic cooking, reconstituting and reheating. Steam cookers are widely used for vegetable preparation. Vegetables prepared under steam are enhanced

TABLE 4.2

PREPARATION DATA FOR THE TILTING SKILLET

Food	Quantity	Thermostat Setting °F	Batches Per Hour	Number of Orders Per Load	Per Hour	Portion Size
Bacon	2 lb	350	12	16	150	3 slices
Eggs						
boiled, hard	50	225	5	50	250	1 egg
boiled, soft	50	225	8	50	400	1 egg
fried	30	400	4	30	120	1 egg
poached	36	225	5	36	180	1 egg
scrambled	18 gal	300 200*	1	720	720	1½ eggs
French toast	35 slices	450	7	12	84	3 slices
Regular oatmeal	10 lb	250	2	320	640	½ cup
Pancakes	30 ea	400	10	15	150	2 each
Clams	10 qt	400	10	20	200	1 pt
Fish cakes	70 3-oz	400	5	35	175	2-3 oz
Haddock fillet	60 4-oz	400	4	60	240	4 oz
Halibut steak	60 5-oz	450	3	60	180	5 oz
Lobster	12 1-1½ lb	350	4	12	50	1-1½ lb
Meat, Poultry						
Beef						
Amer. chop suey	18 gal	400 225*	2	250	500	6 oz
beef stew	17 gal	300	–	280	1½-2 hr	8 oz
corned beef hash	16 lb	400	5	50	250	5 oz
cheeseburger	7 lb	300	12	35	420	3 oz
hamburger	7 lb	300	15	35	525	3 oz
meatballs	12½ lb	400 225*	3	65	200	1 oz
pot roast	120 lb	350 200*	–	500	2-3 hr	2 oz
Salisbury steak	16 lb	400	3	50	150	5 oz
sirloin steak	40 6-oz	400	5	40	200	6 oz
Swiss steak	25 lb	300 200*	1	100	100	4 oz
Chicken						
pan-fried	50 pieces	350	3	25	75	2 ¼'s
whole	16 5 lb	350 200*	–	200	1½-2 hr	2 oz
Frankforts						
grilled	22 lb	300	8	174	1400	2 oz
boiled	16 lb	250	12	128	1536	2 oz
Ham steak	9 lb	400	8	50	640	3 oz
Pork chops	15 lb	350	4	70	280	5 oz
Sausage links	30 lb	350	7	120	840	3 links
Turkey						
off carcass	3 26-30 lb	400 200*	–	200	1-1½ hr	2 oz
on carcass	4 16-20 lb	400 200*	–	175	2½-3½ hr	2 oz
Vegetables						
Canned	30 lb	400	6	125	750	3 oz
Fresh						
beans, wax green	25 lb	400	3	125	375	3 oz
beets	30 lb	400	1	125	125	3 oz
broccoli	25 lb	400	3	125	375	3 oz
cabbage	20 lb	400	5	80	400	3 oz
carrots	35 lb	400	2	150	300	3 oz
cauliflower	12 lb	250	5	75	375	3 oz
corn	50 ears	400	8	50	400	1 ear

TABLE 4.2 CONT.

Food	Quantity	Thermostat Setting °F		Batches Per Hour	Number of Orders Per Load	Per Hour	Portion Size
potatoes	30 lb	400		2	150	300	3 oz
spinach	3 lb	250		10	25	250	4 oz
turnip	20 lb	400		2	100	200	4 oz
Frozen							
French green beans	15 lb	400		6	75	450	3 oz
lima beans	10 lb	250		4	50	200	3 oz
broccoli	12 lb	400		8	50	400	3 oz
sliced carrots	10 lb	250		6	50	300	3 oz
small whole carrots	10 lb	250		3	50	150	3 oz
corn	10 lb	250		18	50	900	3 oz
small whole onions	10 lb	250		7	50	350	3 oz
peas	15 lb	400		10	75	750	3 oz
spinach	15 lb	400		3	75	225	3 oz
Sauces, Gravies, Soups							
Brown gravy	18 gal	350	200*	2	2300	4600	1 oz
Cream sauce	18 gal	250	175*	1	1150	1150	2 oz
Cream soup	18 gal	200		2	375	750	6 oz
French onion soup	18 gal	225		1	350	350	6 oz
meat sauce	18 gal	350	200*	1	575	575	4 oz
Desserts, Puddings, Sweet Sauces							
Butterscotch sauce	18 gal	200		2	2300	4600	1 oz
Cherry cobbler	18 gal	200		2	750	1500	3 oz
Chocolate sauce	18 gal	200		2	2300	4600	1 oz
Cornstarch pudding	18 gal	200		1	575	575	4 oz
Fruit gelatin	18 gal	250		3	750	2250	3 oz
Miscellaneous							
Grilled cheese							
sandwiches	35 sand.	400		8	35	280	1 sand
Macaroni & cheese	18 gal	200		2	300	600	8 oz
Rice	20 lb raw	350	225*	1	320	320	4 oz
Spaghetti	8 lb raw	350	225*	2	200	400	4 oz

*Starting and finishing temperatures, respectively
Source: Market Forge, Bull. No. 46.

in appearance and given individualized "prepared-to-order" appeal. In addition, meat, poultry and numerous other products can be cooked speedily, efficiently and with a minimum of labor. If correctly timed, the steam cooking gives results that are superior to other forms of preparation, since the original flavors, colors and nutritional values are preserved.

Steam cookers are indispensable for a fast food preparation center. High-speed units, small 10- to 20-qt tilting kettles and superheated wet or dry devices, will provide the establishment with a full range of versatile equipment capable of preparing sauces, gravies, soups, stews, eggs, puddings, meat, poultry and vegetables. High-speed pressure units are suitable for reconstitution of prepared frozen foods in original containers and a host of other foods. These devices are available to operate on three types of external energy: steam, gas and electricity. Gas and electric units are capable of generating steam and are fully self-contained. Those operating from an external steam supply require a steady source of power to ensure constant cooking temperature. Depending on size, the steam supply must be able to deliver from 20 to 250 lb per hr. High-speed pressure cookers develop 12 to 15 psi internal pressure.

General Features.—Pressurized steam cookers are safe to operate. They have been used in the home for some 30 years and have a proven safety record. Although the basic principles of the home and commercial equipment are the same, the home cooker is slower and can only prepare one type of food per cycle. Controls on home cookers are not as accurate as those made for commercial application. One of the reasons for the high safety record of domestic units is the built-in safety gasket that will rupture should the internal pot pressure exceed the safe limits.

Commercial steam cookers are fitted with a number of safety devices. These are of paramount importance and should become a prerequisite when selections are being made. Gaskets must be durable and snug-fitting. Grooves should be provided so that the gaskets will not loosen during loading and unloading. Doors should be provided with positive locking devices and interlocks. A safety valve is necessary to limit the internal pressure.

Pressure gauges should be fully visible, easily read, and marked with a danger zone. Gauges should be durable and easy to remove. If several pressure cookers are installed, a spare gauge should be available for checking purposes. Pressure readings should be recorded periodically. If a pressure drop is observed, when preparing identical foods under similar conditions, then the gauge should be tested. If the gauge proves satisfactory, the pressure drop may be caused by a loose or worn gasket, loose door hinge or lock, insufficient steam, or too low voltage.

Stainless-steel construction is advisable for durability and ease of cleaning. Versatile interiors are almost mandatory in order to accommodate pans of various sizes. A safety thermostat is an excellent feature. If the cooking chamber overheats, this thermostat will activate a switch which will turn off the power. Other important features are a timer, buzzer, signal light, defrost cycle, low water cut-off switches, electric browning elements, simmering controls, and an automatic door release.

Steam Cooker Design.—Because of the importance of steam cooking and the increasing role this form of preparation equipment is playing in fast food operations, it is essential to understand the basic designs of each category.

Steam-jacketed Kettles.—Steam-jacketed kettles have been used for many decades. They are the earliest form of steam equipment specially made for this purpose. The double boiler was employed before the steam kettle, and is still used for some forms of conventional preparation.

Steam-jacketed equipment consists of an outer and inner vessel welded together. A space is provided between the two kettles for the flow of steam. Cooking temperatures are controlled by regulating the amount of steam. Capacities vary from a 10-qt counter unit to a 200-gal floor kettle. Variations in the basic design have resulted in the development of many useful types of jacketed kettles. Small tilting units are available which have become an integral part of fast food production.

Most steam-jacketed kettles are easy to keep clean since they are made of stainless steel. If they are installed with sufficient space around the equipment, the burden of exterior sanitation will also be reduced. When not in operation, the kettle's cover should be removed to keep the interior open for full air circulation. This will reduce problems of off-tasting foods as a result of stale food odors. It is also advisable to fill the kettles with water during shutdown for the same reason. A mild solution of detergent should be used for sanitation. A stiff-bristle, long handled brush will facilitate removal of food soil and residues. Several fresh water rinses are necessary to remove all traces of cleaning solution. Covers, faucets, and all exterior sections require the same cleaning procedures. The final step is sanitizing by applying a solution of a product approved for this purpose. It must be remembered that sanitation consists of two steps, cleaning and sanitizing. The latter will prevent the growth of microorganisms. It is not advisable to use steel wool or any abrasive material that may destroy or pit highly polished metal surfaces.

A hot and cold water supply should be located within easy reach of the kettle area. Floor drains should be provided for large stationary kettles. Plastic tubing or hose should be made available for rinsing. Rubber or synthetic rubber hose is not recommended, as these may impart off-flavors to the food.

Table 4.3 illustrates a cross section of foods that can be prepared in steam-jacketed kettles of various sizes. Cooking times are not given, since this is an "open pot" method. Taste and experience are the only guide to the time given to preparation.

Compartmented Steam Cooker.—Compartmented steam cookers resemble an upright chest of drawers or a cabinet. They are constructed of heavy-gauge metal and contain from 1 to 4 compartments, which can be activated individually, as there is a set of controls for each. Compartmented cookers are available in gas, electric, steam-coil and direct steam models. Steam pressure varies between 5 and 8 psi at temperatures of from 200 to 225°F. Gas and electric units generate their own steam. Depending on the model and manufacturer, interior designs may be modified for a specific size pan. For example, a 3-compartment model will hold 6 2½-in. pans; a 2-compartment unit will accommodate 4 4-in. pans. Shelves are either stationary or of the pull-out type. Automatic, semiautomatic and manually operated cookers are manufactured. Automatic models feature a self-releasing door at the completion of the cooking cycle plus a steam-release valve. An audible signal sounds when the food is ready. Automatic models start the time cycle when the pre-heat temperature has been

TABLE 4.3

STEAM-JACKETED KETTLE SINGLE-LOAD CAPACITIES

Food	Cooked Portion		5 Gal	10 Gal	30 Gal	40 Gal	60 Gal
Breakfast Foods							
cereal	6 oz or	Amt. raw	4½ lb	9 lb	24 lb	36 lb	48 lb
	¾ cup	Portions	60	120	320	480	640
scrambled	4 oz or	Amt. eggs	18 dz	36 dz	100 dz	160 dz	220 dz
eggs	2 eggs ea.		(3¾ gal)	(7½ gal)	(22 gal)	(32 gal)	(44 gal)
		Portion	108	216	660	960	1320
*Main Entrées**							
American	6 oz	Yield	3 gal	6 gal	25 gal	35 gal	50 gal
chop suey		Portion	65	130	550	750	1100
baked beans	5 oz or	Yield	3 gal	6 gal	25 gal	32 gal	50 gal
2½ lb raw =	2/3 cup						
1 gal cooked		Portion	75	150	625	800	1250
beef stew	8 oz or	Yield	2½ gal	5 gal	20 gal	30 gal	40 gal
	1 cup	Portion	40	80	320	480	640
macaroni &	5 oz or	Yield	3 gal	6 gal	25 gal	35 gal	50 gal
cheese	2/3 cup	Portion	75	150	625	875	1250
turkey a la	4 oz or	Yield	3 gal	6 gal	25 gal	35 gal	50 gal
king	½ cup	Portion	100	200	800	1120	1600
Miscellaneous							
gravy	2 oz or	Yield	4 gal	8 gal	25 gal	35 gal	50 gal
	¼ cup	Portion	250	500	1500	2000	3000
noodles	4 oz or	Amt. raw	4 lb	8 lb	25 lb	35 lb	50 lb
1 lb raw =	¾ cup	Portion	48	96	300	420	600
4 lb cooked							
rice							
1 lb raw =	3 oz or	Amt. raw	4 lb	8 lb	25 lb	35 lb	50 lb
3 lb cooked	½ cup	Portion	80	160	500	700	1000
spaghetti or	4 oz or	Amt. raw	4 lb	8 lb	25 lb	35 lb	50 lb
macaroni 1 lb	¾ cup	Portion	64	128	400	560	800
raw = 4 lb							
cooked							
Vegetables							
fresh	4 oz or	Amt. raw	15 lb	30 lb	90 lb	120 lb	180 lb
	½ cup	Portion	65	130	375	500	750
frozen	4 oz or	No. pkg.	10	20	60	80	120
loose pack	½ cup	Portion	110	220	660	880	1320
frozen	4 oz or	No. pkg.	5	10	30	40	60
solid pack	½ cup	Portion	55	110	330	440	660

*All main entrée figures are given in terms of raw ingredients. Convenience foods would have a slightly higher yield on the 30, 40 and 60 gallon kettles. A safe increase would be 10%.

Source: Market Forge, Bull. No. 39A.

reached. Door design is important. Some units feature a wheel mechanism, others a hand lever. Wheel locks should not be over-tightened as this practice will destroy the effectiveness of the gaskets. If steam pressures are noted to be below the normal cooking range, gaskets should be inspected. If worn or damaged, they need replacing.

Table 4.4 lists the operating characteristics of a 5 psi rated compartmented steam cooker which holds 6 2½-in. pans or 4 4-in. pans.

High-Pressure Steam Cookers.—High-pressure steam cookers operate at pressures of from 12 to 15 psi at 235–250°F. These units are the "work horse" of the fast food preparation center. Most are small enough to fit on a counter, so that they form an integral part of a flow system (Fig. 4.9). There are many

Courtesy of Market Forge
FIG. 4.9. HIGH SPEED 15 PSI JET COOKER

TABLE 4.4

OPERATING CHARACTERISTICS OF A 5 PSI COMPARTMENTED
STEAM COOKER

Food	Recommended 12 × 20 in. Pan Depth	Approx. Raw Wt per pan	No. of Loads per Hr	Approx No. Cooked 3-oz Serv. per Comp. per Load	Approx No. Cooked 3-oz Serv. per Comp. per Hr.
Frozen, Defrosted					
asparagus	2½″ perf	5	4	150	600
green beans	2½″ perf	5	4	150	600
lima beans	2½″ perf	5	4	150	600
broccoli	2½″ perf	6	5	120	600
Brussels sprouts	2½″ perf	5	4	150	600
carrots	2½″ perf	5	4	150	600
cauliflower	2½″ perf	5	4	150	600
corn (frozen)	2½″ perf	5	4	150	600
peas (frozen)	2½″ perf	5	6	150	900
Fresh					
green beans	2½″ perf	6	2	180	360
beets	2½″ perf	7½	1	150	150
broccoli	2½″ perf	6	3	150	450
cabbage	2½″ perf	5	3	120	360
carrots	2½″ perf	9	2	210	420
cauliflower	2½″ perf	6	3	180	540
corn on cob	2½″ perf	1 doz	4	72	288
onions	2½″ perf	6	2	150	300
peas	2½″ perf	5	4	180	720
French-fried potatoes	2½″ perf	10	3	300	900
regular cut potatoes	2½″ perf	10	2	300	600
spinach	4 ″ perf	3	8	60	480
summer squash	2½″ perf	7	4	180	720
winter squash	2½″ perf	9	2	180	360
turnip	2½″ perf	5	2	120	240
Meat, Poultry, Fish					
chicken, cut up	2½″ solid	8	2	120	240
chicken, whole (4-lb)	4″ solid	12	1	120	120
frankforts	2½″ perf	5	10	240	2400
hamburgers	2½″ solid	5	3	150	450
meatballs	2½″ solid	6	2	150	300
meatloaf	2½″ solid	15	1	300	300
pork chops	2½″ solid	6	2	144	288
sausages	2½″ solid	6	2	120	240
turkey, on carcass	4″ solid	20–22	1	100	2–3 hr
turkey, off carcass	2½″ perf	10–12	1	360	360
fish fillets	2½″ solid	3	4	90	360
fish sticks	2½″ solid	4	3	150	450
lobster	2½″ perf	10	6	60	360
eggs (out of shell)	2½″ solid	48 (eggs)	6	288	1728
eggs (in shell)	2½″ perf	36 (eggs)	5	216	1080
rice	4″ solid	4	2	240	480
spaghetti	4″ solid	3	2	160 (4-oz)	320

TABLE 4.4 CONT.

Food	Recommended 12 × 20 in. Pan Depth	Approx. Raw Wt per pan	No. of Loads per Hr	Approx No. Cooked 3-oz Serv. per Comp. per Load	Approx No. Cooked 3-oz Serv. per Comp. per Hr.
Frozen Entrées					
bulk pack	2½" perf	5	2	72 (6-oz)	144
individual pack	2½" perf	3	4	36 pouches	144
shrimp CPD	2½" perf	3	3	120 (2-oz)	360
shrimp green	2½" perf	3	3	90 (2-oz)	270
lobster tails	2½" perf	6	3	72 (6-oz)	216

Source: Market Forge, Bull. No. 39A.

models and designs to choose from. Some units offer a number of useful features, in addition, there is available a group of specialty cookers which are described under a separate heading.

High-pressure steam cookers are manufactured to operate on four forms of heating energy: self-generating gas or electric models, steam-coil and direct steam-induced units. Those cookers that apply steam directly into the food encompass several designs: one type sends tiny jets of dry steam onto the food; another fills the cooking chambers with a uniform atmosphere of steam. Models can be purchased that offer multiple compartments, so that each section can be timed separately, thus affording the opportunity of cooking different foods simultaneously.

High-pressure steam cookers will prepare many varieties of food, from fresh to frozen, such as vegetables, sea food, rice, poultry, eggs, spaghetti, potatoes and most pouch-packed edibles.

The main advantage of high-pressure steam cookers is speed. During peak periods they will perform efficiently, and if they are located near a service line, preparation can keep up with the service load. Pot washing is reduced, since this method of cooking will not burn pans. To facilitate production, these cookers should be installed near a freezer or cooler storage.

Preparation speed is shown in the following examples: corn and cauliflower require about 30 sec; French cut beans and broccoli spears, 60 sec; chicken parts for frying, 6 min; lobsters, 6 min; onions in water, 6½ min; shrimp, 4 min; boned turkey, 50 min; and hamburger patties, 2 min. Table 4.5 shows cooking times for various food prepared in a 15-lb pressure cooker. This unit will hold 3 2½-in. pans or 2 4-in. pans per load.

This table (Table 4.5) and others should only be used as a guide. Tests must be made on all items prior to production. Even a minor variation in the time will make a difference in the quality. Once a decision has been reached as to the correct cycle, it should be recorded on a chart, hung or placed next to the machine's control box. Time settings for identical foods require periodic checks,

TABLE 4.5

RECOMMENDED COOKING CYCLES FOR A 15 POUND PRESSURE COOKER

Food	Recommended 12 × 20 in. Pan Depth	Approx. Raw Wt per Pan lb	No. of Loads per Hr	Approx No. Cooked 3-oz. Serv. per Unit per Load	Approx. No. Cooked 3-oz. Serv. per Unit per Hr
Frozen, Defrosted					
asparagus	2½″ perf	5	4	75	300
green beans	2½″ perf	5	4	75	300
lima beans	2½″ perf	5	4	75	300
broccoli	2½″ perf	6	5	60	300
Brussels sprouts	2½″ perf	5	4	75	300
carrots	2½″ perf	5	4	75	300
cauliflower	2½″ perf	5	4	75	300
corn (frozen)	2½″ perf	5	5	75	375
peas (frozen)	2½″ perf	5	8	75	600
Fresh					
green beans	2½″ perf	6	4	90	360
beets	2½″ perf	7½	1	75	75
broccoli	2½″ perf	6	5	75	375
cabbage	2½″ perf	5	3	60 (4-oz)	180
carrots	2½″ perf	9	3	105	315
cauliflower	2½″ perf	6	5	90	450
corn on cob	2½″ perf	1 doz.	5	36	180
onions	2½″ perf	6	3	75 (4-oz)	225
peas	2½″ perf	5	6	90	540
French-fried potatoes	2½″ perf	10	4	150	600
regular cut potatoes	2½″ perf	10	2	150	300
spinach	4″ perf	3	10	30	300
summer squash	2½″ perf	7	5	90	450
winter squash	2½″ perf	9	3	90	270
turnip	2½″ perf	5	2	60	120
Meat, Poultry, Fish					
chicken, cut up	2½″ solid	8	2	60	120
chicken, whole (4-lb)	4″ solid	12	1	60	60
frankforts	2½″ perf	5	10	120	1200
hamburgers	2½″ solid	5	3	75	225
meatballs	2½″ solid	6	2	75	150
meatloaf	2½″ solid	15	1	150	150
pork chops	2½″ solid	6	2	72	144
sausages	2½″ solid	6	2	60	120
turkey (on carcass)	4″ solid	20–22	1	50	1½–2 hrs
turkey (off carcass)	2½″ perf	10–12	1	180	180
fish fillets	2½″ solid	3	4	45	180
fish sticks	2½″ solid	4	3	75	225
lobster	2½″ perf	10	6	30	180
eggs (out of shell)	2½″ solid	48 (eggs)	6	144	864
rice	4″ solid	4	2	120	240
spaghetti	4″ solid	3	2	80 (4-oz)	160
Frozen Entrées					
bulk pack	2½″ perf	5	2	36 (6-oz)	72
individual pouches	2½″ perf	3	5	18 pouches	90
shrimp C.P.D.	2½″ perf	3	4	60 (2-oz)	240
shrimp, green	2½″ perf	3	3	45 (2-oz)	135
lobster tails	2½″ perf	6	4	36 (6-oz)	144

Source: Market Forge (1970).

especially where brands have been changed. Where new foods have been introduced, more than one check run is necessary to establish the optimum time.

Browning and Steaming Cookers.—Browning and steaming cookers are specialty models that perform two functions—cooking in steam and browning the surface. A heating element is installed in the cooking chamber that browns the food during the steaming cycle. This eliminates the need of transferring the product to another unit for browning.

Counter-top Specialty Steam Cookers.—Equipment is available, the size of a large battery type bread toaster, which is charged with distilled water and operates on electricity from an ordinary 120-volt AC outlet. Superheated steam is generated that is capable of poaching eggs, melting cheese on a meat patty, heating a meat sandwich, and reconstituting a single portion of prepared frozen entrées. This cooker can be moved from station to station depending on operating schedules.

Another specialty unit is built into a counter and operates on the same principle. This cooker is fully automatic. It injects steam into the cooking chamber every 15 sec. A pulsating timer controls the steam input. The timer can be programmed to 15 min. The cooker is attached to the water system; however, a deionizer is provided that removes water impurities. The ion-exchanger mechanism contains a cartridge filled with an approved resin. A change of color of the resin indicates that a replacement is needed.

General Care of Steam Cookers.—Steam cookers are reliable and with a diligent cleaning program, trouble-free service is ensured. Always read and keep available manufacturer's instructions. Salient points should be recorded on an instruction card and hung in front of the unit. Cleaning should be done with all power off.

In all cases, use a mild solution of detergent, followed by rinsing. Then follow with an application of sanitizing solution. Polish the exterior with a lint free cloth. Never use an abrasive. When washing the chamber, remove all shelves and remove food soil with a brush. Clean strainer and replace. Inspect steam inlet areas and remove any debris that may tend to clog these sections. After cleaning turn on the cooker and run a cycle to ensure proper operation. During the test run check the pressure relief valve and pressure gauges. Check the door for correct sealing.

OTHER EQUIPMENT

Many kinds of labor-saving devices are available that are suited for fast food operations. If space is available and the equipment will generate savings and promote efficiency, it should be considered. At times an excess of mechanical devices can be a waste of space and money if they are not used to full advantage. Guidelines for the selection of equipment are given early in this chapter.

Food Forming Equipment.—Figure 4.10 shows a food-forming machine that is capable of producing 1200 patties an hour. When the patty is formed it drops on a piece of paper which is automatically fed from a magazine. This machine

Courtesy of Hollymatic Corporation

FIG. 4.10. FOOD FORMING MACHINE—HOLLYMATIC MODEL 200

is adaptable to a variety of shapes and weights. It can form meatballs, sausages, mock chicken legs and choppies.

High-Speed Sandwich Production.—Machines are available that are capable of high speed cooking production with consistently good quality. Figure 4.11 shows a machine that will process 500 to 700 sandwiches per hour. Two conveyors move the product over the open flames, broiling the patties and steaming and toasting the buns simultaneously.

Vegetable Preparation.—Versatile equipment is available that reduces to a minimum the labor involved in chopping, dicing, cutting, shredding and slicing vegetables. Figure 4.12 shows a compact portable machine that can perform many labor-saving jobs efficiently and uniformly. Because of its small size it can fit into a production flow plan, and when not in use, it may be stored or moved to other locations. Equipment of this type can slice, shred, chop or grate up to 1000 lb per hr.

Waste Removal.—Waste removal and sanitation are important functions in any type of food service establishment. Waste removal becomes especially

Courtesy of Sani-Serv

FIG. 4.11. HIGH SPEED SANDWICH BROILER MODEL B150-A

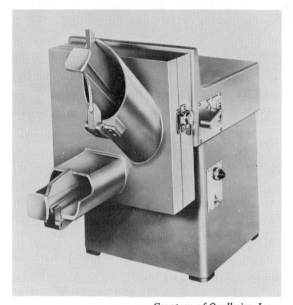

Courtesy of Qualheim, Inc.

FIG. 4.12. VEGETABLE SLICER, GRATER, SHREDDER
MODEL 440

burdensome in a fast food operation because of the vast amount of disposal dishes and wrappings that may be handled. Problems encountered with waste disposal may be reduced by the employment of compactors. Figure 4.13 shows an automatic waste compactor unit. This equipment is movable so that it is possible to position it in any location. The compactor has a compaction ratio of 5 to 1, and can pack 75 lb of compacted trash or the equivalent of 5 average

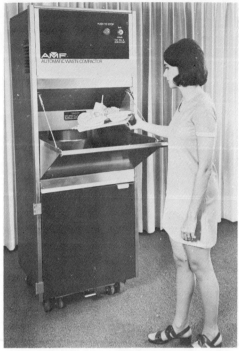

Courtesy of AMF Incorporated

FIG. 4.13. AUTOMATIC WASTE COMPACTOR, MODEL EH-100

waste cans into a single polyethylene bag. Other features of the electro-hydraulic stainless steel model include ease of cleaning, quiet operation, an emergency stop switch, and a rolling dolly-mounted barrel that holds the waste-filled plastic bag.

COUNTER-TOP BLENDERS

Counter-top electric blenders are highly useful, versatile and most suitable for fast food feeding establishments. Small household blenders are not new, and have been on the retail market since before World War II. The food processing and chemical industries employ blenders of various designs and sizes. Commercial blenders used to mix dry ingredients are the ribbon, tumbling, air mixing and vertical shaft propeller types. Equipment to blend liquids consists of a pump or a propeller blade located in the base of a container. Small electric blenders employ a vertical rotating shaft mounted in a motor. The shaft protrudes sufficiently so that it can fit into a metal slot located at the base of the container. The container or reservoir may be constructed from stainless steel or plastic; it houses the propeller located at its base.

Connection between the vertical shaft and propeller is accomplished when the container is brought to rest on the blender's base. Blenders are available in 1-qt, ½-gal and 1-gal sizes.

Functions and Applications.—Blenders can perform a number of diversified operations, such as aerating, liquefying, blending, chopping, crushing, grating, homogenizing, and mixing. These units are both time- and labor-saving devices. They have limitations, as they cannot be used for grinding uncooked meat or for beating egg whites. If used for egg whites, too much air will be absorbed and they will become too fluffy.

Correct timing of each operation is essential. Changes in texture may occur if the optimum time is exceeded.

Hospitals have developed feeding programs around the use of these blenders. They are employed in preparing tube feeding foods, diet and infant foods.

Blenders are useful for the following applications:

(1) To blend beverages and to reduce vegetables to juices and fruits to nectars.

(2) To provide a rapid means of blending and mixing soup ingredients, for borscht, fruit, cream bisques, vichyssoise and tomato vegetable.

(3) To prepare omelet mixes and soufflés.

(4) To prepare sauces, gravy and salad dressing.

(5) To mix efficiently and quickly some desserts and batters, such as waffle, pancake, muffin and popover.

Sanitation.—Proper and complete sanitation is necessary at all times to achieve complete success. After each operation the blender must be cleaned and sanitized. If the bottom portion of the container is inaccessible, a mild detergent should be used to dislodge all food soil. Pour a tepid detergent solution into the container and activate the motor for several minutes. Fill the container almost to the brim so that the motion of the swirling water will splash on the lid. Run at low speed. Rinse the container several times and apply a solution of an approved sanitizing solution. Rinse again and allow to air dry. During overnight or prolonged storage the cover or lid should be removed.

Propeller blades should be treated gently, to prevent injury or misalignment.

Proper sanitation will eliminate one source that may be responsible for off-tastes and off-odors.

VENDING

History and Development

Vending is a prime example of fast and automated food-service operations, combined to form a unique facility that utilizes machine techniques, convenience foods, and for a majority of installations, a highly organized and efficient commissary program. These elements achieve the ultimate goal of lower labor costs, mobility, and quick service to the customer.

Vending is defined as self-service mechanical distribution, metering, or portioning of services, merchandise, edibles, and beverages by the insertion of a coin or coins into a slot. Vending machines were developed in their simplest form around 1900. The early form of motion pictures was a vendable type of entertainment, viewed through a box and activated by a crank. The slot machine, or "one-armed bandit," is an example of vended gambling produced by a mechanical device without human assistance. Bulk vending equipment employed to dispense candy, peanuts, chewing gum and many small dry goods items has been used commercially for over 60 years.

The vending of food and beverages, which forms the backbone of the modern vending industry, had its start with the advent of the Horn and Hardart Automats, just before World War I. This mode of service took hold rapidly and became an immediate success in the New York and Philadelphia marketing areas.

During and after World War II a major industry built entirely around the vending machine emerged. Industrial and in-plant feeding formed the focal point for this method of mechanical food service. Shortages of restaurant employees and the necessity for quick snacks within defense plants located away from urban areas were the essential elements involved in the creation of mechanical feeding facilities. Advances in electronics were responsible for the development and design of sophisticated services, and complete cafeterias, fully contained and automatic, were constructed.

The present vending industry covers a wide range of products and services. Labor shortages and the high cost of labor for menial tasks, coupled with the development of convenience foods, are responsible for the continued sharp growth of vending throughout the world. Although the growth of automated feeding services in Europe has lagged behind that of the Western Hemisphere, Europe's retail vending industry is successful and popular. Vending machines can be found at almost every street corner offering a variety of retail goods for sale.

Classification of Vendable Services

The vending industry, because of its diverse application and complex operation, can best be understood when divided into three service categories: (1) hiring or leasing of services by mechanical means, (2) dispensing of edible or personal services, and (3) dispensing of sundry items and nonedible services, packaged foods and bottled beverages.

(1) The hiring or leasing of services by mechanical means includes telephone pay stations, juke boxes, public toilets, radio and television for hotel and home, auto parking meters, luggage storage lockers and laundry washing machines and manglers.

(2) The dispensing of edible or personal services includes shoe shiners, foot and hotel bed massage machines, soap and towel dispensers, electric and gas meters, perfume and toilet water dispensers, weight scales, ice machines, and all vending machines that dispense portioned food or beverages, e.g., hot and cold drink dispensers, hot and cold food units, and ice-cream dispensers.

(3) Dispensing of sundry items, nonedible services, packaged foods and drinks includes stamps; subway and bus tokens; miscellaneous items, e.g., newspapers, paperback books, magazines, combs, cosmetics, handkerchiefs, postcards, stockings, and contraceptives; flight insurance policies; cigarette and cigar machines; bulk confectionery dispensers; and retail packaged food dispensers, e.g., bread, milk, canned goods.

Operating Principles of Vending Machines

Basically, the operating principles of vending machines or dispensing services are identical regardless of the product or service sold. A coin is the medium of payment, which acts as the key to unlock a mechanism setting the dispenser in operation. Unlocking mechanisms that activate vending equipment are divided into two categories; (1) mechanical or hand-operated, and (2) electrical.

Mechanical or manual operation uses the coin to bridge the lever or button to the interior controls, allowing the product to be released. By moving an exterior lever or push button after the coin is inserted into the machine and accepted by it, the pressure exerted by the customer acts as the power source to set the dispenser in operation. When the external pressure is released the coin drops into the money storage box and the machine cannot be operated again until a new coin is inserted in the slot. This type of vending equipment can be placed in any location, as no external power is required for its operation. The earliest forms of dispensing equipment employed these principles. Bulk vending units dispensing nuts, chewing gum, candy bars, sundry items and cigarettes employ the mechanical system.

Electrically activated dispensers were made possible during and after World War II from the development of electronic components necessary to create operating systems that were fully automated. Machines were built containing a labyrinth of electrical circuits, encompassing microswitches, timers, fractional HP motors, and solenoids. Depending on the product dispensed, interior designs vary. Generally the design of the coin acceptor, coin counter, and change dispenser follow the same basic design. After the coin is deposited in the slot by the customer and the selection of an item made, a master switch is activated that sets the interior components in operation.

Parameters of Vending Machine Design

Modern vending machines must meet certain basic design criteria to satisfy the demands of the consumer, vendor, and if they are used to dispense food or beverages, government sanitation codes. Depending on the product or service rendered, the following items number 1 through 6 apply to all vending machines; items 7 to 10 apply to those dispensers serving food and beverages.

(1) compactness;

(2) attractive and appealing exterior design and decoration;

(3) attractive and presentable display of merchandise;

(4) mechanical reliability and efficient operation;

(5) ease of loading;

(6) ease of repairs and servicing, so that a semiskilled employee can perform on location minor repairs and adjustments;

(7) ease of sanitation and full accessibility to all interior parts for cleaning purposes;

(8) if the vending unit dispenses perishable products or ingredients, the machine must be capable of maintaining a temperature of 45°F or below with necessary temperature controls as required, and shutoff controls should the temperature rise above 45°F.

(9) If the vending unit dispenses hot or heated food of a perishable nature, the machine must be capable of maintaining products at or above 140°F with necessary temperature controls and shutoff controls should the temperature drop below 140°F.

(10) If vending machines are designed to dispense food or beverages, they must comply with regulations set forth by the U.S. Public Health Service 1965 sanitation ordinance and code under the title "The Vending of Foods and Beverages." This code was developed in cooperation with the National Automatic Merchandising Association (NAMA) in 1957 and revised in 1965. In addition, the National Sanitation Foundation (NSF) has also promulgated basic and specific criteria for the evaluation of vending machines for food and beverages.

There are three classifications of coin-operated vending machines: (1) for beverages, (2) for confections and foods, and (3) for sundry and miscellaneous products.

Vending Machines for Beverages

Coffee

instant, freeze-dried or liquid concentrates

fresh brew (batch)

fresh brew (single cup)

The above are manufactured in combination with hot chocolate, soup and tea.

Soft drinks

bottle or canned

cup service (postmix)

cup service (premix)

Milk

packaged (indoors and outdoors)

bulk or cup service

Vending Machines for Confections and Food

bulk

candy bar

hot canned foods and soups
cold foods
fresh fruit
pastry, crackers, cookies and popcorn
chewing gum
ice cream

Vending Machines for Sundry and Miscellaneous Products

cigarette and cigars
postage stamps
ice
cosmetics, toiletries, novelties, detergents, newspapers and books

Selected Examples and Their Operational Aspects

Solid Pack Vending Machines.—Solid pack vending machines are manufactured in a variety of shapes, designs and are adapted for many products, both edible and nonedible. They handle confections, solid food, sundries and miscellaneous products.

Column and Drawer Dispensers.—These machines store their products in stacks. Each stack is set above a drawer. When the machine is filled, the bottom package falls into the drawer. Upon activation the machine mechanism allows the drawer to be opened. After the product is withdrawn and the drawer pushed back into place, a subsequent package falls into it. These units dispense cigarettes and candy bars.

Drop Flap Machines.—As in the column and drawer equipment, packages are stored in columns. Instead of resting one on the other, each package rests on a hinged drop flap or leaf. When the machine is filled, all the leaves or flaps are extended so that each package has its own shelf. When the machine is activated, the lowest shelf drops on its hinge and allows the package to fall by gravity onto the vending chute. These machines are adaptable to cigarettes, candy and packaged sundries.

Cupboard Machines.—Cupboard dispensers consist of a number of small rectangular receptacles or storage spaces covered with a hinged glass door. When the unit is activated, the customer can observe the item desired, open the door, and withdraw the merchandise. Only one door is allowed to open at a time, and once the item is withdrawn the storage space remains empty until reloaded.

Rotary turntable dispensers are available that increase the capacity of a machine. Where a turntable is provided, each shelf, which is divided into segments, can hold up to eight selections. After a sale is completed, the closing of the vend door causes the turntable to move one segment.

There are many variations of cupboard machines. Some are made with conveyors fitted with slots or pockets. The customer presses a button which activates the conveyor. As the conveyor moves, each item is brought into view for selection.

These vending machines are available with refrigeration systems for the dispensing of cold foods or with heating units for hot or perishable foods.

Cigarette Vending Machines.—Cigarette dispensers cover a wide capacity range. Some hold up to 1,200 packs of varying sizes. The cigarettes are loaded into columns, up to 36 columns per machine. Horizontal conveyor type units are available. In these dispensers the package is laid flat. When the machine is activated, the conveyor moves one package length, releasing the merchandise into the chute. Because of the differences in price range of the king, 100, or regular size package, these dispensers require a flexible pricing capability for each size.

Canned Food and Beverage Machines.—These dispensers consist of a series of runways or chutes. When the machine is activated the can is released and rolls or drops to the takeout shelf. Machines of this type can be adapted to heat canned food or to cool canned beverages. Packaged ice-cube dispensers operate on the same principle.

Ice Cream Dispensers.—Dispensers that vend ice cream bricks or pops are completely refrigerated and insulated cabinets, constructed to maintain the product at its proper consistency. In addition, safety controls are incorporated that shut off the machine in the event of refrigeration failure.

Generally, packages are stored in column-type magazines which revolve within the cabinet. When the dispenser is set in motion and the selection made by the customer, the ice-cream package is released from the bottom of the column and drops through a double door—an added precaution to ensure that the inner cabinet is never exposed to the atmosphere.

Coffee Dispensers.—Coffee dispensers are manufactured to provide the beverage by four methods: (1) instant crystals or powder and freeze-dried powder; (2) liquid concentrates; (3) fresh brew (batch brewing); and (4) fresh brew (single cup brewing)

Method 4 is the most popular form of vended coffee. This method is presently the most widely used, as the number of single-cup brewers sold over the last 10 years far exceeds all others. Because of this trend the single cup vending method will be discussed in detail. Most coffee machines have provisions to dispense hot chocolate, soup and tea.

Ground coffee is stored in hoppers, which hold from 8 to 12 lb. A volumetric measuring feed is built into the lower section of the hopper. When the unit is activated, a screw type mechanism or worm gear pushes the coffee out into the brewing chamber. The amount of coffee, measured in grams, is regulated by setting the controls on the hopper. Depending on the brew strength, about 7 to 10 gm are used per cup. A very fine grind coffee is used. The short brew cycle makes this property mandatory so that full extraction can be obtained. Although many of the principles of essential brewing techniques apply to vending machines, those that are tailor-made to meet the unusual conditions are extra-fine particle size, short brew cycles, and blend components which ensure full wettability. About 6 oz of water are added to the coffee at a temperature of 200°F ±5°. Depending on the manufacturer, the water may be heated in open or closed tanks. In any event, a constant source of hot water is necessary, especially during peak serving periods. The total vend time is about 10 sec.

One of the major drawbacks of vended coffee is a lack of proper sanitation, so that off-flavors result from accumulated resins and dirt. Some equipment have provisions for self-cleaning. However, regardless of the machine design, full sanitation is necessary for the vending of a clear, uncontaminated brew.

Soft Drink Vending Machines.—Of the three types of soft drink vending machines in current use, the postmix unit is the most popular. These machines are completely automatic and contain all the components, including ice-making equipment, to produce a finished beverage of high quality. This equipment is the result of man's ingenuity applied to the development of efficient automated dispensers. Postmix cup machines are those that dispense a finished soft drink in a cup with or without ice from a choice of flavored syrups, either carbonated or not. Dispensers of this type are available in a number of sizes and capacities, varying from 500 to 1,500 cups of 7-, 9-, or 10-oz capacity. Carbonation may be adjusted for high, low, or none, depending on the syrup used in the unit. Flavor selections range from 4 to 8.

Depending on the machine's design, flavor selections can be made before or after the coin is accepted by the unit. As with other venders, these machines are equipped with coin changers. After selection is made and the unit activated, the finished beverage is ready for the consumer in about 10 sec. Activation starts a train of events. As the cup falls into place from its storage rack, syrup, carbonated water and ice are metered and delivered to the cup. The amount of each ingredient is controlled by a cam or electrical sensing device.

Premix soft drink machines dispense individual cup size servings. Their use is limited to locations that do not have a water supply, or where temporary installations are required. Portable tanks are filled with syrup and water, and the mixture carbonated. These prefilled tanks are then installed into the machine and hooked into a refrigeration system. Carbonation can also be performed within the dispenser if it is equipped with a carbon dioxide injection system. Although greater uniformity is achieved with this type of equipment, since the filling operation can be controlled more carefully, a major drawback is their limited capacity.

Effect of Water on Vendable Beverages

Water problems that affect beverages also pertain to those dispensed from vending machines. Manufacturers of beverage vending units are building into their machines strainers or screens and activated-carbon water purifiers. However, these do not eliminate problems emanating from brackish or hard water.

Screens and strainers will rid the water of solid particles, such as metal, coarse sand, and dirt. Activated-carbon filters are effective in removing chlorine, metallic tastes, plant life, and sulfur dioxide. Brackish water can be successfully treated by the use of a reverse osmosis filtration system.

Hard water conditions can be corrected by a number of methods, including the ion-exchange process. The ion-exchange process cannot be employed on water fed into coffee brew dispensers, as the side effects will give a finished brew that is bitter and unpalatable. In addition, inconsistency and short-fill cups will also result. The ion-exchange system produces sodium bicarbonate which forms a gel and binds the coffee particles together, thus preventing a full and quick extraction. A polyphosphate system is recommended for the treatment of water fed to fresh brew vending equipment.

The following illustrates the respective effects on soft drinks:

Water Problem	Effect on Drink and Vending Machine
Iron	Imparts metallic taste
Dirt, cloudiness, chlorine, mustiness, fishy tastes and odors	Excessive foaming, reduces carbonation, destroys flavor
Hard water (lime scale)	Plugs valves, reduces cooling efficiency, plugs lines, affects flavor
Acid	Corrodes pipes, causes metallic tastes
Sulfur	Imparts rotten egg odor

The Automated Cafeteria

The automated cafeteria and snack service account for the major dollar volume of the vending industry. A typical automated cafeteria may contain the following equipment.

    (1) pastry dispenser[1] (doughnuts, cakes, cookies, pie);
    (2) dessert dispenser (puddings, fruit salad, fresh fruit);
    (3) soft drink dispenser[1] (postmix, premix, bottles or cans);
    (4) hot food dispenser (stews, prepared dishes);
    (5) soup and canned food dispenser;
    (6) sandwich dispenser;
    (7) cold food dispenser (salads);
    (8) ice-cream dispenser[1];
    (9) milk and chocolate milk dispenser[1];
    (10) coffee, tea, hot chocolate, soup combination vender[1];
    (11) cigarette and cigar dispenser[1];
    (12) candy dispenser[1].

[1] Basic needs for a snack service.

Auxiliary Equipment.
    (1) change maker;
    (2) microwave oven;

(3) condiment table;
(4) can opener;
(5) stirrers, plastic spoons, forks, knives and napkins;
(6) trash receptacle;
(7) water fountain;
(8) utility and storage closets, slop sink, mops and buckets;
(9) water treatment system if required;
(10) tables and chairs.

BIBLIOGRAPHY

ANON. 1969. Flavor-crisp Pressure Fryer. Balantyne Instruments and Electronics, Inc., Omaha, Neb.

ANON. 1970A. How electric char-grilles outperform the oldtime 'pit'. Food Service Magazine *32*, No. 10, 20–24.

ANON. 1970B. Designs for Dining. Designs for Dining, Inc., New York, N.Y.

ANON. 1970C. Char-vec. Harvic Manufacturing Corp., Bronx, N.Y.

ANON. 1970D. Hi-speed Commercial Cooking Equipment, South Bend Range Corp., South Bend, Inc.

ANON. 1970E. Compact Cooking Centers. Market Forge, Everett, Mass.

ANON. 1970F. For Convenience, High Speed Cooking Equipment. Market Forge, Everett, Mass.

ANON. 1970G. Test Kitchen Bull. No. 39A, 41A, 45, and 46. Market Forge, Everett, Mass.

ANON. 1971. Coffee and Cooking Equipment. Cecilware Corporation, Long Island City, N.Y.

CO, D. Y. C. L., and LIVINGSTON, G. E. 1969. Food Technol. *23*, 1568–1579.

COPSON, D. 1962. Microwave Heating. Avi Publishing Co. Westport, Conn.

HALL, C. W. FARRALL, A. W., and RIPPEN, A. L. 1971. Encyclopedia of Food Engineering. Avi Publishing Co., Westport, Conn.

KOTSCHEVAR, L. H. 1970. Principles for Selecting Food Service Equipment. Duke Manufacturing Company, St. Louis, Mo.

LEMOINE, F. K. 1970. Profile of a Restaurant Organization. The Culinary Institute of America, Inc. New Haven, Conn.

MILLER, A. 1970. Char broils 2 sides in 1½ minutes. Food Processing *31*, No. 8, 42–44.

ROGERS, J. L. 1969. Production of Pre-cooked Frozen Foods for Mass Catering. Food Trade Press, Ltd., London.

SHEVLIN, T. S., and MAHLUM, J. M. 1970. Integral heating system reconstitutes frozen meals in 15 min. Food Technol. *24*, 973–986.

TRESSLER, D. K., VAN ARSDEL, W. B., and COPLEY, M. J. 1968. The Freezing Preservation of Foods, 4th Edition, Vol. 4. Avi Publishing Co., Westport, Conn.

WEAVER, M. L. and HUXSOLL, C. C. 1970. Infrared processing improved quality of frozen french-fried potatoes. Food Technol. *24*, No. 10, 1108–1114.

WITCHEL, L. (Editor). 1969. Drive-in Management Guidebook. Harbrace Publications, Inc., Duluth, Minn.

CHAPTER 5

Microwave Cookery

Microwave cookery is synonymous with fast food production. Microwave ovens are considered to be the "darling" of modern high-speed feeding establishments. This form of heating holds the concerted interest of food service personnel. It is a major topic of exploration when systems and rapid methods of preparation are discussed. Even though much publicity has been devoted to this subject, the terminology and proper operation of microwave ovens continue to plague a large segment of the industry and have created an aura of mystery and doubt in the minds of many concerning the merits of this equipment. A reason for this situation is the scanty and superficial information available, notwithstanding the many articles published. Specific instructions emphasizing the full utilitarian value of this mode of cooking would move it out of the realm of "just another heating gadget" to one that deserves full attention in modern fast food installations. It is the intention of this discussion to reduce to practical value the field of microwave cookery so that its usefulness can be realized.

The use of microwave equipment, introduced commercially about 25 years ago, has been sporadic. Since 1962, its popularity has increased because of design improvements. At present, about 75,000 ovens are being sold annually in the United States. It is anticipated that by 1976 sales will reach about one million units annually. This will account for 25% of the oven market. These projected sales figures include the total output for both the domestic and food service market.

Development of Microwave Equipment

Microwaves were known long before 1945, when they were first successfully applied to cooking. At that time, prototype devices were made for aircraft to defrost and heat food. This equipment was capable of heating an 8-oz portion in 1 min. P. L. Spencer, who was responsible for the early development of microwave ovens, holds a number of patents in the field. During that period, three companies began to research the practical aspects of microwave heating: Raytheon, General Electric and Westinghouse. In 1947 the U.S. Navy sponsored an oven development program for submarines which did not make much progress. During the same year, a model emerged which was named the "white range." The cooking chamber was small and the unit was heavy and cluttered with an infinite number of electronic components. This model cooked unevenly and those who tried it became disillusioned with the results.

In 1951 a complicated unit was installed aboard the liner "United States." Because of the complexities of its operation, skills had to be developed to run the oven successfully. The factor of long indoctrination was not practical, although the cooking was considered to be excellent.

During 1954 ovens were designed and marketed for the food service industry. Raytheon sold a practical device named the "Radarange." Uniformity of heating was improved and cooking quality was good. The unit was 6 ft in height and the cavity 20 X 22 X 12 in. in width, depth and height; two magnetrons were located on the top of the cavity. A stirrer, shaped like fan blades, was responsible for energy distribution. Once again, a great deal of skill was required to operate the oven properly. Consequently, its application became limited and the flurry of popularity waned.

Domestic ranges were introduced during 1955 and 1956. These, however, were too expensive and unreliable. The magnetron, the heart of the oven, could not be relied upon and many failures occurred.

The commercial era of microwave cooking actually started during 1960 with the introduction by Litton Industries of an improved and reliable magnetron. Further improvements were developed during 1962 that paved the way for future and sustained growth in this radical departure from conventional cooking methods.

BASIC CONCEPTS OF MICROWAVE HEATING

Basically, microwave cooking employs high-frequency electromagnetic energy called microwave energy, the wave lengths ranging from 0.1 to 30 centimeters. The food absorbs the energy and converts it to heat. Microwaves do not contain heat, but are capable of generating heat when they pass through food and create molecular friction. Conventional or conduction oven cookery employs two factors that affect preparation—time and temperature. Microwave heating is governed by only one factor—time.

The energy is produced by a device known as the magnetron tube. The magnetron operates on high voltage converted from a low-voltage input line. When the magnetron tube is energized, high-frequency energy waves are generated and directed into an oven cavity. The waves move at the speed of light and vibrate at various frequencies.

Microwaves are a form of radiation similar to radio, radar, and infrared. Each has its characteristic wave length and frequency of vibration. Microwaves have a very high frequency, vibrating millions of times per second. When these waves enter a food, their absorption and movement are slowed, the phenomenon being much the same as when light is refracted by water. The absorption of microwave energy causes food molecules to vibrate, creating friction which produces heat. The chemical composition of the food and its physical properties have a direct relationship to the heating time.

An interesting property of microwaves is their ability to be reflected from certain surfaces. If a food is packaged in a metal container, the waves will strike the metallic surface and bounce back, so that the food within the package cannot be heated. Materials, such as paper, certain plastics, plain porcelain, and glass transmit microwaves. During transmission these materials remain cool and unaffected, while the food is being heated.

Microwave Oven Frequency Ratings

Presently, the Federal Communication Commission (FCC) has allocated for commercial use several microwave frequencies of which two are employed in microwave ovens: 915 MHz (megahertz) and 2450 MHz (megahertz). The wave length at 915 MHz is 32 cm or about 12.5 in.; at 2450 MHz it is 12 cm or about 5 in. The term *hertz* stands for the frequency of vibration or number of complete cycles per second. The prefix mega means million; therefore 2450 MHz means 2450 million cycles per second.

In addition to the megahertz rating, a microwave oven is also characterized by its electrical output, measured in kilowatts (kW). An oven with a 1 kW output will require approximately twice the time to cook a food as an oven rated at 2 kW.

THE ANATOMY OF A MICROWAVE OVEN

Figure 5.1 is a diagram depicting the essential components of a microwave oven. They are: (1) cavity or cooking chamber, (2) door, (3) magnetron tube, (4) wave guide, (5) mode stirrer, (6) power supply converter and (7) power input connection.

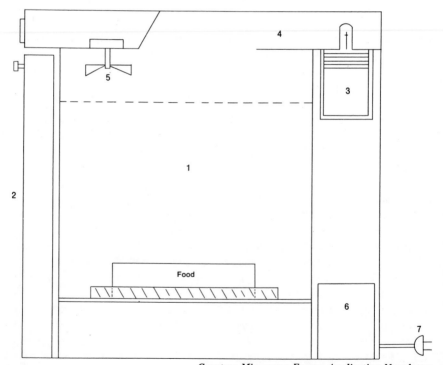

Courtesy Microwave Energy Application Newsletter

FIG. 5.1. ESSENTIAL COMPONENTS OF A MICROWAVE OVEN

Accessories such as switches, timer, door latches, exterior trim, and cavity design may vary according to the manufacturer. In addition, broiler elements may be added for auxilliary heat to brown foods. Fans may also be supplied for exhausting cooking vapors from the cavity.

The power input of 110 or 220 volts is relayed to the power supply converter. The converter has the function of changing the low input voltage to the high voltage required for the magnetron (3) or microwave energy generator. The magnetron then generates high-frequency energy that is transmitted to the cavity or oven chamber by the wave guide (4). The mode stirrer (5) rotates slowly and thus helps to distribute the energy uniformly throughout the cavity. Uniform distribution of the energy within the chamber is mandatory for the production of evenly cooked food. Proper positioning of the product within the cavity is another element that contributes to uniform doneness. However, if the mode stirrer is effective, positioning does not matter. In addition, the food load must be placed on a shelf (glass or plastic) so that the energy will reach its underside. Some manufacturers have eliminated shelves, and in their place have constructed the bottom or floor of the cavity from tempered glass, a sheet of Pyroceram, or in some cases plastic. This provides an unobstructed easy-to-clean chamber. Glass shelves have posed a breakage problem especially with units located in self-service areas.

Construction and Design Features

The oven door (2) is a sensitive and critical part of the microwave assembly. It not only provides access to the cavity, but it must also prevent the energy waves from escaping into the surrounding area. Since this door is opened and closed an infinite number of times during the life of an oven, special consideration has been given to its design and construction. Door tightness and efficiency are achieved by good metal-to-metal contact, in some cases utilizing a quarter-wave slot or electronic "choke" seal around the perimeter which prevents microwave emissions; the slot is filled with a material that is able to absorb any energy escaping from the "choke" seal. Standards of construction enacted by the U.S. Department of Health, Education and Welfare, regulate the construction of doors by requiring that safety interlocks be provided. These are intended to prevent generation of energy when the door is opened. The complete text of these regulations can be found at the end of the chapter.

Strict adherence to sanitary procedures, especially around the door, is essential for prevention of energy leakage. Accumulation of food residue may prevent the door from shutting tightly, so that leakage could become a possibility. Preventive maintenance must be followed. This should include periodic inspections of the locking device, hinges, tightness of the metal-to-metal contact, and door alignment. The oven cavity should be checked for cracks and breaks in the seams and welds.

Accessories and operating controls vary with the manufacturer. Essential accessory components should consist of a durable timing mechanism, master control switch, on-off signal light, and an easily read, permanently affixed panel chart that indicates important operating instructions. An audio alarm that signals the end of the cooking cycle is useful; if several microwave ovens are employed in series, the audio alarm will facilitate production.

Timing mechanisms must be reasonably accurate. Since microwave cooking is based solely on the element of time, an inaccurate device will result in improperly prepared food. Preventive maintenance procedures should include the testing of timers. A reliable stop-watch must be used for this purpose. In addition, timing checks are suggested on all foods prior to production. Purveyor reliability cannot be taken for granted; changes that do occur will be spotted by constant checking.

The life of the magnetron tube can be extended by proper oven operation. Ovens should never be operated unloaded. If it is necessary to check the unit always place a glass of water in the cavity to absorb the energy. When locating or installing ovens, adequate air circulation is advisable around the sides and back.

Advantages of Microwave Ovens

The surge in popularity of microwave ovens during the last 10 years has been due chiefly to their remarkable advantages and the radical departure from conventional heating methods. The following lists these salient attributes:

(1) Reduction in labor costs because of less handling and the elimination of highly skilled personnel.

(2) Rapidity is one of the quickest methods available for reconstitution of frozen uncooked and precooked foods, and is adaptable to the primary preparation of many other forms of food, such as fish, poultry, and bacon.

(3) Versatile production scheduling that will meet peak and low demand periods.

(4) Easy loading and unloading.

(5) Ease of cleaning and sanitizing.

(6) Simplicity of operation; intensive employee training is not required.

(7) Reliability, if testing and preventive maintenance and sanitation procedures are followed.

(8) Adaptability to fast food and automatic production systems.

(9) Excellent mobility due to their compact size and easy installation.

(10) Reduction of power costs.

(11) Minimization of food waste where portion control systems are in operation.

(12) Increased customer turnover realized because of rapid production.

Disadvantages of Microwave Ovens

(1) Microwave ovens are not now adaptable to a full line menu; other means of heating may be required such as convection ovens and pressure steam cookers.

(2) Bulk preparation is not feasible, except where more than one oven is used, or by means of conveyorized continuous equipment.

(3) If more than one item is heated, they must be positioned properly to develop uniform doneness.

(4) The geometry (shape and size) of the food, such as thickness and weight, must be considered for even cooking. Heating time is proportional to the food prepared. The depth or thickness of the product should not exceed 1 in.; 0.5 to 0.75 in. is considered practical. Foods like meat balls or croquettes cook evenly if their shape and weight are uniform.

(5) Foods requiring a crisp and dry surface cannot be properly prepared; breaded fried foods will have a soggy unappetizing crust. This problem may be overcome by using a combination microwave-convection oven, or by partial microwave application, followed by finishing in a convection oven or broiler.

(6) Inconsistent energy distribution within the cavity of the oven will contribute to uneven heating and poor quality.

(7) Uneven thawing will result in inconsistent cooking. The thawed portion will absorb the energy faster, thereby raising its temperature more rapidly, while the unthawed areas will tend to heat more slowly.

(8) Certain plastics and metal containers cannot be used. Plastic dishes, such as Melamine ware, absorb microwaves and may char. Styrene products emit strong noxious odors that will be absorbed by the food.

(9) Certain sauces (Hollandaise) and heavy gravies will break down and form a film. Unless the gravies are composed of waxy rice and wheat flour, they should be prepared separately and added as a garnish.

(10) Items requiring different timing cycles cannot be combined, but should be prepared separately for optimum results.

(11) Placement of the oven must be considered, so that adequate air circulation is available around the exterior.

(12) The effect of radiation on the human body requires preventive safeguards.

APPLICATIONS OF MICROWAVE COOKING

Timing and Timing Test Procedures

It was previously pointed out that time is the one factor which must be controlled for quality production. Continuous testing of all products undergoing microwave preparation must become a fixed function of daily operational activities. The following step-by-step procedures are suggested for this testing program:

(1) Set up a chart in front of the oven. The chart should be placed at eye level for ease of reading. A slate board or magnetic sign set with removable letters is also suggested, so that changes can be made when required.

(2) Manufacturer's instructions should be read. These usually cite methods

for plating and the time necessary for preparation. If instructions are not provided, they should be requested, so that a basis for comparison is available.

(3) Measure the thickness of the food to determine whether it conforms to optimum height requirements of 0.5 to 1 in. Observe the geometry or configuration of the item. If the shape appears irregular it may pose a problem of uneven doneness.

(4) Take a temperature reading of the food. The starting temperature of the food prior to heating should be the same; otherwise the finished food will vary in uniformity. If the product is thawed the temperature should range between 34 and 38°F. Foods heated directly from the freezer should register temperatures of -10 to 0°F. If both heating from the frozen state and heating from the thawed state are used for identical products, then two sets of heating cycles will be necessary. This practice should not be encouraged. It may be required, however, during slow periods when single portions are ordered which must be prepared directly from the frozen stock.

(5) Before actual testing an inspection of the oven cavity and door closure is recommended to ensure that they are throughly cleaned.

(6) When placing the test product in the cavity always place it in the center. After the time cycle is ascertained, retest by placing the food in another location. This will determine if the oven is working properly and is transmitting the energy uniformly throughout the chamber.

(7) Follow the packer's heating recommendations for the first test. At the completion of the cycle, check the temperature of the item. Use a thermometer for this purpose. Insert the stem of the thermometer into the center of the food. Taste the product for palatability, texture, flavor and check for eye appeal. If the packer's recommended time cycle does not meet with approval, another trial must be run. The time and internal temperature of each run should be noted and the reason for rejection (Fig. 5.2).

(8) Once the initial optimum heating cycle has been established, further testing should then be put on a once-a-day schedule. Tests should be made on all new shipments regardless of the supplier's reliability. It is important to perform the tests at the same time of day, preferably in the morning or during a slow period.

(9) A critical factor that is sometimes overlooked and can lead to erroneous results is the type of package or plating material. For uniform results these items should have the same properties. If it is the custom to remove the product from the original container, this procedure must be followed for each test.

Plating and Primary Preparation

Plating and primary preparation of the food before heating are important steps, if quality cooking is to be achieved. In actual production these steps encompass defrosting or thawing, assembly, heating techniques and shielding.

Defrosting.—It is advisable to defrost foods before microwave heating. This procedure will ensure an even doneness. Less energy is required and heating

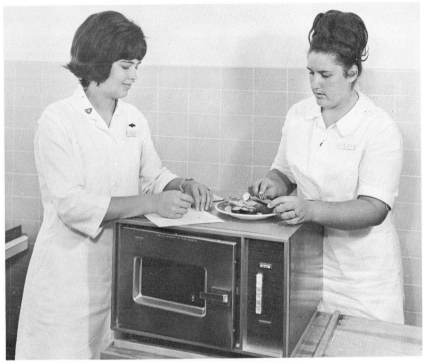

Courtesy Stouffer Food Division of Litton Industries, Inc.

FIG. 5.2. ESTABLISHING MICROWAVE HEAT CYCLES

cycles are shortened. Where microwave cooking is an integral part of the preparation center, a smoother flowing system will result from prior thawing. In this case, defrosting is easily accomplished in thawing refrigerators. These units should be installed between the main freezer storage areas and the preparation center.

If emergencies arise, or for slow demand periods, defrosting can be done successfully in the microwave oven, if certain procedures are followed. For immediate thawing of meat, poultry or fish, each 6 to 10-oz portion should be heated for about 20 sec per side. Set the timer for 20 sec. When the first cycle is completed, remove the product from the oven and turn it over. Do not turn the food in the oven, in order to prevent spilling or spattering interior of the oven. Keep a record of the actual time, so that a reference will be available for future use. In addition, the temperature of the item before and after defrosting should also be noted and compared to the heating time.

After defrosting, the food should be removed from the chamber and allowed to "rest" for 60 to 90 sec, to permit any remaining ice crystals to melt. The product is then ready for the final cooking cycle.

Microwave ovens are adaptable to production flow defrosting, where more

TABLE 5.1

DEFROSTING TIME

Item	Procedure	Time to Defrost
Strip steak (12-oz)	Cover with waxed paper, defrost in microwave by applying 25 sec of time to both sides. Finish off to desired doneness in conventional broiler. Reheating may be done later in microwave.	50 sec
Lobster tails (2 5-oz tails)	Cover with waxed paper, defrost, and cook either in microwave or under broiler.	45 sec
Trout (12-oz)	Cover with waxed paper, defrost, and cook either in microwave or under broiler.	50 sec
Lamb and pork chops (2)	Cover with waxed paper, defrost in microwave, cook under broiler.	50 sec
Doughnuts	Heat uncovered.	5 sec
Cakes	Heat uncovered.	25 sec
Frozen, baked stuffed potato	Depress center before freezing. Cover with waxed paper, defrost. Heat to serving temperature either in microwave or brown under broiler.	45 sec

Source: Litton Industries.

than one oven is installed, or when the final preparation is performed in a broiler or convection oven. Bulk portion packs can be thawed prior to microwave heating, or several portions can be removed from the container and heated. Table 5.1 shows the defrosting time for a variety of foods, heated in an oven with a power output of 1¼ kW.

Plating and Food Positioning.—Casserole type dishes, such as Beef Burgundy and Shrimp Creole, will heat evenly if the product is uniformly positioned around the inner rim of the plate and the center is slightly depressed. Reduction in the thickness of the center area allows the energy to penetrate more uniformly, resulting in an even degree of doneness.

When plating combination platters, such as roast beef, potatoes and buttered brussels sprouts, excellent results will be obtained if food overhanging the dish is eliminated. Microwaves will tend to heat these overhanging sections more rapidly, producing overcooked, dried out or charred conditions. Combination platters will also pose problems of uneven cooking if the percentage of each component is not limited. Entrées consisting of meat or fish, potatoes and a vegetable will heat properly if the percentage of each does not exceed the following: fish or meat 50%; potatoes 25%; and vegetables 25%.

Loose-textured foods will absorb more energy and heat faster than those that are firmer. Meat portions should be sliced and placed flat on the plate. Stacking of solid food items will produce uneven cooking. Before heating, a thin gravy or au jus should be applied to the meat in sufficient amounts to just "top" the surface of the product. If too much gravy is used, the excess will probably boil off, spill over, or give the dish an unappealing and unappetizing appearance. Speedier production is possible by covering the food. Dome covers, waxed paper or inverted unwaxed paper plates can be used for this purpose. Covers should be placed over the dish loosely to allow for venting. Dome sets of various sizes are manufactured. They are designed with side vents to allow the steam to escape, which prevent moisture build-up and soggy food. Finger grips are molded into the dome for easy removal. Most are disposable and therefore will not add to the sanitation load. For increased eye appeal, shallow entrée plates are recommended. Shallow dishes are easier to handle and permit smoother positioning of the food.

Foods packaged in plastic cooking pouches can be heated directly. The top side of the pouch must be punctured before heating. This allows steam to escape and prevents bursting due to an increase of the internal pressure. Pouches should be placed in an upright position, preferably in a serving dish to avoid leakage through the steam escape holes. Plastic pouch heating should actually be performed in two stages. Stage 1 consists of heating for 1 to 2 min, or until the bag begins to expand. The pouch is removed from the cavity (stage 2) and shaken so that the contents rest on the bottom. Holes are then punctured near the top, and the pouch is again inserted in the oven on a dish in an upright position. Heating is continued for an additional period. When the cycle is completed, the bag is opened, by cutting across the top, placing the contents in an appropriate serving dish, garnishing and serving.

Production Assembly Problems.—Production assembly problems may be encountered with items requiring different time cycles or with foods that are similar but vary in size, such as potatoes. If potatoes are of different sizes, they may be separated according to size before cooking; the smaller ones require less preparation time. Another method is to group the potatoes by size in the oven, the smaller ones towards the front, the larger at the rear. The timer is set for the smaller ones which are removed from the oven when cooked. The timer may then be reset for the larger potatoes. However, this may not be necessary: the time cycle can be determined for the larger unit, and at the appropriate time the oven door can be opened and the food removed. When the door is reclosed, the timer will continue until it reaches its final setting. This procedure should be followed when cooking foods that require turning. Items such as turkeys and large roasts may have to be turned 2 or 3 times during a cycle to equalize the degree of cooking.

In cases of volume production, foods requiring similar heating cycles can be assembled and prepared together. It is important to realize that there are no short cuts to quality production. Correct timing in microwave cookery is essential for ultimate success.

Delayed Cooking Procedure.—Delayed cooking procedures or shielding may be necessary when preparing irregular cuts of meat. This method can be compared to the photographic process of enlarging prints, wherein masking or dodging is practiced to increase or highlight a specific area of the picture.

Since metal reflects microwave energy, it is possible to take advantage of this fact by using metal foil to restrict heating of specific areas. When preparing a leg of lamb, the narrow section can be wrapped in foil for a part of the cooking cycle. The same technique can be applied to chicken and turkeys. The wings and legs are wrapped in foil and unwrapped when 3/4 of the cooking cycle is completed. In all cases the foil must be smooth and the edges evenly folded. Shielding prior to microwave cooking has many other advantageous applications, although only a few examples have been cited; improvising should be attempted to supplement standard procedures if uneven cooking of irregular shaped foods becomes a problem.

"Take-Out" Order Procedures.—Microwave heating has become a boon to facilities specializing in "take-out" orders. Ovens are usually used to perform rapid heating chores and are located in areas that are accessible to the customer for self-heating. Items such as sandwiches containing pre-cooked fillings, hot dogs, and French fried potatoes are suited for microwave heating, and are easily handled by the customer. French fries will be hot, but limp.

Sandwiches should be assembled and wrapped in open-end bags; the wrapping keeps the ingredients from drying out prior to and during heating. Portions of French fries should also be placed in bags, which can then be heated along with the other products. Preparation time in a 1½ kW output oven averages about 18 sec. Deep dish apple pie, tarts, turnovers, Danish pastry are all suitable for microwave heating. These products should also be put into waxed bags and heated for 15 sec. Waxed paper will not be affected in the oven. However, the wax may melt or become tacky from the heat of the food.

Primary Cooking Procedures.—Microwave ovens are suitable for cooking raw products, or for finishing partially cooked items. For example, when orders are received for meat that is being roasted in a conventional or convection oven, a portion can be sliced from it and completed in the microwave unit to the required degree of doneness.

Bacon, sausage, pancakes or French toast can be prepared ahead of time and refrigerated. They can be heated and served on demand.

Table 5.2 lists a number of selected foods that can be fully cooked in a 1kW output microwave oven.

Browning in Microwave Cooking

A major disadvantage attributed to microwave cooking is the absence of surface browning, especially with meat products. Foods that are not properly browned or lack a crisp texture are considered unappealing and unappetizing by most consumers, who anticipate browned and crisp food surfaces when dining out, because this tantalizing texture is seldom duplicated in home cooking.

Browning is a result of a chemical reaction between food sugars and amino acids found in protein products. At low temperatures the reaction proceeds slowly. As temperatures are increased the process is accelerated. Temperatures above 350°F are necessary to produce an acceptable brown color on food surfaces.

In microwave cookery, surface temperature rarely exceeds 212°F, and in many cases it is lower. Thus browning does not occur, and the food surface appears gray and unappealing. Under certain conditions, however, browning will take place. Beef roasts, chickens and turkeys, because of their large size, require long cooking cycles. These items and others that contain surface fat will reach temperatures above 212°F at the surface so that some browning will result.

There are alternatives that are capable of overcoming this deficiency. Presearing will promote an acceptable brown surface. After searing, the food is ready for final microwave heating. This method is effective with steaks, chops and small roasts. Another procedure is to remove the food from the microwave oven when 80% cooked and place it in a convection or regular oven or broiler for

Courtesy Stouffer Food Division of Litton Industries, Inc.

FIG. 5.3. MICROWAVE AND INFRARED OVEN COMBINATIONS (A) IS A LITTON MODEL 550 MICROWAVE OVEN (B) IS A LITTON QUARTZ-PLATE INFRARED OVEN, MODEL HE-5000

TABLE 5.2

PRIMARY COOKING OF UNCOOKED AND RAW FOODS

Food	Portion Size	Procedure	Preparation Time*
Meats			
thin-sliced bacon	1 lb	Soften by heating 2 min. Separate slices and finish to order by heating in microwave oven.	30 to 45 sec per slice
link sausage and lamb chops	½ lb 2 at 5-oz each	Heat in a covered, non-metallic dish for 2 min. Brown as needed on grill or under broiler. Partially cook in microwave oven and finish under broiler at time of service, or pre-sear and cook to doneness in microwave oven at time of service.	2 min Approx 30 to 35 sec per chop
pork chops	2 at 4-oz each	Partially cook in the microwave oven and finish under the broiler at time of service, or pre-sear and cook to doneness in the microwave oven at time of service.	Approx 25 to 30 sec per chop
New York, rib or T-bone steak	12 to 14-oz	Pre-sear on hot grill or broiler at time of service; heat to serving temperature in microwave oven.	35 to 45 sec
Rib of beef	1 slice 5 to 6-oz	Pre-cook rib of beef to rare degree. Hold in refrigerator until time of service. Slice and heat each portion as required, to serving temperature in microwave oven.	Approx 30 sec per slice
Seafood			
lobster tail	4 to 5-oz	If frozen, defrost by heating for approximately 30 sec. Split tails, brush with melted butter, season as desired and cook to doneness in microwave oven. If desired, brown before serving under hot broiler.	60 sec

salmon steak	8 oz	If frozen, defrost by heating for approximately 30 sec. Brush with melted butter, season and cook to doneness in the microwave oven. If desired, brown before serving under a hot broiler.	90 sec
halibut steak	8 oz	If frozen, defrost by heating for approximately 30 sec. Brush with melted butter, season and cook to doneness in the microwave oven. If desired, brown before serving under a hot broiler.	90 sec
swordfish steak	8 oz	If frozen, defrost by heating for approximately 30 sec. Brush with melted butter, season and cook to doneness in the microwave oven. If desired, brown before serving under a hot broiler.	90 sec
brook trout	10 oz	If frozen, defrost by heating for approximately 45 to 60 sec. Stuff if desired, season and cook to doneness. If desired, brown before serving under a hot broiler.	105 sec
shrimp	8 oz	If frozen, defrost by heating in a covered, non-metallic dish for approximately 45 sec. Cook in a covered, non-metallic dish one layer deep. After cooking, drain and rinse well in cold water.	2½ to 3 min
Vegetables Idaho potatoes	one 7 oz	Wash and dry. Prick 2 to 3 times. Cook for recommended length of time or until soft. Let stand 5 min before opening.	3 to 5 min
corn on the cob	1 cob	Brush generously with drawn butter, salt and loosely wrap in waxed paper.	45 sec

*For 1 kW output oven.
Source: Litton Industries.

the remainder of the cooking operation. This method will develop the desired brown, crisp surface (Fig. 5.3).

Dual-purpose ovens are being marketed that combine microwave processing with convection or infrared heating. Shallow metal pans may be used in these combination ovens, because the second-stage heating process (convection or infrared) is sufficient to heat all areas to an even degree of doneness. To ensure uniformity, all food prepared in dual-purpose equipment should be turned after the microwave cycle is completed.

SELECTED EXAMPLES OF MICROWAVE COOKERY

Fish

(1) Cut fillets into equal size portions and place on flat dishes. When purchasing precut fillets, it is advisable to have them all cut uniformly.

(2) Whole fillets, when more than one are to be heated, should be positioned equidistant from each other so that the energy is evenly distributed. Turning at the midway point is recommended for uniformity.

(3) For whole fish, remove all excess water before heating. Shielding the tail section will prevent it from overcooking. Turning is necessary for even doneness.

(4) Scallops will cook uniformly if they are about the same size. Irregular or odd shapes should be cut or cubed uniformly. Each piece should be spaced evenly on a flat dish and squeezed lightly to remove excess water.

(5) To enhance eye appeal and flavor, spread a mixture of seasoned bread crumbs and brown butter over the fish. Paprika sprinkled on some varieties, such as blue fish, will improve the appearance. To reduce spattering, apply a thin layer of oil or butter over the surface; these will also produce a slight glaze. Spices and herbs can be mixed in the oil and butter for varied appeal.

(6) Preparation time may change with the species of fish. Loose-textured or spongy structured fish will require less heating time than solid, meaty ones. Haddock, halibut, cod steaks, striped bass, and lemon sole require less heating than salmon steaks, lobster and blue fish fillets.

(7) The weight of the fish has a bearing on the time cycle. Test runs should be made to determine the heating time per pound.

(8) Additional techniques must be followed when cooking lobster. A whole lobster, in shell, is placed in a Pyrex container. Water is added, about 1/2 cup per pound. The eyes are removed and the claws are cracked. Cover the container before heating. A 1½-lb lobster will take about 3 min to cook in a 2 kW output oven. Frozen lobster tails, 8-oz portions, should be defrosted for 25 sec before heating. The preparation time is 1 min in a 2 kW output oven. Aluminum foil shielding may be needed around the narrow section to prevent excessive cooking.

(9) Baked fish can be successfully prepared by microwave. Stuffing will assist the cooking, as the microwaves will penetrate to the center. The stuffing will heat evenly, spreading the heat to the fleshy parts so that a uniform-textured

product results. The interior is first salted and brushed with melted butter. Grated onion is added for flavoring. The fish is cooked for 1 min and removed from the oven. Bread stuffing is then placed in the cavity and the fish is tied. The exterior is brushed with melted butter and sprinkled with onion salt and paprika. During heating the fish should be turned.

(10) Salmon and tuna loaves are easily prepared from the canned product. Various seasonings are added, such as lemon juice and a mixture of pepper. For each cup of fish, one cup of dry bread crumbs and one egg are added. The ingredients are mixed with the fish and formed into a loaf or patties. Cooking time is about 1 min in a 2 kW oven. Tables 5.3A–E give the cooking time for other foods in a 2 kW oven.

TABLE 5.3A

HEATING INSTRUCTIONS FOR MEAT IN A 2 kW OUTPUT OVEN

Food	Portion Oz	Special Instructions	Cooking Time Sec
roast beef slices	8	Pre-roast; cool, slice cold. Shape flat as possible.	35
chopped sirloin	8	Pre-sear on hot broiler. Cool. Heat from refrigerated temperature.	35
sausage	4	Pre-sear on hot broiler. Cool. Heat from refrigerated temperature.	10
barbequed spareribs	6	Cook conventionally, then refrigerate. Cover when heating.	35
Swiss steak w/gravy	8	Cook conventionally, then refrigerate. Baste with sauce. Cover when heating.	40
pot roast (individual serving)	6	Cook conventionally, then refrigerate. Cover when heating.	25

Source: Litton Industries.

TABLE 5.3B

DEFROSTING INSTRUCTIONS FOR MEAT IN A 2 kW OUTPUT OVEN

Food	Portion Oz	Special Instructions	Cooking Time Sec
filet mignon	9	Cover with wax paper. Turn over after 15 sec.	30
rib steak	12	Heat in bag. Turn over after 15 sec.	35
sirloin strip	14	Heat in bag. Turn over after 20 sec.	40

Source: Litton Industries.

TABLE 5.3C

HEATING INSTRUCTIONS FOR VEGETABLES IN A 2 kW OUTPUT OVEN

Food	Portion Oz	Special Instructions	Cooking Time Sec
baked potato (raw)	10	Heat uncovered. Then wrap in foil and allow to stand 2 min. (potato will continue to cook in foil). Break with fork, serve.	130
baked potato (fully baked)	10	Heat uncovered from room temperature.	30
baked potato (pre-baked to 80% doneness)	10	Heat uncovered from room temperature.	50
corn (kernel)	4	Cook conventionally, cool portion, brush with butter and refrigerate. Cover. Heat to order.	15
peas	4	Cook conventionally, cool portion, brush with butter, and refrigerate. Cover. Depress center. Heat to order.	15
broccoli	4	Cook conventionally, cool portion, brush with butter, and refrigerate. Cover. Depress center. Heat to order.	15
carrots	4	Cook conventionally, cool portion, brush with butter, and refrigerate. Cover. Depress center. Heat to order.	15
Italian green beans	4	Cook conventionally, cool portion, brush with butter, and refrigerate. Cover. Depress center. Heat to order.	15
hashbrown potatoes	4	Brown on griddle. Portion, heat to order.	20
corn on cob		Brush with drawn butter, season, loosely wrap in waxed paper.	45

Source: Litton Industries.

TABLE 5.3D

HEATING INSTRUCTIONS FOR CASSEROLES IN A 2 kW OUTPUT OVEN

Food	Portion Oz	Special Instructions	Cooking Time Sec
beef goulash	8	Cover, depress center. Heat in non-metallic dish.	40
beef stew	8	Cover, depress center. Heat in non-metallic dish.	45
beef stroganoff	8	Cover, depress center. Heat in non-metallic dish.	45
cabbage rolls	6	Cover, depress center. Heat in non-metallic dish.	40

TABLE 5.3D CONT.

Food	Portion Oz	Special Instructions	Cooking Time Sec
chicken a la king	8	Cover, depress center. Heat in non-metallic dish.	40
chili con carne	7	Cover, depress center. Heat in non-metallic dish.	40
chop suey	8	Cover, depress center. Heat in non-metallic dish.	40
corned beef hash	6	Slice two 3 oz. portions cold. Cover, heat in non-metallic dish.	35
creamed chicken	7	Cover, depress center. Heat in non-metallic dish.	40
lasagne	8	Bake conventionally, slightly undercook. Keep depth to 2 inches or less. Cover, heat in non-metallic dish.	45
lobster Newburg	7	Cover, depress center. Heat in non-metallic dish.	35
macaroni/beef & tomatoes	9	Cover, depress center. Heat in non-metallic dish.	50
macaroni & cheese	10	Cover, depress center. Heat in non-metallic dish.	55
meat loaf	6	Slice two 3 oz. portions cold. Cover, heat in non-metallic dish.	35
pizza (one 10 in.)		Pre-bake shell conventionally, slightly over-browning. Let air dry on rack. Do not refrigerate. Assemble and heat to order.	45
Salisbury steak	6	Cover, depress center. Heat in non-metallic dish.	35
shrimp Creole	8	Cover, depress center. Heat in non-metallic dish.	40
sliced beef in gravy	4 (meat) 2 (gravy)	Slice meat cold, portion. When order is received, place on plate with 1 oz. gravy under and 1 oz. gravy over meat. Cover, heat in non-metallic dish.	30
sliced pork in gravy	4 (meat) 2 (gravy)	Slice meat cold, portion. When order is received, place on plate with 1 oz. gravy under and 1 oz. gravy over meat. Cover, heat in non-metallic dish.	30
turkey Tetrazzini	7	Cover, depress center. Heat in non-metallic dish.	40
tuna-noodle casserole	7	Cover, depress center. Heat in non-metallic dish.	40
Welsh rarebit	5	Cover, depress center. Heat in non-metallic dish.	30
sliced turkey in gravy	4 (meat) 2 (gravy)	Slice meat cold, portion. When order is received, place on plate with 1 oz. gravy under and 1 oz. gravy over meat. Cover, heat in non-metallic dish.	30

Source: Litton Industries.

TABLE 5.3E

HEATING INSTRUCTIONS FOR BREADS, ROLLS, PASTRIES
IN A 2 kW OUTPUT OVEN
(Pre-baked)

Food	Portion Oz	Special Instructions	Cooking Time Sec
dinner rolls	2	Heat uncovered from room temperature.	5
biscuits	2	Heat uncovered from room temperature.	5
bread, (banana, date nut)	1 (small loaf)	Heat uncovered from room temperature.	15
tarts, fruit	2	Heat uncovered from room temperature.	15
muffins	2	Heat uncovered from room temperature.	6
pie slices	1 slice (6 oz)	Heat uncovered from refrigerated temperature.	15
pie slices	1 slice (8 oz)	Heat uncovered from refrigerated temperature.	20
whole fruit pie	10″	Heat uncovered from refrigerated temperature.	90
doughnuts	2	Heat uncovered from room temperature.	5
brown bread	6 oz	Heat uncovered from room temperature.	12
Indian pudding	6 oz	Heat uncovered from room temperature.	15

Puddings, cereals and other foods that may foam or froth should be placed in a deep dish with ample space between the top of the product and top of the dish to allow for expansion.

Thin gravies will heat uniformly without separation. If gravy separation occurs, use a thickener composed of waxy rice and wheat flour, or prepare separately and add to entrée when removed from the oven. Another method is to add the gravy upon completion of 2/3 of the cooking cycle.

Source: Litton Industries.

Meat and Poultry

Steaks and chops.—Steaks and chops should be pre-seared before microwave heating. This two-step procedure will give the proper degree of doneness and an appealing brown surface. The reverse procedure will produce parallel results. Experiments should be performed to determine the cooking time necessary to produce products that are rare, medium or well done. When running these tests, the cooking time must be recorded.

Poultry.—Poultry products are superb when prepared by microwave heating, as they actually benefit from this mode of preparation. The characteristic poultry flavor is retained and the texture cannot be duplicated by conventional heating. There is also a better control of shrinkage and less bone discoloration. Prepared chicken dishes and parts cook better in a microwave oven. If browning is required, a two-step procedure must be followed, as with steaks and chops.

Many kinds of poultry dishes can be cooked so that a wide menu selection is possible. Those recipes calling for sauces and dressing cannot be handled in the usual manner, but should be prepared separately and added at the final stages of heating. Poultry cooks best without stuffing, as the large cavity actually assists in uniform development. The cavity also helps reduce the "set-aside" period, as little external or post-cooking will occur once the product is removed from the oven. For large whole poultry, turning is necessary at the 1/3 and 2/3 cooking point. When two-thirds of the cycle is completed, the dressing can be placed in the cavity and tied. Sauces and glazes can be applied after one-third of the cycle has been reached. Sauces such as Polynesian pineapple topping will permeate the surface, so that the skin and adjacent areas become saturated with this appealing flavor.

Wings and legs may require shielding during the last third of the cycle to prevent overcooking. If shielding at this point is not feasible because of the high surface temperature, it can be applied at the start and kept on for two-thirds of the heating time. Many distinctive and appetizing garnishes are available to enhance poultry. These are treated separately in Chapter 9.

Roasts.—Solid cuts of meat used for roasting can be successfully cooked in the microwave oven. Several important procedures must be followed for proper development and uniformity.

The shape of the roast must be considered. If the height is uniform, the correct degree of doneness will result. If one end is smaller, shielding may have to be used to cover this section. Frequent turning and basting will assure full flavor and color development. A fat layer about one-fourth inch thick is desirable, as it will help to produce some surface browning. However, it may be necessary to complete the roast in a conventional or convection oven to give a deep brown crispy crust. Meat under the fat layer will reach the highest temperature, while those portions not covered by fat will not receive a proportionate amount of heating. Fat should be trimmed around the bone area.

An important aspect that requires consideration is post-cooking, namely, cooking that occurs after a roast is removed from an oven. The influence of penetrating heat on the roast is to store heat internally. Over-cooking becomes a possibility. This situation is avoidable by reducing the time cycle and allowing the roast to set for a period of time known as the "set-aside" or "stand-by" period. Depending on the roast size, the cut of meat and the internal temperature, this may be from 20 min to 1 hr. During the set-aside period the internal heat has an opportunity to distribute throughout the roast, and this is instrumental in producing the proper doneness. A long, slow cycle will reduce the set-aside period by one-third. Because of the post-cooking problem, it is advisable to run time-study tests to find the optimum cycle necessary to produce rare, medium or well done roasts. This procedure will not only give the desired results, but it will reduce waste and customer complaints due to poor preparation.

Vegetables.—Fresh or frozen vegetables can be prepared by microwave heating and with excellent results. Many fresh vegetables, such as spinach, peas or corn, can be cooked without water as they contain natural water in sufficient amounts. The energy will heat this water, which in turn cooks the product. Because of waterless preparation, the loss of nutrients is reduced to a minimum. Tomatoes and other soft-textured vegetables are prepared rapidly. Depending on the size, heating time will average 30 sec per portion.

Solid vegetables, such as carrots and beets, should be cooked according to size and only one size prepared at a time. If many sizes are involved, slicing, dicing or cutting them into uniform pieces will eliminate the problem. Parts or small unit vegetables like whole-kernel corn, wax beans and peas will produce better results than mashed products.

Frozen vegetables should be defrosted and drained before heating. If thawing is performed in the microwave, these products must be turned, so that the ice remaining on the bottom will melt. Starchy and fibrous vegetables should be treated as fresh vegetables, and require a longer cooking time to make them tender. One-half to 1 cup of water should be added for each pound of starchy or fibrous vegetable.

Certain vegetables are effectively blanched by microwave heating, and are superior to those blanched by other methods of processing. Primarily, blanching is needed to deactivate enzymes. Blanching is usually performed at a temperature of about 185°F. As a result, frozen vegetables lose many of their fresh characteristics. Corn on the cob becomes excessively wrinkled and looks over-cooked, whereas spinach becomes limp. Under microwave heating these deficiencies are reduced, since little or no water is required for blanching and as long as the timing is controlled the energy will reach the center of the product.

MICROWAVE HEATING IN FAST FOOD PREPARATION

Microwave ovens, because of their many advantages, such as rapid heating, mobility and compactness, are being employed by a vast segment of the food service industry. Hospitals, institutions, schools, commissaries and vending companies are finding them useful for primary and secondary heating. Many other categories of feeding establishments are also experiencing excellent results with microwave ovens. The full impact of this method of cooking has not been realized. However, all indications point toward wider use. By the end of this decade, it is projected that 80% of all feeding establishments will have installed one or more units, and that 40% of the households will be employing them.

Because of the present trend toward system motivation, many new food preparation areas are being designed around microwave equipment. By making them the focal point of the preparation center, greater flexibility is engendered for intermediate and terminal heating.

It was previously pointed out that, once the basic techniques are mastered, microwave cooking is easier, and the accuracy with which the correct degree of doneness can be obtained is much greater than with conventional ovens. A common drawback that many food service operators are experiencing is that of not utilizing their equipment to the fullest extent. If all the advantages are to be realized, a greater attempt at planning must be engaged in, to broaden the role of microwave cooking. To properly align a planning pattern to the overall operation requires the coordination of several sub-systems, such as menu planning, personnel instruction and procedural assistance, and purchasing. Actually, greater skill is needed for planning than for the operation of the oven. In addition, if the entire operation revolves around efficiency foods, then proper garnishing and plating techniques must also be developed.

Classification of Microwave Equipment

(1) Classification according to electrical characteristics
110-volt, single magnetron
220-volt, single magnetron
220-volt, two magnetron plus high and low power selectors;
output range 0.7 to 2.5 kW
(2) Cavity dimensions (average of several models)
110-volt, single magnetron: 12 in. wide X 8 in. high X 12 in. deep
220-volt, single magnetron: 16 in. wide X 11 in. high X 14 in. deep
220-volt, single magnetron: 20 in. wide X 15 in. high X 16 in. deep
(3) Continuous conveyor ovens
220-volt, 1 to 4 magnetrons, output range 6 to 50 kW;
dimensions: 27 in. wide, 58 in. high X 130 in. long
(4) Combination ovens
Microwave, infrared combination
Microwave, convection combination
Microwave, steam combination
(5) Door design
Vertical, sliding side-hinged, bottom-hinged
(6) Timing mechanism
Push button timer with 4 to 6 settings (Fig. 5.4)
Dial timer 1 sec to 30 min
With the exception of the industrial continuous conveyor oven, all the others can be installed on counter tops or mobile carts.

Testing for Oven Efficiency

Periodically, microwave equipment should be tested for operating efficiency and food quality characteristics. When purchasing new equipment it is advisable to be in a position to compare efficiency and operating characteristics with others on the market. Cost comparisons and production output should also be determined. The following items are factors pertinent to this survey:

(1) Construction of all new equipment must conform to Federal regulations promulgated by the Department of Health, Education and Welfare (HEW), Department of Labor, and F.C.C. A discussion of these regulations will be found at the end of this chapter.

Courtesy Litton Industries, Inc.

FIG. 5.4. MICROWAVE OVEN, MODEL 500 WITH PUSHBUTTON TIMER

(2) Timing devices should be checked against a reliable stop-watch. This test is extremely important, since the element of time is the guiding factor for quality preparation.

(3) When testing an oven, timer or magnetron, never operate it empty, as damage will result to the energy-producing component. Place a glass of water in the oven before testing to prevent damage.

(4) Selected food items should be used when tests are made to determine energy distribution. Always employ the same type of food for these tests, so that a pattern of the degree of doneness can be developed and compared. A record of each test should be kept for reference. The following data are necessary: food item, weight, geometry of sample, internal temperature at completion, time cycle, degree of doneness, quality comments.

(5) A quick method to check the energy distribution is to place six equal glasses of water in various oven locations. These should always be positioned in a predetermined pattern, equidistant from each other, so that the energy can be checked over the entire area. Check the starting temperatures in each glass and record. Plot the position of each glass on a cardboard template. The dimensions of the plotting board should be the same as the shelf. Save the template for future tests. After each cycle, insert a thermometer into the water and note the temperature of each glass. If the difference between the final and initial temperature is about the same, then the energy distribution is considered satisfactory. If wide temperature variations are noticed, uniform cooking results will be questionable. At this point, a check of the oven's components is necessary. The

mode stirrer may be inoperative and need an adjustment or replacement. The magnetron tube should be checked or replaced.

Extended testing will warrant the employment of different types of food, namely: potatoes; rolls or muffins; chicken parts, preferably legs or wings; or two whole small chickens tied and positioned so that they rest on their back. Refrigerated biscuits produce good results. Thawed frozen entrées are useful for testing purposes. These foods should be carefully placed in glass casseroles and spread evenly to prevent high or low spots. Three portions for each test are sufficient. Spacing and shelf positioning must conform to a fixed pattern following the scheme which was previously discussed.

Commercial Installations

The installation of microwave ovens for mass volume production has made notable strides. Hospitals and schools have benefited economically from the use of this equipment, since it fulfills the objectives of mass feeding through an orderly and well defined production flow system. Chain restaurants and other types of establishments with central commissary facilities are preparing frozen entrées on a mass scale which are later heated by microwave ovens on location.

The Rahway Hospital in Rahway, New Jersey, is an example of a modern institution that serves frozen convenience foods exclusively which are all heated in microwave equipment. Twenty employees and two dieticians cater to 225 patients. Entrées are assembled and heated by microwave units on the patient's floor. These ovens are placed on mobile carts and when not used are stored in alcoves. Ovens are monitored by a closed circuit TV system. The pictures are relayed to screens located in the dietician's office. Each of the two dieticians observes four units. This enables them to see that the ovens are being operated properly.

Menus are scheduled on a 14-day cycle. Patients have the option of selecting up to 12 different entrées for lunch and dinner. An automatic counting machine assorts and tallies the menu selections. Patients have a wide selection of foods, many of which are considered gourmet specialties. In addition, frozen vegetables, fruit, pies, cake, scrambled eggs, meat and poultry are made available to the patient, all of which are heated by microwave. Steaks and chops are purchased fresh and seared before heating in the microwave equipment.

In the kitchen, which is located on the lower level of the hospital, trays are assembled and loaded with the unheated food. Pre-plating is performed by three employees. One places the entrée on a disposable plate, another portions the salads and desserts, while the third distributes the accessories and disposable tableware. The trays are then placed on cold carts and held at temperatures of 38-40°F. The carts are next sent to each floor where they are heated by microwave. When the patient is finished eating, the tray, utensils and uneaten food are dropped into rolling trash carts fitted with a disposable bag. The cold carts are returned to the kitchen area where they are washed, sterilized and held in readiness for the following meal.

The Xerodyne Corporation of Haywood, California, employs conveyorized microwave ovens for volume cooking of chicken parts. These are breaded and cooked for 6 min in a microwave-steam atmosphere. The chicken is then deep-fried for less than a minute to brown the surface. This step may be omitted for customers who wish to perform their own browning. The product is then frozen in a liquid nitrogen tunnel and packaged.

A twin-tunnel microwave oven is used. Each tunnel has separate controls that change the belt speed and temperature. Belts are made of perforated plastic that withstand the effects of the steam and microwave energy. Steam nozzles inside the tunnels provide a controlled-moisture atmosphere. This provision eliminates product desiccation and furnishes up to 10% of the cooking energy.

Breading amounts to 12% by weight of the finished chicken. A superior product results that is juicier and has more flavor. The better quality is attributed to faster cooking and immediate frying. This method of preparation is 2½ to 3 times faster than steam cooking alone, and 40% faster than deep-fat frying.

Microwave heating methods are being used to open oysters. This novel process started under the auspices of the U.S. Department of Agriculture. A commercial line oven consisting of a tunnel and conveyor moves the fresh oysters through the energy section, under highly controlled conditions. The heating is done at

Courtesy Raytheon Company
FIG. 5.5. MICROWAVE MEAT TEMPERING SYSTEM

low intensity so as to not cook the raw oysters, but the heat causes the shell muscle to relax and open sufficiently so that the shucker can easily insert his knife and complete the shucking operation. Production is said to be increased by 33%.

Another industrial application of microwave energy is for meat tempering. A system has been developed to temper frozen raw blocks of meat so that they may be sliced and diced immediately without resorting to the normal 3-day wait in standard tempering rooms. This method has been applied also to fully cooked meat products and to rapid defrosting without cooking of frozen blocks of shrimp and scallops.

Figure 5.5 shows a 25 kW, 915 MHz meat-tempering system, manufactured by the Raytheon Company. This equipment is 36 ft long. The product openings are 6 X 30 in.

MICROWAVE USAGE IN SINGLE UNIT ESTABLISHMENTS

Microwave cooking activities in small or medium-size food service establishments range from ordinary heating to major preparation. In Chapter 2, suggestions were offered for locating microwave equipment within a fast food system. Figure 2.3 illustrates advantageous installations that promote the usefulness of these ovens for a total food production flow pattern.

Ovens can be located near the service post or pick-up counter, or adjacent to the assembly section. In any event, they should be in close proximity to the steam table, warming oven, a pass-through refrigerator, thawing refrigerator and satellite freezer. If foods are to be seared, a broiler or similar equipment should be located in the same general area. In addition, ample counter work space is required for garnishing and plating.

During peak periods, selected items appearing on the day's menu are continuously processed to replenish those foods served from the warming oven or steam table. Depending on the degree of movement, foods being prepared for replenishment should not be fully or totally heated. If they are held for an extended period in a warming oven or steam table the result will be over-cooked products. By undercooking in microwave ovens, this problem will be eliminated.

During normal or slow periods, food can then be prepared to order by following a set flow pattern from freezer or cooler storage to microwave application, garnishing, plating, and finally, serving.

OVEN SANITATION AND MAINTENANCE

Sanitation and basic maintenance are necessary to sustain a successful trouble-free microwave heating program. These activities are related, and should be scheduled together so that they become part of the daily routine. The following steps are recommended for a daily program:

(1) Make a solution of a mild detergent, using warm water. Immerse a clean

lintless cloth in the solution, remove excess liquid, and rub the cavity, walls, doors and shelves until all traces of encrusted food and other foreign matter are removed. If equipment has a glass grease shield, it should also be removed for cleaning purposes. Repeat the procedure for all exterior surfaces. Where food has hardened and cannot be removed by the above method, a soft bristle brush should be used. Rinse all surfaces with warm water. Sanitize the exterior surfaces and door with an approved sanitizing solution, rinse and allow to dry. Wipe spills as they occur.

Never apply steel wool or any other abrasive to metal surfaces. Do not wet any of the exposed electrical components which may be located at the upper section of the cavity. This applies mainly to older models.

(2) Every two weeks the air filter should be cleaned by washing in a mild detergent solution or with soap and water. After rinsing, the filter should be dried.

(3) Daily inspection of the door, hinges and lock is recommended. This inspection is important to prevent harmful injury from the effects of radiation leakage. The door should swing freely and close securely. Loose hinges require tightening or replacement. If the oven is not level, door closure may be affected.

Verify the proper door operating efficiency by using the "1-in. paper test." Partially insert a piece of paper about 1 in. wide by 8 in. long in the oven cavity. While holding the paper, close the door. Attempt to withdraw the paper.

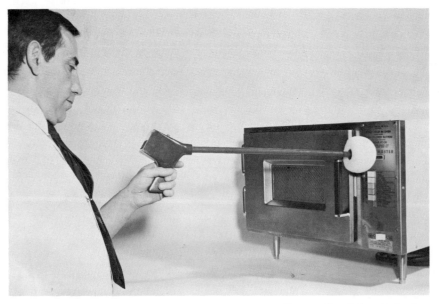

Courtesy Sage Laboratories, Inc.

FIG. 5.6. MICROWAVE ENERGY DETECTOR MICRO-GUARD[T.M.] MODEL MG-1

If the paper cannot be removed, it can then be assumed that the door is tight and properly fitted. Repeat the test on all sides of the door.

(4) As a further guarantee against energy leakage, meters have been developed which register radiation leakage. These instruments register the radio frequency emissions (R.F.) directly on the instrument scale. Figure 5.6 shows a picture of a portable meter developed by Sage Laboratories. A premeasured probe automatically gauges the proper distance of the meter from the oven. The meter is calibrated for 1, 5 and 10 mw/cm^2 in compliance with HEW standards for limiting radiation emission.

(5) Every three months a light oil should be applied to the hinges, latch and blower motor. Remove excess oil so it does not contaminate the food.

(6) Timing devices, switches, voltage and current, inlet plug should also be inspected every three months.

(7) Check the level of the oven, especially if installed on a mobile cart. If noticably off balance, it will not function properly, especially as regards heating of liquid and foods with gravy. Proper door alignment may also be affected by an off-level oven.

(8) Inspection for interior and exterior breaks or ruptures and cracks in the metal seams or walls should be performed periodically.

OVEN CONSTRUCTION REGULATED BY FEDERAL STANDARDS

The Department of Health, Education and Welfare (HEW) promulgated standards and regulations relative to the construction and safety of microwave ovens. These regulations became effective on October 6, 1971, and apply to the manufacture of new ovens. The Federal government deemed it necessary to set standards as a public safeguard against injury caused from exposure to microwave radiation.

Microwaves may be harmful to the human body. The length of time and intensity of exposure have a bearing on the degree of harm caused to the body. Since the effect of microwave absorption is heat, prolonged exposure can result in surface and internal body burns. These injuries are not felt immediately; however, repeated exposure may cause eye burns and cataracts. Other injuries to the body have been reported, but these have been minimized because they were simulated under laboratory conditions and were not observed from actual commercial field operations.

Briefly, these standards require that all new ovens emit no more than 1 milliwatt of radiation per square centimeter, measured 2 in. (5 cm) from the oven. Microwave energy rapidly weakens as the distance from the oven increases. On location, 5 milliwatts of radiation per square centimeter are allowable under normal use. All ovens must be provided with two safety interlocks, operating independently. One of the locks must be concealed and made tamperproof.

HEW REGULATIONS FOR MICROWAVE OVENS

Applicability

The provisions of this standard, unless otherwise indicated herein, are applicable to microwave ovens manufactured after October 6, 1971.

Definitions

(1) "Microwave oven" means a device designed to heat, cook, or dry food through the application of electromagnetic energy at frequencies assigned by the Federal Communications Commission in the normal ISM heating bands ranging from 890 megahertz to 6,000 megahertz. As defined in this standard, "Microwave ovens" are limited to those manufactured for use in homes, restaurants, food vending or service establishments, on interstate carriers, and in similar locations.

(2) "Cavity" means that portion of the microwave oven in which food may be heated, cooked, or dried.

(3) "Door" means the movable barrier which prevents access to the cavity during operation and whose function is to prevent leakage of microwave energy from the passage or opening which provides access to the cavity.

(4) "Safety interlock" means a device or system of devices which is intended to prevent generation of microwave energy when access to the cavity is possible.

(5) "Service adjustments or service procedures" mean those servicing methods prescribed by the manufacturer for a specific product model.

(6) "Stirrer" means that feature of a microwave oven used to constantly change the standing wave pattern within the cavity.

(7) "External surface" means the outside surface of the cabinet or enclosure provided by the manufacturer as part of the microwave oven, including doors, but excluding door handles, latches, and control knobs.

Requirements

(1) **Power density limit.** The power density of the microwave radiation emitted by a microwave oven shall not exceed one (1) milliwatt per square centimeter at any point 5 centimeters or more from the external surface of the oven, measured prior to sale to a purchaser, and thereafter, 5 milliwatts per square centimeter at any point 5 centimeters or more from the external surface of the oven.

(2) **Measurement and test conditions.**

(i) Compliance with the power density limit in this paragraph shall be determined by measurements of microwave power density made with an instrument system which (a) reaches 90 per cent of its steady-state reading within 3 seconds when the system is subjected to a stepped input signal and which (b) has a radiation detector with an aperture of 25 square centimeters or less, said aperture having no dimension exceeding 10 centimeters. This aperture shall be determined at the fundamental frequency of the oven being tested for compliance. The instrument system shall be capable of measuring a power density of 1 milliwatt per square centimeter with an accuracy of plus 25 per cent and minus 20 per cent (plus or minus 1 decibel).

(ii) Microwave ovens shall be in compliance with the power density limit if the maximum reading obtained at the location of greatest microwave leakage does not exceed the limit specified in subparagraph (1) of this paragraph when the leakage is measured through at least one stirrer cycle. Pursuant to para. 78.203, manufacturers may request alternative test procedures if, as a result of the stirrer characteristics of a microwave oven, such oven is not susceptible to testing by the procedures described in this subdivision.

(iii) Measurements shall be made with the microwave oven operating at its maximum output and containing a load of 275±15 milliliters of tap water initially at $20°±5°$ centigrade placed within the cavity at the center of the load-carrying surface provided by the manufacturer. The water container should be a low form 600 milliliter beaker having an inside diameter of approximately 8.5 centimeters and made of an electrically nonconductive material such as glass or plastic.

(iv) Measurements shall be made with the door fully closed as well as with the door fixed in any other position which allows the oven to operate.

(3) **Door and safety interlocks.**

(i) Microwave ovens shall have a minimum of two concealed safety interlocks that are mechanically and electrically independent. A concealed safety interlock on a fully assembled microwave oven must not be operable by (a) any part of the body, or (b) a rod 3 millimeters or greater in diameter and with a useful length of 10 centimeters. A magnetically operated interlock is considered to be concealed only if a test magnet external to the oven, held in place by gravity or its own attraction, cannot operate the safety interlock. The test magnet shall have a pull at zero air gap of at least 4.5 kilograms and a pull at 1 centimeter air gap of at least 450 grams when the face of the magnet which is toward the interlock switch when the magnet is in the test position is pulling against one of the large faces of a mild steel armature having dimensions of 80 millimeters by 50 millimeters by 8 millimeters.

(ii) Failure of any single component of the microwave oven shall not cause more than one safety interlock to be inoperative.

(iii) Service adjustments or service procedures on the microwave oven shall not cause the safety interlocks to become inoperative or the microwave radiation leakage to exceed the power density limits of this section as a result of such service adjustments or procedures.

(iv) Insertion of an object into the oven cavity through any opening while the door is closed shall not cause microwave radiation leakage from the oven to exceed the applicable power density limits specified in this section.

(4) **Instructions.** Manufacturers of microwave ovens to which this section is applicable shall provide or cause to be provided:

(i) For each oven, adequate instructions for service adjustments and service procedures including clear warnings or precautions to be taken to avoid possible exposure to microwave radiation;

(ii) With each oven, adequate instructions for its safe use including clear warnings of precautions to be taken to avoid possible exposure to microwave radiation.

BIBLIOGRAPHY

ANON. 1970A. The microwave oven. American Automatic Merchandiser *12*, No. 3, 68–70.

ANON. 1970B. Remove customer microwave question. American Automatic Merchandiser *12*, No. 10, 76–80.

ANON. 1970C. Hospital utilizes closed circuit TV to monitor microwave ovens. Institutional Quick Frozen Foods *32*, No. 7, 10–15.

ANON. 1970D. The ABC's of Microwave Cooking. Microwave Energy Applications Newsletter, Amherst, N.H.

ANON. 1971. What's Microwave Heating All About? Litton Industries, Minneapolis, Minn.

COPSON, D. A. 1962. Microwave Heating. Avi Publishing Co., Westport, Conn.

THAMER, D. H. 1971. Rapid cook-and-freeze increases fried chicken yield. Food Processing *32*, No. 1, 14–17.

TRESSLER, D. K., VAN ARSDEL, W. B., and COPLEY, M. J. 1968. The Freezing Preservation of Foods, 4th Edition, Vol. 4. Avi Publishing Co., Westport, Conn.

CHAPTER 6

Deep Frying

Food products prepared by deep frying methods are as American as apple pie, the hamburger and frankfurter. Their popularity is nationwide and they are served in all types and classes of food-serving establishments. A reason given for this overwhelming acceptance is that the home is not equipped to properly prepare deep fat-fried foods. Although deep fat fryers have been manufactured for home consumption for many years, the resulting food rarely meets the succulent taste standards of commercially prepared products.

In spite of this generally good acceptance by the public, poor preparation of deep-fried edibles is widespread, so that the end product is soggy and fat-soaked. Basically, two common mistakes or carelessness contribute to poor quality; (1) frying at the incorrect temperature; (2) frying in stale, "broken down" fat. Additional factors are also responsible to a lesser degree. These are discussed in the latter part of the chapter.

Years ago, when deep fat-frying equipment was first introduced, heating control devices were lacking, so that the cook had to guess at the correct preparation temperature. This resulted in inconsistent and usually low quality. Actually, the early fryers consisted of nothing more than a vat to hold some crude form of fat and a basket for the food. The fat, oil or shortening used at that time did not possess the desirable characteristics of those products employed today, since the technological aspects of frying were not developed.

Key Factors for Quality Deep-Fried Food

The following are the key factors that contribute to high quality, appetizing and appealing deep-fried foods:

(1) High quality shortening, fat or oil that withstands high temperature and moisture, has a high smoke point, will not emit unpleasant odors, and will not interfere with the delicate and natural flavors of the food.

(2) Modern frying equipment that has fast temperature recovery and exacting temperature controls.

(3) Proper frying procedures developed by concise training methods.

(4) Easily read and posted operating instructions.

(5) High quality foods, as the initial starting point for a successful program.

Parameters of Deep-Frying Equipment

Deep-frying equipment consists of three basic parts: (1) a deep kettle with sufficient capacity for the fat to cover the food adequately, so that simultaneous cooking of all surfaces takes place; (2) an accurate thermostatic device to control the cooking temperature; (3) a sturdy long-handled basket to hold the food; and

(4) a heat source and uniform heat transfer devices. Many refinements and accessories exist that help to increase production and cooking accuracy.

The following list summarizes the essential factors that should be considered when purchasing deep-frying equipment:

(1) Rapid heat recovery system. A slow recovery will yield soggy greasy food and a low rate of production.

(2) Accurate temperature control and a cut-out mechanism to prevent overheating in case of a thermostat failure. This accessory should be made to cut out at 400°F.

(3) Rapid and simplified sanitation. Fat wells should be removable so that they can be carried to a sink for cleaning. The well should be free of crevices and all corners rounded.

(4) Regardless of the heating source, the heat must be distributed uniformly. Heavy-duty immersion heaters are recommended for fryers heated by electricity. These heaters should be made to swing in an upright position for cleaning purposes. They should be self-cleaning when out of the fat.

(5) All controls should be readily accessible and simple to operate. Controls should be easy to calibrate. Automatic timers and signal lights are desirable to eliminate cooking inaccuracies.

(6) Baskets that are automatically lowered and lifted when the cycle is completed will permit the cook time to perform other duties or to operate several deep fryers.

(7) Baskets should be constructed of heavy-duty stainless steel and provided with a long, sturdy handle as a safety precaution against burning.

(8) A filtration system, either built into the fryer, or an external accessory unit should be provided.

(9) Ample "elbow" work space should be provided on each side of the fryer; 2 or 3 ft of counter space is advisable, to be used for preparation and serving. Locating the fryer at the end of the counter is recommended so that mobile carts can be used to move the fried food.

(10) Frying equipment is manufactured in various models and sizes. A choice of floor and counter models is available. Modular counter types are made so that they fit flush with other cooking equipment of similar overall dimensions. Movable units should be considered, as these will be able to accommodate production loads in various areas.

(11) An important provision that deserves mention is the installation of a collecting area or "cold zone", located at the bottom of the well. This area serves as a collection chamber for charred bits of food and breading materials that would otherwise float in the fat, causing off-flavors.

(12) Adequate hooded ventilation is advisable, even though a properly operated fryer will not emit undesirable fumes or odors. In addition, fryers should not be installed near foods that have a tendency to absorb odors. Coffee under-

going brewing is an example since odors from the fryer can be absorbed by the coffee.

Efficiency and Capacity Ratings

The fryer's capacity or output is rated according to the pounds of product fried in 1 hr. Most manufacturers base their ratings on the hourly production of raw to finished French fried potatoes (3/8″ cut).

There are four basic fryer designs: (1) pressure fryers, see Chapter 4; (2) high production equipment where the food is conveyed through a bed of shortening (Fig. 6.2); (3) nonautomatic fryers ranging in size from a 10 X 10 in. well with a shortening capacity of 15 to 20 lb, to a 24 X 24 in. well that holds 125 to 135 lb of shortening; (4) automatic units activated by pressing a button that starts the cooking cycle. The basket is lowered into the well by mechanical means. When the cycle is completed the basket is raised to the drain position. A fryer of this type measuring 18 X 22 in. is capable of producing 48 lb of raw to finished potatoes per hour, or 70 lb of blanched potatoes per hour (Fig. 6.1). High output models that will prepare 125 lb or more of raw to finished potatoes per hour are referred to as superpowered frying equipment.

When new frying equipment is installed, tests should be performed for tem-

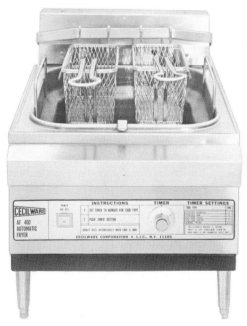

Courtesy Cecilware Corporation

FIG. 6.1. AUTOMATIC FRYER

perature stability and recovery, rated capacity per hour, and efficiency. Figures obtained from these tests can then be compared to the manufacturer's ratings and will serve as a guide to the true characteristics of the equipment.

The efficiency rating is determined by measuring the ratio of the fat capacity to the rated hourly production. For example, if a fryer produces 100 lb per hour of French fried potatoes in 30 lb of fat and another requires 35 lb of fat, the equipment using the lesser quantity of fat is the more efficient.

Continuous Automatic Frying

Figure 6.2 shows a continuous automatic fryer. Designed for volume production, the Fritomat fryer will handle chops, cutlets, liver, sausages, hamburgers, deep-fried breaded fish and other meats, potatoes and onions.

The food is fed into the fryer manually. Temperature regulation, conveying, turning over and delivery of fried pieces are done automatically. Frying time is accurately adjusted. The unit handles up to 1500 pieces per hour or 20 to 30 per min.

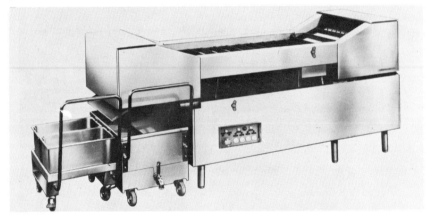

Courtesy Crescent Metal Products, Inc.

FIG. 6.2. A CONTINUOUS AUTOMATIC FRYER, CROWN-X FRITOMAT

The food is conveyed through a controlled height of cooking oil which is automatically cleaned and filtered during the cooking process. The fryer is operated electrically and has four separate thermostatically controlled heating zones.

The finished food is discharged at the lower end of the machine into a mobile cart.

Determining Size and Number of Units per Installation

The question of the size and number of units needed for an efficient frying operation may be difficult to answer. There are guidelines that can be followed, e.g., previous experience gained from a similar situation, or from an established pattern developed from multiunit construction. As a starting point, the following guidelines are suggested:

(1) A guess may have to be made as to the number of anticipated portions of fried food that will be served in one hour. If an establishment specializes in fried foods this may be 80% of the food output.

(2) The size of each portion must be established so that the number of portions that fit into a fryer basket can be determined. When ascertaining the basket capacity, keep in mind that only 2/3 of its capacity is used, and preferably only one-half to avoid overloading. Overloading may affect product uniformity and degree of doneness. In this regard, the volume of the food to be fried is more important than its weight. Food should never be packed tightly, but placed loosely in the basket so that all sides are exposed to the fat. Weigh the number of portions in the basket.

(3) Use as the average preparation time, 5 min for each batch, or 12 cycles per hr. Multiply the weight of food per basket by 12. The resulting answer is the capacity of the fryer required for one hour of continous production.

(4) If production during short peak demand periods warrants a large fryer, it will be wiser to purchase two units equaling the capacity of the larger one. Two fryers will furnish versatility so that two food varieties can be cooked simultaneously, and during low demand periods, one of them can be shut down.

If uncertainty prevails, the installation of multiple equipment should be given serious consideration. In any event, extra space should be allowed at the fryer station so that additional equipment can be installed if needed.

In cases where one fryer is installed, a problem of cooking dissimilar foods at the same time exists. For example, large food portions may need a longer time cycle. Frying temperatures will also vary according to the type of food being fried.

THE FRYING MEDIUM

The use of the most efficient frying medium is as important to quality fried foods as the equipment used for its preparation. Many products of animal and vegetable origin are marketed. Blends of the two are also available. In order to arrive at a satisfactory solution as to which brand will produce quality fried foods, the following characteristics should be evaluated: cost of the product, flavor transfer, smoke point, frying life, and ease of filtration.

The Smoke Point

The smoke point is the temperature at which a fat heated under specific conditions emits a thin, continuous bluish smoke. The smoke point of an acceptable frying medium should be as high as possible. A high smoke point usually indicates prolonged stability. Excessive smoking may be due to deterioration or to the fact that the product is not suitable for the equipment.

The following is a list of various frying products and their respective smoke points.

Product	Smoke Point (°F)
hydrogenated vegetable oil	440–460
standard vegetable shortening	420–440
cottonseed oil	410–430
chicken fat and corn oil	400–430
lard	340–350
olive oil	300–315
bacon fat	290–300
beef suet	235–245

Rendered beef suet is the lowest-priced frying medium; however, a disadvantage is its low smoke point. Hydrogenated lard is economical and has a smoke point of 380°F. If not overheated, this product is relatively stable. Vegetable shortenings and oils have the highest smoke point, a long production life, and a low flavor-transfer factor.

Shortenings are more time-consuming to load in the kettle than liquid frying media. Shortening becomes a solid at room temperature (70°F), whereas oil is a liquid under the same conditions. Shortening has to be packed around the heating elements, and heat applied cautiously to prevent scorching before melting. Filtering must be done at high temperatures or in the liquid state. Oils, on the other hand, are relatively unstable, may cause smoke or foam sooner than shortenings, and increase cleaning chores. Opaque liquid all-vegetable deep-frying fat combines the advantages of both shortening and oil, so that it possesses high stability and is pourable at room temperature.

Quality vs Economy

The saving of a few cents may result in poor, unappealing fried products as opposed to those that are highly acceptable and of superior quality. The science of frying oils and fats has progressed significantly over the years and many products are available today that possess excellent characteristics. When changes are made from one frying medium to another of a different character, the results can be detected. Before such changes are contemplated, tests should be performed to determine the final effect on the taste and flavor properties of the food.

The following is a summary of the desirable characteristics that should be considered when selecting an oil, fat or shortening:

(1) Bland flavor, so that foreign flavors are not imparted to the food.

(2) Long frying life, which will result in an economical frying operation.

(3) Low absorption properties, reducing incidence of greasy food and assuring lower frying costs.

(4) Ability to produce an appetizing, golden brown, non-greasy, crunchy crust.

(5) Resistance to smoking.

(6) Resistance to gumming. A high gum factor will increase cleaning difficulty.

(7) Resistance to the transfer of flavor from one food to another, such as a fish flavor to potatoes.

(8) Resistance to rancidity under normal care and conditions.

(9) The ability to fry uniformly under normal conditions of exacting temperature control and even heating.

(10) Easy digestibility.

Fat Absorption

Proper and careful handling of the frying medium will assure a more economical operation and products of higher quality. The frying medium becomes an integral part of the food. During frying the fat is being replaced by evaporation of surface moisture. Absorption is slowed down by the formation of a crust; however, it continues until the food is removed from the fat. Fat absorption is generally lowest when surface browning or crusting takes place immediately after the food is placed in the kettle. Slow cooking and low temperatures cause a high absorption of fat by delaying crust formation. The amount of fat absorbed varies with the kind and preparation of food being fried, the conditions of the frying fat, and the frying temperature. Table 6.1 shows the range of fat absorption by various foods.

TABLE 6.1

RANGE OF FAT ABSORPTION

Food	Absorption %	Food	Absorption %
French fries	8–12	oysters	10–14
potato chips	32–40	fish	11–15
carrots	7–10	shrimp	12–17
egg plant	9–14	chicken	8–18

Source: Frying Facts, Anderson Clayton Foods.

Absorption is dependent on surface conditions and characteristics of the food, moisture content, and frying temperature. It can be controlled by maintaining the frying medium in satisfactory condition.

Signs of Deterioration

Often one need do no more than step inside the front door of a restaurant to detect signs of spoiled fat. An irritating, unappealing, rancid odor is proof that either the fat must be changed or the fryer's temperature checked. The color of the fat is a useful index of deterioration. Usually the color of a fresh frying medium varies from water-white to pale amber. Dark color is a sign of deterioration in a fat, and will produce darker fried foods. A color test kit is available containing five vials, each with a different-shaded liquid. A sample of fat is drawn from the kettle and matched to a vial of similar color to obtain the score.

A final determination is made by means of a taste test. This test should be performed on a daily basis. If the flavor is rated unpleasant, acid, burnt or reveals foreign characteristics, the medium needs changing. Other signs of detection are foaming, a gummy or syrupy condition, and excessive smoking. If deterioration is abnormally high an attempt should be made to trace the causes of the rapid breakdown.

Investigation of Excessive Deterioration

The following factors contribute to fat deterioration:

(1) The main causes of fat spoilage arise from chemical changes induced by oxidation, hydrolysis and polymerization. *Oxidation* is the result of a reaction between oxygen and the fat. It begins the moment air comes in contact with the frying medium and is speeded up as the temperature rises. *Hydrolysis* is caused by the presence of water in the fat; it splits the fat molecules, altering the structure of the fat and reducing its usefulness. *Polymerization* (two or more molecules joining together to form one large one) results from high temperatures. The formation of gums and resin in the kettle is a result of *polymerization*.

(2) Contamination by foreign materials, such as bread crumbs, potato ends, and other pieces of food debris contributes to oxidation. It is for this reason that daily straining or filtering is mandatory. Fryers with built-in collection or cold zones reduce the problem of rapid oxidation from this source. Built-in filtering systems or external accessory equipment make the job easier. For expediency, the use of cheesecloth or filter paper placed in a funnel are recommended.

(3) Contamination by metal such as brass and copper will contribute to fat breakdown; these metals should not be permitted to come into contact with the kettle.

(4) The use of detergents to clean the kettle is recommended; however, complete rinsing is necessary before replenishing the kettle. Soaps and detergents are injurious to fat.

(5) Deterioration is also caused by holding the fat at preparation temperatures for prolonged periods when not in use. During low demand or slack periods the temperature should be reduced to 200°F.

(6) A continuously operating fryer will keep the fat in good condition. Fryers that are infrequently used contribute to a faster rate of fat deterioration. Fat is continually removed from the kettle by absorption. To maintain a constant quantity of frying fat in the kettle, fresh fat must be added. The rate at which this is done is designated as "fat-turnover". A satisfactory daily measure of fat turnover is 15 to 20% of the fat content. Rapid fat turnover keeps the frying fat in good condition through frequent replenishment. In a well-balanced

frying operation with adequate turnover, it is seldom necessary to discard any used frying fat.

Consumer Preference for Frying Fats

In February, 1971, a research report was published showing the results of a nine-month study of consumer preferences for food fried in various types of cooking fats. This work was performed at the School of Hotel Administration, Cornell University.

Four commercial types of cooking fat were employed in this study:

(1) an opaque liquid all-vegetable product;
(2) a winterized cottonseed oil;
(3) a hydrogenated solid all-vegetable fat;
(4) an animal-vegetable solid fat.

The results of these extensive studies revealed a difference in the fat performance of the various products tested under similar conditions. The opaque liquid all-vegetable frying fat was the most efficient, with equal or superior food acceptance ratings over an extended period. The consumer was able to recognize differences between French fried potatoes cooked in the various fats. The consumer's choice was indicated by ranking the test products singly or in pairs.

DEEP-FRYING PROCEDURES

Deep-frying procedures are simple, especially when using automatic equipment. However, simplicity in itself will not produce quality food unless a rigid schedule of operating and sanitation procedures are followed. The following procedural pointers should be incorporated into a well-defined operational program:

(1) Determine if the cooking time and temperature settings recommended by the manufacturer are adequate. Periodic checks should be made of the time and temperature factors to determine if changes have occurred because of a malfunction of the timer and thermostat. Use an accurate thermometer to check cooking temperatures and a stop-watch to test the timer. Determine the temperature drop when the kettle is loaded; a sharp decrease in temperature may cause prolonged heating so that the food will become greasy. Observe the time necessary for the temperature to reach its cooking setting. Reduce the food load in the basket until the recovery period is reduced, to assure optimum performance. Hang a time-temperature chart in front of the equipment for reference.

(2) Before putting food in the fry kettle, wipe off or shake all excess moisture, crumbs and loose breading. All portions or pieces of food should be about the same size. Food having a high moisture content, like fish, oysters or thawed items, should be drained carefully before frying.

(3) Always keep the fat content of the kettle at the proper indicated level. Add additional fat when level drops.

(4) Fill basket only half full of food and never exceed two-thirds of the capacity. Never overload as a means of increasing production. Overloading will delay heat recovery and will also result in excessive absorption due to the inability of the heating equipment to maintain proper frying temperatures. A good ratio to maintain is 1 lb of raw food to each 6 lb of frying fat.

(5) When frying frozen foods, do not thaw, but place in kettle directly from the freezer. Below-counter freezers are ideal for temporary storage. These units should have removable stainless steel drawers. Counter fryers can be installed directly over the freezer box.

(6) Do not salt food over the kettle or use excess salt. Addition of salt to the frying oil will tend to shorten its usefulness and retard browning.

(7) Turn kettle off or set at 200°F during slow periods. Most fryers will recover rapidly.

(8) Allow the finished fried food to drain. Where excess fat is observed, blot food on absorbent paper.

(9) If charred pieces of food are floating on the surface of the fat, gather them together with a long-handle mesh filter and remove.

(10) For foods that are breaded on the premises, the following procedures are suggested. Start breading when food reaches room temperature. Dipping and breading should be done by using both hands—one hand for dipping, the other for breading. Heavily breaded foods require additional frying time. Certain wet or moist foods, such as oysters, scallops, fish or fillets, should be allowed to "set" or "rest" for several minutes before frying, so that the breading and dip mixture can seal. If necessary, redip and bread. When frying breaded foods, place them flat in the basket without touching.

(11) To ensure continuous high-quality production, taste the fat for signs of deterioration. This should be done at the beginning of each shift or at the start of the day's business.

Selected Examples of Frying Procedures

Table 6.2 lists a number of popular deep fried foods, their preparation temperature and cooking time.

The time cycle shown in Table 6.2 will change with the initial temperature of the food, moisture content, condition of the fat, efficiency and condition of the frying equipment, size of the portion, and the amount of food loaded in the basket.

Many gourmet, specialty and nationality semiprepared frozen foods are being marketed. A number of these products are made for finishing in a deep fryer. This trend is an outgrowth of the increasing use of convenience foods. Examples are breast of chicken Kiev, stuffed potato balls, and breaded Italian style eggplant.

TABLE 6.2

FRYING TEMPERATURES AND TIME

Product	Size In.	Temperature °F	Approx. Time Min
French fries			
raw to done	3/8	350	5–6
blanching	3/8	350	3
browning	3/8	350	3
frozen blanched	3/8	350	3–4
frozen breaded shrimp	–	350	4
fresh breaded shrimp	–	350	3
frozen breaded fish fillet	–	350	4
fresh breaded fish fillet	–	350	3
frozen breaded fish sticks	–	350	3–4
fresh breaded fish sticks	–	350	3–4
breaded clams	–	350	1–2
breaded oysters	–	350	4–5
breaded scallops	–	350	4
breaded pork cutlet	–	350	4–5
breaded veal cutlet	–	350	3–4
frozen breaded onion rings	–	350	3–4
fresh breaded onion rings	–	350	3–4
chicken	–	325	12–15

Source: Deep Frying Procedures. Procter & Gamble Co.

Potatoes.—Potatoes are marketed in four forms: blanched and frozen, blanched and refrigerated, potato powder, and fresh raw. The most popular are the blanched and frozen. This popularity stems from a more uniform product and high-quality yield.

To ensure a quality product, potatoes should be kept frozen at all times. The amount of "frost" on their surface is an indication of the product's temperature. If blanched and frozen potatoes are permitted to thaw, they will absorb twice the normal amount of fat. This will produce a greasy, limp and unappetizing finished product.

Blanched and refrigerated varieties do not present preparation problems. However, they do not have the eye appeal or crisp texture of frozen potatoes. Blanching can be accomplished in the fryer at 300°F for 3 to 5 min. After draining and cooling they are placed in a covered plastic or waxed container and stored in a refrigerator for about 72 hr. Never allow sliced potatoes to touch metal or remain uncovered, as they will turn dark.

The raw to fresh type result in an excellent product during certain periods of the year. Because of changes within the potato as it ages, it is not possible to produce a uniformly high-quality finished product 12 months of the year.

Seafood.—Seafoods are best prepared from the frozen state. Most seafoods are breaded before frying. The product can be purchased with or without breading. A disadvantage of breading on the premises is the appearance of uneven brown or dark spots on the fried fish. This problem is attributed to a moist breading product. If the breading is not dry, the fish must be rebreaded to obtain a uniform surface color.

Onion Rings.—Onion rings are a popular deep-fried item. These products are available fully breaded and frozen. The extruded onion ring is gaining in popularity. These rings are formed by an extrusion process and are uniformly sized and firm. Because of the firmness, their shape is retained, whereas most other onion rings are fragile and may fall apart. For optimum results, onion rings must be fried in the frozen state and served hot.

Breading on the premises is time-consuming and the resulting product does not usually measure up to the final quality standards of the pre-breaded variety. If breading is to be performed on location, freshly sliced sweet Spanish onions should be used. These are dipped in bread flour and then into an egg-milk batter (6 medium size eggs for 1 pt milk) and finally into a commercial breader or cracker meal. Depending on the amount of coating desired, the last two steps can be repeated; however, allow a few minutes "set-time" between applications.

Chicken.—Broilers weighing from 1½ to 2 lb should be cut into several pieces. Poultry of this size will yield about 4 to 6 uniform pieces. Roll the chicken in seasoned flour (salt and pepper added). Chicken frying is performed at lower temperatures than for most other foods. Temperature should be 325°F and fried for 12 to 15 min.

Sanitation

High-quality fried products are contingent on proper and complete sanitation of the deep fryer equipment. Procedures recommended for a daily and for a weekly program follow:

Daily.—(1) After power is turned off and the fry basket removed, raise heating elements to half position to drain, then move them to the upper limit or until they lock in place.

(2) Remove fat well (for safety, wear heat-retardant gloves or use a pot holder) and filter the fat. If fryer contains filtering device, turn it on.

(3) Wash baskets and tank and rinse. Remove all traces of soap or detergent. Allow to dry. After drying, replace tank and refill with the filtered fat. Replenish with fresh fat to proper level.

Weekly.—(1) Drain and clean kettle.

(2) Replace kettle and fill with water mixed with a fry-kettle cleaning agent (2 oz to 1 gal water).

(3) Lower the heating elements into the cleaning solution and turn on the power until the liquid comes to a boil.

(4) Turn off the power and allow to stand for 10 min or overnight.

(5) Rinse and dry the heating elements, fry tank and baskets. Apply a final rinse of a vinegar water solution to "sweeten" the metal surfaces.

(6) After drying, replace the filtered fat and replenish to the proper level.

(7) Turn the unit on and check the thermostat and temperature with a hand thermometer.

CAUSES OF COMMON FRYING PROBLEMS

Fat Darkens Excessively and Prematurely:

(1) use of inferior or wrong type of fat;
(2) overheating;
(3) faulty thermostat;
(4) inadequate filtering of fat;
(5) improper and inadequate cleaning of equipment;
(6) hot spots in kettle;
(7) food may be improperly prepared, too much moisture;
(8) foreign matter entering the fat.

Excessive Smoking:

(1) inadequate filtering of the fat;
(2) improperly prepared food;
(3) use of wrong type of fat, smoking point too low;

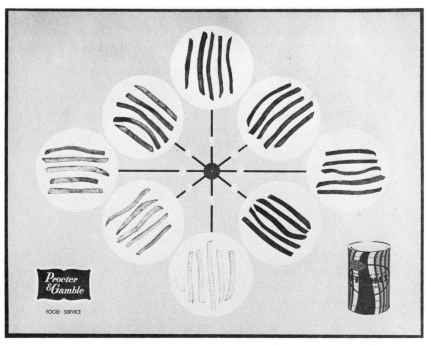

Courtesy The Procter and Gamble Company

FIG. 6.3. AN EXAMPLE OF A COLOR MATCHING CHART TO DETERMINE DEGREE OF DONENESS; OTHER CHARTS ARE AVAILABLE FOR FISH STICKS AND CHICKEN LEGS

(4) overheating of the fat;
(5) faulty thermostat;
(6) inadequate cleaning;
(7) hot spots in kettle;
(8) poor ventilation.

Poor Browning and Undercooked Food:

(1) excessive foam development;
(2) overloading kettle;
(3) faulty thermostat;
(4) frying temperature too low;
(5) improper preparation of food;
(6) poor or slow recovery of the temperature;
(7) check cooking procedures for time and temperature.

Excessive and Persistent Foaming:

(1) use of wrong type of fat;
(2) overheating or faulty thermostat;
(3) hot spots in kettle;
(4) fat being held at frying temperatures for long periods without cooking;
(5) improper sanitation and failure to remove gum from equipment before replenishing;
(6) overfilling the kettle with fat;
(7) kettle too large for the operation;
(8) salt in fat;
(9) poor or no filtering;

Greasy Foods:

(1) frying temperature too low;
(2) overloading kettle;
(3) frying in foaming fat;
(4) improper preparation of food;
(5) overcooking;
(6) improper draining of food after frying (Fig. 6.4);
(7) slow temperature recovery.

Obnoxious Odors from Kettle:

(1) use of inferior fat;
(2) use of deteriorated or spoiled fat;
(3) use of poor quality food;
(4) excessive debris (crumbs, charred food) in fryer;
(5) foreign matter in kettle.

Courtesy American Spice Trade Association

FIG. 6.4. CORN POPS BEING PROPERLY DRAINED OF FAT

Objectionable Flavor of Fried Foods:

(1) use of inferior fat, deteriorated or spoiled fat;
(2) foreign matter in kettle;
(3) use of poor quality food;
(4) inadequate filtration and presence of debris in fat;
(5) excessive fat absorption;
(6) poor turnover.

DAILY RECORD OF DEEP FRYING OPERATION

For economy, continued quality and trouble shooting, records of the deep frying operation should be maintained. The following data should be recorded:

(1) Date...... ——
(2) Time of test...... ——
(3) Fryer number if more than one...... ——
(4) Location ...... ——
(5) Fat capacity of kettle (lbs) ...... ——
(6) Brand fat ...... ——
(7) Daily fat replenishment (lbs)...... ——
(8) Percent of fat used for replenishment...... ——
(9) Filtered time, AM, PM...... ——
(10) Fat taste test...... ——
(11) Color comparison test...... ——
(12) Frying temperature...... ——
(13) Type food fried...... ——
(14) Temperature of food prior to frying...... ——
(15) Appearance of finished food...... ——
(16) Color wheel comparison test (see Fig. 6.3)...... ——
(17) Odor, taste, texture of finished food...... ——
        (greasy, crisp, off-flavor, off-taste)...... ——

(18) Date of last complete cleaning. . . . . . ____
(19) Date of last fat change. . . . . . ____
(20) Date of last check of thermostat. . . . . . ____
(21) Date of last check of timer. . . . . . ____
(22) Remarks . . . . . . ____

BIBLIOGRAPHY

ANON. 1966A. Significant savings on frozen French fries over preparation from fresh potatoes. Quick Frozen Foods 23, No. 7, 76–77.
ANON. 1966B. Deep Frying Procedures. Procter and Gamble, New York, N.Y.
ANON. 1969. Frozen Food Institutional Encyclopedia. National Frozen Food Association, New York, N.Y.
ANON. 1970. Electric automatic lift fryer operational guide. Cecilware Corp., New York, N.Y.
ANON. 1971A. Frying Facts. Anderson Clayton Foods, Dallas, Texas.
ANON. 1971B. Electric frying machines. Food Service Magazine 33, No. 2, 32–40.
MORGAN, W. J. 1971. Deep fat frying. Cornell Hotel and Restaurant Administration Quarterly 11, No. 4, 82–88.
POTTER, N. N. 1968. Food Science. Avi Publishing Co., Westport, Conn.
TRESSLER, D. K., VAN ARSDEL, W. B., and COPLEY, M. J. 1968. The Freezing Preservation of Foods, 4th Edition, Vol. 4. Avi Publishing Co., Westport, Conn.

The Control, Evaluation and Handling of Efficiency Foods

CHAPTER 7

Quality Control

Quality control is a broad, encompassing and significant activity for fast and convenience food establishments. It is assuming a major role in the development of consistent and high-quality food. Quality control should be instituted on all levels of a food service operation, so that maximum benefits can be achieved. Programs of this sort have rarely been expanded to embrace all the activities of food service. They are usually developed for a small segment of the overall operation, for example, the inspection of incoming products. To be meaningful, quality control must be applied to all steps and equipment that come in contact with food. Once an agenda is evolved covering all food and food contact points, problems contributing to unsavory and unpalatable edibles will be drastically reduced or completely eliminated. Moreover, a strong program will increase the profits and contribute to greater customer satisfaction.

Management of small or medium-size establishments is generally averse to such a program, because it feels incapable of fulfilling the required tasks intelligently. Others are of the opinion that quality control can only be performed by food technologists or highly trained technicians. Many multiple-unit organizations which operate fully equipped laboratories have not developed comprehensive in-store programs. In this respect, the emphasis has been placed on formulations, specifications and the testing of incoming products, leaving a wide gap between the initial phase of quality control and service to the consumer.

In this chapter, there is presented the blueprint for a quality control plan, derived from the day-to-day activities of most food service establishments. In-store problems and solutions are stressed. Procedures and testing methods are reduced to easily understood steps so that they can be interpreted without difficulty and without the need of technical training other than the normal expertise necessary to run the feeding unit.

It will be noted that two terms, in accord with present usage, are used interchangeably. These terms are, *quality control* and *quality assurance*. The latter term is the more recent, and is gaining acceptance; however, both have the same meaning.

DEVELOPING A COMPREHENSIVE PROGRAM

The prime reasons for a comprehensive quality assurance program within a fast and convenience food unit are: (1) Since convenience products are prepared elsewhere and/or by other companies, and since there is no control over their preparation or formulation, tests must be performed to assure product consistency and expected quality. (2) Fast food preparation is performed in new modes of heating equipment and involves different handling techniques from those used for traditional foods. Therefore, quality production is generated by optimum equipment performance and exacting preparation techniques. These can only be achieved by a strong quality control program.

A quality control calendar consisting of simplified procedures can be fulfilled without the services of skilled technicians. Many tests and controls can be competently performed, and the data evaluated by most supervisory personnel. Special equipment and instruments are not required other than the basic tools, such as scales, thermometers, timer or stopwatch, hydrometer and certain test kits (water analysis). The services of food technologists are needed for food spoilage evaluations, special formulations, and for drafting plans for quality control within a multi-unit company. Depending on the scope of the program, it would be beneficial to retain the services of a technologist or food laboratory technician on a call or per diem arrangement.

Basic Segments of the Program

The fundamental operational aspects of most feeding establishments are identical, though there are variations in volume, size, food preparation, form of service, and location. Purchasing, storage, food preparation, serving and sanitation are common to all food service units. However, differences exist with the extent and scope of a quality assurance program. The convenience food-oriented unit requires a more elaborate plan than the conventional type restaurant. The following are the basic suggested segments of an all-inclusive program:

(1) Purchasing
   (a) Prepurchasing: comparison shopping, price evaluation, quality grading, delivery efficiency, supplier reliability, and a continuing market survey to keep informed of all new developments.
   (b) Establishing specifications and formulations for each food item that will be purchased. Where Government Standards of Identity exist, they should be incorporated into each specification. (Standards and specifications are discussed in detail later in this chapter.)
   (c) Establishing procedures for test panels.
(2) Inspection of delivered products
   (a) Record temperature of the food, if frozen, and the condition and temperature of the refrigerated delivery truck.

   (b) Run comparison tests to check the delivered products with purchase specifications.
   (c) Product weight determination.
   (d) Product count determination.
   (e) Record pack date and code of product.
 (3) Dry, freezer and cooler storage control
   (a) Storage temperature evaluations.
   (b) Stock-rotating schedules.
   (c) Orderly stacking procedures.
   (d) Sanitation control.
   (e) Procedures for proper storage of left-over food.
 (4) Food preparation
   (a) Efficiency checks of all cooking equipment for timing, temperature and physical condition of each unit.
   (b) Sanitation control to eliminate problems of off-flavors, off-tastes and food spoilage.
   (c) Preparation control, testing quality of finished food, beverages, garnishing and plating.
   (d) Control of warming and holding units to ensure against over-cooked foods.
 (5) Ware-washing control to assure that soap residues and grease are completely removed.
 (6) Control of sanitation for refuse collection and disposal area.
 (7) Rodent, vermin control.
 (8) Water quality control.
 (9) Review new procedures and methods that may pertain to food production and packaging.
 (10) Review and disseminate local, state and Federal health codes and other food regulations pertinent to the establishment.

THE MEANING OF QUALITY

The word *quality* in reference to edibles has many significant meanings and interpretations. Two distinct and divergent definitions exist, one for the consumer or "end-user", and the other for the technician or technologist.

The average consumer associates quality with personal preferences, as something that is liked, disliked, excellent, superior, great or good. These descriptions are both subjective and abstract, and do not produce concrete evidence as to the degree of quality, from the standpoint of actual grade. Many factors exert an influence on the consumer's decision, such as inherited habits, locality, ethnic characteristics, advertising, "gimmicked" sales promotions, and price. In addition to these psychological pressures, positive sensory stimulations play an important role in establishing quality parameters. These include an appealing flavor, a pleasing mouth feel or texture, an attractive natural color or appearance, general palatability, product consistency, and to many consumers the nutritional values of the food. Additional factors that determine consumer quality preferences are the ambient or surrounding character of the restaurant, the type and efficiency of the service, plating methods, and cleanliness. These contribute to mood appeal and have a decided effect on the final determination of quality.

For the analyst or technologist, quality is usually referred to as a gauge of measurement, as the result of grading in accordance with certain specific and predetermined specifications. These may be established by the U.S. Department of Agriculture, the Food and Drug Administration, other government agencies, trade associations or by a company's own testing and consumer evaluation panel.

Quality, from a scientific standpoint, can therefore be defined as an orderly classification of a product's chemical and physical characteristics (Thorner and Herzberg, 1970). Flavor, texture, color or appearance, consistency, palatability, nutritional values, safety, ease of handling, convenience, storage stability, and packaging are the essential elements that must be evaluated in establishing a product's quality rating.

Quality is also equated with certain economic factors, such as the cost of the product, profits generated, and consumer acceptance within the intended selling price range.

It is interesting to note the dictionary definition of quality as a characteristic, an attribute of something, a property or feature, or the degree of excellence of a product or thing.

Regardless of the exact definition, there are two dominant features: the actual chemical or physical measurements of the product, and acceptance of the product by the consumer based on whether it will fulfill his "wants" with complete satisfaction.

What Is Quality Control?

Quality control or quality assurance is an activity, procedure, method or program that will ensure the maintenance and continuity of a product's specifications and standards within prescribed tolerances during all stages of handling, processing, preparation and packaging; and to further ensure that all the original and desirable characteristics are sustained during storage, processing or preparation and will remain unaltered until consumed.

Tools for Quality Determination

The tools required to perform practical and reliable quality testing are basic and uncomplicated. Intensive training is not necessary to use them in a proper, meaningful manner. Although sophisticated testing equipment can be purchased that will yield results of infinite accuracy, they are not required for routine tests and simplified methods of evaluation. The following are the basic tools: (1) human senses; (2) scales; (3) various types of thermometers; (4) hydrometers or hand refractometer; (5) stop-watch or timer; (6) sieves; (7) periodicals containing the latest regulations and specifications.

Development of the Human Senses

Odor and taste sensations play an important and almost indispensable role for those engaged in the food service industry. The self-development of sensory determinations can be a long and arduous task. Without the full maturity and realization of this growth, personnel engaged in the food service industry lack an essential working tool. Those who have mastered the culinary arts have done so because they have also mastered the art of precise identification of odors and tastes, and have applied this knowledge to their craft.

Proper handling of foods and beverages of all categories requires a full understanding of one's smell and taste functions. Application of these senses will not only help to maintain consistency of the product, but will forestall customers' complaints, and will make it easier to understand complaints if they arise. The economic aspects of our sophisticated food establishments make it mandatory to continually sustain and upgrade quality, thus maintaining and increasing consumer satisfaction as well as profits.

Sensory perception is complex. It involves the senses of taste, smell, touch and sight. According to experiments carried on by Georg von Békésy in 1964, hearing, the fifth sense, is also involved in combination with the other four. An important factor that contributes to customer dissatisfaction and annoyance is excessive noise. Noise levels have a decided bearing on the customer's moods, so that high-quality food can be mentally downgraded if the decibel level is too high. However, for our purposes we shall consider only the senses of taste and smell in conjunction with touch and sight, as the tools of self-evaluation.

Delicacy and receptivity of the human senses are yet to be fully duplicated by modern scientific means. Scientific instruments such as the gas chromatograph are being used successfully to identify and classify the chemical structure of many odors. However, the mechanisms of sensory perception within the human body are still considered to be the most delicate and most discriminating for these evaluations. Human ability to identify and differentiate concentrations of odor-producing substances as low as 1 part per billion is possible. The average person can identify about 2,000 odors and tastes, the trained technician 5,000 or more.

Proficiency in sensory evaluation is the result of habit and prolonged indulgence. This can best be understood by tracing a sensory effect from source to recognition. Electrical impulses are transmitted from the point of reception to a central nerve area. Finally it is supposed that from this nerve center the impulse is relayed to the brain, where the sensation is correlated and defined.

This physical process sets up within the body a conscious realization of the sensory event. In many instances a person cannot verbally define smell or taste, especially if it is a new experience. In such a case a mental comparison must be made to imprint the sensation with a known or past experience. For example, orange juice has its own characteristic flavor, and a mental imprint was developed in us in all probability during childhood. However, if the orange juice turns rancid, thus obliterating its true character, the mental imprint would be reclassified to a sensation of sourness or rancidity.

Various adjunct factors have an important effect on sensory evaluation. Sex, age, locality, ethnic groupings, income, physiological and psychological influences all have a bearing on the process of sensory registration. Likes and dislikes play a major role in sensory orientation. Food service personnel whose childhood experiences led to a like or dislike of a certain food are motivated to reflect the same attitudes into adulthood. As an example, those restaurant managers who liked and enjoyed their own coffee were found to maintain the highest efficiency of coffee service, both in coffee brewing and sanitation.

Mechanisms of Sensory Perception

There is no chronological order by which a person may react to a sensory experience. Since we are exploring the interplay of sight, touch, smell and taste as determining evaluators, the sense that comes into action first is of little importance. It all depends on the substance under investigation.

As with color blindness, some people are partially taste- and odor-blind, and therefore cannot register full and concrete sensory judgement. If a person has a stuffed nose or the common cold, a blocking of the olfactory passage will result, negating total sensory effects, since the sum of the taste-odor combination is required for registration.

The Nose.—The nose is the center of odor evaluation. A relatively few molecules of an odor-producing substance will excite this organ sufficiently to yield a determination with speed and precision.

When we breathe or sniff, the air enters through our nostrils. These are separated by a thin wall constructed of gristle and bone, known as the septum. The air passes from the lower nostrils up through the two tunnels or nasal passages and down to the region of the throat.

Each nasal passage is lined with soft, moist, mucous membranes covered with fine hairs called cilia. The hairs act as an air filter. Tiny blood vessels located in the nasal passages warm the incoming air. This function increases the volatility of odor-producing substances so that finer dispersion of the molecules results.

The area controlling the sense of smell is located in the highest part of the nasal cavity. This section is known as the olfactory bulb tract. A moist mucous membrane containing an infinite number of nerve fibers comprises this small section. The olfactory nerve connects with the olfactory lobe on the lower surface of the front part of the brain. This part of the brain registers and classifies incoming odor sensations.

Although the olfactory tract is the center of odor detection, the entire nasal cavity comes into play as an evaluator. The lower part of the nose perceives

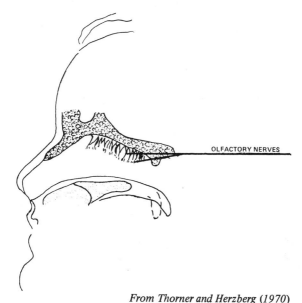

From Thorner and Herzberg (1970)

FIG. 7.1. OUTLINE OF THE NOSE SHOWING LOCATION OF
OLFACTORY NERVES

tactical sensations, such as cold, heat and pain and reacts vigorously to some substances (e.g., pepper) having unusual tactile properties (Fig. 7.1).

The Mouth.—The cavity of the mouth, which contains the tongue, can be considered as the focal point for flavor or taste perception. Flavor is a complex sensation. It encompasses the sense of taste and smell, together with the sense of feeling.

The taste response is primarily intercepted on the tongue. Items which are analyzed for taste must be in a moist state; or if dry, the saliva, acting as the diluent, suspends or dissolves them for sensory action. This sensory action is induced on receptors known as taste buds.

The function of the taste buds is primary in nature, registering four responses: sweet, salty, sour and bitter. The sense of touch acts as the intensifier or limiting agent to the four basic sensations. Temperature gradients have a direct relationship to the resulting stimulus. The sense of touch influences all areas of the mouth and throat. Figure 7.2, a diagram of the tongue, shows the location of the taste bud receptors for saltiness, bitterness, acidity, and sweetness.

The boundary or interaction surfaces mingle the taste sensations so that subtle stimuli are achieved. However, unless the odor-producing areas are activated in combination, the complete emotive response will fall short of a true identification. Since flavor or taste is the nonvolatile portion of the item under identi-

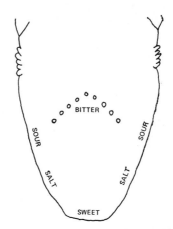

From Thorner and Herzberg (1970)

FIG. 7.2. AREAS OF THE TONGUE THAT ARE SENSITIVE TO
THE FOUR TASTE SENSATIONS

fication, the volatile portion, even though it is not sniffed directly into the nasal cavity, will permeate into it through connecting channels located at the rear of the mouth (Fig. 7.3).

Touch (Feeling).—The sense of touch can be described as the threshold of pain. This response falls into categories of temperature variations, texture, and the sensations of burning or bite produced by spices or condiments.

The role of touch in odor and flavor identification is extremely important, since these senses are modified or intensified, so that the final determination can be altered or misinterpreted.

The entire mouth cavity is affected by touch, as well as the lower nasal cavity. Carbonated beverages, if tested too cold (below 40°F) will prevent subtle flavor detections. Coffee, if too hot (above 140°F) or too cold, will negate the true and accustomed character. The acid-indicating area of the tongue will not give a true taste of sourness if the temperature of a food is above 100°F.

If the food texture changes from its expected normal sensation, the result is usually detected. The quality is downgraded and the consumer becomes dissatisfied. Texture embodies such sensations as firmness, softness, juiciness, chewiness, and grittiness. Customer comments denoting dissatisfaction may include such descriptive terms as tough, undercooked, mushy, pre-cast like iron, gristly, or hard-tack.

Sight.—The sense of sight is the visual indicator of a number of conditions and characteristics of the product being tested.

Color, density, texture, sanitation and product deterioration can be observed visually before application of the senses of smell and taste. Conditions of visual spoilage can be pinpointed by the observation of mold formation.

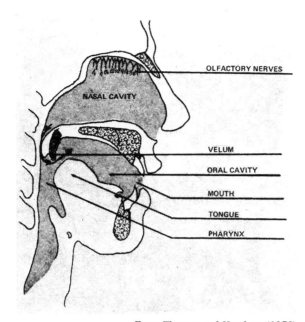

From Thorner and Herzberg (1970)

FIG. 7.3. DIAGRAM SHOWING CONNECTING CHANNELS BE-
TWEEN THE NASAL CAVITY AND THE MOUTH

The color of the food will influence a quality determination, and a customer's reaction to it. Proper shape, natural color, particle size, visual consistency and sanitation are some of the sensory detections influencing quality.

Techniques of Sensory Detection

Methods of sensory detection may vary from person to person; however, several fundamental rules must be followed.

Concentration followed by repeated application is recommended, especially if the item under test is a new taste experience. Regardless of the personal likes or dislikes as to the taste or odor of a certain food, each experience should be so concentrated upon that an indelible imprint of its sensory character can be made a basis for total recall.

Visual Observations (Appearance).—As a first step, the sample should be observed for color, density or viscosity, and visual evidence of spoilage. Sanitary conditions should also be noted, such as cleanness of dishes and dispensers.

Smelling Techniques (Aroma, Odor).—As indicated previously, flavor is perceived as a combination of smell and taste. The smell or odor character is established first, since this sense is the keener of the two, and will assure a more positive as well as a speedier identification.

A deep sniff at short intervals using both nostrils is advisable. If possible, the sniffing should be done with the mouth open, waving the sample from the region of nostrils to the mouth. This procedure will permit full penetration of the volatile material into the entire sensory area, and will ensure full coverage of the olfactory section of the upper nasal cavity. The surrounding ait should be still and free from interfering aromas.

If a comparison of similar substances is being made, a whiff of one sample, followed by a whiff of the other, the sequence being repeated several times, should be sufficient for positive identification. If a control sample is used, this should be analyzed first, followed by the unknown.

Odor determinations of dry substances can be performed by first blowing on the sample with moist breath. The aroma of the dry material can then be studied since its volatiles will be released.

Tasting Techniques.—Prior to the actual testing, an inexperienced taster should perform a series of examinations using solutions of foods having the four basic tastes. Dilute solutions of pure substances exhibiting the effects of sweetness, sourness, bitterness and saltiness should be prepared. As each solution is tested, a mental note should be made of the reaction and the location of the stimulus on the tongue.

Before actual testing, the mouth should be rinsed with warm water. This preliminary step will freshen the mouth cavity and prepare the taste buds for sharper perception.

The sample should be drawn into the mouth with a "slurp" or whirling action, so that all areas of the cavity are moistened. Immediately after the mouth is fully moistened and the sense registered, the liquid must be expelled. If the impression was not clear, a second or third test should be made. Between tests of the same or different substances, the mouth should be flushed with warm water.

The sense of touch plays an important role in taste evaluation. The temperature of the material must be noted and if not in the proper range it must be adjusted to meet its physical character.

Taste Panels

It is not unusual to find one person with the responsibility of selecting brands of food using his own personal likes or dislikes as the sole indicator. This system may once have been feasible for small restaurants or where a chef, by tradition, had the full authority to direct purchasing and preparation activities. However, if this scheme is used for a pre-prepared food operation, it may lead to consumer dissatisfaction. Regardless of the size of restaurant, a taste panel consisting of three or more people should have the authority to make the necessary selections.

The subject of taste panel procedures, programming and test evaluations is broad. Many procedures and methods of scoring are used. Professional tasters are employed in a number of industries, e.g., the coffee, tea, wine and liquor industries. Federal and state agencies use trained testers for such products as butter and cheese. Consumer panels are occasionally called upon to provide an insight into customer preferences for particular products.

Many companies operate taste panel laboratories provided with separate booths to isolate the panel members. Isolation prevents individual influence, either by facial expression or conversation. Subdued or colored lights are installed so that the color of the food will not affect the final decision. Test or scoring reports cover a wide range of formats. Some use a numerical ranking scale known as a hedonic scale. Descriptive terms such as *like definitely, like mildly, neither like nor dislike, dislike mildly,* and *dislike definitely* are frequently employed. The taster checks his opinion for each sample, and may make additional comments. The terms are given number rankings, such as 5 for *like definitely,* down to 1 for *dislike definitely.* When the forms are completed the results are averaged.

The *triangle* procedure test is another scheme that can be used when two samples are submitted for evaluation. This is practical for two- or three-member panel groups and can be readily adapted to a convenience food program. The samples are submitted to each panel member. Two samples may be identical and one different. Each sample is coded and all are plated in the same way. The taster is asked to select the two samples that are similar and the one sample that is different. The panelist must also indicate the samples or sample he prefers.

Taste testing can be exhausting, resulting in a gradual dulling of perception. Depending on the product, the limit of tasting endurance is about 5 to 6 samplings. The time of day, ambient conditions, and physical condition of the panelist should be taken into consideration when scores are evaluated. Professional panelists are more proficient during the early part of the morning than at any other time of day.

Typical Applications

Sensory evaluation has many applications within a food service center. The following list indicates the areas where this method of testing is applicable.

(1) Evaluating supplier's samples and comparison shopping.
(2) Evaluating deliveries against specifications.
(3) Checking flavor and taste deterioration as a result of prolonged storage.
(4) Checking for superficial signs of food spoilage.
(5) Checking the taste characteristics of deep fry fat.
(6) Checking the degree of doneness from microwave oven preparations and from other equipment.
(7) Checking the effects of food additives, such as spices, herbs and garnishes.
(8) Checking sauces and gravies.
(9) Checking complaints.
(10) Checking and investigating reasons for off-flavors and off-tastes.

(11) Checking the taste and flavor of beverages, such as coffee and soft drinks.

Evaluation of Complaints

Perhaps one of the most difficult evaluations that food service personnel have to make is that related to complaints. Coping with customer complaints is considered an art. To understand a customer's feeling and to judge the value of superficial descriptive statements, such as *no good, poor, doesn't taste right, lousy, not bad, not good,* and *can be better* is frustrating and requires patience and a knowledge of human reactions.

Complaints can be separated into three categories: (1) psychological, (2) physiological, and (3) pressure or business competitive patterns.

Psychological complaints are those which arise from the sensory effects of the product. These involve the senses of feel, smell and taste. Under this category, criticism may occur from the mode of service, incorrect temperature of the food, color or shade of the product, texture (mouth feel). For example, a customer may be accustomed to a cup of coffee with cream added, exhibiting a straw-like color. If for some unknown reason the color is darker or lighter than usual, a complaint may be lodged that the beverage is poor or just not good.

Various food combinations which are not compatible will cause distressing reactions. Examples of this are maple syrup and coffee, a combination that renders a bitter aftertaste, or onions on a hamburger and coffee, which will alter the flavor of the coffee. Condiments and relishes can also create abnormal reactions.

Physiological complaints are those which arise from the physical condition or health of the customer. The customer may have a hangover, upset stomach, common cold, or some other ailment which will completely change his typical sensory sensation. Foods or beverages consumed under these conditions will have an unusual taste, which may result in unmerited complaints.

Pressure or business competitive pattern complaints are annoying because they cannot be rationally traced or solved. These are an outgrowth of unethical business practices among vendors (suppliers) for the sole purpose of creating a beneficial atmosphere for their sales efforts. This is a form of business sabotage. Representatives or agents are sent to establishments to make complaints which are unfounded about a food or beverage. Tracing the source or origin of complaints originating under this scheme can be difficult. However, if management has confidence in its ability to evaluate complaints through the process of sensory determination, then a solution becomes an easy matter.

Frequency of complaints must also be taken into consideration. If there is an abnormal number within a short period, a full investigation of the possible causes must be made. Although there are no statistics available on this subject, a "rule of thumb" measurement is that complaints should not exceed 1% of the patronage on the average.

MEASURING DEVICES

Scales

Scales are manufactured in a variety of models, shapes and capacities. Their uses are unlimited, not only for quality assurance tests, but for portion control, receiving and preparations. Weighing devices have been used for food preparation since Biblical times. They are a basic tool, and together with the thermometer and timer, form the essential devices for preparation and quality assurance.

Weighing devices are available to fill all needs, such as portion control scales, floor scales, hanging platform scales, built-in scales, table or counter top devices, and built-in conveyor or track units. Capacities range from 1 gram to several tons. Models are built that print the weight on a tape. These may be connected to computers for automatic portioning. Others register the weight on a direct-reading dial, cast a magnified image of the weight, or indicate the reading by sliding a weight along a beam.

Scale Characteristics.—Technical developments have provided the means of determining weight accurately, quickly and simply. An association of scale manufacturers has assisted all types of industry in the proper use and maintenance of weighing devices. Selecting scale equipment can become a burdensome and frustrating task because of the number of models on the market.

Good scales, regardless of capacity, are expensive. It is not advisable to purchase cheap weighing equipment. Scales can last indefinitely if they are handled properly and kept clean. Scales of high quality will prove more advantageous and less expensive than numerous cheap ones over a period of time. A useful weighing device should have the following features: compactness, rust resistance, ease of cleaning and adjustment, durability, accuracy, quick readability, prompt damping action for speedy weighing, tare reset device, positive protection of parts from dirt and grease, tamper proof where necessary, leveling device for uneven surfaces, and built-in illumination where required.

Scale Location.—Scales should be placed in strategic locations so that they are a useful part of a forward flow system. They should not be installed in remote areas, as they are used frequently. Convenience food systems require the services of a number of portion-control scales to check the weights of incoming products and to monitor production at various locations, such as assembly and preparation areas. Quality cooking by microwave ovens can only be accomplished if the weight of the product is determined beforehand, and the time cycle set accordingly. Subsequent weighing is then necessary to check the consistency of each portion. If changes in weight are observed, the cooking cycle must be increased or decreased. Scales have proved invaluable as a means of detecting weight shortages of delivered merchandise. They can also be used to determine shrinkage losses due to prolonged freezer storage, and to assist in securing an accurate inventory and cost-control schedule.

Portion-control scales of various capacities are recommended for quality con-

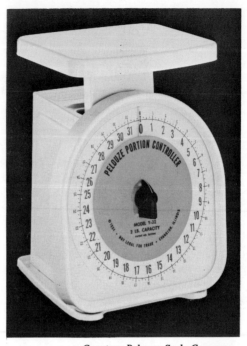

Courtesy Pelouze Scale Company

FIG. 7.4. PORTION CONTROL SCALE, 2 LB CAPACITY

trol tests, formulations and portioning. Figure 7.4 shows one type of portion-control weighing device. This scale has a 2-lb adjustable weight capacity in ¼-oz increments. The knobs located at the center of the scale can be rotated to zero to compensate for the weight of a plate or platter. Similar models are available for dietetic control portions. These register in grams and have a 500 to 1000-gm capacity with 1-gm accuracy. Other portion-control devices are available that register under or over weight tolerances by means of a pointer encased in an upright housing. The weight is adjusted by means of a beam graduated in ¼-oz. For additional capacity 1 or 2 lb weights are supplied that are placed on a platform.

Scale Maintenance and Sanitation.—Scales that are dirty, dusty or encrusted with grease and soot will not give accurate results. Scales should be kept clean and dry. A daily cleaning schedule is advisable to avoid buildup of foreign matter. Scales that are sealed require that all exterior surfaces and parts be cleaned. Those with exposed parts must be cleaned carefully, so that knife edges and other sensitive mechanisms are not disturbed. Never use force or pressure when cleaning or adjusting a scale. This may cause unrepairable damage and inaccurate results. Cleaning should be done with a lint-free cloth and a mild detergent solution. A low-pressure air hose can be used for removing dust and drying. The air should be dry.

It is recommended that a set of weights be purchased to check the accuracy of all scales. The test for accuracy should be performed monthly. Scales that have adjustable compensating or balancing devices can then be reset according to the degree of inaccurancy indicated by the check weights. These check weights should be kept separate and stored in a dust-proof box. Each scale should be tagged and the date of the test recorded.

Scale Requirements.—It is difficult to establish a plan encompassing the number of weighing devices that are required. A fast food, portion control and convenience food establishment may need many small scales and only 1 or 2 larger scales for receiving. For a medium-size operation the following scales may be required:

(1) Receiving area: 1 platform scale 500- or 1000-lb capacity and 1 50-lb capacity counter scale.

(2) Receiving office and/or quality control section: 3 portion-control scales of 2-, 5- and 10-lb capacity.

(3) Storage areas: 1 counter scale 25-lb capacity and 1 platform scale 500-lb capacity.

(4) Assembly: 1 counter scale 25-lb capacity, several portion-control scales.

(5) Preparation and garnishing section: 1 counter scale 25-lb capacity, several portion-control scales.

Thermometers

One of the basic tools used in the food service industry is a temperature-measuring device or thermometer. Almost every function within a food serving establishment, regardless of size or mode of operation, is dependent on a thermometer. The demands of the culinary arts make it mandatory that temperatures be known, set, and held at required levels. Beverages, hot or cold, refrigerators, dishwashing operations, deep fryers, griddles, and storage facilities are but a few of the many areas where accurate temperatures must be maintained. Unfortunately, temperature-measuring devices are taken for granted, and little thought is given to the possibility of inaccuracy. Unless an appreciation is developed for the applications, limitations, and accuracy of thermometers, inconsistent and erroneous readings will develop.

Testing for Accuracy.—One of the first rules governing thermometer application is accuracy. A new thermometer is not necessarily accurate. Old instruments as well as new ones require periodic checks for accuracy. If an instrument is improperly handled or dropped, the results will be affected.

Testing the accuracy of a thermometer involves the use of elaborate equipment, such as a calibrated liquid bath in which the device is suspended for a period of time. Although this method is highly accurate, it is unnecessary for the food service thermometer.

The simplest method is to check one instrument against another. The thermometer used in this procedure is a high-accuracy precalibrated bimetallic device. This thermometer should only be used for testing. If reserved for this purpose and properly handled, it will retain its accuracy indefinitely.

Another procedure which can be followed if the bimetallic type is not available is use of boiling water. However, there are limitations to this method. Even though water has a boiling point of 212°F, altitude and impurities affect this temperature.

Errors Caused By Improper Reading or Placement.—Errors of incorrect reading can occur, especially if the dial is small or the numbers have been rubbed off the glass column. Holding the instrument properly so that the eye is directly in line with the scale will reduce reading errors. Thermometers must be placed correctly. Stems should be immersed sufficiently so that the entire bulb is completely covered. Time is an important factor. Readings cannot be rushed, as it takes time for the instrument to reach its maximum registration. There is no hard-and-fast rule to apply to the time factor. Experience is the best criterion.

Types of Thermometers.—(1) Mercury or fluid column (Fig. 7.5) is provided with a metal protecting case. Overall length is 6 in.

Courtesy Fischer Scientific Company

FIG. 7.5. MERCURY OR FLUID COLUMN THERMOMETER

(2) Bimetallic, all-metal type, utilizes a precision bimetal helix which responds quickly to changes in temperature. The coil is located in the end of the stem. Changes in temperature cause a rotary action of the helix, turning a shaft on which a pointer is mounted (Fig. 7.6).

(3) Cup type measures the temperature of liquids in tanks, barrels, and similar vessels (Fig. 7.7). The thermometer is lowered into the liquid, allowed to

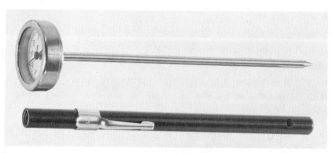

Courtesy The Cooper Thermometer Company

FIG. 7.6. BIMETALLIC THERMOMETER

Courtesy Fischer Scientific Company
FIG. 7.7. CUP TYPE THERMOMETER

remain for about 1 min and then withdrawn. The cup will bring up a small amount of fluid which prevents the reading from changing before it is observed.

Checking Thermostats and Built-in Thermometers.—In various sections of Chapters 3 and 4 thermometer applications were discussed, and methods of reading the internal temperatures of frozen foods described. The need to test thermostats installed on such equipment as deep fryers, steam-pressure cookers and other units containing these devices is essential to quality production. Tests of this sort should be put on a weekly schedule and records kept each time a test is performed. Built-in thermometers found on coffee brewers and refrigerators require periodic checks. Many of these have a metallic stem or bulb. If dirt, grease, or salts resulting from hard water become encrusted on the stem, temperature accuracy will diminish.

The Abbe Refractometer

An instrument of value to the food service operator is the Abbe refractometer. With it, one can determine the percentage of sugar in syrup, the total solids in juice products, and the purity of fats and oils used in food preparation.

The Abbe refractometer comprises two glass prisms between which the refractive index is a measure of the "bending" or refraction of light as it passes through a fluid. Under standard conditions of temperature and pressure, the refractive index of a substance remains constant. It does vary with concentration.

The principle of refraction, or bending of light, can be demonstrated by placing a pencil in a glass of water. If one looks at the glass from the side, the pencil appears to be broken at the surface of the water. This illusion is caused by the fact that light passes at different rates through the water and through the air above the water.

The Abbe refractometer comprises two glass prisms between which the sample to be tested is placed, a telescope for observing the extent to which the light is bent, and a scale from which the refractive index is read. Some refractometers also have a scale calibrated in sugar percentage, which saves the operator the time necessary to convert refractive index to percent sugar, using tables supplied with the instrument.

The expense of a standard Abbe refractometer prevents its widespread use in food service establishments.   However, a modified Abbe refractometer, called a hand refractometer, is inexpensive and within the budget of many. It is very simple to use and sufficiently accurate for food service operations.

The hand refractometer consists of a prism, a prism cover and a telescope with a built-in scale. The sample to be tested is placed on the prism and the cover closed (Fig. 7.8). The instrument is held toward the light and the re-

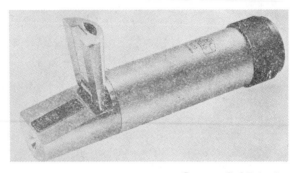

Courtesy Carl Zeiss, Inc.

FIG. 7.8. VIEW OF A HAND REFRACTOMETER SHOWING EX-
TENDED PRISM WHERE SAMPLE IS PLACED

fractive index is read directly from a scale built into the instrument. Since the hand refractometer is not accurate over a wide range, two types, one each for high and low indices, are necessary to cover the complete range.

Using the refractometer and appropriate tables, the food service operator is able to rapidly determine the percentage of sugar in fountain syrups, maple syrup and honey. He can also check the sugar content in premix and postmix carbonated beverages to ascertain if dispensing equipment is operating properly. The quality of tomato products is a function of total solids, and this can also be obtained with a refractometer. A food service operator who uses corn oil for his salads can determine by this means if the oil he is purchasing is pure.

The refractometer is one of many tools available to the food service operator enabling him to provide the best possible foods for his customer.

The Hydrometer

A hydrometer is a weighted spindle with a graduated neck that floats in a liquid at a height related to the density of the liquid.   The neck contains a numerical scale from which the measurement is obtained. This scale gives the percentage of soluble solids in .the liquid. Hydrometers are available to measure many different solutions by various systems, such as Brix, Baumé, Twaddle, API and Salimeter (Fig. 7.9). The Brix hydrometer is used to measure the percentage of sugar by weight at a specified temperature. This device will produce the same results as a refractometer. The higher the Brix, the greater the sugar concentration in the liquid. Hydrometers of this type are helpful in determining the density of fruit syrups, juices and the operating efficiency of postmix soda and juice dispensers.

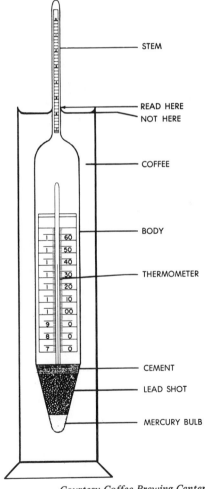

Courtesy Coffee Brewing Center

FIG. 7.9. AN EXAMPLE OF A HYDROMETER

Stopwatches and Timers

Stopwatches and timers are essential to check the timing cycle of equipment. Most equipment used for fast food preparation have built-in timing devices. Since these are mechanically operated they require constant checking to determine their accuracy. Microwave cooking depends on precise time cycles for the proper degree of doneness. It is not advisable to check automatic timers with an ordinary wrist watch, especially where the cycle is less than 1 min. Stopwatches are available that are graduated in 1/5 sec, 1/10 sec, and 1/100 min. A timer graduated in 1/5 sec is sufficient. Interval timers with an alarm are useful for checking longer cooking cycles. Figure 7.10 shows a pre-programmed product key timer for fast food operations.

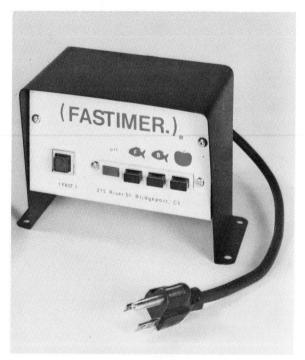

Courtesy Fast Automation Service Techniques, Inc.
FIG. 7.10. PRE-PROGRAMMED PRODUCT KEY TIMER

Sieves

The use of sieves is limited in fast food operations. They are employed in USDA and FDA specification evaluations. Figure 7.11 shows a typical sieve used for this purpose. In the section of this chapter dealing with specifications will be found the procedures employing several sizes of sieves.

Courtesy Fischer Scientific Company

FIG. 7.11. SIEVE

SPECIFICATIONS

Purchasing is a highly skilled art, requiring the knowledge of many products. The common denominator for purchasing, regardless of volume, is to buy smartly and to obtain the best value for the money. Buying involves a number of techniques and a vast amount of data. Due to the rapidly expanding market involving new foods and prepared items, the amount of data required for purchasing these products can fill a good sized library. Purchasing techniques embody comparative shopping, evaluation of new products, wise judgement in timing large purchases of seasonal products and in selecting the right purveyor. In addition, a buyer must understand foods, specifications, formulations, and be able to evaluate these in terms of price and quality. Purchasing also requires integrity and the ability to cooperate with management, suppliers, and kitchen employees.

One of the means devised to assist buying is the specification. Specifications are important tools for both buyer and management; they are guidelines detailing a product's characteristics, including such properties as quality grade, weight, count, contents, packaging and other data pertinent to a specific item.

Specifications make the task of comparison shopping easier, since the specific guidelines of a product's characteristics become a common language and can be used for evaluation. They are effective in submitting purchase proposals to suppliers for quotations (bid purchasing). Specifications, if properly used, provide an excellent means of cost control and product uniformity. The latter is significant for convenience food purchases. Pre-prepared foods should be bought according to specifications and nutrient content. The knowledge of nutrient content is essential for hospitals and other establishments where dietetic balance prevails.

Specifications should be reviewed and revised periodically. During periods of short supply, revisions may be necessary to maintain the same food costs. In addition, new and improved products may be offered which are less expensive or possess some decided advantage over those in current use. Finally, specifications are management's silent guardian of security. Where large purchases are involved, management has the means at its disposal to cross check the price, quality, and other factors against the specifications.

Commercial Bribery

Commercial bribery is a gentle term for unethical practices, such as kick-back, payoff, or thievery. Regardless of the description, the activity harms management and makes those involved accessories to the crime. This form of doing business only enriches the person on the receiving end. A company can be severely hurt by such practices. Many bankruptcies have occurred as a result of commercial bribery. Quality deteriorates, short weights or short counts are delivered, and prices may be increased to compensate for the situation. Those readers who wish to delve deeper into these illegal practices are referred to *The Meat Handbook* by Albert Levie (Avi Publishing Co.) which contains an excellent treatise on the subject.

Methods of Preparing Specifications

The first step in preparing a set of specifications is to list all the products that will be purchased. If menus are available they can be used as a guide for the foods to be served. The list should be separated into the various product categories, such as meat, dairy, desserts and beverages. Subdivisions will be helpful to segregate those products that have similar characteristics. The meat list will show all the cuts of beef and pork products, followed by pre-prepared meat items, and those entrées containing percentages of meat, like stew and pot pies.

The second step is to compare the list with existing government and trade association specifications and standards. If these do not exist for specific items, they will have to be written, in order to round out the program. It is important to include all items to be purchased, such as paper goods, soaps and detergents. Equipment specifications should also be considered, especially where repeat purchases are made for a multiunit organization. If this is the first attempt at writing specifications, help may be required. One way of obtaining this assistance is to start a collection or library of all regulatory food specifications emanating from Governmental sources. This library will also assist in quality control testing.

At present a number of Federal agencies are involved in the promulgation of food standards. Several of these agencies have overlapping regulations of identical foods. The following are the agencies: General Service Administration, Food and Drug Administration, Public Health Services, Department of the Interior, Department of Defense, and the Department of Agriculture.

Food and Drug Administration (FDA).—This agency has the responsibility for preventing adulteration and the misbranding of foods. Its objectives are to assure that food is safe, pure, wholesome, sanitary, and honestly packaged and labeled. The responsibility applies to interstate movement and sales. The agency also assists in the prevention of milk-borne and shellfish diseases and in the control of sanitation related to shellfish production. FDA sets and issues reasonable definitions and legal standards for most staple foods.

Department of Agriculture.—This Department has the responsibility for inspecting meat and meat plants. It aids both the consumer and industry in disseminating food specifications and in quality improvement. It provides a basis for trading, using standards of quality or grades.

It issues guidelines on prepared meat and poultry products, and it inspects and grades poultry. These operations apply only to interstate transactions.

Department of Defense.—This agency is mainly concerned with military purchases. All food is purchased on specification. These are handy references and may be obtained from the Government Printing Office, Washington, D.C. They also publish menus and recipes which are available for a small fee. The Army operates a food research and development facility located at Natick, Mass. Publications are issued which are available to the public.

Department of Interior.—This department works with the fish industry and assists in quality improvement. It operates an inspection service and establishes grade standards for fishery products.

State and Municipal Laws.—All states and many municipalities have food laws and health codes. These supplement Federal regulations, which apply only to interstate transactions. These state and local laws usually follow Federal regulations. Changes are made to provide enforcement for specific local situations.

Trade Associations and Other Agencies.—Many trade associations have self-regulatory voluntary grading operations. Members agree to abide by these regulations and the association monitors the products accordingly. International food standards exist, established under the auspices of the United Nations through FAO/WHO; they are known as the Codex Alimentarius Commission. The Commission develops international and regional standards and publishes them in a food code form.

Food Labels, an Important Source of Information.—The "Fair Packaging and Labeling Act" of 1966 and the recently enacted truth-in-labeling regulations are for consumer protection. These laws apply to all packaged food regardless of where they are sold. Most labels list the ingredients of the food (Fig. 7.12). This information provides a deeper understanding of the product's quality and contents.

Labels reveal whether or not spices, coloring, flavors, preservatives or other additives have been added to the food. The ingredients contained in meat and poultry products must be listed in descending order of predominance, as used in the formulation of the product. Foods with geographic names must contain products from the stated locality; for example, Idaho potatoes must be grown in Idaho. A food is misbranded if its label expresses or implies a false geographic region in words or pictures. Exceptions are made for geographical names indicating a class of food, rather than a place of origin, such as Swiss cheese, Irish potatoes, and Gouda cheese.

Recently the FDA announced proposals to require food manufacturers to

FROZEN
BEEF STEW

FOR MODIFIED DIETS: SODIUM CONTROLLED, FAT CONTROLLED, SOFT, BLAND, DIABETIC DIETS.

HEATING INSTRUCTIONS
Minimum recommended serving temperature 160°F.
Remove label. Pierce center of cover.

CONVENTIONAL OVEN
Preheat oven to 450° F.
Heat 55 to 70 minutes.

CONVECTION OVEN
Preheat oven to 450° F.
Heat for 30 to 45 minutes.

INFRA RED OVEN
Set temperature control at #6 or #7.
Place tray in oven. Heat for 30 to 45 minutes.

PRESSURE STEAMER
Low pressure 4 # to 7 #.
55 to 65 minutes.
High pressure 15 #.
30 to 45 minutes.

EXCHANGES: One 8 oz. serving (by volume) will supply 3 meat exchanges (less 5 grams of fat) and 1 bread exchange.

TABLE OF ANALYSIS	Per 100 Grams	Each 8 fl. oz. Serving
Carbohydrates (gms.)	5.6	15
Protein (gms.)	8.6	23
Fat (gms.)	3.7	10
Available Calories	90	242
Sodium (mg)	20	53

COOKED MEAT CONTENT 23.88%.

INGREDIENTS: Gravy (water, tapioca starch, wheat flour, paprika, natural liquid caramel coloring), cooked cubed beef, cooked carrots, cooked potatoes, cooked peas.

NET WT. 5 LBS.

8—9.4 OZ. SERVINGS BY NET WT.
8—8 OZ. SERVINGS BY VOLUME

MEDI-DIET T.M.

DISTRIBUTED BY NATIONAL HOSPITAL FOODS, INC. 540 FRONTAGE RD., NORTHFIELD, ILL. 60093
SPECIALISTS IN PREPARED ENTREES FOR MODIFIED DIETS

Courtesy National Hospital Foods, Inc.

FIG. 7.12. AN EXAMPLE OF A LABEL THAT INCLUDES ALL NECESSARY INFORMATION

disclose on labels the names and source of all fat ingredients, including the kinds of fatty acids that may be present. These regulations will allow the consumer to distinguish between foods high in "polyunsaturated" vegetable fats and low in or free of "saturated" animal fats. Another important feature of these proposals would require all labels of processed foods to show the animal source, e.g., beef or chicken fat, or the vegetable origin, such as cottonseed or corn oil. At present, oils and fats are labeled as "shortening" or vegetable oil.

Prepared Meat and Poultry Products Standards

The United States Department of Agriculture has recognized the need for prepared meat and poultry products standards to protect the consumer and food service industry. Although hundreds of prepared foods are offered for sale and new ones are introduced daily, standards are now available for many products. New standards are in constant preparation as new items emerge and new processing techniques are developed.

When Federally inspected processed meat or poultry products are purchased, it is assured that they were examined by the USDA for wholesomeness and label accuracy. These inspections are performed at each step of the processing. The Consumer and Marketing Service branch sets standards and examines formulas for product characteristics and label description.

These standards describe the product's content, such as the minimum amount of meat, the maximum amount of water, and other components contained in the item.

Exacting Procedures Followed to Prepare Standards.—The USDA test kitchens examine and test similar products processed by various manufacturers. The data obtained from these tests provide information about the product trend, general properties and quality factors. Information is gathered from restaurants, cook books and other reference material. Test panels composed of representatives from different segments of the food industry are used. The data gathered from these sources are evaluated and a product standard definition is evolved.

In addition, technical work is performed in laboratories to finalize the product's standard based on such components as allowable fat and moisture content.

If a manufacturer develops a new processing technique, it must be checked to determine whether it will produce a wholesome product. Additives, if used, must be safe and effective. All processors are required to register their complete formulas, which must be approved prior to commercial distribution. If a manufacturer markets a product similar to one for which requirements are established, but with some slight variation, then the new varied item must be labeled by another name.

USDA Performs Continuous Product Inspections.—Between the time a product's formula, label and packaging are approved, and the time it reaches its final destination, inspectors check the product through all phases of the processing operation. This program guarantees that the standard is followed, the label is used correctly, and the product is wholesome.

At the outset, the inspector examines the raw meat or poultry that will be used to make the product to be certain that these perishable ingredients are fresh and wholesome. He also checks all the other ingredients, such as the spices and vegetables. During processing the inspector follows the USDA approved formula or recipe. He observes measurement of the ingredients to make sure that the amounts added comply with the approved formula.

If the processing includes cutting, chopping, mixing, stuffing, slicing or forming, the inspector watches each operation to assure that the formula is being followed. If the product is cooked, he checks the cooking time and temperature to ensure the proper degrees of doneness. Smoking and curing are also checked. The inspector continues his vigil during the freezing operation to see that the products are properly frozen.

Finally the product's packaging material is inspected for soundness and safety. Can closures are inspected for proper sealing and soundness. The inspector follows the USDA's previously approved packaging specifications. Samples from each lot of canned products are tested for presence of microorganisms. These samples are incubated, or held for a specific length of time at high temperatures, to check for microbial safety.

Labels and weights are then checked to determine if they meet the standard. It was previously stressed that labels must be read, since they form a composite guide of the product's contents. The item weighing the most is listed first, and that weighing the least is at the bottom. This scheme helps to evaluate the cost of the product. For example, the label of a certain brand of meat pie lists the water content first, followed by potatoes, carrots and finally the legal percentage of meat. Another brand lists the meat first, followed by carrots, potatoes and beef stock. The net weight of both brands is identical; however, the latter brand costs 4¢ more because it contained a higher percentage of meat and carrots, and it was therefore considered the better value.

Labels should also be checked for the USDA stamp of approval (Fig. 7.12, upper left hand corner).

Grading

Grading of foods is a vast undertaking conducted jointly by USDA's Consumer and Marketing Service and the departments of agriculture of the various states. Grading is a voluntary service and is self-supporting. It is provided to those companies requesting it on a fee-for-service basis.

During the fiscal year 1970 the following products were certified: 80% of the poultry, 69% of the butter, 67% of the lamb and mutton, 64% of the beef, 50% of the fresh fruits and vegetables, and 20% of the shell eggs. During the same period the following foods were certified for quality and/or wholesomeness: 87% of the dried eggs, 80% of the frozen fruits and vegetables, 77% of the processed liquid eggs, 46% of the nonfat dry milk, and 40% of the canned fruits and vegetables.

Grade Standards.—Grade standards define differences in quality that affect the usefulness and value of a food. They cover the whole range of a product's natural qualities. The number of grades for a particular food depends upon its variability; for instance, eight grades are necessary to span the range of beef quality, while only three are needed for turkey. The beef and lamb grades usually encountered are USDA Prime, Choice and Good. Choice is the grade most widely available; it denotes a high degree of tenderness, juiciness, and flavor. Chicken and turkey are often sold with the USDA Grade A shield affixed to the package. Lower grades, such as B and C are seldom offered for sale, but are used in soup, pies, etc. Grade A poultry has more meat and a better appearance.

Eggs are graded for both quality and size. Top quality eggs—USDA Grade AA and A—have a firm yolk and thick white content and stand up well for frying and poaching. Grade B eggs may have a flatter yolk and a thinner white content. Egg sizes are based on weight per doz, such as Extra large, weighing 27 oz per doz; Large, weighing 24 oz per doz; Medium, 21 oz per doz; and Small, 18 oz per doz.

Examples of FDA Standards of Identity

The increasing role of pre-prepared foods of all types in the food service industry has stepped up the policing activities by the Food and Drug Administration to protect the consumer against misbranding, adulteration and to assure wholesomeness. In order to give a clearer understanding of the Standards of Identity, selected examples follow:

§27.15 Canned prunes; identity; label statement of optional ingredients.

(a) Canned prunes is the food prepared from dried prunes, with or without one of the optional packing media specified in paragraph (b) of this section. Such food may be seasoned with one or more of the following optional ingredients:

(1) Spice.
(2) Flavoring, other than artificial flavoring.
(3) A vinegar.
(4) Citric acid.
(5) Lemon juice.
(6) Unpeeled pieces of citrus fruits.

Such food is sealed in a container. It is so processed by heat as to prevent spoilage.

(b) (1) The optional packing media referred to in paragraph (a) of this section are:

(i) Water.
(ii) Light sirup.
(iii) Heavy sirup.
(iv) Extra heavy sirup.

(2) Each of packing media in sub-paragraph (1) (ii) to (iv), inclusive, of this paragraph is prepared with water and one of the optional saccharine ingredients specified in paragraph (c) of this section.

§20.3 Ice milk; identity; label statement of optional ingredients.

Ice milk is the food prepared from the same ingredients and in the same manner prescribed in § 20.1 for ice cream and complies with all the provisions of § 20.1 (including the requirements for label statement of optional ingredients), except that:

(a) Its content of milk fat is more than 2 percent but not more than 7 percent.

(b) Its content of total milk solids is not less than 11 percent.

(c) Caseinates may be added when the content of total milk solids is not less than 11 percent.

(d) The provision for reduction in milk fat and total milk solids from the addition of bulky ingredients in § 20.1(a) does not apply.

(e) The quantity of food solids per gallon is not less than 1.3 pounds; except that when the optional ingredient microcrystalline cellulose specified in § 20.1 (f) (6) is used the quantity of food solids per gallon is not less than 1.3 pounds, exclusive of the weight of the microcrystalline cellulose.

(f) When any artificial coloring is used in ice milk, directly or as a component of any other ingredient, the label shall bear the statement "artificially colored," "artificial coloring added," "with added artificial color," or "_____, an artificial color added," the blank being filled in with the common or usual name of the artificial color; or in lieu thereof, in case the artificial color is a component of another ingredient, "_____ artificially colored."

(g) The name of the food is "ice milk."

(h) If both artificial color and artificial flavoring are used, the label statements may be combined.

§19.525 Cottage cheese; identity.

(a) Cottage cheese is the soft uncured cheese prepared by the procedure set forth in paragraph (b) of this section. The finished cottage cheese contains not more than 80 percent of moisture, as determined by the method prescribed under "Moisture—Official," on page 210 of "Official Methods of Analysis of the Association of Official Agricultural Chemists," Ninth Edition (1960). [Ed. note, 10th edition, 1965, p. 247, 15.157.]

(b) (1) One or more of the dairy ingredients specified in subparagraph (2) of this paragraph is pasteurized; calcium chloride may be added in a quantity of not more than 0.02 percent (calculated as anhydrous calcium chloride) of the weight of the mix; harmless lactic-acid-producing bacteria, with or without rennet, are added and it is held until it becomes coagulated. The coagulated mass may be cut; it may be warmed; it may be stirred; it is then drained. The curd may be washed with water and further drained; it may be pressed, chilled, worked, seasoned with salt.

(2) The dairy ingredients referred to in subparagraph (1) of this paragraph are sweet skim milk, concentrated skim milk, and nonfat dry milk. If concentrated skim milk or nonfat dry milk is used, water may be added in a quantity not in excess of that removed when the skim milk was concentrated or dried.

(3) For the purposes of this section the term "skim milk" means the milk of cows from which the milk fat has been separated, and "concentrated skim milk" means skim milk from which a portion of the water has been removed by evaporation.

[24 F.R. 6482, Aug. 12, 1959, as amended at 28 F.R. 3022, Mar. 28, 1963]

USDA Standards for Prepared Meat and Poultry Products

Standards for meat and poultry products are pertinent guidelines to assist in the task of quality interpretation and cost evaluation. To fall into this classification, a food must contain a *minumum* amount of meat or poultry prescribed by the USDA. For example, ready-to-serve chicken soup must contain at least 2% chicken. Condensed chicken soup must contain 4% or more, since it would then contain at least 2% when diluted with water. But chicken-flavored soup, which is not considered a poultry product, may contain less chicken.

The standards for meat ingredients usually are based on the fresh weight of the product, whereas those for poultry are measured on the weight of the cooked, deboned product. Since meat and poultry shrink during cooking, standards take this factor into account. For instance, beef pot pie must contain at least 25% fresh beef. Turkey pot pie must contain 14% or more cooked turkey. Chicken burgers must be 100% chicken; a product containing fillers must be called chicken patties. Following is a current list of product standards:

Red Meat Products

Note: All percentages of meat are on the basis of fresh uncooked weight, unless otherwise indicated.

1. *Barbecued Meats:* Weight of meat when barbecued cannot exceed 70% of the fresh uncooked meat; must have barbecued (crusted) appearance and be prepared over burning or smoldering hardwood or its sawdust.

2. *Barbecue Sauce with Meat:* At least 35% meat (cooked basis).
3. *Beans with Bacon in Sauce:* At least 12% bacon.
4. *Beans with Frankfurters in Sauce:* At least 20% franks.
5. *Beans with Ham in Sauce:* At least 12% ham (cooked basis).
6. *Beans with Meat Balls in Sauce:* At least 20% meatballs.
7. *Beef and Dumplings with Gravy or Beef and Gravy with Dumplings:* At least 25% beef.
8. *Beef Burgundy:* At least 50% beef.
9. *Beef Sauce with Beef and Mushrooms:* At least 25% beef and 7% mushrooms.
10. *Beef Sausage* (raw): No more than 30% fat.
11. *Beef Stroganoff:* At least 45% fresh uncooked beef or 30% cooked beef, and at least 10% sour cream or a "gourmet" combination of at least 7.5% sour cream and 5% wine.
12. *Beef with Barbecue Sauce:* At least 50% beef (cooked basis).
13. *Beef with Gravy:* At least 50% beef (cooked basis).
14. *Gravy with Beef:* At least 35% beef (cooked basis).
15. *Breaded Steaks, Chops, etc.:* Breading not to exceed 30% of finished product weight.
16. *Breakfast Sausage:* No more than 50% fat.
17. *Brunswick Stew:* At least 25% meat.
18. *Burritos:* At least 15% meat.
19. *Cabbage Rolls:* At least 12% meat.
20. *Cannelloni with Meat and Sauce:* At least 10% meat.
21. *Capelletti with Meat in Sauce:* At least 12% meat.
22. *Chili Con Carne:* At least 40% meat.
23. *Chili Con Carne with Beans:* At least 25% meat.
24. *Chili Hot Dog Sauce with Meat:* At least 6% meat.
25. *Chili Hot Dog with Meat:* At least 40% meat in Chili.
26. *Chili Macaroni:* At least 16% meat.
27. *Chili Pie:* At least 20% meat.
28. *Chili Sauce with Meat:* At least 6% meat.
29. *Chop Suey (American Style) with Macaroni and Meat:* At least 25% meat.
30. *Chop Suey Vegetables with Meat:* At least 12% meat.
31. *Chow Mein Vegetables with Meat:* At least 12% meat.
32. *Condensed, Creamed Dried Beef or Chipped Beef:* At least 18% dried or chipped beef (figured on reconstituted total content).
33. *Corned Beef and Cabbage:* At least 25% corned beef.
34. *Corn Dog:* Must meet standards for frankfurters; batter not to exceed the weight of the frank.
35. *Cream Cheese with Chipped Beef* (Sandwich spread): At least 12% meat.
36. *Croquettes:* At least 35% meat.
37. *Curried Sauce with Beef and Rice* (Casserole): At least 35% beef (figured on beef and sauce part only).

38. *Deviled Ham:* No more than 35% fat.
39. *Egg Foo Young with Meat:* At least 12% meat.
40. *Egg Rolls with Meat:* At least 10% meat.
41. *Enchilada with Meat:* At least 15% meat.
42. *Frankfurters, Bologna, Other Cooked Sausage:* May contain meat and meat by-products; no more than 30% fat, 10% added water, and 2% corn syrup; no more than 15% poultry unless its presence is reflected in product name; no more than 3.5% cereals and nonfat dry milk, with product name showing their presence. *All Meat:* Only muscle tissue with natural amounts of fat; no by-products, cereal, or binders. *All Beef:* Only meat of beef animals.
43. *Fried Rice with Meat:* At least 10% meat.
44. *Fritters:* At least 35% meat.
45. *Frozen Breakfasts:* At least 15% meat (cooked basis).
46. *Frozen Dinners:* At least 25% meat or meat food product (cooked basis, figured on total meal minus appetizer, bread and dessert).
47. *Frozen Entrées: Meat and One Vegetable:* At least 50% meat (cooked basis).
48. *Frozen Entrées: Meat, Gravy or Sauce, and One Vegetable:* At least 30% meat (cooked basis).
49. *Goulash:* At least 25% meat.
50. *Gravies:* At least 25% meat stock or broth, or at least 6% meat.
51. *Ham, Canned:* Limited to 8% total weight gain after processing; if gain is up to 8%, must be labeled *Ham, with Natural Juices;* if between 8% and 10%, it must be labeled *Ham, Water Added, with Juices.*
52. *Ham, Not Canned:* Must not weigh more after processing than the fresh ham weighs before curing and smoking; if contains up to 10% added weight, must be labeled *Ham, Water Added;* if more than 10%, must be labeled *Imitation Ham.*
53. *Ham a la King:* At least 20% ham (cooked basis).
54. *Ham and Cheese Spread:* At least 25% ham (cooked basis).
55. *Hamburger or Ground Beef:* No more than 30% fat; no extenders.
56. *Ham Chowder:* At least 10% ham (cooked basis).
57. *Ham Croquettes:* At least 35% ham (cooked basis).
58. *Ham Salad:* At least 35% ham (cooked basis).
59. *Ham Spread:* At least 50% ham.
60. *Hash:* At least 35% meat (cooked basis).
61. *High Meat Baby Foods:* At least 30% meat.
62. *Lasagna with Meat and Sauce:* At least 12% meat.
63. *Lima Beans with Ham or Bacon in Sauce:* At least 12% ham or cooked bacon.
64. *Liver Sausage, Liver Loaf, Liver Paste, Liver Cheese, Liver Pudding, Liver Spread, and similar liver products:* At least 30% liver.

65. *Macaroni and Beef in Tomato Sauce:* At least 12% beef.
66. *Macaroni Salad with Ham or Beef:* At least 12% meat (cooked basis).
67. *Manicotti* (containing meat filling): At least 10% meat.
68. *Meat Balls:* No more than 12% extenders (cereal, etc.)
69. *Meat Balls in Sauce:* At least 50% meat balls.
70. *Meat Casseroles:* At least 25% fresh uncooked meat or 18% cooked meat.
71. *Meat Pies:* At least 25% meat.
72. *Meat Ravioli:* At least 10% meat in ravioli, minus the sauce.
73. *Meat Salads:* At least 35% meat (cooked basis).
74. *Meat Taco Filling:* At least 40% meat.
75. *Meat Tacos:* At least 15% meat.
76. *Meat Turnovers:* At least 25% meat.
77. *Omelet with Bacon:* At least 12% bacon (cooked basis).
78. *Omelet with Ham:* At least 18% ham (cooked basis).
79. *Paté de Foie:* At least 30% liver.
80. *Pepper Steaks:* At least 30% beef (cooked basis).
81. *Pizza Sauce with Sausage:* At least 6% sausage.
82. *Pizza with Meat:* At least 15% meat.
83. *Pizza with Sausage:* At least 12% sausage (cooked basis) or 10% dry sausage, such as pepperoni.
84. *Pork Sausage:* Not more than 50% fat.
85. *Pork with Barbecue Sauce:* At least 50% pork (cooked basis).
86. *Pork with Dressing and Gravy:* At least 30% pork (cooked basis).
87. *Pork and Dressing:* At least 50% pork (cooked basis).
88. *Sandwiches* (containing meat): At least 35% meat.
89. *Sauce with Meat,* or *Meat Sauce:* At least 6% meat.
90. *Sauerbraten:* At least 50% meat (cooked basis).
91. *Sauerkraut Balls with Meat:* At least 30% meat.
92. *Sauerkraut with Wieners and Juice:* At least 20% wieners.
93. *Scalloped Potatoes and Ham:* At least 20% ham (cooked basis).
94. *Scallopine:* At least 35% meat (cooked basis).
95. *Scrapple:* At least 40% meat and/or meat by-products.
96. *Spaghetti Sauce and Meat Balls:* At least 35% meat balls (cooked basis).
97. *Spaghetti Sauce with Meat:* At least 6% meat.
98. *Spaghetti with Meat and Sauce:* At least 12% meat.
99. *Spanish Rice with Beef or Ham:* At least 20% beef or ham (cooked basis).
100. *Stews* (*Beef, Lamb,* and the like): At least 25% meat.
101. *Stuffed Cabbage with Meat in Sauce:* At least 12% meat.
102. *Stuffed Peppers with Meat in Sauce:* At least 12% meat.
103. *Sukiyaki:* At least 30% meat.
104. *Sweet and Sour Pork or Beef:* At least 25% fresh uncooked meat or 16% cooked meat, and at least 16% fruit.
105. *Swiss Steak with Gravy:* At least 50% meat (cooked basis).

106. *Gravy and Swiss Steak:* At least 35% meat (cooked basis).
107. *Tamale Pies:* At least 20% meat.
108. *Tamales:* At least 25% meat.
109. *Tamales with Sauce (or with Gravy):* At least 20% meat.
110. *Taquitos:* At least 15% meat.
111. *Tongue Spread:* At least 50% tongue.
112. *Tortellini with Meat:* At least 10% meat.
113. *Veal Birds:* At least 60% meat and no more than 40% stuffing.
114. *Veal Cordon Bleu:* At least 60% veal, 5% ham, and containing Swiss, Gruyère or Mozzarella cheese.
115. *Veal Fricassee:* At least 40% meat.
116. *Veal Parmagiana:* At least 40% breaded meat product in sauce.
117. *Veal Steaks:* Can be chopped, shaped, cubed, frozen. Beef can be added with product name shown as *Veal Steaks, Beef Added, Chopped, Shaped, and Cubed.* No more than 20% beef or must be labeled *Veal and Beef Steak, Chopped, Shaped and Cubed.* No more than 30% fat.

Poultry Products

All percentages of poultry (chicken, turkey, or other kinds of poultry) are on cooked deboned basis unless otherwise indicated.

1. *Breaded Poultry:* No more than 30% breading.
2. *Canned Boned Poultry:*
   (a) *Boned (kind), Solid Pack:* At least 95% poultry meat, skin and fat.
   (b) *Boned (kind):* At least 90% poultry meat, skin and fat.
   (c) *Boned (kind),* with Broth: At least 80% poultry meat, skin and fat.
   (d) *Boned (kind), with Specified Percentage of Broth:* At least 50% poultry meat, skin and fat.
3. *Chicken Cacciatore:* At least 20% chicken meat, or 40% with bone.
4. *Chicken Croquettes:* At least 25% chicken meat.
5. *Chopped Poultry with Broth (Baby Food):* At least 43% meat, with skin, fat, and seasoning.
6. *Creamed Poultry:* At least 20% poultry meat.
7. *Poultry a la King:* At least 20% poultry meat.
8. *Poultry Barbecue:* At least 40% poultry meat.
9. *Poultry Burgers:* 100% poultry meat, with skin and fat.
10. *Poultry Chop Suey:* At least 4% poultry meat.
11. *Chop Suey with Poultry:* At least 2% poultry meat.
12. *Poultry Chow Mein, without Noodles:* At least 4% poultry meat.
13. *Poultry Dinners:* At least 18% poultry meat.
14. *Poultry Fricassee:* At least 20% poultry meat.
15. *Poultry Fricassee of Wings:* At least 40% poultry meat (cooked basis, with bone).
16. *Poultry Hash:* At least 30% poultry meat.

17. *Poultry Noodles or Dumplings:* At least 15% poultry meat, or 30% with bone.
18. *Noodles or Dumplings with Poultry:* At least 6% poultry meat.
19. *Poultry Pies:* At least 14% poultry meat.
20. *Poultry Ravioli:* At least 2% poultry meat.
21. *Poultry Rolls:* Binding agents limited to 3% in cooked roll.
22. *Poultry Salad:* At least 25% poultry meat.
23. *Poultry Soup:* At least 2% poultry meat.
24. *Poultry Stew:* At least 12% poultry meat.
25. *Poultry Stroganoff:* At least 30% poultry meat.
26. *Poultry Tamales:* At least 6% poultry meat.
27. *Poultry Tetrazzini:* At least 15% poultry meat.
28. *Poultry with Gravy:* At least 35% poultry meat.
29. *Gravy with Poultry:* At least 15% poultry meat.
30. *Sliced Poultry with Gravy:* At least 35% poultry.

Meat Products Having Complete Standards of Identity

Complete standards of identity currently exist for three meat products. These standards require specific ingredients to be present as follows:

(1) *Corned Beef Hash:* Must contain at least 35% beef (cooked basis). Also it must contain potatoes (either fresh, dehydrated, cooked dehydrated, or a mixture of these types), curing agents, and seasonings. It may be made with certain optional ingredients such as onions, garlic, beef broth, or beef fat, but may not contain more than 15% fat nor more than 72% moisture.

(2) *Chopped Ham:* Must contain fresh, cured, or smoked ham, along with certain specified kinds of curing agents and seasonings. It may also contain certain optional ingredients in specified amounts, including finely chopped ham shank meat, dehydrated onions, dehydrated garlic, corn syrup, other chemical substances as permitted in the Federal standard, and not more than 3% water to dissolve the curing agents.

(3) *Oleomargarine or Margarine:* Must contain either the rendered fat, oil, or stearin derived from cattle, sheep, swine, or goats; or a vegetable food fat, oil, or stearin; or a combination of these two classes of ingredients in a specified proportion. It must contain individually or in combination, pasteurized cream, cow's milk, skim milk, a combination of nonfat dry milk and water or finely ground soybeans and water. It may contain optional ingredients specified in the standard, including butter, salt, artificial coloring, vitamins A and D, and permitted chemical substances. Fat in finished product may not exceed 80%. Label must indicate whether product is from animal or vegetable origin or both.

Food Additives

Food additives include a wide variety of substances. The various agents are classed according to their function and the property they impart to a food.

Presently there are 30 different groups of additives totalling about 3000 substances. The most widely employed are flavoring agents, accounting for 1200 assorted compounds. Food additives are constantly undergoing evaluation and review, as to their merits and effects on the human body. This review is often instigated by people who are of the opinion that food additives, regardless of their merits, are harmful to health.

Proponents point up the need for additives, because of the increasing role of efficiency foods to both the consumer and the food service industry. The key to the success of many of these efficiency or ready-to-serve foods is the additive which often extends shelf life and reduces preparation time.

Definitions of food additives are as diverse as the subject. One definition interprets them as "nonnutritive substances added intentionally to food, generally in small quantities to improve its appearance, flavor, texture, or storage properties." Another source defines them as "substances or mixtures of substances, other than a basic foodstuff, which is present in a food as a result of some aspect of production, processing, storage, or packaging." Spices, natural seasonings, baking powder, fruit and beverage acids are among the food additives widely used.

The control of food additives is exercised by the Food and Drug Administration, under the Amendment of 1958 which formed a part of the Federal Food, Drug and Cosmetic Act of 1938. The amendment states that no additive can be used until the FDA is convinced by scientific evidence that such additives are safe at the intended level of use in specific food applications. The burden of proof regarding the safety of a new additive rests with the organization. Exempted from the above are items which by prior evaluation, or from experience based on long consumer usage, are "generally recognized as safe." These additives are referred to as the GRAS list, which includes some 600 substances. The entire list of GRAS substances is undergoing a reclassification and review, authorized by a Presidential order.

Categories of food additives are preservatives, antioxidants, sequestrants, surface-active agents, stabilizers and thickeners, acids and alkalies, food colors, dietary sweeteners, nutrient supplements, flavoring agents, anticaking and antifoaming agents, antisticking substances, meat-curing agents, and enzymes.

Preservatives.—Preservatives are added to foods to prevent spoilage due to microorganisms and enzyme action. These substances prevent the growth of bacteria, yeast, and molds. Sodium benzoate is used in soft drinks and acidic foods. Calcium propionate and sorbic acid inhibit the growth of mold. Chlorine is used as a germicidal wash for fruits and vegetables. Fumigants control microorganisms on spices, nuts, and dried fruits. Sulfur dioxide is used to prevent browning of fruits and vegetables caused by enzymes.

Antioxidants.—Antioxidants prevent the oxidation of fats. Without the addition of antioxidants, rancidity would develop, resulting in extreme off-flavors and off-tastes. Foods such as potato chips, breakfast cereals, salted nuts, and dehydrated foods containing fat would all have short shelf life if antioxidants were not added.

Stabilizers and Thickeners.—These are gums, starches, dextrins and other substances that stabilize (prevent separation) and thicken food by absorbing water, thus increasing viscosity and forming gels. Gravies, pie fillings, cake toppings, chocolate milk drinks, jellies, puddings and salad dressings are among the many foods containing these additives.

Food Colors.—Food colors are added to numerous foods to improve appearance and to make them more eye-appealing. Those derived from coal-tar origin are all certified and are added to foods in minute quantities. Maraschino cherries, hard candies, soft drinks, and gelatin desserts are some of the foods colored with certified coal-tar dyes.

Flavors.—Flavoring agents are the most widely used additives and include both natural and synthetic substances. Spices, herbs, essential oils and plant extracts are employed for this purpose. Food colors and flavoring agents are not added to deceive the public, but to enhance the appeal of the item. In some instances these agents are required to replenish natural flavors that are lost during processing, e.g., from heating and drying operations.

Flavor enhancers that act to intensify flavors present in foods are employed on a wide scale. Monosodium glutamate is a flavor enhancer or potentiator.

Nutrient Supplements.—Nutrient substances such as vitamins and minerals are added to supplement and enrich certain foods. Vitamin D is added to milk, iodine to salt, vitamin A to margarine, and vitamin C to fruit juices and soft drinks. At the present time nutrients are undergoing an intensive review and study by the FDA, both to reevaluate and determine their merits and to see whether the daily requirements prescribed for human beings are accurate.

Commissaries Must Conform to Federal Regulations

Vending and restaurant commissaries that process meat and poultry products for off-the-premises sales must now conform to Federal regulations governing these operations. Previously, the regulations applied only to intrastate transactions. Many state and municipal laws were not sufficient to cover commissaries. Commissaries must now conform to the new laws that upgrade and control food handling and sanitary conditions.

In 1906 a Federal Meat Inspection Act was passed. This law provides for mandatory inspections of animals, slaughtering conditions and meat-processing facilities. This act helps to ensure that meat and meat products are clean, wholesome, unadulterated, free from disease and properly represented. In 1957 the Federal Poultry Act was instituted; it is essentially the same as the meat act, except that it applies to poultry and poultry products.

In December 1967 the Wholesome Meat Act was passed, followed by the Wholesome Poultry Act in August 1968. Both laws contain provisions to regulate commissaries that manufacture and prepare meat and poultry food products for sale elsewhere. All meat and poultry items, including entrées, meat pies, meat or poultry soup and casseroles, that are cooked or portioned in a central kitchen are covered under these regulations. Presently, the law does not apply to central kitchens that supply satellite units in the same building or complex.

All states are required to follow the Federal acts and to establish a uniform enforcement and inspection program. Included in these laws are commissary layout, design, installation and labeling nomenclature. Not affected are non-meat and poultry products and sandwiches. Labeling and formulation procedures must be followed according to methods provided by the USDA. Labels must conform to the 1966 Federal Fair Packaging and Labeling Act.

FACTORS AFFECTING FOOD QUALITY

Many factors are responsible for poor quality food. Most of them can be traced to poor sanitation, faulty handling, malfunctioning of equipment, incorrect preparation and carelessness. Although additional elements exert a deleterious effect on quality, only those that occur from in-store situations will be discussed here. For purposes of confining these problems to practical applications, it will be assumed that the food undergoing preparation was purchased according to predetermined and exacting specifications. When delivered, the products were checked and found to be in good condition and within the bounds of the quality expected.

The properties of food considered when making a quality evaluation are: flavor, which is a combination of taste and aroma perception; nutritional content; texture; appearance, and consistency. In addition, attributes such as shelf life, convenience, packaging and price form a secondary group that tends to influence quality evaluation.

A feeding establishment, regardless of size, is a complex manufacturing center. From the time the food is delivered until it is served, a myriad of steps and handling operations are involved. The preparation center and adjunct operations can be compared to a highly organized chemical processing facility. Many of the physical and chemical unit operations and instrumentations that enter into the production of fine chemicals or drugs are also involved in food preparation. Most foods can be likened to delicate products such as perfume, where the valuable essences are easily destroyed by improper handling or processing. The following are the prime factors responsible for significant quality changes:

(1) spoilage due to microbiological, biochemical, physical or chemical factors;

(2) adverse or incompatible water conditions;

(3) poor sanitation and ineffective warewashing;

(4) improper and incorrect pre-cooking, cooking and post-cooking methods;

(5) incorrect temperature;

(6) incorrect timing;

(7) wrong formulations, stemming from incorrect weight of the food, or its components;

(8) poor machine maintenance program;

(9) presence of vermin and pesticides;

(10) poor packaging.

Any of these factors, either singly or in combination, will contribute to poor quality, and effect changes that will be evident in the food's flavor, texture, appearance, and consistency.

Food Spoilage and Contamination

It is unfortunate that the process and results of food and beverage spoilage cannot be readily observed. The adage "what you don't know, won't hurt you," applies to the thinking of the majority of food service personnel. If the wording were changed to "what you don't know *can* hurt you," a greater awareness of food and beverage deterioration, its problems and solutions might be achieved.

All foods will deteriorate, some more rapidly (dairy products) than others. Measures must be taken and procedures instituted to ensure the correct handling and storage of foods, otherwise spoilage will result, profits will diminish, and customer dissatisfaction will occur.

The importance of preventing spoilage cannot be minimized. The customer demands and has every reason to expect that the food and beverage served will be safe, wholesome, and good in taste. The consumer has been well informed through the various news media as to the restrictions and safeguards enacted by the Federal, state and local governments, and supposes that all the items served him are free of contamination.

It is the purpose of this discussion to show in outline how to prevent spoilage and what can occur if the basic rules of good housekeeping, sanitation, and product handling are neglected.

The study of microbiology is a broad, complex subject. Without at least an elementary knowledge of its scope one cannot comprehend the significance, importance and effect of microorganisms on food spoilage. Since this book is limited in coverage, only brief mention can be made of this subject but the attempt will be made to couple the underlying reasons for spoilage of foods to their corrective measures.

The following list designates the major types of spoilage of foods and beverages: (1) microbiological spoilage, (2) biochemical spoilage, (3) physical spoilage, and (4) chemical spoilage.

Microbiological Spoilage.—There are thousands of species of microorganisms in existence. All are not harmful; many are valuable and are used in the preservation of food, in the production of alcohol, or to create special flavors. Those used in food production are specially cultivated and employed under controlled conditions. Microbiological spoilage is considered to be the primary cause of food and beverage spoilage. Microorganisms are found everywhere: in the soil, air, water, and on fruit and vegetables. All food-processing equipment that has not been fully sterilized, as well as the human body and clothing, are contaminated by these spoilage organisms. The main factors that induce the growth of microorganisms are suitable temperature, moisture, and a substrate for them to feed on, such as foods and beverages. There are three principal forms of microorganisms: (1) bacteria, (2) molds, and (3) yeast.

Bacteria.—Bacteria are microscopic unicellular plants of varying shape and size. The three shapes most commonly encountered are spherical, rod and spiral. A number of bacteria produce spores which resemble seeds and are resistant to heat and chemicals. Sterilization temperatures will deactivate these highly resistant spores. Bacteria are measured in units called microns. One micron is equivalent to 1/25,000 in. The size of most common bacteria range from 1 to 10 or more microns in length; and about ½ micron in diameter.

Molds.—Molds are larger than bacteria and are more complex in structure. They are members of the plant family, are composed of many cells, and are usually cylindrical or shaped like tubes. They grow in a network of hairlike fibers called mycelia and send up fruiting bodies that yield spores. These organisms can penetrate the smallest opening. They are tenacious and become anchored to a substance by their hair-like fibers. Molds are probably the most common type of spoilage organisms that can be seen by the naked eye. They are distinguishable by a majority of food service personnel. An example is the bread mold and the mold that forms on the surface of meats and cheese products. An outgrowth of mold contamination that is generally readily identifiable is the odor referred to as *mildewy*.

Yeast.—Yeast cells are larger than either molds or bacteria, measuring about 20 microns in length. They are unicellular plants and are of spherical or ellipsoidal shape. Yeasts play an important role in the food industry. They produce enzymes that have a favorable effect on certain chemical reactions, such as leavening of bread and the production of alcohol and glycerol. Yeasts can induce undesirable reactions on such items as citrus juices and fruit-flavored drinks by a process known as fermentation. The result of uncontrolled fermentation is generally identifiable by the sour or vinegary taste of the beverage.

Biochemical Spoilage.—Biochemical spoilage, probably the second greatest source of food deterioration, is caused by natural food enzymes. These are complex chemicals that bring about many complicated reactions by assuming the role of catalysts. If enzymatic reactions are not controlled, off-flavors, off-odors, and off-colors will develop in foods and beverages. Many foods contain natural enzymes which under certain conditions produce significant changes. An example is the apple. When it is peeled and the meat exposed to the air, the apple turns brown. This change is brought about by enzymes in the apple that are dormant until activated by the oxygen in the air. However, these reactions must be controlled; otherwise deterioration occurs from the weakening of the tissue structure setting up conditions favorable to the growth of microorganisms.

Microorganisms as they grow in various foods and beverages secrete enzymes that produce significant changes in the product. An example is the production of alcohol by the enzymes derived from yeast.

Enzyme formation can be controlled in much the same manner as microorganisms. Heat, cold, drying, the addition of certain inhibiting chemicals, and radiation are the principal means used to control and inactivate damaging natural food enzymes.

Physical Spoilage.—Physical spoilage can be brought on by temperature changes, moisture and dryness. Excessive heat destroys emulsions, dries out food by removing moisture, and destroys vitamins. Extreme cold can also cause deterioration. A common example is the freezing of milk, which results in an emulsion break, causing the fat to separate. Some sauces exhibit a like tendency.

Excessive moisture in powdered beverage concentrates, such as tea or hot chocolate, can support the growth of mold or bacteria. The moisture content need not extend throughout the entire product to allow growth. Surface moisture will cause lumping and caking, stickiness, and crystallization of the product. These conditions are prevalent in vending machines and counter-served iced tea or hot chocolate dispensers. Entrapped moisture in protective film packages can damage the contents. If this moisture is condensed, conditions may be ripe to support the growth of microorganisms.

Chemical Spoilage.—Chemical spoilage may be caused by the interaction of certain ingredients contained in the food or beverage with oxygen of the air, by light or by time (extended storage). Temperature changes can accelerate reactions producing undesirable chemical changes. In addition, the reaction of incompatible substances with the food or beverage can lead to chemical spoilage. Examples of this are the effects of certain metals on the brewing of coffee and in deep fat frying; and the effect of iron, copper, or other impurities, such as high alkalinity, from water used for carbonated beverages.

Algae.—Algae are plants that live in fresh and salt water, and on moist surfaces. They are not parasitic, as they manufacture their nourishment by photosynthesis. Algae play an important role in food processing. Irish moss, a form of algae, is used in chocolate milk to hold the chocolate in suspension. In some parts of the world, algae are used as a food (kelp). Certain varieties of algae contain iodine, bromine and potassium and are used as fertilizer. However, algae can produce disagreeable side effects on foods and beverages.

If they grow in large masses and die, their residues will impart putrid odors and tastes to the water. If the water is used for cooking, the brewing of coffee, or for soft drinks, off-flavors and off-odors will be noticeable. Old city water systems may contain large quantities of algae. Steps must be taken to treat water containing impurities, such as those caused by algae residues.

Prevention of Foodborne Contamination.—Contamination that results in foodborne illnesses can be prevented. Spoilage of food is the end result of careless handling, innocent and unconscious unsanitary habits of the food handler, and a lack of control to check infection at the source of the problem.

The majority of foodborne illnesses result from the introduction of causative organisms by employees and or customers and are caused by (1) handling or contact with food or food-serving utensils, and (2) contamination of food-serving utensils with oral or nasal discharge or skin infection.

Attributable Illnesses.—Illnesses associated with foodborne contamination are:

(1) *Handling contamination* (hands in direct contact with food) *Staphylococcus* toxin

   Salmonellosis (mostly gastrointestinal illness; less commonly typhoid fever, paratyphoid)

   Amoebic dysentery

   Bacillary dysentery (shigellosis)

   Enteric (intestinal) viruses (infectious hepatitis)

(2) *Respiratory contamination* (mouth, nose, and throat discharges) *Staphylococcus* infection

   Scarlet fever

   Streptococcal sore throat

   Tuberculosis

   Diphtheria

(3) *Chemical poisoning,* although not classified in the airborne group, occurs as a result of certain toxic chemicals that come into contact with foods or beverages. Examples are copper, cadmium, zinc, and cyanide. Copper poisoning is caused by contact between copper and acid foods or carbonated beverages. Many governmental agencies have enacted laws outlawing the use of copper in vending machines and soda dispensers for this reason. Cadmium and zinc poisoning result when acid foods dissolve these metals from containers in which they are stored. Cyanide poisoning is caused by the failure to thoroughly wash and rinse polished silverware.

Introduction of Contaminants Into Food.—Three areas where foods or beverages will be subjected to contamination are:

(1) at the source, e.g. the processor, canner or manufacturer;

(2) in storage, in the freezer, in transit, or in the food establishment's refrigerators;

(3) in preparation in the commissary, kitchen or counter.

Methods of Prevention.—*Health habits* of personnel involved in food preparation should reflect a number of basic rules of hygiene including: the washing of hands in hot water, using plenty of soap; drying hands on a clean cloth or paper towel; keeping fingernails short and clean; using hair net or cap; remaining away from the food when the person has an infected cut, boil, or other infection of the exposed skin; using transfer tools that are properly cleaned and sanitized; covering sneezes and coughs by means of a tissue or handkerchief; and reporting to management cases of diarrhea, fever or other serious symptom so that a job replacement can be made. In addition, all food service personnel should receive a periodic medical checkup and all new personnel should be given a medical examination to determine freedom from tuberculosis or whether he or she is a typhoid carrier.

Insects and rodents, such as flies, roaches, rats and mice, are carriers of disease and spoilage-producing organisms. Provisions must be made to eliminate them. Vermin control is necessary as a precautionary measure and should be performed by specialists. Entry points, like loose-fitting doors, pipes, tiles and broken screens, should be repaired, filled in or replaced.

Overhead and airborne sources of contamination are areas generally neglected. These become breeding grounds for contaminants. Overhead pipes, stairwells and casings, fans, blower blades, stove hoods, window frames and skylights are areas requiring periodic and systematic cleaning and sanitizing.

Preparation equipment (items used in the preparation of foods and beverages) include grinders, slicers, choppers, dicers, blenders, mixers and can openers. An item such as a can opener is rarely sanitized, yet it is one piece of equipment that is in constant use. It is a prime spawning area for microorganisms.

Work surfaces require constant attention, especially if made of wood. Usually a damp cloth is used to wipe the surface, and little thought is given to its sanitary condition. Tables, sandwich boards, meat blocks, bread boards, and other items upon which food is prepared comprise this type of equipment.

Transfer containers and utensils (items which come in intimate contact with foods and beverages for a long period of time) include pots, pans, beaters, scoops, spoons, knives, ladles and liquid-measuring vessels. All are carriers of bacteria and unless they are completely sanitized they become potential sources of food-spoilage organisms.

Salmonella and Staphylococcus.—Pathogenic organisms such as *Salmonella* and *Staphylococcus* have received a great deal of attention in recent years.

Salmonella is a bacterium most commonly related to typhoid fever in terms of identification. Only 3 of some 1,300 known strains of *Salmonella* cause typhoid and paratyphoid fevers. Salmonella organisms, when taken into the body, multiply in the intestinal tract and produce an infection resulting in nausea, vomiting, cramps, diarrhea and fever. To protect against false claims of food poisoning, the food service operator should be knowledgeable as to the symptoms. It is usually between 12 and 30 hr after ingestion before the symptoms appear.

Since 1946, statistics have shown an increase from 723 to over 20,000 reported cases of Salmonella poisoning per year. It should be realized that many cases are unreported, leading one to believe the figure of 20,000 per year is conservative. Better methods of isolation and reporting may have contributed to this meteoric rise; however, the increased incidence of Salmonella poisoning has caused widespread concern. Regulatory activity has increased proportionately. Laws have been passed and enforcement agencies created to guarantee that all efforts are taken to keep Salmonella poisoning at a minimum.

Salmonella organisms have been found in a wide variety of foods which may have become contaminated during production, handling or storage. Poultry,

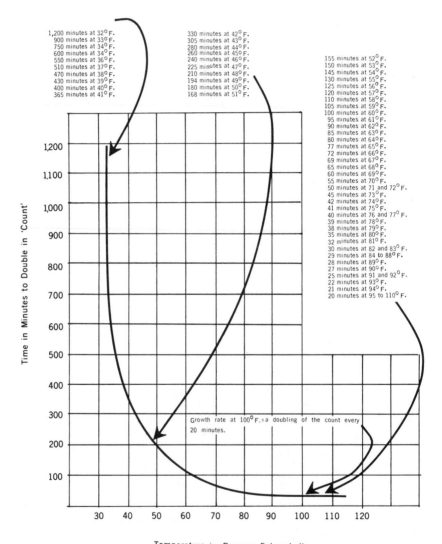

Temperature in Degrees Fahrenheit

Courtesy National Association of Frozen Food Packers, Washington, D.C.

FIG. 7.13. GROWTH RATES FOR BACTERIA

meats, eggs and dairy products are among the foods most frequently found to harbor Salmonella. However; items such as imported plastic drink coolers have in the past been recalled from the market because they were discovered to be a source of contamination.

The U.S. Public Health Communicable Disease Center, established because of the alarming increase of Salmonella food poisoning, lists poor handling in the food establishment as a major problem source. Minute amounts of contamination in foods can be greatly increased by improper cooking, processing and refrigeration (Fig. 7.13).

Staphylococcus contamination differs from *Salmonella* in that the food poisoning is caused by the toxin produced by certain strains. All pathogenic organisms are destroyed during the normal pasteurization process. However, the toxin produced by *Staphylococcus* is heat-resistant. Common sources of post-processing contamination are traceable to improper handling of raw meats within the food service establishment, coupled with poor cleaning and sanitizing of cutting boards and table tops.

Figure 7.14 is a reference chart of foodborne illnesses, and their causes, source and effects. This chart was compiled by the National Restaurant Association as a quick guide to the causes of these illnesses, with the intent that it will be used to help eliminate the source of contamination.

Effect of Water on Food Quality

Water is a complex chemical solution rarely encountered in nature in the pure state. It is one of the main ingredients for sustenance and a highly prized natural resource. There is much to be learned about water, and scientists, realizing this, continue to research and study the mysteries surrounding many of its unique characteristics.

To the general public water is water, and any variation in its chemical components do not become apparent until problems arise. Current consumption of water for industrial purposes in the United States is estimated at about 130 billion gallons per day. Less than 1/10 of this quantity is supplied by municipalities. Surface sources account for 91% and ground water furnished 9% (Mc-Clelland, 1965).

Water is the major component of beverages. It lends its properties to those substances for which it is a solvent, and has a direct bearing on the quality of all foodstuff and food preparations. Water in its pure state is a simple combination of two familiar gases, hydrogen and oxygen. When the two gases are chemically united, the liquid is formed. Unfortunately, water that is universally consumed contains many other substances in an infinite variety of combinations and amounts. These materials, if present in relatively large quantities, will cause unusual tastes, odors and discolorations. These substances are called dissolved or soluble materials because they form an intimate and complete mixture with the water. In addition, water also contains undissolved or insoluble items over a

ILLNESSES OF FREQUENT OCCURRENCE

NAME OF ILLNESS	CAUSATIVE AGENT	FOODS USUALLY INVOLVED	HOW INTRODUCED INTO FOOD	PREVENTATIVE OR CORRECTIVE PROCEDURES
Staphylococcus Food Poisoning	Staphylococcus entero-toxin — a poison developed by staphylococcus when it grows in food	Cooked ham or other meat, chopped or comminuted food, cream filled or custard pastries, other dairy products, Hollandaise sauce, bread pudding, potato salad, chicken, fish, and other meat salads, "warmed-over" food	Usually food handlers through nasal discharges or purulent local skin infections. (Acne, pimples, boils, scratches and cuts)	Refrigerate moist foods during storage periods; minimize use of hands in preparation. Exclude unhealthly food handlers (having pimples, boils and other obvious infections)
Perfringens Food Poisoning	Clostridium perfringens	Meat which has been boiled, steamed, braized, or partially roasted, allowed to cool several hours and subsequently served either cooled or reheated	Natural contaminate of meat	Rapidly refrigerate meat between cooking and use
Salmonellosis	Over 800 types of Salmonella Bacteria, capable of producing gastro-intestional illness.	Meat and poultry, comminuted foods, egg products, custards, shell fish, soups, gravies, sauces, "warmed-over" foods	Fecal contamination by food handlers. Raw contaminated meat and poultry, liquid eggs and unpasteurized milk	By good personal habits of food handlers; sufficient cooking and refrigeration of perishable foods Eliminate rodents and flies
Salmonellosis a) Typhoid Fever b) Para-typhoid A	Salmonella typhosa S. paratyphi A	Moist foods, dairy products, shell fish, raw vegetables and water	By food handlers and other carriers	Prohibit carriers from handling food; require strict personal cleanliness in food preparation; eliminate flies

ILLNESSES OF LESS FREQUENT OR RARE OCCURRENCE

NAME OF ILLNESS	CAUSATIVE AGENT	FOODS USUALLY INVOLVED	HOW INTRODUCED INTO FOOD	PREVENTATIVE OR CORRECTIVE PROCEDURES
Streptococcus Food Infection (Beta type Scarlet Fever & Strep Throat	Beta hemolytic Streptococci	Foods contaminated with nasal or oral discharges from case or carrier	Coughing, sneezing or handling	Exclude food handlers with known strep infections
Streptococcus Infection (Alpha type) (Intestinal)	Enterococcus group; Pyogenic group	Foods contaminated with excreta on unclean hands	By unsanitary food handling	Same as above; thorough cooking of food and refrigeration of moist food during storage periods
Botulism	Toxins of Clostridium botulinum	Improperly processed or unrefrigerated foods of low acidity	Soil and dirt. Spores not killed in inadequately heated foods	Pressure cook canned foods with PH over 4.0; home canned foods boil 20 minutes after removal from can or jars; cook foods thoroughly after removing before serving; discard all foods in swollen unopened cans
Bacillary Dysentery (Shigellosis)	Shigella Bacteria	Foods contaminated with excreta on unclean hands	By unsanitary food handling	Strict personal cleanliness in food preparation; refrigeration of moist foods . Exclude carriers
Amoebic Dysentery	Endamoeba histolytica	Foods contaminated with excreta on unclean hands	By unsanitary food handlers	Protect water supplies; insure strict personal cleanliness with food handlers. Exclude carriers
Trichinosis	Larvae of Trichinella spiralis	Raw or insufficiently cooked pork and pork products (also whale, seal, bear or walrus meat)	Raw pork from hogs fed uncooked infected garbage	Thoroughly cook pork and pork products over 150°, preferably to 160°
Fish Tape Worm	Parasitic Larvae	Raw or insufficiently cooked fish containing live larvae.	Fish infested from contaminated water	Cook fish thoroughly. Avoid serving raw fish
Arsenic, Fluoride, Lead Poisoning (Insecticides, Rodenticides)		Any foods accidentally contaminated	Either during growing period or accident in kitchen	Thoroughly wash all fresh fruits and vegetables when received; store insecticides and pesticides away food; properly label containers; follow use instructions; use carefully; guard food from chemical contamination
Copper poisoning	Copper food contact surfaces	Acid foods and carbonated liquids	Contact between metal and acid food or carbonated beverage	Prevent acid foods or carbonated liquids from coming into contact with exposed copper
Cadmium and zinc poisoning	Metal plating on food containers	Fruit juices, fruit gelatin and other acid foods stored in metal plated containers	Acid foods dissolve cadmium and zinc from containers in which stored	Discontinue use of cadmium plated utensils as food containers. Prohibit use of zinc coated utensils for preparation, storage, and serving of acid fruits and other foods or beverages
Cyanide	Silver Polish		Failure to thoroughly wash and rinse polished silverware	Discontinue use of cyanide base silver polish or wash and rinse silverware thoroughly

Courtesy The National Restaurant Association

FIG. 7.14. FOODBORNE ILLNESSES, THEIR CAUSES, SOURCES AND EFFECTS

considerable range of shapes and sizes. Some of these are living organisms such as bacteria, mold, fine dirt, and sand. For practically every use of water, an attempt is made to remove all the undissolved or suspended material by means of filters or fine screens. Water containing dissolved materials must be treated chemically so that it can perform its specific function more easily and efficiently.

The chemical composition of water can change dramatically from one locality to another. In fact water changes may occur within relatively short distances. Day-to-day and seasonal variations in mineral content, turbidity and temperature have an added effect on water quality.

Properties and Sources of Water.—Water has a number of unique properties that enhance its usefulness but also add to its complexities.

(1) Water occurs on earth in three forms: liquid, vapor and solid (ice).

(2) It expands when it freezes, whereas most substances contract.

(3) It is lighter as a solid than as a liquid.

(4) It has a high heat capacity, in that it absorbs a great deal of heat without much rise in temperature.

(5) It has a higher surface tension than any other common liquid except mercury. This property becomes apparent with dish washing, when rinsing or wetting agents are required to reduce surface tension.

(6) It is the prime solvent, universally employed or related to nearly every aspect of man's existence.

The source of all water is from precipitation in the form of rain or snow. Rain is practically pure water, but as it falls it collects such airborne contaminants as dust, sulfur dioxide and other air pollutants, and microorganisms. After reaching the ground the rain either runs over the surface or into the ground. During this process, it dissolves any soluble and many sparingly soluble materials with which it comes in contact, among which are common salt (NaCl), sodium sulfate, salts of calcium, magnesium, iron, and manganese, as well as carbonates and silicates. All these soluble substances dissolved in the water are termed as "solids," "total solids" or "minerals."

Hardness.—Two types of water hardness are encountered, (1) carbonate (formerly called temporary hardness) due to calcium and magnesium bicarbonates and carbonates, and (2) noncarbonate (formerly called permanent hardness) due to calcium and magnesium sulfates, chlorides and nitrates.

A quantitative classification of hardness based on calcium carbonate is as follows:

	Ppm	Gpg
soft	0–60	0–4
moderately hard	61–120	4–8
hard	121–180	8–12
very hard	Over 180	Over 12

The terms used in reporting analytical results are:

(1) Parts per million (ppm). A unit weight of material per million weight units of water.

(2) Milligrams per liter (mg/l). The same as ppm, also expressed as grams per cubic meter.

(3) Equivalents per million (epm). A unit chemical equivalent weight of material per million weight units of water.

(4) Grains per gallon (gpg). The number grains of solute per 1 U.S. gal of water.

$$1 \text{ grain} = 1/7000 \text{ lb}$$
$$1 \text{ U.S. gal} = 8.33 \text{ lb}$$
$$1 \text{ gpg} = 17.1 \text{ ppm}$$

Brackish or Saline Water.—Water that contains large amounts of dissolved minerals but is less salty than sea water is termed brackish or saline water. Such water occurs in many inland localities. The following list shows the concentrations of dissolved solids in saline water.

Description	Ppm of Dissolved Solids
brackish	1,000–3,000
saline	3,000–10,000
sea water	33,000–36,000
brine	over 36,000

An American Water Works Association report on the extent of brackish and saline water in the United States and Canada indicated that of 20,215 municipal water utilities surveyed, 1,066 had raw water with a total dissolved solids content of 1,000–3,000 ppm, and 31 had water containing 3,000–10,000 ppm.

The drinking water standards of the U.S. Public Health Service recommended that water containing more than 250 ppm of chlorides or sulfates, or 500 ppm of dissolved solids is not fit for human consumption.

Highly mineralized water is usually unsuitable for general use due to its high hardness, its corrosiveness, its bitter and saline taste, its laxative action, and its adverse effect on the flavor of beverages and food. Treatment of these conditions is now possible by a process called reverse osmosis.

Impurities Affecting Water.—The following is a list of impurities which if present in sufficient amounts will have a direct influence on the quality of beverages, will affect food quality, and cause mechanical problems with equipment: (1) dissolved minerals, (2) dissolved gases, (3) free mineral acid, (4) oils and greases, (5) turbidity and sediment, (6) color-producing substances, (7) organic matter, (8) tastes and odors and (9) microorganisms.

Dissolved Minerals.—Calcium and magnesium compounds are the most common contaminants of fresh water, causing hardness. These ingredients are responsible for scale, excessive soap consumption, the formation of undesirable films such as scums and curds, the plugging of valves, lines, heater tanks, burn-out and failure of thermostat relays.

Calcium carbonate is the salt found in scale and may be deposited at temperatures less than 150°F. At every temperature, an equilibrium exists between free carbon dioxide in the water and the amount of calcium bicarbonate which can be held in solution.

Iron and manganese are usually present in rocks and soil in the oxidized form. When rain water percolates through the soil, decaying matter consumes the dissolved oxygen. Iron and manganese deposits are then reduced to a soluble form and dissolved. These minerals are likely to be found in water drawn from the lower reaches of reservoirs, where dissolved oxygen is expected to be absent. The presence of iron causes metallic tastes. As little as 0.1 ppm of iron will cause staining of dishes. It can be detected in coffee, particularly if cream is added. Manganese will appear as a gray to black deposit on dishes and glasses.

Sodium ion (Na^+) is found in nearly all natural waters. At high concentrations and at elevated temperatures, it may cause foaming. It can be removed by hydrogen-ion exchange, demineralization or distillation.

Alkalinity is generally considered to be due to bicarbonates, carbonates, hydroxide, phosphate and silicates. Alkalinity will cause scaling (Fig. 7.15) and foaming. Its effect on coffee is pronounced, as it destroys its acid character, resulting in a flat, insipid brew. Alkalinity affects soft drinks by reducing the flavor and tang, and the antispoilage potential of acids. It also creates off-tastes.

Courtesy Everpure Inc.

FIG. 7.15. VIEW OF INTERIOR OF LINE FITTING SHOWING SCALE BUILDUP (LEFT) AS A RESULT OF ALKALINITY IN WATER, AND FITTING (RIGHT) AS A RESULT OF WATER TREATMENT

Scale on equipment as a result of water hardness will act as an insulator and decrease the transfer of heat. This problem will lead to erratic cooking temperature, especially where the thermostat is responsible for maintaining exacting preset heat levels. Scale deposits will become spawning areas for bacteria and also tend to make equipment sanitation more difficult. Hard water may also contribute to textural defects and subdue the subtle flavor characteristics of spices and herbs.

Chlorides may not only cause corrosion but also destroy flavor. They are found in domestic and industrial wastes and oil-field brines. Sulfates enter water from the soil or industrial wastes. They combine with calcium to form calcium sulfate scale. Demineralization will remove this from the water, or it can be retained in solution by treatment with surface-active agents.

Dissolved Gases.—Oxygen is picked up by rain water as it falls through the atmosphere. Carbon dioxide and nitrogen are absorbed in the same manner. Oxygen is also contributed by photosynthesis. At low pH values, oxygen causes iron, steel, galvanized iron, and brass to corrode. The highest rate of corrosion occurs at 160°–180°F. At high pH values it encourages scale formation. Mechanical or chemical deaeration techniques can be used to remove oxygen from water.

Carbon dioxide is absorbed by water from decaying matter, rocks, soil or from the atmosphere; it is a factor in corrosion. Its removal can be brought about by aeration, deaeration, neutralization and lime-soda softening.

Hydrogen sulfide may be picked up by water from the atmosphere, from sulfur containing bacteria, or from nearby oil or gas fields. It causes corrosion and has a repulsive "rotten egg" odor; it will combine with any iron present to precipitate black ferrous sulfide. It can be removed from water by aeration at low pH, chlorination or by a highly basic anion exchange. It becomes evident in foods and beverages at very low levels, 0.05–0.12 ppm.

Ammonia is present in water as a result of the decomposition of organic matter. It corrodes copper, zinc and their alloys. Removal is accomplished by hydrogen-ion exchange or by "breakpoint" chlorination.

Free Mineral Acids.—Free mineral acids may be present in water as a result of the discharge of industrial wastes, particularly acid mine drainage or waste pickle liquor. These are a direct cause of corrosion, and produce metallic and sour tastes in beverages and foods.

Oils and Greases.—Oils and greases, if present in minute quantities, will cause foaming and formation of sludges. Films will also be deposited on the surfaces of dispensers and brewing equipment. Oily deposits will become apparent in beverages and will interfere with carbonation. Some foods prepared in oily or greasy water will appear glossy, and an after-taste of the impurities may become apparent. Domestic and industrial wastes and newly installed pipes contribute these contaminants to the water supply.

Turbidity and Suspended Solids.—The problems of turbidity and suspended solids in water are the result of domestic and industrial wastes, old water systems and land erosion. Sedimentation and foaming are caused by this situation. Coagulation is the process employed to remove these conditions. Finely divided particles are agglomerated into larger masses to effect rapid settling. Aluminum sulfate (alum) is the coagulant most commonly used in water conditioning; other agents include ferrous sulfate, ferric sulfate, and ferric chloride. Polyelectrolytes are becoming more widely used as coagulants. These products are high molecular weight, water-soluble polymers which form ions; some types are called ion-exchange resins.

Color and Organic Matter.—Color and organic matter in water are caused by farm runoff, domestic and industrial wastes, and flooding of swamps and river beds. Color of natural waters range from very light yellow to dark brown. Iron in excess of about 0.3 to 0.5 ppm will cause water to appear rusty. These conditions can also be attributed to old water systems and rusting pipes. Color and organic material will affect all beverages by imparting off-tastes, color changes, foaming, and staining of utensils. Natural food coloring may be affected, especially with vegetables. Organic matter can impart off-tastes and change the flavor character adversely. Activated carbon filters, chlorination and coagulation act to remove these conditions.

Tastes and Odors.—Tastes and odors are caused by many of the impurities previously discussed. Domestic and industrial wastes and living microorganisms also contribute to this problem.

Microorganisms.—Microorganisms are the result of domestic wastes, farm runoff, and flooding; they grow in reservoirs and old water systems. These organisms may be algae, diatoms and protozoa. Floral odors emanating from the water are usually caused by diatoms or protozoa. Fishy, earthy and grassy odors may be traced to this source. Slime and scum will cause fouling of equipment and corrosion.

Water Treatment.—Considering the many impurities in water, treatment is a necessity, no matter how minor. When water is used for drinking purposes, it should be safe; it should not carry disease; it should be free of undesirable tastes and odors; and it should be clean, without color, dirt and other unsightly material.

Every industry has its own water problem. A careful study of each aspect of an operation must be made to determine whether impurities or the results of the treatment will affect the product.

The food service industry—which includes restaurants, hotels, vending machines, industrial caterers, airline feeding and steamships—uses water for many different purposes. The two important areas for water in relation to public feeding are in the preparation and serving of beverages, and in maintenance and cleaning operations. Hard water must be softened to protect equipment and make cleaning easy. Large volumes of hard water in all parts of the United States are softened during the course of a year. The water-softening industry is providing excellent methods and equipment for this program. However, serious problems can result with incorrect treatment: water that is suited to one type of treatment may not be equally suited to another.

Many companies exist that will render expert guidance in solving water problems. After the proper water-treating equipment is installed, maintenance schedules must be followed to keep it in top operating condition. Treatment chemicals and cartridges require periodic changing or replenishment for effective elimination of water problems.

Water Testing.—Water testing was once considered an art for the experienced chemist. Although the role of the chemist is still regarded as important for the more sophisticated examinations, analysis kits are available that provide for fast, simplified testing of water.

The Hach Chemical Co. manufactures a variety of test kits, packaged in plastic cases, covering a complete range of analyses. Each test is devised for simplicity. Bottles of solutions are numbered. By following the instruction sheet, the numbered bottles of solution are selected and used for a specific test.

The high and low range total hardness test employes three reagents, a buffer solution, a stable indicator and a titrating solution which is added drop by drop until the color changes. Water hardness is determined by counting the number of drops required to bring about the color change: 1 drop equals 1 ppm of hardness.

Water testing should be performed on a quarterly basis, so that year round determinations can be compared and steps taken to eliminate or forestall problems. If extreme or severe conditions exist, testing may have to be scheduled more frequently.

Effects of Poor Sanitation and Ineffectual Warewashing on Quality

Poor sanitation heads the list of all contributing factors responsible for low quality beverages and becomes a dominating element in the reduction of food quality. In many instances incomplete sanitation leaves behind enough contaminants on equipment to cause definite off-tastes and off-flavors. A lack of understanding for the need of sanitation, improper procedures on automated equipment, along with little or no personnel training are the three basic factors of this widespread problem.

Sanitation consists of two parts: (1) cleaning and (2) sanitizing.

Cleaning means the removal of residues of food, dirt, dust, foreign material or other soiling ingredients or materials.

Sanitizing means the effective bactericidal treatment of clean surfaces of equipment and utensils; effective treatment is defined as one that is equivalent in effect to that of a solution containing 50 ppm of available chlorine.

Sanitation within food service establishments can be best understood if it is separated into the following four divisions, each requiring a different approach and procedure: (1) warewashing and sanitizing, (2) equipment cleaning and sanitizing, (3) interior cleaning (tables, counters, floors, toilets, and storage areas), and (4) exterior cleaning (sidewalks, parking areas, trash storage areas, and windows).

Detergents.—Detergents are classified as cleaning agents. They may be soaps, synthetic powders, liquids, solvents, or abrasives, such as sand. Generally, detergents are referred to as cleaners that are packaged for laundering, dishwashing and surface scouring. They are products which have soapy characteristics without having the disadvantages commonly found when soap is used in hard water.

Soap is the product formed by the saponification or neutralization of fats, oils, waxes, rosins or their acids, with organic or inorganic bases (alkalies). Under acid conditions or in hard water, the detergent properties of soap are destroyed. Soap forms a curd with the hardness components of the water, resulting in undesirable precipitates and a considerable waste of soap. For example 1.5 lb of pure soap is destroyed per 100 gal of water per grain of hardness.

Detergents are formulated from a number of different compounds, and include the following.

(1) *Alkalies,* which help soften water by precipitation of the hardness ions, and saponify fats. Alkalies used are caustic soda, sodium metasilicate, soda ash, or trisodium phosphate.

(2) *Complex phosphates,* which emulsify, disperse and suspend fats and oils, soften water by sequestering, and provide rinsability characteristics without being corrosive. Sodium tetraphosphate, sodium tripolyphosphate, sodium pyrophosphate, or sodium hexametaphosphate are used for this purpose.

(3) *Organic compounds* used in detergents are chelating and wetting agents, and mineral or organic acids. Chelating agents soften water, prevent mineral deposits, and peptize proteins without being corrosive. Wetting agents emulsify and disperse fats, help water to wet solids, form suds, and are rinsable without being corrosive. Organic acids (citric, gluconic, or hydroxyacetic acid) prevent mineral deposits and soften water without being corrosive. Inorganic acids prevent mineral deposits and soften water; hydrochloric, sulfuric, nitric, and phosphoric acids are used for this purpose.

Detergents are grouped according to the kinds of work they perform. There are three types: (1) neutral, (2) alkaline and (3) acid. Neutral types are used for cleaning floors, similar structures and walls. Alkaline types are used for routine and heavy-duty cleaning. Most food deposits are slightly acid and require an alkaline detergent to neutralize and dissolve food deposits. This type is employed on beverage dispensers, glasses and most preparation equipment. Acid types are used to remove lime deposits and to neutralize or dissolve deposit accumulation. Deposits in coffee urn jackets, heaters and inside washing machines are removed by acid detergents.

Germicides or Sanitizers.—Germicides and sanitizers are chemicals that kill or deactivate bacteria on dishes, pots, pans, tables, floors and all equipment surfaces contacting food or beverages. For products to meet this classification they must be registered with the U.S. Department of Agriculture. Sometimes a sanitizer is combined with a detergent: the product is then called a "detergent-sanitizer."

Sanitizing agents must be used correctly to be effective. Too little will not do the job and too much is wasteful. Instructions should be written and posted for its proper formulation with water and subsequent use. These agents, if properly used, are a prime safeguard against the growth of microorganisms. In addition to those areas listed above, germicidal agents should be used when cleaning storage rooms and all refrigerating equipment.

Hot Water.—Hot water in sufficient quantities and at correct temperatures is essential for sanitation of equipment and warewashing.

Food service establishments need large volumes of $140°-195°F$ water so that all peak demands can be met. Capacity and recovery are essential to an efficient hot-water system. When the selection of a hot-water system is made, several basic criteria should be considered.

(1) The system should be oversize to allow for business growth and unforeseen demands.

(2) Domestic heaters should not be considered, as they will not produce hot water in quantity or the temperature range necessary for commercial application.

(3) A two-temperature system should be installed, one for general-purpose water at $140°F$, and the other at $180-195°F$ for sanitizing; the latter is called high-temperature water.

Water Heaters.—Three hot water heating systems are available, including: automatic, instantaneous, and circulating tank equipment.

Automatic storage water heaters are self-contained, thermostatically controlled units which supply hot water for immediate use upon demand at a rated flow, and require no separate external tank.

Circulating tank water heaters are units requiring a separate external storage tank; these units heat water as it passes through the heater and is being returned to the storage tank. The temperature of the water in the storage tank is thermostatically controlled.

High-temperature Water.—An adequate dependable supply of high-temperature water $(180-195°F)$ is essential for final rinse operation of dishwashing machines. The high temperatures required for effective sanitization make it uneconomical and unsafe to maintain general-purpose water at such temperatures. Therefore, a separate hot water generating system is normally required; this should be properly sized, installed, and operated to deliver the water volume at the flow pressure and temperatures required as specified (Section 6, NSF Standard No. 5, Commercial Gas Fired and Electrically Heated Hot Water Generating Equipment for food establishments using dishwashing machines).

Strict Cleaning Schedules Are Important.–Cleaning chores are usually the most difficult to maintain on a strict schedule. Regardless of the size of an operation, a sanitation schedule must be evolved that will include every area, machine and preparation equipment within the premises. A schedule should reveal the following information: (1) area or name of equipment to be cleaned, (2) steps necessary for daily sanitation, (3) steps necessary for weekly or monthly cleaning, (4) names of employees assigned to each task, (5) period of the day or shift when chores should be performed. One employee should be assigned the task of caring for the cleaning equipment, such as rags, sponges, mops and brushes. When not in use, these should be stored in a utility closet, with a sink provided. Cleaning equipment should be rinsed and cleaned before storage. Cleaning fluids and powders must be handled in a careful manner and kept far removed from the food preparation area. They should be mixed in the utility closet and dispensed from it when needed. Rags should be lint-free, enough being available so that each job can begin with clean cloths. Good rags are expensive and should be laundered and stored in the same manner as table cloths and napkins. Sponges should be rinsed in a sanitizer and allowed to dry. Greasy, sour or dirty sponges, if used, will only increase the sanitation wash load.

It should be remembered that faulty sanitation will downgrade food quality. Grease, soap or detergent residues that adhere to dishes, glasses, pots or other equipment which contacts food will contaminate the food in varying degrees. This can result in a flavor or taste defect (Table 7.1).

Pre-cooking, Cooking and Post-cooking Effects on Quality

Pre-cooking procedures include storage, assembly, thawing, portioning and other food handling activities prior to heating or other means of preparation. This category includes all products that require little or no preparation, and are served directly to the customer, such as salads, sandwiches, some desserts, bread, rolls, condiments, juices and cold beverages.

Cooking applies to all modes of heating, either partial (warming) or complete (raw to finish). Examples are steam pressure, convection ovens, microwave ovens or any other type of oven, deep frying, broiling, and griddle preparation. Coffee and tea brewing are considered to be in this category, since they require heat for extraction of the desirable essences.

Post-cooking includes plating, portioning, holding in steam tables or hot cabinets, storing of leftovers, and foods that were previously prepared and held in temporary cool storage.

Pre-cooking.–Improper and careless storage techniques will downgrade quality (see Chapter 3, Storage Areas). Poor stock rotation and prolonged storing in any of the storage areas (dry, cooler or freezer) may lead to flavor and texture changes. Positive storage control procedures will tend to eliminate these problems.

Haphazard food assembly methods, such as piling or stacking of food prod-

TABLE 7.1

SUMMARY OF FACTORS WHICH CAN CAUSE DISHWASHING
AND EQUIPMENT CLEANING PROBLEMS

Symptom	Possible Cause	Suggested Cure
Films	Water hardness	Use an external softening process. Use more detergent to provide internal conditioning. Use a chlorinated cleaner. Check temperature of wash and rinse water. Overheated water may be precipitating film.
	Detergent carryover	Maintain adequate pressure and volume of rinse water.
	Improperly cleaned or rinsed equipment	Prevent scale buildup in equipment by adopting frequent and adequate cleaning practices. Maintain adequate pressure and volume of rinse water.
Greasy films	Low pH	Maintain adequate alkalinity to saponify greases.
	Insufficient detergent	
	Low water temperature	
	Improperly cleaned equipment	Unclog all wash sprays and rinse nozzles to keep any greases carried in the steam from depositing on dishes. Clogged rinse nozzles will also interfere with wash tank overflow, allowing surface scums to remain in the machine.
Streaking	Alkalinity in the water	Use an external treatment method to reduce alkalinity.
	Improperly cleaned or rinsed equipment	Maintain adequate pressure and volume of rinse water. Alkaline cleaners used for washing must be thoroughly rinsed from dishes.
Spotting	Rinse water hardness	Provide external or internal softening.
	Rinse water temperature too high or too low	Check rinse water temperature. Dishes may be flash drying, or water may be drying on dishes rather than draining off.
	Inadequate time between rinsing and storage	Allow sufficient time for air drying.
Staining	Iron in water	Check for corrosion. Retain iron in solution with surface active agents.
	Color in water	Provide external treatment for iron or color removal.
Foaming	Detergent	Change to a low sudsing product.
	Dissolved or suspended solids in water	Use an appropriate treatment method to reduce the solids content of the water.
	Food soil	Adequately remove gross soil before washing. The decomposition of carbohydrates, proteins, or fats may cause foaming during the wash cycle.
	Alkalinity, oils, or color in water supply	Use an appropriate treatment method to reduce or remove these factors.
	Improperly cleaned equipment	Keep all wash sprays and rinse nozzles open. Keep equipment free from deposits or films of materials which could cause foam buildup in future wash cycles.

TABLE 7.1 (Continued)

Symptom	Possible Cause	Suggested Cure
Dirty dishes	Insufficient detergents	Use enough detergent in wash water to ensure complete soil suspension.
	Wash water temperature too low	Keep water temperature high enough to dissolve food residues.
	Inadequate wash and rinse times	Allow sufficient time for wash and rinse operations to be effective.
	Improperly cleaned equipment	Unclog wash sprays and rinse nozzles to maintain proper pressure and flow conditions. Overflows must be open. Keep wash water as clean as possible.

Source: National Sanitation Foundation.

ucts; spillage and mixing of liquids, such as sauces and gravies so that they become contaminated with each other, will help to destroy the inherent character of the food. Spices, condiments and herbs should be labeled properly to avoid a mix-up (Fig. 7.16). All ingredients should be assembled in an orderly neat fashion until needed for preparation. Sandwich spreads should be kept re-

Courtesy American Spice Trade Association

FIG. 7.16. PROPERLY LABELED SPICES TO AVOID A MIX-UP

frigerated and stored in tight containers during slack periods. Sandwich meats, fish and other products that have a tendency to form a crust or hard surface when exposed to air should be mixed in small lots or covered. Improper thawing procedures for certain foods will affect quality. Items intended for microwave oven heating may require special thawing techniques to prevent uneven doneness (see Chapter 5, Microwave Cookery). Foods that are to be cooked in the frozen state, like French fries, should not be allowed to thaw, but should be held in a freezer until used.

Cooking.–Although cooking refers to all modes of food heating (fully or partially), factors affecting quality, such as temperature, timing, formulations and equipment maintenance, are all involved in the final outcome. For example, a faulty timer on a microwave oven will yield inconsistent quality; unfiltered fat for deep frying will produce low quality fried products; a loose door or a worn gasket on a steam pressure cooker may give unsatisfactory results.

Employment of proper utensils is essential for consistent quality. The use of a 10-gal container to heat 1 gal of a product will cause excessive shrinkage, texture changes and flavor losses.

Salad dressings should be added just prior to serving. Tossed or mixed salads containing soft-textured components (tomato slices) should not be allowed to stand for long periods of time. Lettuce and other salad vegetables should be kept dry to prevent loss of crispness and browning. Tossed or mixed salad ingredients should be stored in coolers until used. Before storage they should be wrapped in plastic film or placed in a covered vessel.

Forcing or inducing rapid heating by the use of high temperatures or exposed flames will reduce flavor, decrease tenderness, increase shrinkage and may produce a burnt character. Cooking should always be performed cleanly and within the prescribed time cycle.

Formulations or recipes should be written clearly and precisely. All quantity measurements should be listed together with the size of the measuring device to be used, such as ladle or scoop size and number. Heating cycle and equipment should also be posted.

Post-cooking.–Holding food in a steam table, cabinet or under infrared lamps for excessive periods of time will reduce quality, by affecting food texture, flavor, increase shrinkage and loss of nutrients. Foods will become mealy, mushy, soggy or dried out. Over production should be avoided for identical reasons. The time between preparation and service should be held to a minimum. Coffee should not be held over 1 hr and at temperatures of 185–190°F. Desserts like cream or custard pies require refrigerated storage to prevent spoilage.

Leftover foods should be properly refrigerated, and packed loosely in shallow covered pans, labeled and dated. Food that will not be used should be thrown away. Fresh produce should always be washed before serving or use in salads or soup. Washing will remove excess soil, dust, insecticides and surface bacteria.

Effects of Packaging on Food Quality

Fast and convenience food service systems depend on efficient packaging, so that the package becomes an "employee" and does the work within the program. Packages must provide maximum protection during storage. It must be easily opened, well labeled and be rigidly constructed. The module type container that remains intact throughout the entire operation has reduced handling. By decreasing the number of transfer operations, fewer errors are made, waste is reduced and the original quality is maintained.

Effective packaging must protect the food from microorganisms, and prevent evaporation or dehydration and oxidation. All these factors, if present, will affect the quality of the foods.

Many novel packaging devices are being introduced to aid fast food systems. Clear plastic covers are being placed on some frozen food products so that the contents can be observed at all times. Frozen fresh fruit, like orange slices, are now being packed in aluminum foil trays. Edible or dissolvable plastic materials, made from hydroxypropyl cellulose, a thermo-plastic, has been granted FDA clearance. This product is being used to package dry materials or oil-based items. Besides being edible, it is also biodegradable, non-caloric, and non-nutritive. It passes through the body without being digested or metabolized and does not support the growth of mold or bacteria.

THE QUALITY ASSURANCE PROGRAM

Location of the Laboratory or Office

The question of locating a quality assurance office or laboratory so that centralization is achieved is important. The amount of area devoted to this facility requires consideration, since space is usually limited and at a premium. A combination receiving and quality assurance office is feasible for a small- to medium-volume operation. The functions of both receiving and quality control can be handled by the same person. Usually for this size operation, the distance from the receiving section to the preparation area is close enough, so that all activities can be performed without too much movement. For larger installations or commissaries, the laboratory office should be located between the storage areas and preparation center. Space needs can be minimal, unless a full laboratory program is to be instituted. For normal routine tests an area measuring 8 by 8 ft is ample. This will allow sufficient space to install the following equipment: small desk and chair, filing cabinet, bookcase, laboratory bench or work table with stainless steel top 8 ft long, provided with a stainless steel sink. Cabinets should be installed under and over the counter area.

Equipment Requirements

(1) **Thermometers.**—(a) Several accurately calibrated thermometers to be used to check the accuracy of those instruments employed for daily routine

tests. One of each of the following are suggested: −30 to +125°F, 0 to +230°F, +20 to +500°F. These should be long-stem mercury-filled devices. They should be used only for checking purposes and should be stored in a safe place when not in use.

(b) For routine temperature readings the following are recommended: Three thermometers (−30 to +125°F) for recording frozen food cooler storage temperatures. For frozen foods, metal-stem thermometers are needed to penetrate the product and to record its internal temperatures. Three 0 to +230°F thermometers for routine checking of coffee brew water, and holding temperatures of foods stored in cabinets and steam tables. Two deep-fat thermometers, +20 to +500°F. A surface-activated pyrometer is useful to check griddle temperatures. Thermometers should be of high quality. The style is not important, as long as they are accurate and can be easily read.

(2) **Stopwatch or Timer.**—An accurate stopwatch, graduated in 1/5 sec, that will register 60 sec and 30 min. One revolution of the hand will equal 60 sec, while a second dial will show the number of minutes. Stopwatches are valuable devices to check timers. As microwave heating is dependent on accurate timing, a high-quality watch is necessary to check the accuracy of the cycle. These should be calibrated once every 6 months.

(3) **Refractometers.**—These instruments were discussed. They are useful for checking sugar content of syrups, syrup measurement of soft drinks, sugar content of jams, jellies, ketchup, fruit juices and other products containing sugar substances.

(4) **Hydrometers.**—These weighted spindles have been described in this chapter. Their use is similar to the refractometer. Specialty equipment can be purchased to test for the soluble solids of brewed coffee. In addition to the spindles, several glass cylinders are needed. Two of each of the following are recommended: scale reading 0 to 12° Brix, 9 to 21° Brix and 0 to 35° Brix.

(5) **Scales.**—Two portion scales, a 32 oz by ¼ oz capacity and a 5 lb by ¼ oz capacity, and 1 beam scale calibrated in grams, equipped with a pan to accomodate an 8-in. diameter sieve. An effective, inexpensive model is the Harvard Trip Balance single beam scale.

(6) **Sieves.**—Several sieves are required to determine drained weight (Fig. 7.11). One U.S. Standard No. 8 sieve, 8-in. diameter and one 12-in. diameter. A 2-mesh screen is necessary for checking canned tomatoes. The 8-in. diameter sieve should be used for can sizes of 2½ or smaller, while the 12-in. diameter sieve is required for the number 10 size can.

(7) **Miscellaneous Equipment.**—Various glass graduates calibrated in ounces (8-oz, 16-oz, 32-oz), stainless steel pans, spatulas, spoons, absorbent paper, lint-free towels, and racks or supports to hold the screens and sieves in position during draining.

(8) **Fat Analyzer.**—To check fat content of hamburger meat, a Hobart fat analyzer is recommended. This equipment is discussed in detail later.

Testing Procedures

Quality assurance procedures that are considered to be essential for a meaningful program follow:

(1) Sampling
(2) Sensory evaluation
    (a) Appearance of the product
    (b) Texture
    (c) Flavor (taste and aroma)
    (d) Evaluation of the results with the specifications and USDA and USDI scoring methods
(3) Drained weight tests
    (a) Simple procedure
    (b) USDA procedure
(4) Determination of the percent of breading
(5) Determination of the percent of fat contained in chopped meat
(6) Fill of container determination

Sampling.—Sampling is an important segment of quality control. Proper sampling is a highly specialized art and must be accomplished with infinite care. Many industries employ the services of professional samplers, who are licensed to perform the job. Rigid testing procedures are required by authorities before a license is issued. Commodities like spices, coffee and tea are sampled prior to acceptance of an order. A sampling firm is issued authority to draw samples of the product. These are then tested according to predetermined procedures.

Precise procedures should be followed when taking samples for testing purposes. For example, the USDA provides detailed sampling methods. These indicate the exact number of samples that are to be drawn according to the size container and the number of containers in a specific product lot. For example, if a shipment contains 2400 cans or less, 3 samples are drawn; if 2401 to 12,000, 6 samples; and if 12,001 to 24,000 units, 13 samples.

When sampling a delivery, do not remove all the samples from the same carton. If three samples are needed, draw them from different containers. Always mark or label the sample with the date and code. Samples should be kept in a freezer until tested. It is advisable to set aside a shelf or some specific space to store the samples. This may avoid a mixup or their disappearance.

Determining Drained Weight.—The following procedures can be used to determine the drained weight for most canned, glass and frozen fruits and vegetables:

(1) Quick method (for approximate results): Product is first thawed and is then emptied on a previously weighed mesh screen or U.S. Standard mesh sieve #8, and allowed to drain for 2 min. At the end of 2 min the product remaining on the screen is weighed. The weight of the screen or sieve is subtracted, and the difference is the drained weight of the product.

(2) For a more precise method, and to conform to procedures prescribed by the USDA, the following is recommended:

(a) *Thawing:* thaw samples in closed containers so that air can circulate freely. Open the container periodically and take a reading of the temperature at the center of the mass. Drain the product as soon as possible, after the temperature at the center of the container has reached 28°F.

(b) *Draining:* open the container and if the product is a fruit packed in syrup, remove any hard caked sugar from the top. Do not disturb the product while removing the sugar cake. If any loose granulated sugar remains, gently stir the top of the liquid to dissolve it.

Place the screen or sieve, which has been previously weighed, in a horizontal position on the rack, tripod ring, or other suitable support, and pour most of the free liquid through the screen. This will partially drain the product. Pour the remainder (balance) of the product uniformly on the sieve, and allow to drain for 2 min. Time with a stopwatch or accurate laboratory timer.

Weigh the product remaining on the sieve, subtracting the weight of the sieve. The difference is the drained weight.

Three tests should be performed. Add the results and divide by 3 for the average drained weight of the shipment.

Halves of apricots, peaches and pears should be turned "cups down" on the sieve or screen.

Fill of Container.–Fill of container tests apply to foods packed in cans and glass containers. As a rule of thumb, the container must be filled to 90% or more of its total capacity. When products have an unusually high specific gravity (viscous syrup) it is necessary that the fill or contents of the can be of a higher net weight, to prevent slack-fills or under weights. The percentage of fill is determined by measuring the headspace inside the can. Fill of container standards form a part of a product's quality grading specification.

The Brix Hydrometer.–Hydrometers as previously explained, are instruments for comparing the weight of a quantity of solution with the weight of a similar quantity of pure water. The scales on a hydrometer vary according to their use, although all readings are based on specific gravity. Hydrometers are useful tools for food service personnel. They can be used to measure the uniformity of soft drinks delivered through a dispenser, and the consistency of syrups and juices.

Readings on hydrometers, other than those used for coffee are expressed in degrees. These are merely points of reference on an arbitrary scale, adopted to obtain uniformity of results. Two methods are employed: the Baumé and Brix. Bottlers of soft drinks express their results in degrees Baumé when measuring syrups. Soft drinks, juices and light syrups are measured in terms of percentage sugar. For this purpose the Brix hydrometer is used, since 1 Brix degree is equal to 1% sugar by weight. Although a refractometer can be used for the same purpose, these are expensive and are not always available.

TABLE 7.2

TEMPERATURE CORRECTIONS TO READINGS OF BRIX HYDROMETERS
STANDARDIZED AT 68°F

Temperatures, °F	Observed Percentage of Sugar, Degrees Brix								
	0	5	10	20	30	40	50	60	70
	Subtract								
32	0.30	0.49	0.65	0.89	1.08	1.24	1.37	1.44	1.49
41	0.36	0.47	0.56	0.73	0.86	0.97	1.05	1.10	1.14
50	0.32	0.38	0.43	0.52	0.60	0.67	0.72	0.75	0.77
59	0.20	0.22	0.24	0.28	0.32	0.34	0.36	0.38	0.39
68	No correction								
	Add								
77	0.27	0.28	0.30	0.32	0.35	0.38	0.39	0.39	0.40
86	0.61	0.62	0.63	0.68	0.73	0.78	0.79	0.80	0.81
95	0.99	1.01	1.02	1.10	1.16	1.20	1.22	1.23	1.22
104	1.42	1.45	1.47	1.54	1.60	1.64	1.65	1.66	1.65
113	1.91	1.94	1.96	2.03	2.07	2.10	2.10	2.10	2.08
122	2.46	2.48	2.50	2.56	2.58	2.59	2.58	2.56	2.52
131	3.05	3.07	3.09	3.12	3.12	3.10	3.07	3.03	2.97
140	3.69	3.72	3.73	3.72	3.67	3.62	3.57	3.50	3.43

Source: Tressler and Joslyn (1961).

A limitation on the use of hydrometers is temperature. The instrument is accurate only at the single temperature for which it has been designed. If the temperature varies more that a few degrees above or below the standard reading, errors will occur in the results. For this reason a temperature correction table has been developed (Table 7.2). This table will correct readings on those instruments standardized at 68°F.

Directions for Using a Hydrometer.—The equipment needed for the measurement is: (1) Brix hydrometer, (2) glass cylinder, (3) thermometer (reading to 212°F) and (4) several clean absorbent towels. Handle these pieces of equipment with extreme care to prevent breakage. They must also be kept clean. Fill the cylinder to the engraved line above the diamond with warm water containing a small amount of detergent. Suspend the hydrometer in the solution. Force the hydrometer down into the solution by pushing gently on the top of the hydrometer stem with a finger. Remove finger and let hydrometer rise. Repeat several times. Holding the hydrometer only at the very top, remove it from the solution. Rinse it thoroughly under warm but not hot running water. Dry with a clean absorbent towel. Do not touch the body of the hydrometer or any part of the stem except the top. Lay it down gently on the clean towel.

Pour the detergent solution from the cylinder. Rinse it out thoroughly with warm water.

The thermometer stem should be washed and rinsed also.

Now make sure the sample to be tested is well mixed.

Fill the hydrometer cylinder with the sample and then pour it out. This removes any traces of material that might affect the measurement.

Fill the cylinder with the sample to the engraved mark. Insert the thermometer.

Check the cylinder to make sure it is standing on a level surface and that the hydrometer is floating without touching the walls of the cylinder.

Add more liquid until it fills the cylinder exactly to the brim.

Check the body and submerged portion of the stem to see whether any small bubbles are adhering to them. If any are seen, the hydrometer must be removed and wiped with a clean towel, and lowered again gently into the liquid.

After the hydrometer has been in the sample for at least 2 min, gently push it down into the cylinder nearly to the bottom and allow it to rise. Repeat this once or twice. On the last rise, stop the bobbing motion of the hydrometer with a finger. Read the stem as rapidly as possible after the hydrometer stops. Precise reading, which is essential, comes only after much practice.

Notice that the liquid is drawn up slightly around the stem. Read the stem where the liquid meets it, not at the level of the liquid away from the stem. (Refer to Fig. 7.9.)

Immediately after reading the stem, insert the thermometer and read it. Record both readings. (First reading)

Mix the sample again as above, bringing the hydrometer to a rest away from the walls of the cylinder. Take another stem and temperature reading.

Record both readings. (Second reading)

Repeat again for a third reading.

Remove hydrometer, rinse it off, dry it, and lay it on the towel.

If other samples are to be tested, pour out the one already in the cylinder, rinse it out with the next sample. Proceed as above.

Average the three readings (hydrometer and temperature). Make a temperature correction by referring to Table 7.2. Add or subtract the figure found in the table. For example:

Average of 3 readings   20.00°Brix at 86°F
Add correction factor (Table 7.2) 0.68
Percentage of sugar at 68°F   20.68°Brix

The USDA has designated four categories of syrup densities to be used for fruit products and sweet potatoes. Each category is determined by measuring the degree Brix of the syrup.

Extra heavy syrup means that a syrup tests 25° or more, but not more than 40°Brix.

Heavy syrup means that the syrup tests 21° or more, but less than 25°Brix.

Light syrup means that the syrup tests 16° or more, but less than 21°Brix.
Slightly sweetened water means that the syrup tests less than 16°Brix.
Although the categories are the same, the degrees Brix for the syrup of various products differ. The examples shown above apply to the syrup of canned apricots. USDA Quality Grade Standards designate the liquid media and Brix measurements for the product.

Determination of the Percentage of Breading.—The amount of breading that can be used to coat certain food products is regulated by the Food and Drug Administration, and by the Department of the Interior Bureau of Commercial Fisheries. Breaded shrimp, fish portions, fish sticks, oysters and scallops are regulated by these agencies.

The percentage of breading is a troublesome area when costs between one brand and another are being evaluated and the price differences justified. It therefore becomes an important aspect of quality assurance to determine the amount of breading, in order that cost evaluation can be made on the unbreaded product.

The Food and Drug Administration, for example, promulgated regulations for breaded shrimp in June, 1965. This regulation refers to all forms of shrimp such as "fantail" or butterfly; butterfly with tail off; round with tail; round with tail off; pieces; and composite units. Regardless of the form, the regulation limits the amount of breading material to 50% or less of the raw shrimp. Frozen raw lightly breaded shrimp is another category. If the label states "lightly breaded," the product must be 65% shrimp material. Frozen fried scallops must contain a minimum of 60% by weight of scallop meat. Frozen raw breaded fish portions must contain not less than 75% by weight of fish flesh. Frozen fried fish portions must contain not less than 65% by weight of fish flesh. Frozen raw breaded fish sticks must contain not less than 72% by weight of fish flesh.

Exacting methods of analysis to determine the percent of breaded material on a product have been established by the FDA; however, for routine purposes it is not necessary to follow them. Simplified procedures have been developed by the National Frozen Food Association. Since these tests are suggested for spot cost evaluations and as a means to cross check deliveries, the results will be reasonably accurate and can be performed without elaborate laboratory equipment.

Simplified Procedures for Breaded Shrimp and Scallops.—Select one pound of the product at random from several packages. If there is a significant amount of loose breading in the carton, include a portion of it with the sample. Weigh the sample immediately, before moisture condenses on them or before they thaw. Use a scale that is accurate to 0.1 oz.

Place the weighed sample in a bucket or large pot that contains 2 or 3 gal of tepid (70-80°F) water. Gently stir the sample with a ladle, large spatula or paddle for 10 min. This will separate the bulk of the breading from the seafood. If any of the breading remains, wash it off under a moderate spray of water. If necessary, gently brush off any remaining material with the fingers.

Next lay the debreaded pieces on a sloping screen or paper towel and allow to drain for 2 min before weighing.

The percentage of seafood is calculated as follows:

$$\frac{\text{Weight of debreaded product}}{\text{Weight of breaded product}} \times 100 = \text{percentage of seafood}$$

The percentage of breading is calculated as follows:

100% minus the percentage of seafood = percentage of breading

In the case of shrimp a cutback of 5 percentage points is allowed to compensate for "inaccuracy of method." This provision does not apply to breaded scallops.

Procedure for Breaded Fish Sticks and Portions.—Select one pound of the product at random from several packages. Weigh the sample. Place each piece individually in a tepid water bath and allow to remain for 10 to 80 sec (the larger the portion the longer the dip). Remove from the bath; blot off lightly with a double thickness of paper toweling. Then scrape off or pick off the breading from the fish flesh with a small spatula or tweezer. Weigh the debreaded portions and calculate the percentage of breading by the method illustrated above. Make no adjustment for "inaccuracy of method."

Procedure for Breaded Oysters.—Breading percentages that are determined for frozen breaded oysters do not have too much significance because the raw shucked oysters, before being breaded, are both high in water content and highly variable in the amount of water content. The breading acts almost as a sponge, absorbing some of this water before freezing, so that the breading weights are correspondingly high and variable.

The following procedure is suggested by the Bureau of Commercial Fisheries' Technological Laboratory on the basis of limited experimentation.

Weigh 1 pound of a randomly selected sample. Hold the frozen oysters individually under a stream of cold water and remove most of the breading by rubbing the surface. Stop the washing before the oysters thaw. Blot quickly and weigh. After thawing, check for additional breading left in the folds. If a significant amount remains, weigh it, and subtract this weight from the previously determined debreaded weight. Do not wait until oysters are thawed and breading has been removed from the folds to determine the debreaded weight. During thawing the oysters will lose a considerable amount of fluid, so that a weight determined after thawing will not be correct. Apply the previously described formula to determine the amount of breading. No allowance is made for "inaccuracy of method."

If specific procedures do not exist for products that require an evaluation of the percentage of breading, improvisations can be made by referring to any of the above methods. Once a procedure has been established it should be closely followed, so that continuity and uniform results are achieved.

Determination of Fat Percentage in Ground Beef.—A simplified method exists for measuring the fat percentage of ground beef. The Hobart fat percentage measuring kit is devised for a rapid, accurate and simplified analysis (Fig. 7.17). One kit will provide a continuous series of tests at 15-min intervals.

Courtesy The Hobart Manufacturing Company

FIG. 7.17. FAT PERCENTAGE MEASURING KIT

A 2-oz sample of ground beef is inserted in the kit under a heating element. The sample must be ground at least twice through a 1/8-in. plate. The heater is activated when the timer is set for a 15-min interval. The fat and juices are collected in a test tube located under the heater. A specially calibrated scale with a movable pointer is mounted vertically next to the test tube. This scale measures the column of fat and is expressed in terms of the percentage of fat in the meat. The heating element is automatically turned off at the end of the 15-min cycle. A bell is sounded indicating the end of the cycle.

The kit is manufactured to analyze the content of ground beef samples that contain 10 to 40 percent fat. Test results are within ±1% when operated in accordance with suggested procedures.

Sensory Evaluation.—The mechanism of sensory evaluation have been discussed in this chapter. Sensory perception is a major laboratory tool for quality assurance. Once the art is mastered, it can be employed to good advantage at almost every phase of the food establishment. It is suggested that sensory evaluation procedures that form a part of the USDA and USDI quality grade standards be followed and used as a basic guide.

USDA and USDI quality grade standards are established by assigning a grade score to such factors as color, uniformity of size, defects and product character. When an evaluation is made, the scoring for many of the factors is determined by the use of sensory analysis. *Appearance* characteristics are scored from a product's color, uniformity of size, and defects. The product's *character* is scored from an evaluation of texture, taste and aroma. Each of the quality grade standards have incorporated in them factors that only relate to specific characteristics of the product.

The following example will serve to illustrate these points:

U.S. Standards for Grades of Frozen Whole Kernel (or Whole Grain) Corn
Color (varietal)—Golden or Yellow; White

U.S. Grade A (or Fancy)

Similar varietal characteristics, good flavor and odor, minimum score of 90 points for good or reasonably good color, practically free from defects, tender.

U.S. Grade B (or Extra Standard)

Similar varietal characteristics, good flavor and odor, minimum score of 80 points for reasonably good color or fairly good color scoring no less than 7 points, reasonably free from defects, reasonably tender.

U.S. Grade C (or Standard)

Similar varietal characteristics, fairly good flavor and odor, minimum score of 70 points for fairly good color, fairly free from defects, fairly tender.

Grade A

Color (quality factor): practically uniform, typical of tender sweet corn, product bright, practically free from "off-variety" kernels.

Defects: practically free from pieces of cob, husk, silk and harmless extraneous vegetable matter; pulled, ragged, crushed, damaged, seriously damaged kernels, loose skins.

Tenderness and Maturity: kernels in milk or early cream stage of maturity, tender texture.

The standards for grades of frozen whole kernel corn show the extent to which sensory perception is employed. The senses of sight, odor, feeling and taste are involved and must be applied if a meaningful evaluation is to be made.

Fish and shellfish are graded by the U.S. Department of the Interior, Bureau of Commercial Fisheries. This is a voluntary service offered to the fish industry. The basic techniques employed for fish and shellfish parallel those for vegetables and fruit. Sensory evaluation is required for scoring. For example, grades for frozen breaded fish sticks are U.S. Grade A and U.S. Grade B. U.S. Grade A requires good flavor and odor, and means that the cooked product has the typical flavor and odor of the indicated species of fish and of the breading;

and is free from rancidity, bitterness, staleness and off-flavors and off-odors of any kind.

Condition of the package, ease of separation, broken or damaged sticks, uniformity of size and weight, distortions, coating defects, blemishes, bones and texture are the factors that require evaluation for grading.

PREPARING THE SPECIFICATIONS

The development of specifications can be a monumental task. At the onset of the program, specifications should be prepared for those products accounting for the largest volume of purchases. Since specifications are merely simplified rules relating to a product's description, they should be brief and clearly written. In case of emergencies, due to short crops, strikes or other unforeseen problems, alternative specifications should be prepared. Although Federal specifications should be included wherever possible, they should be used only to form the base of the formulation. Specifications may have to be "tailor-made" to fit a specific operation, if additional factors have to be added, such as the average nutritional composition, or a certain spice or herb or method of packing.

Product Grouping

A specification program will become easier if all the items are separated into various food groups. The following is an example of a product grouping list:

(1) Milk and milk products: fresh fluid, processed, milk drinks and soups. Cream, frozen desserts, non-frozen desserts, ice cream, milk desserts. Cheese (all types).

(2) Meat, poultry, fish:
Beef: cooked, canned, dried, soups, mixtures.
Pork: cooked, cured, fresh, mixtures.
Veal, lamb: fresh, cooked, mixtures.
Variety meat: liver, sweetbread; fresh, cooked, mixtures.
Lunch meats.
Poultry: chicken, soups, mixtures.
Fish, shellfish: soups, mixtures.

(3) Eggs: raw, cooked (scrambled).

(4) Vegetables: potatoes, dark green, deep yellow, tomatoes, soups, mixtures.

(5) Condiments, pickles, olives.

(6) Fruits: citrus, raw, processed, juice (single strength and concentrated); punches; dried, dehydrated.

(7) Grain products (enriched and non-enriched): flour, cereals, pastes, breads, rolls, biscuits, crackers, cakes, cookies, pastry.

(8) Fats and oils: butter, margarine, lard, vegetable fats, salad and cooking oil, salad dressings, imitation cream products.

(9) Sugars and sweets: syrups, jellies, candies, dessert powders.

(10) Beverages: coffee, tea, soft drinks, cocoa and hot chocolate.
(11) Soaps, detergents, cleaning supplies.
(12) Paper goods.
(13) Accounting and office supplies.

Most of the above groupings may include the following subheadings: frozen, pre-prepared frozen, dehydrated, fabricated, and freeze-dried.

Specification Fact Form Sheet

The fact form sheet is the finalized version of a product's specifications. Certain items or fact headings will apply to all products. These are: name or general description of the product; packing; method of packaging, quantity, shipping instructions, supplier, price and terms.

Depending on the product, the following are examples of pertinent data that will serve to further describe the item:

Federal or state grade;
trade association recommendation;
coding;
count;
weight per portion;
weight per case;
container size;
drained weight;
moisture content;
geographical location of food's origin;
percentage of breading;
percentage of principal ingredients per portion;
percentage of other ingredients (spices, herbs);
nutrient composition, such as number of calories per portion, protein, mineral content, and vitamins;
methods of reconstitution or heating—conventional, convection, microwave, quartz, or infrared oven preparation;
time cycle and temperature, and whether the product will be prepared from the frozen or defrosted state;
items such as anticipated flavor, texture and appearance can also be made a part of the specification;
special instructions pertaining to gravy sauces, kind of spices or herbs.

The Frozen Food Critic

The Frozen Food Critic is a feature presentation, appearing in *Quick Frozen Foods* magazine. Each month Laura K. Track presents her comments on frozen prepared foods. Although these analyses are primarily devoted to retail frozen products, the methodology is concise and can be readily adapted to a quality assurance program. Figure 7.18 shows an example of this interesting feature.

The Frozen Food Critic

FROM QFF'S TESTING KITCHEN

Since the proof of the pudding is in the eating, QFF each month tests various frozen products on the market under conditions equivalent to those in the housewife's kitchen. QFF's testing kitchen reports on the adequacy of the packer's cooking instructions, appearance, flavor, palatability and general consumer appeal of the product

Analyzed by LAURA K. TRACK, QFF Home Economist

Baked Ziti with Cheese in Sauce

Weight and Price: 12 oz.; 55¢
Description: Aluminum baker with crimped-on foil-lined cardboard cover in rectangular carton showing cut of finished product and directions on reverse, or bottom side. Closure, both ends, adhesive-sealed.
Ingredients: Enriched Ziti macaroni (cooked) in a sauce containing tomato puree, fresh onions, mozzarella cheese, sugar, salt, vegetable oil, Romano cheese (made from cow's milk), fresh celery, spices, garlic, fresh carrots, wine.
Directions: *In oven,* at 425°. Remove aluminum casserole from box and bake with foil cover slightly loosened for 30 minutes. Remove cover and bake 5 minutes longer. *On top of stove,* over low flame. Place covered aluminum casserole in pan, add half-an-inch of water and heat 35 minutes. *In electric skillet,* at 380°. Heat covered casserole 25-30 minutes with skillet lid on. *Serve* piping hot in its own casserole or on a heated serving dish. Top with grated Parmesan cheese.
Comments: The oven method of heating was used. Heated as per directions, the macaroni was beginning to brown nicely on top and the cheese was melted.
Yield: Weight of the baked Ziti was 360 grams net—sufficient for 2 generous portions.
Flavor: Ziti was not waterlogged, but nicely cooked, a little on the al dente side, which is good. The sauce, while ample, was not soupy, but nicely coated the macaroni. The cheese was ample.
Suggestions: None.

T 1914

Sweet and Sour Beef

Weight and Price: 14 ozs.; $1.19.
Description: A long rectangular carton, highly enameled finish, adhesive-sealed ends, holding a large plastic bag containing vari-colored mixture.
Ingredients: Water, beef, vinegar, sugar, winter melon, cucumber, catsup, bell peppers, onion, pineapple celery, carrots, corn starch, water chestnuts, paprika, soy sauce, (soy beans, wheat, salt, water), salt vegetable oil.
Directions: 1. Boil water first. 2. Remove bag from carton and place it in uncovered pot of boiling water. 3. When water resumes boiling con-

tinue heating for 10 to 20 minutes. 4. Use utensil hole to remove bag from boiling water. 5. After heating remove contents immediately. Serve while steaming hot. 6. Do not refreeze. Serve with fried rice or fried noodles.
Comments: Heated 15 minutes after the second boil, the product was nicely heated through.
Yield: The weight was 391 grams, of which 55 grams was meat. By measurement there were 1½ cupfuls.
Flavor: Not too sharp nor oversweet. The vegetables were, for the most part, cooked through except the carrots which were in ⅜ in. cubes and too crisp for the average palate.
Suggestions: None

T 1915

Speckled Butter Beans

Weight and Price: 10 oz. 31¢.
Description: Small rectangular carton overwrapper with wax paper showing photo of a mound of speckled beans, shaded from a reddish brown to a grayish tone, measuring ⅝ in. wide x ¹⁵⁄₁₆ in. long, and of the shape of rather large lima beans.
Ingredients: Contains slight amount of salt.
Directions: *Southern Style*—Place frozen speckled butter beans in 1½ cups boiling, salted water. Add desired amount of Bacon Drippings or Salt Pork and cook 45 to 50 minutes. *Serving Suggestions*—Place frozen speckled butter beans in one cup of boiling salted water. When water again boils, cover, reduce heat and cook gently (35 minutes or until tender.) Avoid over-cooking.
Comments: With the latter method used and adding ½ teaspoon salt to the boiling water before adding beans, and following directions, the beans were cooked to a nice tenderness in the time given.
Yield: The beans, of lima-size, weighed 296 grams before cooking. After cooking, they weighed 396 grams (beans and cooking liquor), the beans weighing 327 grams and measuring 1¾ cupfuls and the liquor, 49 grams, measuring 3¾ tablespoonfuls.
Flavor: Somewhat mealy with a rather alkaline flavor and a peppery afterbite.
Suggestions: A clarification as to the nomenclature, which would be somewhat beneficial to most of our Northerners. To most of us in the northern part of the United States,

butter beans are also known as wax beans and are the long string beans similar to the familiar green beans but yellow in color. It seems, however, that in some sections of the South, and perhaps in other areas, the small limas are designated "Butter Beans," while in some others all limas while undried are called "Butter Beans." Dictionaries are not too helpful. The 1943 edition of *Webster's New American Dictionary* cites: Butter Bean. Yellow string bean; wax bean. The 1936 edition of *Noah Webster's Unabridged Dictionary*: Butter-bean. The Lima bean. *Phaseolus lunctus.* Funk and Wagnall's *Standard Encyclopedic Dictionary*, gives: butter bean. 1. The wax bean. 2. In the southern U.S., the lima bean. Also: wax bean. A variety of string bean of a pale yellow color, cultivated in the U.S.; also called butter bean.

T 1916

Crab Cakes

Weight and Price: 6 oz.,; 69¢.
Description: Unlined shallow square carton with bottom closure with zip-type opening device containing four round cakes deep-fried.
Ingredients: Crab meat bread crumbs, eggs, mayonnaise, onion, celery, green bell peppers, shortening, mustard, salt, leavening, monosodium glutamate, parsley, seasoning, and spices. Coated with non-fat dry milk solids and bread crumbs. Precooked in pure vegetable oil.
Directions: Place on foil in preheated oven for 20-25 minutes at 400 deg.
Comments: The crab cakes heated to a good brown in the time recommended.
Yield: The crab cakes measured 2⅜″ in diameter and were ¾° thick. They each weighed 45 grams, totaling 180 grams before heating and 40 grams each, totaling 160 grams, after 25 minutes at 400°.
Flavor: The crust was crisp, somewhat thick, completely intact, the centers soft somewhat similar to the consistency of a poultry stuffing, grayish in color, with flecks of celery and green peppers showing through. The crab could not be identified as in pieces but seemed to be in a mashed form and very mild in flavor, the whole a little too salty.
Suggestions: None.

T 1917

Courtesy Quick Frozen Foods Magazine

FIG. 7.18. THE FROZEN FOOD CRITIC

BIBLIOGRAPHY

ANON. 1962A. A Guide to Sanitation of Food Service Establishments. Nutrition Service, Iowa State Department of Health, Ames, Iowa.

ANON. 1965. Food Service Sanitation Manual. Public Health Service Publication No. 934. U.S. Department of Health, Education & Welfare, Washington, D.C.

ANON. 1968. Meat Buyers' Guide. National Association of Meat Purveyors, Chicago, Ill.

ANON. 1969. Meat and Poultry Standards For You. Home and Garden Bulletin No. 171, U.S. Department of Agriculture, Washington, D.C.

ANON. 1970A. Grading America's Foods. Consumer and Marketing Service. U.S. Department of Agriculture, Washington, D.C.

ANON. 1970B. Inspection for Consumer Protection. Consumer and Marketing Service, U.S. Department of Agriculture, Washington, D.C.

ANON. 1970C. Nutritive Value of Foods. Home and Garden Bulletin, No. 72, U.S. Department of Agriculture, Washington, D.C.

ANON. 1971A. Standards for Meat and Poultry Products. Consumer and Marketing Service Bull. 85. U.S. Department of Agriculture, Washington, D.C.

ANON. 1971B. GRAS classifications set, origin of substances stressed. Food Processing. 32, No. 2, 10-12.

ANON. 1971C. The Almanac of Canning, Freezing, Preservation Industries. Edward E. Judge & Son, Westminister, Md.

DE FIGUEIREDO, M. P. 1970. Microbial indices for quality assurance. Food Technol. 24, 157-159.

FLANAGAN, T. 1968. School Purchasing Guide No. 7. American School Food Service Assoc. and Research Corp. of the Assoc. of School Business Officials. Denver, Col.

FOSTER, E. M. 1969. The problem of salmonellae in foods. Food Technol. 23, 1178-1182.

HARJES, C. F., and SMITH, R. J. 1970. Nutritive analysis of frozen cooked institutional foods. Food Technol. 24, 989-992.

HARMS, E., and TRESSELT, M. E. 1970. Third Conference on the Fundamentals of Psychology. Various Approaches to the Study of Perception. Annals of New York Academy of Science 169, No. 3, 595-738.

HARTLEY, D. E. 1970. Commissaries, labeling and the law. Vend 24, No. 2, 23-26.

KERR, R. G. 1964. Fish Cookery for One Hundred. Test Kitchen Series No. 1. United States Department of the Interior, Washington, D.C.

MCCLELLAND, N. I. 1965. Water Quality Considerations and Related Dishwashing Problems. The National Sanitation Foundation, Ann Arbor, Mich.

POTTER, N. N. 1968. Food Science. Avi Publishing Co., Westport, Conn.

PYKE, M. 1970. If it's poisonous . . . why eat it? Food Technol. 24, 652-658.

ROSSMAN, J. 1971. Now: a plastic to eat—or simply dissolve in water. Package Eng. 16, No. 7, 54-58.

SEMLING, H. V. 1970. Stop overlapping food inspection—GAO. Food Processing 31, No. 8, 64.

SPIVAIC, J. 1971. Use of more chemicals in food products stirs a heated controversy. The Wall Street Journal 177, No. 8, 1 and 20.

THORNER, M. E., and HERZBERG, R. J. 1970. Food Beverage Service Handbook. Avi Publishing Co., Westport, Conn.

WIESMAN, C. K. 1971. Identifying and controlling product quality attributes. Food Product Development 5, No. 2, 15-22.

WILLETT, R. 1970. Never mind the product; how is it packaged? Institutional Distribution 17, No. 6, 36-44.

CHAPTER 8

Concepts of Efficiency Foods

EFFICIENCY AND CONVENIENCE FOODS

The word "convenience," when applied and defined in reference to pre-prepared food service or foods for home consumption, refers to only one segment of a broad spectrum of food forms and products. It is difficult to work out an exact definition for foods in this category. Basically, a pre-prepared food is one that can be served and consumed with little or no preliminary preparation other than heating or cooling operations that increase its palatability and refreshment threshold.

Although "convenience" has become the accepted term for all pre-prepared frozen foods, many in the industry are now referring to the entire group as "efficiency" products, with "built-in chef service." Other forms of pre-prepared or semi-prepared edibles cannot be ignored, since they complement the fundamental aspect of overall convenience food service. There are, for example, the adjunct items necessary to complete a menu based on an efficiency program. Freeze-dried, naturally and artificially dried, fabricated or engineered, textured vegetable protein, canned, natural, fermented, intermediate or semi-moist, sugar-concentrated, convenient or component, and convenient packaged items are the categories of adjunct efficiency foods which complement convenience products. These foods form the full spectrum of products with which the pre-prepared and semi-prepared food industry is concerned.

It is important at this juncture to place the relationship of efficiency and convenience or component foods in its proper perspective. For reasons of clarity and to provide a fuller understanding of the subject matter, convenience or pre-prepared foods are treated separately, since they now occupy a dominate role. Chapter 9 is devoted to pre-prepared frozen entrées; Chapter 10 is focussed on pre-prepared desserts and beverages.

The present chapter discusses all adjunct and convenient efficiency foods. Those product categories that have been used for a long time, and require little or no preparation, such as canned goods, semi-moist items, edibles obtained from fermentation, and sugar-concentrated foods are mentioned briefly. Freeze-dried foods, textured vegetable protein products, and convenient form items are treated in depth. Examples of each are characterized and aligned with the overall subject matter of this book.

A New Language Concept for Efficiency Foods

An interesting and practical method of describing efficiency foods has been introduced by Bruce Smith, editor of *Food Service Magazine.* The following are the definitions of the terms that are based on this concept:

(1) *The Raw-to-Ready Scale:* This is the first measuring tool available to the industry. It rates, on a scale of from 1 to 10, the efficiency (amount of labor-input needed) for both food and equipment products.

(2) *Readiness Values:* This is the point on the Raw-to-Ready scale at which a given product exists. For example, a frozen pre-prepared Spanish Rice Flamenco, which requires only re-heating, is at the peak of the scale and is assigned a Readiness Value of 9.

(3) *Patron-Ready:* This is a simple term used in place of such former terms as "cooked and plated, served."

(4) *Value-Added Foods:* This term is suggested in place of the formerly used "convenience" in that it once again stresses consumer awareness. From management's side, the "values added," are labor cost reductions.

Associated with the new language concept for efficiency foods are workable definitions for various forms of heating, also presented by *Food Service Magazine.*

(1) *Primary cooking* is generally accepted as meaning all the way from "raw to ready."

(2) *Re-heating* involves the processing of pre-cooked foods to serving temperatures.

(3) *Reconstituting* means "to build up again by putting back together," e.g., freeze-dried and dehydrated food products.

(4) *Holding* means to maintain foods at ideal serving temperatures pending waitress or customer pickup.

ADJUNCT EFFICIENCY FOODS

To round out a menu which has been constructed on a convenience pre-prepared frozen entrée food program, it is necessary to employ various forms of semi-prepared and other types of prepared products. The most widely used group of adjunct efficiency products is that categorized as convenient or component foods.

Convenient or component foods include a large variety of products. These are pre-cut or pre-portioned uncooked foods. They may also be basic combinations of prepared canned or dehydrated products that require additional preparation or mixing with other components. Examples of convenient foods are: portion-cut fish, meat and poultry; frozen blanched vegetables; cleaned and packaged fresh vegetables; cake mixes; soup, gravy and sauce bases. Additional convenient foods are chopped fresh and canned celery for salads; shredded cabbage for cole slaw; chopped fresh parsley; Caesar salad, tossed salads, peeled whole or sliced fresh onion; fresh hard boiled eggs for salads or garnishes; and diced, rissolé and French-cut fresh or frozen potatoes; cold-pack fresh fruit, such as orange, grapefruit and pineapple segments, cantaloupe, honeydew and watermelon balls used for fruit salads and garnishes or sold as pre-mixed fruit cocktail. Also included are uncooked breaded products like shrimp, fish sticks, and onion rings.

Vegetables

Frozen vegetables comprise a large segment of convenient food forms. This popularity stems from the fact that when served they look and taste like the fresh product and are wholesome and nutritious. In many instances their flavor and succulence are superior to the fresh variety and they have excellent storage stability. Waste is minimized, labor reduced, and preparation procedures are easily adapted to fast food service. For example, steam-pressure cookers are an excellent means for their preparation. Another advantage of frozen vegetables is that seasonal varieties are available throughout the year.

Some frozen vegetables are in reality cooked products. Winter squash, pumpkin and a percentage of corn on the cob have been steamed sufficiently before freezing to cook them. Most vegetables are blanched before freezing; this treatment partially precooks vegetables and makes them porous. Blanching is beneficial, as it is effective in deactivating enzymes which cause the development of off-flavors, undesirable textures, and the rapid loss of carotene and vitamin C during storage.

Pouch packed or "boil-in-the-bag" frozen vegetables with sauces added are interesting and appealing items. These products may be considered as either fresh or pre-cooked. Usually sauces such as butter, cream or cheese, have already been cooked. Preparation procedures are simple, requiring heating in a hot water bath, in a microwave oven, or in a steam pressure cooker. Pouch-packed frozen vegetable products with sauces added can also be classified as convenience foods, since they are fully prepared and may require only garnishing to dress them up.

Potatoes are the most important frozen vegetable, leading all frozen foods in volume consumed. Because of the important role of potatoes in the food service industry, the subject is treated separately.

Purchasing frozen vegetables should be carried out according to procedures developed in the chapter on Quality Control. Labels should be checked for grade, e.g., U.S. Grade A or U.S. Fancy. Grade A vegetables are carefully selected for color, tenderness, and freedom from blemishes. They are the most tender, succulent and flavorful vegetables produced. If vegetables are to be used for soup, casseroles, or soufflés, U.S. Grade C or U.S. Standard may well serve the purpose, since appearance is not too important. Besides indicating the grade, the label will describe variety, size, seasonings, number of servings, cooking directions and net content.

There are many varieties of frozen vegetables. A partial listing follows:

artichokes	beans, cut green and French green
asparagus, spears and cut	beans, cut wax

broccoli, spears and chopped
Brussels sprouts
cabbage
chestnuts, water
collard greens
corn, cut and cob
egg plant
kale
lima beans, baby and Fordhooks
mixed vegetables
mustard greens
okra

peas and carrots
peas, blackeyed and green
pepper
potatoes, diced, French-fried, mashed
rice, brown and wild
soybean sprouts
spinach, leaf and chopped
squash, winter and crookneck
succotash
turnip greens
zucchini

Selection and inventory of frozen vegetables may pose a problem because of the numerous varieties and forms available. Selection depends on several factors, such as the regional popularity or preference, price, ease of preparation, availability and entrée compatibility. Vegetables should be purchased that have dual applications. For example, some vegetables can be served with an entrée, as an entrée, or in a salad. A good illustration of this is asparagus, which is popular when served either hot or cold. Asparagus, as a multipurpose vegetable, will not only enhance the main dish, such as steak or poultry, but it can also be served as an attractive entrée. Many sauces are compatible with this vegetable. Lemon-butter sauce, hollandaise sauce, mild flavored cheese sauce, or a garnish of crisp bacon bits or toasted blanched almonds over hot buttered asparagus are all attractive, appealing, and tasty. The asparagus can be placed on different toasted breads, such as raisin, cinnamon, or white. Chive cream cheese sauce over hot asparagus is another example of an unusual and tasty dish. Salad dressings blend with asparagus very nicely, and so do varieties of seasoned butters.

Carrots, acorn squash and sweet potatoes blend well with the following spices: cloves, cinnamon, ginger, basil, curry or chili powder; blended maple and light corn syrup.

Celery, onions, spinach, potatoes and asparagus will mix with almost all herbs, plus curry, chili, garlic or onion powder, nutmeg, dry mustard, grated cheese, and salad dressing.

Broccoli, Brussels sprouts, cabbage and cauliflower are compatible with dill, celery salt, basil, curry powder, nutmeg, lemon juice and horseradish.

Peas, lima beans, corn, green beans are enhanced with dill, mint (except on corn) ginger, dry mustard, garlic, chili, onion powder, pimiento, sugar, grated cheese, and horseradish.

Minted glazed carrots are unusually delicious. The glaze consists of honey and butter, slowly cooked with the carrots. The mint is added when served.

Another different preparation is mushroom-cheese sauce used on green beans, cauliflower or broccoli. Additional information on garnishing and seasonings will be found in Chapter 9.

Asparagus should be slightly defrosted before cooking. Cooking time in boiling water is 8 to 10 min after the salted water reaches its second boil. Steam pressure time is about 1½ min. Over-cooking should be avoided, as it causes the appealing green color to fade rapidly.

Frozen asparagus spears are usually packed in 1½ lb cartons and are available in two styles: all green, and green and white. Classification is according to the thickness of the stalk, as shown in Table 8.1.

TABLE 8.1

CLASSIFICATION OF ASPARAGUS

Classification	Diameter In.	No. of 5 Inch Stalks per Carton
Small	less than 3/8	up to 125
Medium	3/8 to 5/8	70 to 90
Jumbo	5/8 to 7/8	40 to 60
Colossal	larger than 7/8	30 to 35

Many other vegetables fit the same pattern as asparagus and can be prepared in a number of ways. Mushrooms, carrots, celery, beets and wax beans are examples of multi-purpose vegetables.

Potatoes.—Potatoes are considered to be the "backbone" staple commodity of the food service industry, and as a vegetable have long been a basic part of the American diet. Potatoes are available in many convenient forms, and are prepared, cooked and employed in more recipes than perhaps any other food. It was French-fried potatoes that renewed the popularity of prepared frozen foods. Their success led to many other potato specialties, as shown in Table 8.2.

About 70% of the potatoes used for French fries are grown in the West. Idaho, Washington and Oregon are the three major potato-producing states. In the East, northern Maine accounts for a smaller share of the market. The largest percentage of the crop is processed from the Russet variety. This species has a lower water content than other types, and because of its larger size the finished product is more uniform in length and color.

Styles of Frozen Potatoes.—Many styles or configurations of frozen potatoes are marketed. These are recognized by the Department of Agriculture and form a part of the U.S. Standards for grades of Frozen French-fried Potatoes. The following styles are set forth in these Standards:

(1) *Straight Cut* refers to smooth cut surfaces of potatoes that are sliced into strips. Dimensions vary from 3/8 by 3/8 in. to 1/2 by 1/2 in.

(2) *Crinkle Cut* refers to corrugated cut surfaces with cross-sectional dimensions of 3/8 by 3/8 in. to 3/4 by 3/4 in.

TABLE 8.2

LIST OF FROZEN POTATO PRODUCTS PACKED INDIVIDUALLY AND/OR AS INGREDIENTS OF PRECOOKED FROZEN FOODS.

French-fried	Miscellaneous
regular cuts	potato rounds (shredded and extruded)
crinkle cuts	baked stuffed
pan-fries	puffs
Patties	au gratin
regular	boiled
onion-flavored	rissolé
Mashed	creamed
riced	scalloped
whipped	Delmonico
cuts for mashing	cottage-fried
shredded for mashing	roasted
dehydrofrozen	dumplings or pirogen
Diced	knishes
regular	blintzes
onion-flavored	pancakes
dehydrofrozen	hashed in cream
Hashed brown	cream of potato soup
Southern style, loose frozen	potatoes and peas in cream sauce
prescored-portion control	stew mix

Source: Tressler, Van Arsdel, and Copley (1968).

(3) *Strips* consist of elongated pieces of potato with practically parallel sides and of any cross-sectional shape. This style may be further identified by the approximate dimension of the cross-section, for example 1/4 by 1/4 in., 1/2 by 1/4 in., or 3/8 by 3/4 in.

(4) *Shoestring* refers to strips, either straight-cut or crinkle-cut, with a cross-sectional area predominantly less than that of a square measuring 3/8 by 3/8 in. This style is preferred by those wanting a thinner and crisper product. They are also more economical, since more servings per pound are obtained.

(5) *Dices* consist of pieces of potato cut into approximate cubes.

(6) *Rissolé* are whole or nearly whole potatoes.

(7) Other styles are acceptable when the description of the size, shape or other characteristic differentiates it from the other forms.

(8) *Steak or Ranch* fries refers to wedge-shaped cuts. These produce a golden brown exterior when fried and an interior resembling the texture of baked potatoes.

(9) *Hashed Browns* are sliced rounds, and are available in pan size or individual portions. This style is usually prepared on a griddle or in a tilting skillet.

(10) Frozen French-fried potato strips are designated as to length in accordance with the following criteria:

(a) *Extra long:* 80% or more are 2 in. in length or longer; 30% or more are 3 in. in length or longer.

(b) *Long:* 70% or more are 2 in. in length or longer; and 15% or more are 3 in. in length or longer.

(c) *Medium:* 50% or more are 2 in. in length or longer.

(d) *Short:* less than 50% are 2 in. in length or longer.

Fully Prepared and Blanched Potatoes.—Frozen French fries are available fully prepared and blanched. Fully prepared varieties are completely cooked at the factory and require only heating in an oven for serving. This type is preferred for home consumption because they can be prepared without frying in a deep oil bath. They are also used to advantage for large volume institutional feeding programs, such as schools. Regular and crinkle cuts can be prepared in a standard oven at a temperature of 475°F. Preparation time is 15–18 min. In a convection oven the time is about 1 min per lb at a temperature of 450°F. Shoestrings require 10 to 12 min at 450°F in a standard oven, and about 1 min per lb at 425°F in a convection oven. When heating is completed, the finished product should be drained on absorbent paper.

The oil-blanched variety are partially cooked at the factory. They are also called parfried potatoes. This type is prepared in a deep fryer.

Other Potato Products.—Other frozen potato products are available that are prepared as by-products from the manufacture of frozen French fries.

Potato patties are formed from shredded or chopped material. Seasoning, MSG, rice or potato flour and salt are added. The mixture is fed into a forming machine for different shapes. These are easily prepared in deep fat, tilting skillet, baked, broiled or as an au gratin.

Whipped, mashed, puffs, diced and baked potato forms are available. The baked style are made from whipped potatoes which are stuffed into a container shaped like a half of a whole potato. These may have to be seasoned before browning in an oven or broiler. Diced and sliced forms are excellent for salads, lyonnaise, and soups.

Dehydrated Potato Products.—Dehydrated potatoes are manufactured by two processes: dehydrofreezing and drying by heat. Dehydrofreezing is a method of food preservation developed about 1957. It involves the dehydration of a fruit or vegetable until about one-half of the moisture content has been removed, after which it is packaged and frozen. Since dehydration is not carried to the point where the quality is damaged, the reconstituted product retains a high quality. Dehydrofrozen potatoes are dehydrated to approximately 15% moisture content. Before dehydration, the potatoes are mashed and mixed with nonfat milk solids and then extruded in a thin layer on a continuous belt drier. This process gives a highly desirable product. Boiling water is added to the product for reconstitution. Seasonings, additional milk and butter can also be introduced into the mix. These potatoes can then be whipped or served as mashed.

Potatoes obtained by dry-heat dehydration contain about 6–7% moisture. This product is not frozen but is packaged dry in a moisture-proof container.

Several forms of dehydrated potatoes are available: flakes, granules, cubes and slices.

Slices of dehydrated potatoes can be prepared in 15 min for country-fried potatoes, scalloped and au gratin products, potato salads, hashed browns, and stews. Manufacturers' preparation recommendations must be followed for quality reconstitution. Over-cooking should be avoided for potatoes that are to be used in recipes that require further cooking.

Flakes and potato granules can be prepared in a short time. The amount of liquid added to the product will determine the final texture. These products will retain their original quality when held for several hours in a steam table. They will not discolor. In addition to mashed and whipped forms, flakes and granules can be used for patties, pancakes, baked and stuffed in foil boats, dumplings and soups.

Potato cubes have a number of interesting uses, such as for hashed brown, lyonnaise, chowders and soups, cold potato salad, in chicken and beef pies, and au gratin. Once again, preparation instructions must be followed for uniform and quality results.

Extruded potatoes are made from those parts of the potato not used when French fries are cut from them. The left-over pieces are ground up, made into a powder, and then reshaped into various forms by extrusion. Precise shapes are possible as a result of this process. Extruded potatoes can also be flavored, if desired, for snacks and other dishes.

Onions.—The onion is a remarkable vegetable. Not only has it been a favorite flavoring vegetable for centuries, but its importance within culinary areas is increasing. Onions are a multi-purpose vegetable in that they can be used as flavoring agents, as a garnish, and as a side dish with an entrée.

Two forms of onions are being used in fast food operations: frozen onion rings, breaded or unbreaded, and dehydrated onion products. Dehydrated onion products have been on the market since 1935. These consist of instant minced onion, chopped onions, granulated onion, onion flakes, toasted onion flakes, instant onion powder, onion salt and sliced onions. Onion salt is the only form which is not full strength, as it is mixed with table salt.

Onions grown for dehydration have been specially developed for high solids and low moisture; California is the leading growing state.

The number of available forms of dehydrated onions increases their usefulness for a variety of recipes where onion flavor is desired. The powder is suited to dishes requiring no onion texture. The minced and flaked forms are used where particles are required. Toasted flakes impart the flavor of browned onions, and onion salt makes possible a rapid addition of onion flavor.

In addition to their versatility the dehydrated product and frozen onion rings offer many interesting advantages: (1) storage loss is minimized, (2) they are easy to use, (3) flavor and quality can be controlled, (4) labor is reduced, (5) uniform flavoring can be achieved once the quantity measurements have been established.

Onion Rings.—Onion rings are marketed in two styles: precooked and raw. The sweet Spanish variety of onion is most commonly used in preparing rings. The onions are peeled and sliced. The resulting onion rings are breaded and then either frozen directly or cooked before freezing. U.S. Standards for grades of frozen breaded onion rings were established in 1959. Two grades were designated: (1) U.S. Grade A or (U.S. Fancy); (2) U.S. Grade B or (U.S. Extra Standard). Imperfect rings, according to these Standards are defined as: (1) units that have not been separated into a single or double ring of the slice; (2) portions of rings or rings not joined to form a continuous circle; (3) slices that lack a hole in the center; (4) rings that are extremely irregular in shape.

Onion rings are available that have been processed and pre-formed by extrusion. Fresh onions are peeled and cut and then made into a slurry that is fed into an extrusion machine. The resulting rings are firm, uniform, and are not as brittle as the conventional type. Onion rings are also sold that are fully cooked and frozen. These require only oven heating for preparation. They are similar to the fully prepared French fries and are finding favor for mass feeding operations.

Table 8.3 is a condensed fact sheet showing the description and uses for the types of dehydrated onion products available to the trade.

Chives, Shallots, Green Onions and Leeks.—Green onions, shallots and leeks are sometimes called "scallions." Green onions are ordinary onions harvested very young. They have very little or no bulb formation and their tops are tubular. Shallots are similar to green onions, but grow in clusters and have practically no swelling at the base. Leeks are larger than shallots, have a slight bulb formation and broad, flat, dark green tops.

Shallots.—Shallots impart a mild delicate onion flavor to a food. This flavor is distinctive. It blends well with a variety of dishes, and imparts a mild yet robust flavor, whereas onion or garlic, if added in the same proportions, would produce an overpowering effect. Because of their unusual flavor and affinity for sauces, they are widely used in French and Continental cuisine. Their popularity increased in the United States when they became available in the freeze-dried form.

Freeze-dried shallots are marketed diced. Each flake measures about 1/4 to 3/8 in. Shallots are also sold as a powder. Their versatility offers a wide range of applications, as in soups, casseroles, vegetables, salad dressings, sauces, and rubbed on meats.

Chives.—Chives, like shallots, are marketed in the freeze-dried form. This product is in the multi-purpose class; it can be used as a garnish for color and as an interesting seasoning. Chives have been favored for centuries for their ability to impart a delicate, mild, onion-like flavor and color to foods. The applications of this product are limitless, especially since they are available in the freeze-dried form. The following are a number of applications:

(1) sprinkled over cooked vegetables, with butter or oil;

TABLE 8.3

DEHYDRATED ONION PRODUCTS—DESCRIPTION AND APPLICATION

Form	Description	Applications
Powdered	Finely powdered white onion, free-flowing.	Meat products, canned foods, gravies, sauces; seasonings, soups, cheese, and wherever fresh onion flavor is required without the appearance of onion particles; 1 lb of powder is equivalent to 10 lb of raw prepared onions.
Granulated	Coarse particles, processed from pungent white onions, free-flowing.	Same as for the powdered form.
Ground	Coarser particles than granulated, free-flowing.	Same as for the powdered form.
Minced	Small pieces, about 1/8 in.	Soups, sauces and prepared foods, meat loaves, vegetables, casseroles, relishes and wherever some onion texture is required. Replaces 8 lb. of raw onions. Reconstituted by adding 3 parts of cold water to 1 part of minced onion by volume. Allow to soak for a minimum of 30 min, drain excess water. Also add dry where sufficient liquid is present.
Small Chopped	Small uniform pieces of white onions.	Vegetables such as seasoned peas, green beans, enhance some prepared canned or frozen foods. Reconstitution same as for minced onions.
Chopped	Medium uniform pieces of white onion.	Soups, sauces, canned and prepared foods, meat loaves, vegetables, casseroles, relishes. Reconstitution same as for minced onions.
Large Chopped	Larger than chopped, uniform coarse pieces.	Soups, on hamburgers, relishes, casseroles, Chinese and Spanish rice dinners. Reconstitution same as for minced onions.
Onion Salt	Onion powder with table salt added.	Hamburgers, steaks, fried chicken, French fries, and as a table condiment.
Diced ¼ in.	Uniform pieces, ¼ in.	Relishes, vegetables, Chinese food, casseroles, hamburgers, hot dogs, chili burgers, sloppy joes, for sautées, and wherever texture and appearance are factors.
Diced ½ in.	Uniform large pieces, ½ in.	Stews, chicken a la king, Chinese food, vegetables, Italian food, Spanish rice, soups, on roasts, and wherever a very pronounced presence of onion is needed. Reconstitution same as for minced onion.

TABLE 8.3 (Continued)

Form	Description	Applications
Sliced	Long pieces, sliced pieces and rings.	Salads, hamburger, liver, onion soup, Chinese dinners and wherever a large piece of onion is required visually and as well as for flavor. Reconstitution same as for minced onions.
Large Sliced	Longer pieces and rings than sliced variety.	Same uses as for the sliced variety.
Browned or Toasted	Available in many forms.	Use where sautéed or fried onions are required. Soups, gravies, stews, poultry, fish, vegetables and casseroles.

Source: Gilroy Foods (1971).

(2) added to sour cream as a topping for baked potatoes, green cooked vegetables, omelets and pancakes;
(3) as a garnish over fish, chicken or in fish sauces;
(4) directly in omelets or the sauces used with omelets, or in scrambled eggs;
(5) in creamed dishes or casseroles;
(6) in soups;
(7) in cheese dishes;
(8) in cream cheese or cottage cheese.

Celery Flakes.—Dehydrated celery flakes provide an appetizing flavor to many mixed dishes. This seasoning is used successfully in soups, stews, sauces, stuffings and salads. Reconstitution is necessary. This is done by adding an equal amount of water to the mix and allowing it to stand for about 15 min.

Mixed Vegetable Flakes.—Mixed vegetable flakes are considered an all-purpose seasoning, since they provide the flavor characteristics of a number of vegetables such as onions, celery, green and red peppers, and carrots. This seasoning is excellent for enhancing the flavor of many frozen pre-prepared entrées, such as stews and meat loaves; it is also excellent for soups, sauces, stuffings and salads. Rehydration is the same as for celery flakes.

Sweet Pepper Flakes.—This product provides a convenient way of adding green or red pepper flavor to sauces, salads, vegetables, casseroles, and to any dish where diced pepper is desired. It is excellent for certain frozen pre-prepared entrées such as meat loaf, Chinese and Italian dishes.

Garlic.—Ever since garlic became available in the dehydrated form its popularity has increased many fold. Table 8.4 shows the forms of garlic in use and some suggested applications. The addition of garlic to any food should be limited, since too much will tend to overpower the true character of the preparation. It is advisable to experiment with each application until the desired effect

TABLE 8.4

DEHYDRATED GARLIC PRODUCTS—DESCRIPTION AND APPLICATIONS

Form	Description	Applications
Powdered	Fine powder, free-flowing.	Wherever fresh garlic flavor is required. Meat products, gravies, sauces, seasonings, cheeses, salads.
Granulated	Coarser particles, free-flowing.	Same as for powdered product.
Ground	Coarser than granulated, free-flowing.	Same uses as for powdered garlic and where particle size is desirable.
Minced	Small pieces about 1/16 in.	Soups, sauces, prepared foods, meat loaves, vegetables, casseroles, relishes and sautéing.
Chopped	Pieces about ¼ in.	Same as for minced, including bread and rolls. An all-purpose product.
Large sliced	Solid slices, the size of a nickel or dime.	Same as for minced, also used by pickle and relish packers.

Source: Gilroy Foods (1971).

is obtained. Garlic is an excellent means for off-setting the blandness of frozen pre-prepared foods and is especially useful for some nationality dishes.

Convenient Egg Products

About 1 out of 10 shell eggs produced in the United States today is processed into liquid, dried or frozen forms. These products are true convenient items, providing the fast food operation with many advantages, e.g., savings in storage space; reduced labor costs; elimination of waste; reduced sanitation and garbage loads; ease of measurement and use; and uniform color and quality.

These products are not new. Dried eggs have been marketed for many decades. They came into prominence during World War II. Although they provided the Armed Services with egg dishes, they were not popular because of their rubbery texture and off-flavor. However, since that time, processing has been improved and methods of rehydration have become more accurate, so that the end product is much more palatable and compares favorably with its fresh counterpart.

Egg products are available in the following forms:

(1) Dried eggs, powdered, yolks and whites.

(2) Frozen eggs, whole, whites, yolks. Combination products, e.g., a mixture of eggs and non-fat milk for scrambled and omelets. Combination omelet mixes, egg custards, and fried eggs.

(3) Frozen hard-cooked eggs.

(4) Preserved hard-cooked eggs in gallon jars.

Frozen raw eggs have excellent freezing qualities; however, frozen cooked eggs may become tough and rubbery.

Defrosting frozen egg products should be carried out well in advance of preparation. Defrosting should be slow and never at room temperature. Any thawed eggs that are not consumed should not be refrozen, but stored overnight in a holding refrigerator at temperatures of 38°F.

Hard-cooked eggs should also be refrigerated promptly. They should be put into a tightly closed container or wrapped in plastic. Sometimes hard-cooked eggs will develop a green discoloration between the white and the yolk. This greenish color is harmless; it results from a chemical reaction between the sulfur in the white and the iron in the yolk. Both sulfur and iron are natural, wholesome components of the eggs.

Hard-cooked frozen eggs are marketed diced and also in the form of a 12-in. cylinder, resembling a baloney. It provides about 75 center-cut slices, or it can be diced or chopped. Thawing is accomplished by submerging the product in boiling water for 7 min, or in hot tap water for 15 min. Unused portions can be refrigerated for up to 3 days.

Eggs can be used in an almost unlimited number of ways. Within the convenience food establishment, hard-cooked eggs are adaptable for salads and as a garnish. Frozen or dried whites can be used for sauces. Frozen whole eggs can be cooked alone for scrambled, baked, omelets, or shirred dishes, for soufflés, fondues, and in meat loaves.

Manufacturers' instructions must be followed to assure quality results. Generally, moderate to low temperatures with proper timing should be followed to produce uniformly tender, attractive egg dishes. High temperatures and long cooking causes the egg protein to shrink with an accompanying loss of moisture, making the protein rubbery or tough.

Portion-Cut Meats

Portion-cut meats are a positive asset for the fast food eating establishment. Many advantages can be gained by their use. Among the more notable are: (1) purchases are limited to a desired cut; (2) cost per portion is known and can be accurately calculated; (3) the purchaser orders only what is required. Other significant advantages are: (1) they meet the convenience and flow pattern of the preparation center; (2) labor is reduced; (3) uniform quality is assured; (4) service is speeded up; (5) the problem of using trimmings for secondary dishes is eliminated; (6) specifications are easy to write; (7) deliveries can be easily checked; (8) inventory control is simple and pilferage can be reduced or eliminated; (9) spoilage is eliminated or greatly reduced; (10) ageing is not necessary, since the cuts can be ordered according to the age desired. Table 8.5 shows examples of portion cut meats.

The Series 1000 Specifications.—There are so many different kinds and cuts of meat available that a new meat dish could be featured every day of the year. Since meat commands a large share of the total food purchases, it is important that exacting specifications be followed to ensure uniform quality and good value for the money spent.

TABLE 8.5

EXAMPLES OF PORTION-CUT MEATS

Cut or Description	Portion Size (Oz)	Suggested Methods of Preparation
Strip loin, boneless	6 to 14	Broil, pan broil, pan fry or grill
Pin bone strip		
boneless	6, 8, 10, 12	Broil, pan broil, pan fry or grill
Butt strip	6, 8	Broil, pan broil, pan fry or grill
Sirloin, butt	3, 4, 6	Pan fry or grill
Sandwich cut, round		
or oblong	2, 3	Pan fry or grill
T-bone	8, 10, 12, 14, 16	Broil, pan broil, pan fry or grill
Rib club, boneless	8, 10, 12	Broil, pan broil, pan fry or grill
Rib eye	4, 5, 6, 8	Broil, pan broil, pan fry or grill
Tenderloin (filets		
mignon)	4, 6, 8, 10	Broil, pan broil, pan fry or grill
Twin beef (filet		
mignon)	2, 4	Broil, pan fry or grill
Beef filet or sirloin	4, 6, 8	Broil, pan broil, pan fry or grill
Beef Swiss	4, 5	Braise
Sirloin beef cubed	3, 4, 5, 6	Pan fry or grill
Floured beef steaks	4	Grill or pan fry
Pepper beef steaks	2¼, 3, 4	Grill or pan fry
Mushroom beef	2¼, 4	Grill or pan fry
Pizza patties with		
cheese slice	3½	Grill or pan fry
Chuck wagon steaks	2¼, 3, 4, 6	Pan fry or deep fat fry
Cubed dinner beef		
steaks	6	Pan fry or grill
Salisbury steaks	6	Pan fry or grill
Chopped beef steaks	6, 8	Pan fry, grill or broil
Beef patties	2, 3, 4	Pan fry, or grill
Sirloin beef kabobs	6, 8	Broil, pan fry or grill

Source: Colonial Beef Company, Phila., Pa.

One method is to specify the quality grade of the primal cuts from which the individual portions will be taken. However, other considerations may arise when the primal cuts are processed. For example, what are the percentages of unwanted bone and fat? Another question concerns the substitution of cheaper cuts for more expensive ones.

The answers to the above questions are provided by the USDA Institutional Meat Purchase Specifications Series 1000, which have become the industry's guidelines of comparison. The following are several examples of these exacting guidelines: Porterhouse steaks may have no more than 4-in. tails and the diameter of the tenderloin muscle must be not less than 1¼ in., T-bone steaks may have no more than 3-in. tails and the diameter of the tenderloin muscle must be not less than 1/2 in. of surface fat and a maximum thickness of 3/4 in. at any one point.

Specifications are also designated for ground beef. Two styles are mentioned: regular and special. For both the fat content must not exceed 25%.

If breaded meats are purchased, the quantity of breading should be determined by methods outlined in Chapter 7.

Cooking Pointers.—Most frozen meat may be cooked either thawed or frozen. The frozen meat will require additional cooking time. Meats cooked in a deep-fat frier should not be thawed before cooking. This applies primarily to breaded products, where the breading may flake off in the fryer, increasing fat absorption. Thin meats 1/2 in. or less in thickness should be cooked in the frozen state. If defrosted, they will cook too rapidly so that the degree of doneness cannot be controlled. Most operators prefer to cook their meat thawed, since cooking from the frozen state requires more skill, especially for microwave oven heating.

Slow thawing is advisable and should be performed in a refrigerator. Once the meat is thawed it can be kept in a cooler for several days. Rapid thawing causes rupture of the meat cells and thus allows the flavorful juices to escape.

Meat Tenderizing.—Meat that is cooked by pan frying, grilling, broiling, and deep frying must be tender to start with because the heating process will not change the chewy texture. Stewing meat and Swiss steak cuts will become tender during braising. This method of preparation tends to break down the connective tissues. Some choice grades of loin and rib cuts are naturally tender; however, other parts and cuts may need to undergo a tenderizing process.

Tenderizing may be accomplished by putting the meat through a cubing machine, slicing into thin strips while in the frozen state and then laminating several pieces together to form a single steak. Ageing is still another tenderizing method. Meat can be ordered aged. For this purpose, it is put into a plastic bag, or dry-aged. Those cuts which are boneless are aged in plastic bags, whereas meat with bone-in cuts are dry-aged.

Tenderizing may also be done chemically. The substance commonly employed for this purpose contains papain which is extracted from papaya fruit. Papain is an enzyme that breaks down the connective tissues. The action takes place during cooking at temperatures between 140° and 175°F. Over-tenderization and loss of flavor may occur if the meat is cooked at too low a temperature, reheated, or held at serving temperatures for a prolonged period of time. Lower grades of meat, such as commercial or utility steaks, that have been tenderized at the meat packer, can be purchased at substantial savings over choice grades.

Poultry Products

Poultry is high on the list of popularity in American meals. Convenient and convenience forms of poultry cover a wide range of products. With today's modern production, processing, and marketing methods, chicken, turkey, duck, and geese are available the year around for roasting, broiling, frying, and stewing.

Packaged, cut-up poultry, heat-and-serve fried chicken, breaded uncooked frozen and freeze-dried products, turkey and chicken rolls, and roasts stuffed or unstuffed are just a small part of the vast convenient and convenience poultry market.

The terms or definitions for poultry include *chickens, turkeys, geese, guineas,* and *duck*. Broiler-fryer chickens are produced mainly in the Del-Mar-Va Peninsula, where Delaware, Maryland, and Virginia converge. Other growing areas include Georgia, Mississippi, Alabama, Arkansas, and the Carolinas.

Stewing hens, a byproduct of the egg industry, are produced in the Southeast, Midwest, parts of the Northeast and in California. Turkeys are raised in Rhode Island, the Midwest and California. The major producing area for ducks is Long Island, New York.

Young poultry is marketed at an early age. Broiler-fryers are ready for market in about 9 weeks and a 20-lb tom turkey in about 5 mo.

Poultry and poultry products come under the inspectional jurisdiction of the USDA. Congress enacted two laws to protect the consumer against unhealthy and unwholesome poultry—the Poultry Products Inspection Act of 1957 and the Wholesome Poultry Products Act of 1968. The latter requires inspection of all poultry products whether they move in interstate or intrastate commerce. In addition, the USDA has specified minimum meat requirements for many processed products. These were listed in Chapter 7.

Poultry is graded for quality. After inspection, a USDA grade seal is affixed to the product. The top poultry grade is U.S. Grade A. To attain a Grade A rating, the poultry must have good overall shape and appearance, must be meaty, should be practically free from defects and have a well-developed layer of fat in the skin. Other grades exist, such as B and C. Birds receiving these ratings are used in processed foods. In 1965 grade standards were developed for raw, ready-to-cook poultry rolls, roasts, and bars.

Poultry is usually labeled according to age. This is important, since age indicates tenderness and suggest ways to cook the poultry. It is important to remember that cooking poultry in intense heat toughens the protein, causes abnormal shrinkage and loss of juice. The following are the age groups:

(1) Mature chickens may be labeled *mature chicken, old chicken, hen, stewing chicken,* or *fowl.*

(2) Mature turkeys may be labeled *mature turkey, yearling turkey,* or *old turkey.*

(3) Mature ducks, geese, and guineas may be labeled *mature* or *old.*

(4) Young chickens may be labeled *young chicken, Rock Cornish game hen, broiler, fryer, roaster,* or *capon.*

(5) Young turkeys may be labeled as *young turkey, fryer-roaster, young hen,* or *young tom.*

(6) Young ducks may be labeled *duckling, young duckling, broiler duckling, fryer duckling,* or *roaster duckling.*

Although not included in the above, mention should be made of squab and squab chicken. These are popular items considered to be gourmet. Squab are immature pigeons weighing about 1/2 to 1 lb each. Squab chickens are young chickens, while Cornish hens are a cross breed of a Cornish bird and a chicken.

Cuts and Forms.—Poultry is probably one of the most popular, convenient, versatile, and profitable foods served. Fried chicken with the bone-in is accepted on a national scale. For the convenience, fast food operation, prepared raw or cooked poultry presents a wide selection of cuts and forms. The basic forms are chilled raw poultry, frozen raw poultry, smoked poultry, freeze-dried products, and canned varieties. In addition, poultry cuts or parts are available, such as breasts, legs, splits, wings, and chicken livers. Poultry is often boned and marketed in cans. Both chicken, turkey and game fowl are available in this form. Broilers or fryers are boxed one dozen to the case. Turkeys are usually dressed and ready to cook. Weights vary from 20 to 25 lb. Turkey rolls have a weight range of 8 to 10 lb and will yield about 30 to 35 servings.

Storage Suggestions.—Chilled raw poultry or ready-to-cook fowl is bled, picked, with head, feet and viscera removed. This form should be stored promptly and used within 48 hr. Frozen poultry or parts must be handled like other frozen foods. At $0°$ F maximum storage is 12 mo. Frozen cooked poultry slices or pieces covered with gravy or broth can be stored at $0°$F for 6 mo, while fried chicken has a 4-mo storage life at $0°$F, and cooked poultry dishes a 6-mo storage period. Canned poultry should be stored in a dry place at temperatures not exceeding $70°$F and for a period not exceeding 1 yr. Freeze-dried poultry may be held at room temperatures up to 2 yr if the container has a good, solid seal.

Thawing.—Thawing should be done in a refrigerator ($36°$-$40°$F) in the original wrap, on trays or platters for 18 to 24 hr, or until pliable. Turkeys weighing 20 to 25 lb may take 3 days to thaw. Whole frozen fowl can be hung on a rack for air circulation. Quick thawing can be performed in a bath of cold water, the water being changed to hasten the process. This method requires constant surveillance. The original wrapper must be kept in place, and as soon as the fowl becomes pliable it must be removed. Do not thaw in hot water or in a heated room. Do not thaw frozen stuffed poultry before cooking. In all instances read and understand the packer's preparation instructions printed on the label. Poultry is extremely perishable, and proper handling is required to prevent spoilage. Do not attempt to partially cook poultry and hold it for completion of the cooking process the following day, as this gives bacteria an ideal opportunity to grow. Strict compliance with proper methods of sanitation is advisable. Avoid cross-contamination with other foods or surfaces in the preparation area.

Portioning.—For whole broiler-fryers, stewing chicken, turkey or duck, the average serving per person is about 3 to 4 oz of cooked meat without the bone, or from 0.5 to 0.75 lb of fowl. Cut-up poultry will yield the following servings: 1 breast half, 1 leg, 2 drumsticks, 2 thighs, or 4 wings. A 2-lb broiler, split, will give 2 portions (Fig. 8.1). Combination dishes such as casseroles and pies should contain about 0.33 lb of poultry meat.

Pre-prepared frozen poultry and poultry dishes are discussed in Chapter 9.

Courtesy American Spice Trade Association

FIG. 8.1. PREPARING CHICKEN SPLITS FOR HEATING

Portion Control Fish Products

Fish and shellfish products provide a vast variety of choices. There are more than 240 species sold in the United States, which puts this food group ahead of all others with regard to the number of products offered for sale. Fish and shellfish can be purchased frozen, canned, cured fresh and in a wide selection of convenience, convenient, and specialty items.

The number of fish and shellfish products which can be successfully handled and merchandised in a fast and convenience food operation is much less than that for the general market. Frozen, canned, cured, and an interesting variety of pre-prepared frozen entrées that need only to be heated before serving are the main products used. In addition, there are frozen raw fish products that are stuffed or breaded and then baked or deep-fried.

Forms of Fish Products.—Whole fish are sold just as they come from the water. Before cooking they must be scaled, eviscerated, and the head, tail and fins removed. Small fish like smelt are often cooked with only their entrails removed.

Dressed fish are scaled, eviscerated and, sometimes the head, tail and fins removed. The smaller fish are called *pan-dressed* (Fig 8.2).

Steaks are cross-section slices from a large dressed fish cut 5/8 to 1 in. thick. A cross-section of the backbone is usually the only bone in a steak. Chunks are cross-sections of a large dressed fish with a cross-section of the backbone included.

Single fillets are practically boneless and may or may not be skinned. The most common type are the sides of the fish cut lengthwise away from the backbone.

Butterfly fillets are the two sides of the fish cut lengthwise away from the backbone and held together by the uncut flesh and skin of the belly. These fillets are practically boneless.

Frozen raw or fried breaded fish portions are cut from frozen fish blocks, coated with a batter, breaded, packaged and frozen. Portions weigh more than 1½ oz and are at least 3/8 in. thick. Raw portions must contain not less than 75% and fried portions not less than 65% fish flesh, according to U.S. Department of the Interior (USDI) standards. They may be purchased raw or partially cooked.

Frozen fried fish sticks are cut from frozen fish blocks, coated with a batter, breaded, partially cooked, packaged and frozen. Fried fish sticks weigh up to 1½ oz., must be at least 3/8 in. thick, and contain not less than 60% fish flesh, according to USDI standards.

Canned fish are packed in a large variety of convenience and specialty products. These include three popular items; tuna, salmon and sardines.

Tuna is packed from six species; namely, albacore, blackfin, bluefin, skipjack, yellowfin, and little tuna. Albacore has lighter meat than the others and is the only species permitted to be labeled "white meat" tuna. The others are labeled "light meat". Canned tuna is packed in oil or water. Solid packs are the most expensive, followed by chunk and flaked, while the grated is the least expensive pack.

Salmon, packed from five species, is sold by the name of the fish, since there is a difference in the color, texture, and the flavor of each. Higher-priced varieties are deeper red in color and have a higher oil content. The most expensive is the red or sockeye, followed by chinook or king, the medium red, silver or coho, pink, the least expensive being the chum or keta.

Cured fish are processed from many different species. Some of the more common cured fish on the market are pickled and spiced herring and salmon;

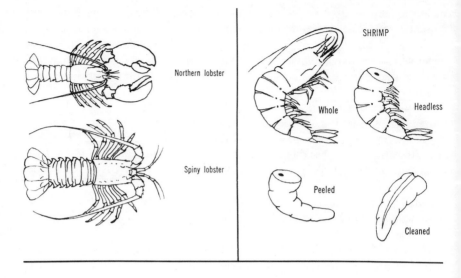

MARKET FORMS OF FISH

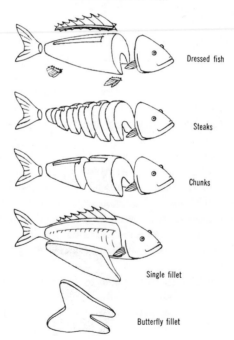

From Kerr (1969)

FIG. 8.2. MARKET FORMS OF FISH AND SHELLFISH

salt cod and salmon; smoked chubs, salmon, white fish and sturgeon. Cured fish have remarkable versatility. They may be served as hors d'oeuvres, in sandwiches, in salads, or as an appetizing entrée. Smoked salmon or lox is highly regarded in many sections of the country. This product is available in cans and is packed in oil with protective paper separating each slice.

Forms of Shellfish.—In this country shellfish means crustaceans and mollusks. Crustaceans include crabs, lobsters, and shrimp; mollusks are clams, oysters and scallops.

Clams are available fresh in the shell or shucked, that is, the meat removed from the shells. The meat is pale to deep orange in color and has a fresh, mild odor. Fresh shucked clams are packed in little or no liquid. Frozen raw or fried breaded clams are shucked clams coated with a batter, breaded, packaged and frozen. They may be purchased raw or partially cooked. Canned clams are sold whole, minced, or in chowder, bouillon, broth, and nectar.

Crabs consist of three principal species—blue, Dungeness, and king. Frozen crab legs are the legs of cooked king and tanner crabs which have been frozen and split or cut into sections. The meat is white, with an attractive red tint on the exterior. Crab meat is the meat removed from cooked crabs. The meat is packed and chilled, frozen, pasteurized, or canned. King crab meat is primarily leg meat. It is white with an attractive reddish tint. The packs of blue crab are: lump meat, obtained from the two body muscles which operate the swimming legs; flake meat, small pieces of white meat from the body; a combination of flake and lump meat; and claw meat, brownish tinted meat from the claws.

Lobsters consist of the northern variety and spiny lobster. The northern lobsters have large, heavy claws, whereas the spiny lobsters have no claws.

Lobsters in the shell are sold fresh, frozen, or cooked (Fig. 8.3). The cooked lobster should be bright red and have a fresh, mild odor. Lobster meat is the meat removed from cooked lobsters. The meat is packed and chilled, frozen, or canned. It is white, with an attractive reddish tint on the outside.

Oysters consist of three main species: Eastern, Pacific and Western. The oyster meat is referred to as shucked and should be plump and have a natural creamy color and clear liquid. The meat is packed with little or no liquid. Oysters containing an excess amount of liquid should be avoided, as this indicates poor quality and careless handling. Frozen raw or fried breaded oysters are shucked oysters coated with a batter, breaded, packaged, and frozen. They are available raw or partially cooked. Canned oysters are sold whole and for stew.

Scallops are shellfish, a mollusk with two shells. They are active swimmers and move about the ocean bed freely. The two principal species marketed are bay and sea scallops. The adductor muscle is excellently flavored and is the only part of the scallop eaten by Americans. The sea scallop's muscle may be as large as 2 in. across, whereas that of the bay scallop measures about 1/2 in.

Shucked scallops are the adductor muscles removed from the shells. The meat is a creamy white, light tan, orange, or pinkish. Fresh scallops should have

Courtesy American Spice Trade Association

FIG. 8.3. PREPARING HERBED LOBSTER TAILS FOR HEATING

a sweetish odor and be packed in little or no liquid. Fried scallops must contain not less than 60% scallop meat, according to USDI standards. They are available raw or partially cooked.

Shrimp as marketed in the United States are the common or white shrimp, which is greenish-gray; brown or Brazilian shrimp, which is brownish-red; pink or coral shrimp; and Alaska, California, and Maine varieties, which vary in color and are relatively small. However, when cooked, all shrimp assume the same color—a reddish tint. There is very little difference in the appearance and flavor of cooked shrimp. Shrimp are sold according to size; the larger the size, the higher the price.

Headless shrimp are, as would be expected shrimp with the heads removed. "Green shrimp" is a trade term used to describe raw shrimp.

Peeled and cleaned shrimp are headless shrimp with the shell and intestinal tract removed. They are sold raw or cooked, fresh, frozen, and canned.

Frozen, raw or fried breaded shrimp are peeled and cleaned shrimp coated with a batter, breaded, packaged, and frozen. Breaded raw shrimp must contain not less than 50% shrimp meat according to USDI standards. They are available raw or partially cooked.

Shrimp vary in average count per pound from under 10 to over 70. Trade nomenclature for the different sizes are: under 10 to the pound, extra colossal; 10 to 15, colossal; 16 to 20, extra jumbo; 21 to 25, jumbo; 26 to 30, extra large; 31 to 35, large; 36 to 42, medium large; 43 to 50, medium; 51 to 60, small; 61 to 70, extra small; and over 70, tiny or tidi.

Grade Standards.—Grade standards have been established by the Bureau of Commercial Fisheries, U.S. Department of the Interior for a total of 15 processed fishery products. These include frozen raw and fried breaded fish portions, frozen fried scallops, frozen raw and fried fish sticks, frozen headless dressed whiting, frozen ocean perch fillets, frozen sole and flounder fillets, frozen haddock fillets, frozen fish blocks, and frozen raw or fried breaded shrimp.

Quality grades for fish products are Grades A, B, C and substandard. When purchases are planned, specifications should include the USDI grade standard. In addition the amount of fish or shellfish to buy per serving varies with the recipe to be used, size of serving, and amount of bone or shell in the product. Allow approximately 3 to 4 oz of cooked, boneless fish or shellfish per serving.

Preparation Hints.—Fish and shellfish are excellent sources of high quality protein and other nutrients. Pre-prepared frozen and portion-controlled frozen raw fishery products are important to the fast and convenience food service operation. They are popular and generate good profits; there is no waste; and they are easily prepared. They lend themselves well to a variety of preparations, such as baked, broiled, fried, poached, grilled, and steamed. They are excellent for almost any course; appetizer, cocktail, soup, salad, sandwich and entrées.

Regardless of the fish form, successful preparation is possible at all times by employing moderate temperatures and short cooking time. Seafood is naturally tender, so that cooking it at too high a temperature or for too long a time toughens it, dries it out, and destroys the fine natural flavor.

Knowing when seafood is cooked may pose a problem, especially with unthawed frozen raw products which are stuffed. Raw fish have a watery, translucent appearance. During cooking the watery juices become milky colored, giving the flesh an opaque whitish tint. This color change is quite obvious. When the flesh is opaque in the center of the thickest part, the fish is cooked. At this point the flesh will flake easily when tested with a fork and will separate readily.

Cooked fish is tender and delicate. Handle it as little and as gently as possible during and after cooking. Holding cooked seafood at serving temperature is the same thing as overcooking. The best policy to follow is to prepare the fish to order to avoid overcooking. In addition, read all labels and preparation instructions. Run several tests to check their accuracy.

Butter helps to draw out the appealing fish flavors. Use it generously when basting, or add it to the accompanying sauces.

When preparing clam or oyster dishes, or any hot lobster meat or crabmeat, the shellfish meats should be added towards the finish of the cooking cycle. This practice will preserve the full flavor and retain the natural tenderness of the product.

Do not overcook shrimp products. Shrimp should always be simmered and never boiled. Place the shrimp in a covered pan and simmer for about 5 min.

Surveying the Portion-Control Market.—Many forms of frozen fish and shell-

TABLE 8.6

FISH AND SHELLFISH
Approximate Yield and Approximate Amount to Purchase Per Serving

	Fish and Shellfish as Purchased	Yield %	Amount to Purchase Oz
Fish	Whole	27	11
	Dressed or pan-dressed	38	8
	Fillets, steaks, and chunks	61	5
	Portions and sticks	90	3½
	Pickled and spiced	100	3
	Salted	72	4¼
	Smoked	66	4½
	Canned tuna	100	3
	Canned salmon	81	3¾
Clams	In the shell:		
	Hard	14	21½
	Soft	29	10½
	Shucked	48	6½
	Breaded, raw or fried	84	3¾
	Canned minced clams	100	3
Crabs	In the shell:		
	Blue	14	21½
	Dungeness	24	12¼
	Soft-shell	66	4½
	King crab legs	52	6
	Cooked meat	97	3¼
	Canned meat	85	3½
Lobsters	In the shell	25	12
	Spiny lobster tails	51	6
	Cooked meat	91	3½
Oysters	In the shell	12	25
	Shucked	48	6½
	Breaded, raw or fried	88	3½
	Canned whole	100	3
Scallops	Shucked	63	5
	Breaded, raw or fried	87	3½
Shrimp	Headless	50	6
	Peeled and cleaned	62	5
	Cooked, peeled, and cleaned	100	3½
	Breaded, raw or fried	86	3½
	Canned whole	100	3

Source: Kerr 1969.

fish are available, so that variations in menu listings can be achieved throughout the year (Table 8.6).

Fish fillets that are boneless and skinless offer a number of interesting and choice dishes, such as poached in an appropriate sauce, fried, broiled, and sautéed (Fig. 8.4). Fillets are also packed stuffed with crabmeat. These are portioned in 4-oz and 6-oz servings.

Courtesy American Spice Trade Association

FIG. 8.4. FISH ROLLS PROPERLY PLATED AND GARNISHED

Shrimp are packed breaded fried or raw, cooked, raw frozen, or freeze-dried. The forms of shrimp products are limitless. In addition to the conventional shrimp forms, stuffed shrimp are sold stuffed with crabmeat, breaded and frozen. This product can be served with a seafood sauce or with an Oriental sweet and sour sauce.

Frozen fish are sold raw breaded and pre-cooked. Species such as cod, haddock, sole, flounder, pollock and perch are packed in this manner.

Deviled crab are available in natural or aluminum shells. Portions average about 3 oz.

Shrimpburgers, fish patties, breaded oysters and breaded scallops are other products available for fast food preparation.

Chapter 9 contains a discussion of fish products that are pre-prepared and frozen.

FOODS PRESERVED BY FERMENTATION

Preservation by fermentation is an ancient art, dating back almost 4000 years. This method of preservation makes use of microorganisms under controlled conditions. Wine production, beer brewing, bread baking, cheese processing, salting and pickling of various edibles all involve fermentation.

Salted or cured foods are produced by the beneficial effects of salt. By sorting, the permissible organisms are enabled to grow. The amount of salt employed determines and controls the fermentation activity. The process applied to cucumbers and other fruits and vegetables is known as pickling. Pickling combines salting, selective-control microorganisms, and fermentation. The process stabilizes the tissues of the fruit or vegetable.

Cheese is a product obtained by inoculating milk with suitable organisms to control fermentation.

Meat is preserved by curing or pickling. This is accomplished by dry curing, or with a pickling solution at temperatures ranging from 35° to 38°F. Chemicals used in this process are sodium nitrate, sodium nitrite, sodium chloride, sugar, citric acid and vinegar.

Foods from fermentation are important adjunct items for the fast and convenience food service organization. All these foods are excellent in themselves, but when used properly with other compatible items, they tend to enhance the taste. They add sparkle and zest to a salad, a sandwich, an entrée, or dessert, provide a change in the texture and flavor of many foods, and are appealing and attractive as garnishes.

This discussion is centered around the following products: pickles, relishes, olives, sauerkraut, pickled fruits, such as peach, pear, crabapple, and watermelon rind; pickled vegetables like onion, okra, peppers, tomatoes (ripe or green), and green beans.

Pickles and Relishes

Items such as pickles and relishes are extremely useful to the convenience and fast food service organization. They are not only appealing, appetizing and refreshing, but are also colorful and serve as excellent garnishes. For unknown reasons these highly regarded products are sometimes abused and mishandled. In addition, an incorrect relish or pickle may be served which is not compatible with the accompanying dish. This is a vast subject, since there are a limitless variety of these products. Briefly stated, here is a list of recommendations that will serve to illustrate applications of relishes and pickles:

(1) Mix into sandwich spreads.

(2) Sprinkle chopped pickle or relish in almost any soup.

(3) Add the diced products in stuffing, meat loaves, meat dishes, fish, salads, and creamed or buttered vegetables.

(4) Add diced pickles, olives or relishes to scrambled eggs.

(5) Add pickles or their liquids to sauces for meats, fish, fowl, and egg dishes.

(6) Add pickle liquid to almost any dressing or to baste meat.

(7) Add sweet fresh cucumber pickles to hamburgers or chopped dill pickles to stuffed peppers.

Storage and Holding Qualities.—Fermented products possess excellent keeping qualities. Opened containers should be stored in a refrigerator. Make sure that the packing liquid covers the contents. The natural acids in the food and the liquor tend to inhibit the growth of molds and bacteria. Discard any opened product if it is very discolored, if it has an offensive odor, if gas bubbles appear, or if there is unusual softness, mushiness or slipperiness.

Pickle Categories.—There are two basic categories of pickles: cured and fresh pack. Each has its own characteristic of flavor and texture. Both classes are mostly cucumber pickles or contain cucumber pickles in a mixture.

(1) *Cured pickles* are those that have been slightly fermented in salt brine for several months. They are then desalted, washed, and the process completed in a vinegar solution. Various seasonings are added to impart the desired flavor characteristics. The curing process creates subtle flavor changes and edible acids. These pickles are usually crisp, dark green, and somewhat translucent.

(2) *Fresh-pack* pickles, as the name implies, are produced by packing cucumbers directly into a container. The contents of the container is covered with a pickling solution containing vinegar, other acids, flavorings, and ingredients to produce a desired characteristic. The containers are sealed and pasteurized with heat to preserve them. These pickles retain some of the flavor of fresh cucumbers; they are usually a light yellow-green color. They are not as salty or as acid as the cured type. The words "Fresh-pack" often appear on the label.

Typical Varieties.—Typical basic varieties are the dill, sour, and sweet pickles. Each of the basic varieties is defined as follows:

(1) *Dill pickles* are flavored with dill, an aromatic herb, which may be supplemented by spices. The three variations of this product are the genuine dill, processed dill, and quickly fermented dill. Labels may indicate terms, such as "kosher" or "kosher style." These are highly spiced and include onion and garlic flavors. Most dill pickles are large or medium in size and may be cut into strips, slices, cubes, or chips.

(2) *Sour pickles* are brine stock products which have been finished in vinegar and spices. These may be packed whole or cut into strips, slices, or in any manner. There are a number of styles, such as sour mixed, which is a combination of pickles with pickled vegetables, like onions, peppers and cauliflowers. These are also cut into many forms. In addition there are *sour relish* or *piccalilli* products, and *chow chow*. Chow chow is similar to sour mixed pickles, with the addition of a flavored spicy mustard sauce.

(3) *Sweet pickles* start as sour pickles from which the vinegar has been drained. They are finished in sweet spicy liquors that are added periodically, until the desired degree of sweetness is attained. The varieties of sweet pickles are endless. These may be had as sliced sweet pickles, chips or wafers; plain sweet pickles, cut crosswise into discs; candied chips; sweet dill pickles made

from processed dills instead of the sour type; mixed sweet pickles with vegetables added.

Other Pickled Products.—A large selection of pickled fruits and vegetables is available which blend well with other foods and make excellent attractive garnishes. In addition there are tasty relishes such as corn, tomato-pear chutney, horseradish and pepper-onion.

Sauerkraut obtained from brined, fermented cabbage has a pleasant, tart and tangy flavor. It is crisp and firm in texture, and has a creamy white color. It can be cooked in many ways or served cold. The cooked sauerkraut can be served as a main dish with meat, or as a vegetable with pork. When used cold it can be added to sandwiches, on a salad plate, or in a mixed pickle and relish platter.

Cured olives are a member of this class of foods. These products are versatile and can be employed in many ways. A detailed discussion of olives can be found in the following chapter.

Making a Selection.—It is considered worthwhile when making a selection of pickled products to explore and test as many styles and forms as can be obtained. If your wholesaler has a limited supply, then go to a supermarket and a gourmet specialty shop and examine the displays. Many so-called gourmet packs are interesting and offer a large selection of products not usually found elsewhere. It may be possible to order these retail items through a distributor. Most packers also have a line of institutionally packed sizes.

When perusing the stocks of pickle products, read the labels, since they reveal a great deal of information, and may even suggest different uses for the item. Note the size of the pickle; they come in seven regular sizes from *midget* to *extra*

TABLE 8.7

USES FOR A SELECTED LIST OF PICKLE PRODUCTS

Pickle Product	Suggested Uses
Sweet, all styles	Salads (fish or meat), sandwiches, cold cuts
Dill, genuine	Cold cuts, sandwiches, roast meats, barbecued meats, corned and processed meats
Dill, quick-process	Sandwiches, potato salad, egg and cheese dishes cold cut meats (pastrami, corned beef, tongue)
Dill, kosher style	Same as for dill, quick-process type
Mustard, chow chow	Frankfurters, cold meats, ham, cheese, roast pork
Sweet relish	Most salads, meat loaf and roast meats, hamburgers, fishburgers, ham sandwiches
Dill relish	Most salads, stews, pot pies, barbecued products corned beef, cole slaw
Frankfurter relish	Hamburgers, frankfurters, meat salads, cold cuts, fish sticks
Hamburger relish	Hamburgers, frankfurters, deep fried products, meat and fish salads

Source: Thompson 1969.

large. Also examine the mixed pickles and relishes to see what ingredients are used and in what proportions. Table 8.7 is a handy reference guide for use in deciding which of the more common pickle products harmonize with selected dishes.

CANNED FOODS

The boundary line or hypothetical line of demarcation between ready-to-eat foods in cans and their frozen counterpart is often difficult to draw. The forerunners are those products packed in cans. Arguments for and against the use of each category are endless. However, what is definitely known is that a vast variety of canned edibles, regardless of the inroads being made by frozen foods, will continue to be popular. In a number of instances they are increasing in volume. Notable are portioned packed canned foods for vending, fish products, salad mixes, and soup. In addition, the use of individually portioned canned foods for hot lunches under Federal funded sponsorship has won recent approval by the USDA for Type A school lunch programs. Canned puréed foods specially packed for elderly people are another important addition to canned packed products.

Canned foods are those items which are packed in hermetically sealed containers, and then subjected to a heat-processing treatment, which destroys microorganisms that would cause spoilage. The amount and length of heating varies with the nature of the product being processed and the size of the container.

The art of canning was discovered by a Frenchman, Nicolas Appert, during the latter part of the eighteenth century. This discovery was perfected after some years of experimentation, and soon altered the eating habits of the Western World. Canning continues as a key resource for providing a sound, nutritious food supply in many areas of the world. In the United States a vast industry has been built around the canning of edible and non-edible products. Research and development continues as a cornerstone of this industry, touching upon every phase of the canning process. Innovations in cans and canning became available near the end of the last decade, i.e., easy-open cans, aluminum cans, new protective inner coatings, and aseptic canning.

Canned Products for Fast Food Service

The list of products available to and in use by fast and convenience food service operations is endless. Included are a complete line of fish products like tuna, salmon, gefilte, mackerel, salmon, sardines, crab meat, lobster meat, clams, oysters, shrimp; meat and poultry products, including processed meat, such as chicken, turkey and ham; canned milk, whole eggs, canned ready-to-bake biscuits, soup bases, olives, prunes, pickles, nut pastes, syrups and toppings, and a complete array of vegetables and fruits.

In addition, prepared products and component parts are marketed such as mixed salad products. These include tuna, salmon, ham, shrimp, crabmeat, egg, chicken, potato, macaroni, bean and beet salads. Many of the same products are freeze-dried and packed in cans. Component products for salads are celery, peppers, onions, and relish.

Prepared foods that are packed in cans are spaghetti and spaghetti sauces of all types, chicken and beef pot pie fillings, sauces, corned beef hash, pie fillings, stews, chili con carne, meat balls, chicken and dumplings.

TEXTURED VEGETABLE PROTEIN FOODS

Textured vegetable protein foods are additional sources for man's search to solve the hunger crisis that is plaguing many areas of the world. Once considered the food of the future, vegetable protein products that contain all the essential amino acids or body-building elements are now being manufactured with success. Advanced applications of food science and technology are responsible for these notable achievements in transforming products that are rich in nutritional values into forms that resemble traditional foods.

The importance of this new industry has not been fully realized by most food service personnel. Textured vegetable protein foods present an unlimited potential and an entire horizon of new and exciting efficiency products compatible with fast food service. Anticipated sales by 1980 are expected to exceed two billion dollars annually.

These foods, referred to as fabricated or engineered, derive their protein from plants, such as soybean, peanuts, cottonseed, sunflower, safflower, coconut and alfalfa. Soybean protein has been used since 1940. However, it was not until the early part of the last decade that increased attention was focused on these plant proteins as an inexpensive source of food for underdeveloped countries. During the mid-1950s, manufacturing methods and processing procedures were developed to transform plant protein into food products. These products covered a wide range, but their acceptance was slow and the entire program was viewed with skepticism. Today the marketing picture has changed completely, and considerable interest has been aroused at all levels of the food industry. The underlying reason for this turn of events was a decision of the United States Department of Agriculture to allow the addition of vegetable protein in Type A school lunches.

The words *fabricated* or *engineered* which are employed to designate this group of foods is as confusing and misleading as the term *convenience foods* when it is applied to pre-prepared frozen products. Fabricated or engineered foods are also referred to as mock-meat, simulated products, synthetic edibles and textured vegetable protein items. The last term was adopted by the USDA in its notice allowing the use of these foods in school feeding programs. The FDA is considering the use of the term *textured protein products* in its proposed standard of identity.

Definitions

Analogs.—The word analog is emerging from the cloisters of food science into general public usage. Analogs are similar or like products in function only, not in origin. When applied to textured vegetable protein products, the analogs are similar to the traditional food forms, e.g., bacon, turkey, chicken, ground beef and ham.

Isolated Vegetable Proteins.—This is a highly concentrated form of vegetable protein. The protein content averages 95%. This product is employed to reduce shrinkage, to improve appearance, and to provide a solid structure or form to a finished food.

Expanded Vegetable Proteins.—These are small particles of protein matter resulting from an extrusion process. When flavored and colored, they resemble chunky, diced, or cubed products such as chicken bits, beef parts, and pork chunks.

Spun Vegetable Proteins.—These proteins result from a spinning process similar to the methods employed for making synthetic cloth fibers such as nylon.

Soy Products.—There are five types of soy products: (1) full-flat soy flour containing 40% protein; (2) defatted soy flour containing 50% protein; (3) soy concentrate containing not less than 70% protein; (4) soy milk, extracted from cooking soy beans; and (5) isolated soy protein containing 90% protein.

Textured Vegetable Protein.—The definition of this term is contained in the USDA Food and Nutrition Service Notice FNS 219, allowing for its use in Type A school lunch programs. The text of this notice follows:

"Textured vegetable protein products are used in combination with meat for use in lunches and suppers served under child feeding programs."

"Textured vegetable protein products are food products made from edible protein sources and are characterized by having a structural integrity and identifiable texture such that each unit will withstand hydration and cooking, and other procedures used in preparing the food for consumption."

"Textured vegetable protein products meeting the following requirements may be used as an alternate to meet part of the minimum requirements of 2 oz of cooked meat specified for the Type A school lunch."

"The vegetable protein product shall be prepared and served in combination with ground or diced meat in the form of meat patties, meat loaves, meat sauces, meat stews, or in similar foods made with poultry or fish. Ratio of hydrated vegetable protein product of moisture content 60 to 65%, to uncooked meat, poultry or fish in the combination shall not exceed 30 parts per 70 parts, respectively, on basis of weight."

Processing

Spun Vegetable Protein.—This process is also referred to as weaving, looming or textiling. The material is extruded through spinnerettes and into a coagulating bath, producing fiber-like material. The diameter of the fibers can be varied from 1 thousandth to 30 thousandths inch. The diameter can be used to gauge the texture of the fibers as to the degree of tenderness or toughness. The strands or fibrils are mixed with flavors, colors, or other enhancing substances. The mass is further treated with a coagulating protein to bind it together into a cohesive form and give it an appropriate texture.

Fibers that have the same texture as meat fibers can be mixed with ground meat to complement the natural texture. These are referred to as meat extenders; they have a shelf life longer than meat and are more stable under refrigeration. They contain no enzymes that accelerate deterioration.

Extruded and Expanded Vegetable Proteins.—Products such as soy flour and soy concentrates are mixed with water, flavor and a coloring agent, and cooked under pressure. After cooking, the mass is extruded into the air, where it expands like cereal-based snack foods. The dimensions of the product are controlled by the shape of the die and speed of the cutting knife. These proteins, when dried, are used as extenders, and added in small quantities to traditional foods, replacing all or part of the natural meat components. Examples where these vegetable proteins are added are chili, sloppy joes, spaghetti sauce, and patties.

Merits of Textured Vegetable Protein Products.

Textured vegetable protein foods offer many advantages. The following are the significant merits that have contributed to their rapid growth:

(1) Raw materials are plentiful and resulting products are less expensive than meat or poultry.

(2) They are versatile and can be fabricated into any desired form.

(3) They can be flavored and colored to resemble natural foods.

(4) They can be dehydrated, frozen or canned.

(5) They have excellent storage stability. They do not become mushy on prolonged refrigerated storage.

(6) Their nutritional composition can be controlled and kept uniform.

(7) Raw materials are available worldwide, which means that they can be produced in localities where the population is underfed.

(8) Shipping costs are reduced, since they occupy less space than conventional foods. Elaborate packaging is not required, except for products requiring refrigeration.

(9) Fat content is controllable and therefore, they are excellent for reducing diets and for reduction in cholesterol intake.

(10) They have a stabilizing effect on comminuted meat products. They hold fat and other ingredients in a matrix of protein particules, thereby eliminating weeping and flavor losses.

(11) Natural foods are improved, especially those low in protein content.

(12) When used as extenders, they help to reduce shrinkage and aid in the retention of natural juices.

(13) They are excellent efficiency foods. Labor is reduced since cutting and trimming are not necessary.

(14) Food costs are reduced and waste is eliminated.

(15) Fabricated products will retain their shape and texture indefinitely.

(16) They are tender, chewable, bland and have a high degree of flavor and color acceptance.

(17) They absorb fats and oils when required.

(18) Harsh cooking and handling will not destroy their texture or flavor.

(19) Rehydration of the dried protein is simple. Water is readily retained. Three parts of water are required for one part of protein.

An Endless Array of Food Applications.—Textured vegetable proteins offer an endless array of food applications. Their versatility is so unique that imagination and ingenuity are the main ingredients needed to create a variety of formulas or recipes employing these food forms.

The following are examples of foods containing textured vegetable proteins: analogs of beef, chicken, ham, pork, sea food, bacon and bacon bits, and cheese. A part of all of the meat content is replaced with vegetable proteins for the following dishes, sloppy joes, spaghetti sauce, chili, pizza topping, meat balls, and meat loaves. Meat balls and meat loaves are excellent when 60% of the meat is replaced with vegetable protein. Diced protein forms can be used in chow mein, meat or chicken pies, chicken a la king and casseroles. Many nationality dishes, e.g., Italian, Russian, French and Spanish, can be improved by replacing a percentage of the meat or poultry content with an equivalent amount of textured vegetable protein.

Bacon bits have become a valuable garnish and a seasoning additive. They add a pleasing flavor and provide appetite and eye appeal to many preparations. They can be used as a garnish on salads, baked potatoes, cooked vegetables, scrambled eggs, soufflés and omelets, and as a seasoning for canapés, meat loaf, meat patties, stuffed eggs, biscuits, and dips.

The following show the percentage of textured vegetable protein in typical recipes:

(1) Macaroni and cheese sauce with ham-flavored protein, 11%.

(2) Pizza topping, with beef-flavored protein, 15%.

(3) Chili with beef-flavored protein, 6.50%.

(4) Meat patties with seasoned chunks or minced protein, 10%.

(5) Barbecue sauce with seasoned chunks of protein, 10%.

(6) Snack dip with ham-flavored minced protein, 8.50%.

(7) Scrambled eggs with bacon-flavored protein bits, 5.5%.

(8) Irish style stew with beef-flavored protein chunks, 7.25%.

(9) Sukiyaki with beef-flavored protein chunks, 10.50%.

(10) Stroganoff with seasoned protein chunks, 4.50%.

(11) Veal-type patties with seasoned protein chunks, 25.0%.

(12) Sweet and sour pork with pork-flavored protein chunks, 19%.

(13) Meat loaf with beef-flavored chunks or minced protein, 10.5%.

(14) Tuna fish salads with unseasoned protein chunks, 25%.

Cautious Handling and Experimentation Required.—Excellent results will be obtained with textured vegetable proteins. Manufacturers' instructions must be read and understood. Recipe cards should be developed for each food. If the finished food develops off-tastes, off-flavors or peculiar looking textures, it can be assumed that the fault was in the preparation.

Over-cooking will produce insipid foods. Off-flavors will result and the texture will assume a mealy or gritty character. Stews and casseroles require frequent stirring during heating to prevent a flat tasting and cereal-like character. Textured vegetable protein should be added to these products when the cooking cycle is two-thirds complete.

Spices and herbs are readily accepted by the proteins. Experimentation will be necessary to determine which seasoning will produce the desired effects. The result should be a mellow taste, not sharp or biting. However, the spices or herbs should be added in sufficient quantities to accent their individual trait. Flavor enhancers should also be added. These products require experimentation to achieve proper flavor development.

Textured vegetable protein foods are adaptable to all forms of heating. Microwave oven heating produces excellent results. The absence of fat tends towards a juicier food. If microwave oven heating is attempted, the product should contain more moisture than normal. The extra fluid will yield a high quality, juicy and tender food.

Rehydration cannot be rushed. Allow 30 to 45 min for this operation. Most protein products absorb up to three times their weight of water. Some manufacturers recommend that their product be rehydrated in ice water ($40°F$); others suggest using hot water ($160°F$).

OTHER PROTEIN PRODUCTS

Because of the intense interest being shown in edible proteins, other substances are being employed commercially as protein sources, among them petroleum, autolyzed yeast, whey, fish, deglanded cottonseed, and seaweed colloids.

Seaweed Colloids

Seaweed colloids comprise a group of substances that possess a number of useful and outstanding characteristics. The group consists of agar, algin and carrageenan. As the name implies, these colloids are obtained from seaweeds or marine algae.

Agar.—Agar has many names, such as Chinese moss, seaweed isinglas, and Japanese gelatin. In the form of a sweetened gel, it has been eaten by Orientals for centuries. The Japanese were responsible for the commercial development of agar products. Agar has been used as a culture medium for microorganisms since 1882.

Agar is prominently employed in foods. The bakery and confectionery industry use it in icings, as a moisture barrier to retard the drying of unwrapped products, and to prevent the running of icing in packed items.

Carrageenan.—Carrageenan, or Irish moss, is used in ice cream to control ice crystal formation and in evaporated milk to prevent separation and sedimentation. It is used in chocolate milk to help form a suspension of the cocoa particles and milk. As a thickening and gelling agent, it plays an important role in the quick preparation of certain prepared foods. It is used to thicken sauces, to form a gel in aspics and salads, and in butter sauces for frozen vegetables to increase the cohesiveness of the sauce on the vegetables.

Algin.—Algin, obtained from kelp or brown algae, is the most important of the seaweed colloids. It is employed as an emulsion stabilizer. When added to ice-cream it produces a smooth body and texture. It also helps to prevent coarsening due to ice crystal formation during storage. When added to salad dressings it helps to hold the oil and water in suspension. It is also used as a stabilizer in chocolate milk; as a gelling agent in puddings; as a thickener in imitation whipped cream, margarine and sauces; and as a coating on food to prevent moisture and flavor loss.

When used in canning, it helps to reduce the cooking time by keeping the viscosity of the food at low levels and thus increasing heat transfer. It is employed in foods to reduce caloric content, as in spaghetti and spaghetti sauce, since it imparts an appealing mouth feel due to the gel formation. Other products that have benefited from this property are fabricated meat balls, artificial caviar, shrimp, extruded onion rings, and fabricated potato chips.

Cottonseed Protein.—Concentrated protein from cottonseed has been made possible by the commercial removal of a toxic material contained in the pigment gland. The gland, which is also named gossypol, is completely removed. The cottonseed is then reduced to a defatted flour, protein concentrate or protein isolate. The protein is bland and has an off-white color. It is used in the same manner as soybean protein.

Whey Protein.—Whey protein is obtained from raw whey, a by-product of cheese manufacturing which was previously discarded. This protein effects freeze-thaw stability in a food, and is a foaming agent. Because of the foaming action it can be used in desserts and foods that require whipping. Whey proteins are bland and odorless.

Other Proteins.—Protein from petroleum has entered the commercial stage in France. It is produced from yeasts and bacteria that are grown on crude oil.

Fish proteins (FPC) are made from fish that are either discarded or have no commercial value because of their small size.

Autolyzed yeast protein is produced from a selected strain of brewers' yeast. This product is being used as a flavor carrier for a variety of textured protein foods. It is claimed that as a flavor carrier, increased stability is achieved under extreme processing conditions.

FOOD FORTIFICATION

Food fortification or enrichment is becoming an important aspect of fabricated products. Simply stated, fortification is the addition of vitamins, minerals and protein to food to enhance its nutritional content. Although food enrichment is not new, a concerted effort is under way to produce edibles of all types that are wholesome and nutritionally beneficial. Foods such as cereals, rice, dairy items, bread, flour and macaroni have undergone enrichment for decades. Addition of iodine to salt to prevent goiter has been practiced since 1924.

Food is eaten because of a personal choice. It is rarely consumed voluntarily just because it is known to be nutritious. The goal of nutritionists, food scientists and some segments of the government concerned with nutrition is to provide edibles that are not only highly nutritious, but are appealing to the consumer. Many consumer groups and lobbies are also endorsing these principles.

Over the past ten years the level of nutrition has decreased, not because of food alterations, but because the consumer has shifted preference to more convenience products, prepared desserts, punches, ades, and soft drinks. Foods high in nutritional value have decreased in popularity. Those foods adversely affected are milk, vegetables, fruits and grain products. As a result of this dramatic shift in buying patterns to less nutritional foods, methods of fortification are being evaluated. Foods of all types are being appraised on the basis of what constitutes a sufficient vitamin and mineral content, so that consumers at all economic levels may benefit.

Fabricated snack foods are being enriched. Vitamins destroyed during processing are being returned to finished foods. For example, vitamin C is being added back to potato chips to supplant that lost in processing. Tid-bits, corn-chips, pretzels, snack nut meats, pre-packaged popcorn and puffed and extruded fat-fried items are all undergoing evaluation for enrichment purposes.

FLAVOR ENHANCERS

Flavor enhancers or potentiators such as monosodium glutamate (MSG) and mertaste (GMP) have assumed significant roles in the flavor development of convenience pre-prepared foods and textured vegetable protein products. Flavor enhancers are not spices, herbs or flavoring agents. Nonetheless, they appear to possess the unusual ability to make foods taste better, without adding any distinctive character, aroma, or flavor of their own. They intensify flavors already present, and then act to blend them together into a single entity.

MSG was discovered in 1908 by a Japanese who found that small pieces of dried seaweed accentuated the natural flavor of foods. However, it wasn't until World War II, when spices were in short supply, that MSG became popular. Today the dollar volume of these enhancers leads that of all condiments and flavoring agents with the exception of salt.

The mechanism by which flavor potentiators act on the human body has not been fully established. One theory suggests that these substances stimulate the nerve ends in the mouth. However, disagreement continues concerning the real facts underlying this phenomenon.

Advantages of Flavor Potentiators

(1) MSG exhibits a slightly sweet and salty taste to meats and meat products. In small quantities these traits are not sensed. MSG increases salivary secretion, creates a general sense of satisfaction, and a pleasant aftertaste. The increase in salivary secretion is probably responsible for the comment that foods prepared with these substances are more juicy and appealing.

(2) Mertaste, when added to soup or gravies, creates a sense of fullness, viscosity or body. Dried soup mixes become more appealing with the addition of this enhancer.

(3) Mertaste when combined with MSG will enhance the action of the MSG.

Disadvantages of Flavor Potentiators

(1) Flavor potentiators are not effective in sweet products like baked goods and desserts, in cereals, fruits, fruit juices, or dairy products.

(2) They may tend to accent disagreeable characteristics. The aroma of fish for instance, is accented to a disagreeable level; however, potentiators have no effect on freshly caught fish. They reduce the aroma of sulfury aromatics in meat, but increase the sulfur aroma of mustard to an uncomfortable threshold.

(3) Testing by trial and error is required to find the optimum amount to be used in a specific product. Guidelines are available, but these must be tested prior to serving.

(4) They tend to suppress sour, fatty, oily, starchy, burnt, and bitter food characteristics. Under certain conditions these factors may not require the suppressing action of MSG; thus care must be exercised to retain these traits when it is added to foods.

Using Flavor Enhancers Such as MSG

(1) For beef, veal, pork, lamb, and mutton: sprinkle the meat with the substance together with other spices. For steak, sprinkle on both sides and rub into the surface.

(2) For poultry: sprinkle in the cavity and on the surface.

(3) For vegetables: when they are prepared with little or no liquid, MSG can be added during cooking. For vegetables prepared in liquid, add MSG with final seasoning or added to a butter sauce.

(4) For fresh fish: sprinkle on both sides and in cavity before preparation.

(5) MSG will restore some of the freshly cooked flavor of foods held in a steam table. Sprinkle on the portion before serving.

(6) Highly flavored or highly seasoned foods may require more MSG than blandly spiced or seasoned foods.

(7) For sauces, gravies, soups, stews, casseroles, and salads: add MSG along with other required seasonings.

(8) Suggested quantities for meats, fish, shellfish, poultry and vegetables: 25 lb, add 2/3 oz; 50 lb, add 1 1/3 oz; 75 lb, add 2 oz.

For soups, sauces, gravies:-1 gal, add 1/2 tablespoon; 3 gal, add 1 1/3 tablespoon; 6 gal, add 2 2/3 tablespoon.

Other Types of Flavor Enhancers

Maltol.—Maltol is isolated from the bark of larch trees, pine needles and roasted malt. This substance imparts freshly baked odors and flavors to bread and cake. It also enhances the flavor of artificial fruit flavors and allows for a reduction of the sugar content in soft drinks without affecting the sweeteners.

Maltrin.—Maltrin is a hydrolyzed cereal solid that is made from pure starch using a gentle conversion process. It has many interesting features: it is soluble in tepid water, it has low hygroscopicity, its sweetening factor is low compared to sucrose, and it contributes a firm, appealing body texture without masking flavors. It can be used as a partial substitute for non-fat dry milk and egg solids. Maltrin can replace starch and flour fillers and it has a rapid dispersion rate. It is a mild flavor enhancer, so that less flavors and spices are used. This product can be used in soup, cake mixes, as a carrier for spices, sauce mixes, many pre-prepared frozen convenience entrées, glazes, instant sauces which require no prior heating, and in coffee whiteners.

MISCELLANEOUS TYPES OF EFFICIENCY FOODS

Sugar-Concentrated Foods

Jelly, jam, preserves, fruit butters, sweetened condensed milk, candied and glacéed fruits are the products in this category.

The raw products are concentrated by evaporation to a point where microbial spoilage cannot occur. After concentration, sugar is added. Mild heat is applied to products containing 65% or more soluble solids and having a high acid content. With more than 70% solids, high acid content is not required for preservation against bacterial spoilage.

Semi-moist or Intermediate Moisture Products

Semi-moist or intermediate moisture products include partially dehydrated foods that have a suitable concentration of dissolved solids to bind the remaining water sufficiently to inhibit the growth of bacteria, mold and yeasts. Foods in this category can be pre-cooked or raw, and are stable at room temperature. Examples of products treated by this process are diced white chicken meat, diced carrots, beef stew, barbecued pork, apple pie filling, beef cubes and coarse ground hamburger beef. Figs and dates, both of which are air-dried, are in this category. Soft candies, marshmallows, fig newtons, fruit cake, peperoni, and dry sausage are other products within this group.

Convenient Packaged Foods

Convenient packaged foods are any category or form of pre-prepared or semi-prepared products. The majority of these products are individually wrapped portions of ready-to-eat foods. Examples are sugar packets, tea bags, butter patties, individual portioned coffee cream or non-dairy whitener; packets of salad dressing, mustard, salt, pepper and ketchup, and one-cup servings of instant coffee.

Dehydrated Foods

These are foods in which the free water content is reduced sufficiently to control microbial growth. Two methods are available: (1) dehydration by nature, as in sundrying, and (2) dehydration by artificial means.

Natural dried foods have been consumed since biblical times. These include grains, legumes, nuts, many varieties of dried fruit, fish and meat.

Artificially dried foods are produced by hot air, superheated steam, under vacuum, in inert gas, and by direct application of heat. Examples of food in this segment are potato chips; spaghetti products; fruits, such as apples, pears, grapes (raisins), figs, cherries and bananas; vegetables like potatoes, onions, celery, parsley and cabbage; meats, such as bacon, beef and pork; fish and fish products; milk products, either whole milk or non-fat skim milk; whole eggs, yolks, and egg white; instant coffee and tea. In addition, many combinations of food products are obtained by employing dried components, such as milk shake powder, salad dressings, soup mixes, lemonade and other soft powdered drinks. Artificial drying was developed in France about 1795, using hot air as the drying medium.

Many of these products are discussed in Chapter 9, in conjunction with garnishing.

Freeze-dried Foods

Freeze-dried foods have become an essential part of the fast and convenient food service scene. Major developments in the techniques of freeze drying during the last decade have paved the way for the formulation, production, and marketing of many useful and novel food products. The use of freeze-dried items is increasing in popularity because of the many advantageous characteristics that these foods offer. Flavor, color, texture and nutrient composition are practically unaffected by the rigors of processing. Storage stability is excellent and reconstitution is simple and rapid. Bacteria, molds and yeasts have little chance to multiply in sturdy air tight packages.

Processing.—Freeze-dried foods are products that have undergone high-vacuum processing while in a frozen state and under the influence of specific conditions of temperature and pressure. Within certain controlled conditions water can exist as a liquid, solid and vapor. These simultaneous properties are referred to as the three point or triple stage. At $32°F$, and at a pressure of 4.7 mm of mercury, waters enter the triple point stage. Below 4.7 mm of mercury the ice sublimes from the frozen product and is emitted in the gaseous form as water vapor. Sublimation is the phenomenon by which a solid or gas changes its physical state without becoming a liquid. In this case the ice becomes a vapor without passing through the liquid phase. Successful freeze dehydration is performed at a pressure of 4 mm or below to bring about rapid sublimation. The major difference between freeze drying and its conventional counterpart, thermal drying, is that the foods are not subjected to extreme high temperatures, which usually results in a loss of quality.

Freeze-drying is time-consuming and expensive. The approximate drying time, depending on the product being processed, ranges from 6 to 24 hr. Products which are diced, cubed or powdered may require only 4 to 6 hr. Ten to 24 hr are needed for drying strawberries; peaches, 10 to 18 hr; chives, 12 hr; beef, diced and cooked, 7 to 10 hr; and shrimp, whole and cooked, 7 to 14 hr.

Preparation Prior to Processing.—The food is prepared in the form required of it after processing. This may include trimming, peeling, sizing, grading, and portion control measures. The product may be blanched or cooked, and then diced, sliced, or pulverized. They are then frozen before drying.

Drying.—Conventional freeze-drying is performed in a cabinet, on trays, using steam for heat, and refrigerated condensers for water removal. Other methods include continuous freeze-drying, and the use of microwave systems which reduces the processing time.

Packaging.—After the food is dried it must be protected from moisture, oxygen and light. For this purpose it may be packed in cans, aluminum foil-polyethylene laminated bags, or plastic pouches. Products such as meat are flushed with nitrogen gas to prevent oxidation. This step is particularly important for foods with a high fat content.

Product Characteristics

Freeze-dried products are unique in that they are smaller and lighter than the original food. The smaller size and lighter weight reduces packaging, shipping costs and storage space. For example, 1 lb of freeze-dried chives is equivalent to 12 lb of the fresh product; 1 lb of freeze-dried shallots is equal to 7 lb of fresh shallots.

Freeze-dried foods can be recognized by their appearance. They look somewhat like the initial frozen product insofar as shape and size are concerned. However, they are much lighter in weight and have a spongy texture. Color is also lighter, but it returns to normal when rehydrated. A disadvantage is brittleness. Some freeze-dried foods are so friable that they can be completely pulverized between the fingers. Rough handling or poor packaging can contribute to the destruction of product's shape.

Preparation and Rehydration.—Rehydration is an easy one-step operation.

Water is added in sufficient quantities to restore the food to its natural state. Correct rehydration techniques are essential to ensure high quality. Before preparation the product label and fact sheet must be read and understood. These instructions must be followed. Since the field of freeze-drying has broadened, numerous products are available from a variety of manufacturers. Each company has provisions for its own optimum methods of handling and preparation developed by prior testing and field experience.

Rehydration should not be rushed. Where freeze-dried products are being used regularly, rehydration should be scheduled on a preset basis, well ahead of the actual serving period. Some products will require two hours for quality rehydration; other items, such as shrimp, shallots, and chives can be rehydrated within minutes. Shrimp requires about 6 min; diced shallots, 4 min; chives 60 to 90 sec; and coffee is instantaneous.

Foods in almost every category are available in the freeze-dried form. They include shrimp, herbs, onions, garlic, potatoes, shallots, chives, crab meat, mushrooms, many green vegetables, fruits, coffee, tea, scrambled eggs, meat parts (slices and cubes for soup and stews) and salad mixes. Salad mixes are useful items, including tuna, ham, egg, shellfish, and salmon. These are mixed with freeze-dried celery and onion and are blandly seasoned. They come in No. 10 cans and have long storage stability.

Rehydration of salad mixes is simple, but it must be scheduled about two hours in advance of serving. Water is added and the mixture is allowed to rehydrate slowly. This process will take between 90 and 120 min. The development of the flavor and texture becomes readily apparent since the rehydrated mix closely resembles all the characteristics of the freshly prepared salad. After rehydration the mixes are handled like those prepared from fresh ingredients. They may be mixed with salad dressing, mayonnaise, or served with oil and vinegar or lemon. Varieties of seasonings can be added because most of these products are not highly spiced or salted. Freeze-dried fruits such as strawberries, blueberries, prunes and others are available for garnishes and salads. Fruit pie fillings are made that are easy to handle and can be added to frozen pie crusts and heated in convection ovens.

Compressed Freeze-Dried Foods.—Compressed freeze-dried foods have been developed by the U.S. Army Food Laboratories, Natick, Mass. Spinach, carrots, and other vegetables are compressed under pressures ranging from 1,000 to 2,000 psi. This process produces vegetable bars 3 in. long, 1 in. wide and 1/2 in. thick. Upon rehydration these foods expand to 11 times the size of the compressed bar.

Advantages of Freeze-Dried Products.—A wide range of products are being marketed. During this decade, the development of cheaper processing methods are anticipated which will reduce costs substantially. Presently, those foods that have been processed and reconstituted properly are excellent. Nutrient retention, color, flavor, and texture factors are natural, and storage stability is good. These are the plus factors. However, on the negative side are high processing costs, expensive packaging, and the need for cautious handling and prudent preparation, since freeze-dried foods are easily damaged.

BIBLIOGRAPHY

ANON. 1962. MSG Enhances Natural Flavors. McCormick and Company, Inc., Baltimore, Md.

ANON. 1966. A Glossary of Spices. American Spice Trade Association, New York, N.Y.

ANON. 1968. Portion Control Service from Treasure Isle. Ocean Products, Inc., Tampa, Fla.

ANON. 1970A. TVP, a fabulous new food. Archer Daniels Midland Co., Decatur, Ill.

ANON. 1970B. The Easy Way With Bontrae. General Mills, Minneapolis, Minn.

ANON. 1970C. Enrichment. Merck and Company, Rahway, N.J.

ANON. 1971A. High-protein foods from cottonseed. Food Processing 32, No. 4, F4–F6.

ANON. 1971B. Fabricated foods from the sea. Food Processing 32, No. 7, F4–F6.

ANON. 1971C. Tureen flavors from Miles. Miles Laboratories, Inc., Marschall Division, Elkhart, Ind.

ANON. 1971D. Temptein, the obedient protein. Miles Laboratories, Inc., Marschall Division, Elkhart, Ind.

ANON. 1971E. Heller's soy protein blend No. 200 for patties, Bull. 19. B. Heller and Company, Chicago, Illinois.

ANON. 1971F. A Discussion on Food Fortification. Hoffman-La Roche, Inc., Nutley, N.J.

ANON. 1971G. Maltrin, applications for the convenience food industry, Bull. 1003-2. Grain Processing Corp., Muscatine, Iowa.

ANON. 1971H. The Canning Industry. National Canners Association, Washington, D.C.

ANON. 1971 I. Introducing a real breakthrough in school feeding. Ore-Ida Foods Company, Boise, Idaho.

ANON. 1971J. Onion and Garlic Facts. Gilroy Foods, Inc., Gilroy, Calif.

ANON. 1971K. Easy-open, new markets, new convenience, new profits. Vend 25, No. 8, 19–30.

ANON. 1971L. Seamark 27. Ocean Products, Inc., Tampa, Fla.

BATCHER, O. M., and MURPHEY, C. E. All about meat, that key item in food buying, meal planning. U.S. Dept. of Agriculture Yearbook, 94–116.

BIRD, K. 1965. How Freeze-Drying Works. U.S. Dept. of Agriculture, Washington, D.C.

BIRD, K. 1969. Key factors in successful new foods. Food Technol. 23, 1159–1168.

CASTILLE, M. A., DAWSON, E. H., and THOMPSON, E. R. 1969. The vegetable round up–from buying to cooking. U.S. Dept. of Agriculture Yearbook, 174–195.

CROSBY, V. B., and GULICH, A. R. 1969. Poultry: a tasty anytime delight that's popular dozens of ways. U.S. Dept. of Agriculture Yearbook, 117–126.

DESROSIER, N.W. 1970. The Technology of Food Preservation, 3rd Edition. Avi Publishing Co., Westport, Conn.

GUISLEY, K. G. 1968. Seaweed Colloids. Encyclopedia of Chemical Technology, 2nd Edition, 17, 763–784. John Wiley & Sons, New York.

HANDY, A. E. 1969. Eggs–nature's prepackaged masterpiece of nutrition. U.S. Dept. of Agriculture Yearbook, 139–145.

HENNESSEY, G. R., STANSBURY, M. F., PERSELL, R. M. 1971. USDA creates nutritive functional products. Food Eng. 43, No. 4, 71–74.

JACKSON, R. H. 1970. Convenience food. Feeding the Military Man, 22, No. 1, 50–54.

KAPLOW, M. 1970. Commercial development of intermediate moisture foods. Food Technol. 24, 889–893.

KERR, R. G. 1969. Savvy with seafood. U.S. Dept. of Agriculture Yearbook, 127–130.

LACHANCE, P. A. 1970. The "new" proteins. Food Technol. 24, 239–240.

PECKHAM, G. C. 1969. Foundations of Food Preparation. Macmillan Company, Toronto, Ontario.

ROBINSON, R. F. 1971. Plant proteins. Meat Processing *10*, No. 2, 68.
SMITH, B. 1971. A new language for today's system implementation. Food Service Magazine *33*, No. 6, 8.
THOMPSON, E. R. 1969. The pedigreed pickle is here: new quality in old favorites. U.S. Dept. of Agriculture Yearbook, 244–248.
TRESSLER, D. K., VAN ARSDEL, W. B., and COPELY, M. J. 1968. The Freezing Preservation of Foods, 4th Edition, Vol. 4. Avi Publishing Co., Westport, Conn.
WANDERSTOCK, J. J. 1970. Meat purchasing. The Cornell Hotel & Restaurant Administration Quarterly. *II*, No. 3. 60–64.

Convenience Foods

For reasons of clarity, definition and identification, convenience foods are pre-prepared and frozen foods that require a minimum of preparation, such as heating, garnishing and plating. It was pointed out in Chapter 8, that only a thin dividing line exists between convenience foods and other categories of pre-prepared products, like the endless varieties of edibles packed in cans or jars.

Convenience food forms are gaining general acceptance throughout the entire food service industry. Towards the end of the last decade, a majority of feeding establishments in the United States were using some type of efficiency and convenience products. Surveys recently conducted by the National Frozen Food Association demonstrate the extent to which these products are being used in the food service industry (Fig. 9.1 and 9.2). The meteoric rise of frozen foods is graphically shown in Fig. 9.3. This chart illustrates the growth of 44 food products over a 10 year period.

Noticeable changes in attitude are occurring within the industry, so that the pace of acceptance is dramatically accelerating. New products and innovative ideas are saturating the market. As a result, management that has been glued to tradition is now taking a more objective view of the feasibility of using convenience foods.

Advances in food technology, production and freezing techniques are the underlying reasons for the shift from traditionally prepared to convenience foods. Foods used to manufacture convenience products are harvested at the peak of maturity, or are freshly killed. These are rapidly and uniformly processed and quickly frozen, providing the end user with flavorful and nutritious foods, foods that are superior in many respects to those prepared in the home or restaurant. These are not all ordinary, nor are they haphazardly prepared foods. Many of the products are highly sophisticated concoctions spanning the continents and ethnic backgrounds. They are the result of fully equipped test kitchens and the combined efforts of a number of world-famous chefs. Food service personnel who have been using convenience foods successfully have achieved their goals by proper handling, interesting garnishes, and attractive plating.

Craig Claibourne, former food editor of *The New York Times* and noted culinary authority, is of the opinion that frozen entrées properly manufactured, and correctly prepared and served, are as palatable as those that are freshly cooked. Mr. Claibourne also thinks that "a variety of frozen entrées might upgrade the American palate, which now runs heavily to steak and French fries. Besides such ordinary dishes as pot roast, creamed chicken and spaghetti, there are frozen precooked versions of beef burgundy, coq au vin rouge, sauerbraten, beef Stroganoff and chicken Kiev" (Prestbo 1970).

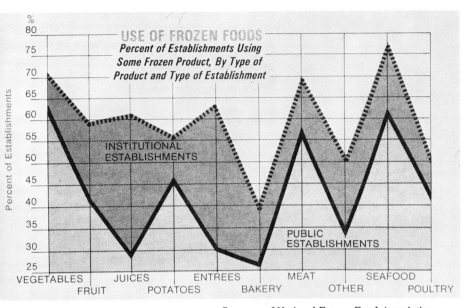

Courtesy of National Frozen Food Association

FIG. 9.1. USE OF FROZEN FOODS BY FOOD SERVICE ESTABLISHMENTS

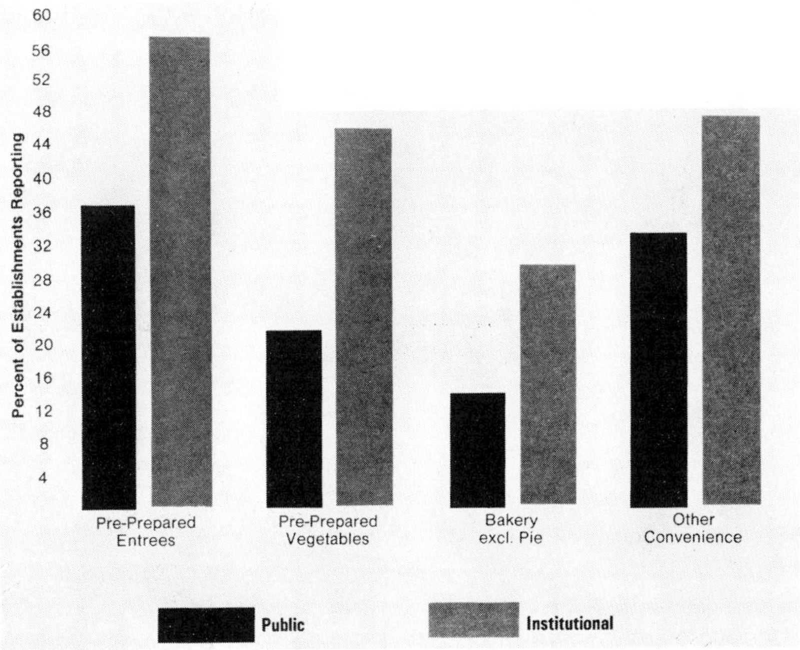

Courtesy of National Frozen Food Association

FIG. 9.2. ACCEPTANCE OF CONVENIENCE PRODUCTS BY FOOD SERVICE INDUSTRY

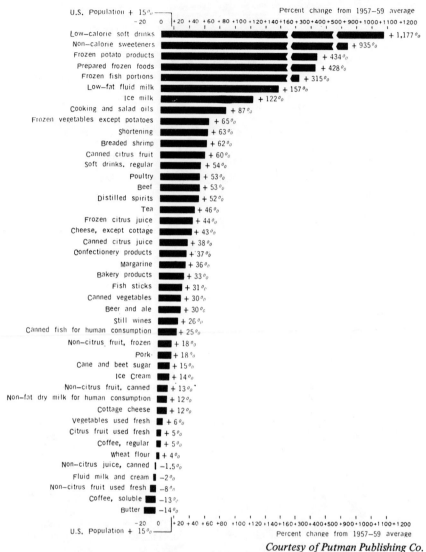

Courtesy of Putman Publishing Co.

FIG. 9.3. A DECADE OF GROWTH: 44 FOOD PRODUCTS

A New Art of Cookery Emerges

Since we are dealing with new concepts of food service, the approach to preparation and mode of serving should be oriented in this direction. Conventional foods and traditional handling should be separated from the new concepts. A fundamental knowledge of cooking is necessary to obtain a fuller understanding of product development.   If this dual idealogy is followed, the role of pre-

prepared foods will become more meaningful. When embarking on a study in this field, the first step, therefore, is to develop it as another branch of the art of cookery.

To further implement this approach, garnishing and plating have emerged as the principal arts within the convenience food field, for they provide the avenues for imagination, creativeness and showmanship. When the art of exploiting these elements is mastered, the opportunity lies open to serve the customer an exciting, effective, and palatable menu, that is both tasty and varied.

Convenience Food Service Base Broadens

All segments of the food service industry are moving into convenience foods, including posh restaurants and hotels. Heretofore, their employment was limited to schools, hospitals, industrial feeding establishments, diners, and drive-ins. This move was necessary because of shrinking profits, increasing labor costs, and lack of suitable employees. Moreover, there has been a concerted effort to streamline operations. Many operators who are engaged in running prestige units are tailoring convenience foods to the image of the establishment. In addition, management is giving greater emphasis to quality assurance techniques than that formerly accorded to conventional service.

A number of food service personnel have become disenchanted with pre-prepared frozen items. However, as proper equipment is installed and methods of handling, heating, reconstitution, garnishing and plating are improved upon and understood, dissatisfaction with this mode of service should lessen.

ADVANTAGES OF CONVENIENCE FOODS

The following are the major advantages of convenience foods:

(1) Intricate culinary skills are not required, since most of these foods are simply heated, garnished and plated. Recipes are not required; in their place, production and preparation instructions are substituted (Fig. 9.4 and 9.5).

(2) The time lag between preparation and final service is reduced.

(3) Over-production is reduced or eliminated, and the use of "left-overs" is no longer a problem.

(4) Waste due to shrinkage and theft is minimized and can be more efficiently controlled.

(5) Portion sizes can be standardized and are more easily controlled. Their costs are more accurately determined.

(6) The environment of the kitchen and/or preparation areas is cleaner and more orderly. Odors are reduced, and temperature and humidity are lower. All these result in better working conditions.

(7) Management has more time to devote to merchandising to provide the customer with added satisfaction. Unique garnishing and plating techniques coupled to efficient service will move the customer into a more relaxed spirit and frame of mind.

Courtesy of Stouffer Food Division of Litton Industries, Inc.

FIG. 9.4. SIMPLE HEATING OF CONVENIENCE FOODS AT CORRECT TEMPERATURE AND TIME FOR QUALITY PRODUCTION—A BASIC REQUIREMENT

(8) Greater flexibility in menu planning and an opportunity to keep up with periodic fads, eating crazes, and the use of nationality foods result.

(9) Foods and beverages are more uniform after the art of handling and preparation have been mastered.

(10) Reduction of raw material inventory, no investment in slow moving merchandise, and easier record keeping result.

(11) Ordering is simplified and receiving is less involved. Both these functions are more orderly and efficient, with fewer employees involved.

(12) Production space is reduced. An efficient and effective work system can be achieved.

(13) Production costs and their respective accounting procedures are less involved and can be determined with greater accuracy.

(14) Flexibility to meet emergency situations is possible, such as raw material shortages, strikes, or sharp price increases.

(15) Greater versatility is possible in handling production during off-hour service and unexpected surges in business.

(16) Sanitation chores relevant to pots, pans and other cooking utensils are reduced.

Courtesy of Stouffer Food Division of Litton Industries, Inc.

FIG. 9.5. AFTER HEATING, FOOD IS PLACED IN STEAM TABLE AND HELD AT PROPER SERVING TEMPERATURE, UNDER STRICT HOLDING PROCEDURES

(17) Packaging requirements can be specified to fit into a particular production flow system.

(18) Nutritional contents of products are available for dietetic control.

(19) Custom or private label formulations are possible to meet the specific needs of large-volume operations.

(20) Purchases can be made in many different quantities and product assortments.

(21) Reliable purveyors can provide uniform and consistent products.

DISADVANTAGES OF CONVENIENCE FOODS

Presently convenience foods offer a number of disadvantages. Many of these, however, are gradually being corrected by better educated, more experienced managers, and by improved products, better distribution, and handling procedures.

A list of those disadvantages follows:

(1) Little or no product standardization, size or type of packaging.

(2) Poor, ineffectual and inadequate training of personnel.

(3) Packages do not have complete instructions for recommended preparation procedures.

(4) National distribution is limited to major cities and their suburbs; many outlying or remote areas cannot obtain a steady flow of merchandise.

(5) A high capital investment is necessary to purchase new equipment to replace existing conventional kitchen facilities.

(6) The initial phases and subsequent introduction of a convenience food system requires cautious and careful planning for ultimate success. Guidance towards this end is often fragmentary and contradictory.

(7) Preparation equipment requires standardization and should be less complicated.

(8) The lack of highly skilled mechanics needed to repair equipment is creating bottle-necks and equipment down-time.

(9) Improper handling of frozen foods, such as incorrect storage temperatures, intermittent thawing, and faulty preparation, is resulting in spoilage, off-flavors, and general low quality.

(10) The need for greater appreciation and imagination on the part of preparation personnel in order to properly garnish and plate foods and make them more appealing and appetizing.

(11) Prolonged power failures may result in business disruptions, hardships, and loss of business.

(12) Discontinuance of established items by manufacturers once they have been merchandised and accepted by the restaurant has created a hardship on the operator.

(13) Operators have become disenchanted if the changes in convenience service do not show an immediate uptrend in profits and business.

(14) Shortages due to labor strikes at the manufacturers or by teamsters can cause numerous hardships.

(15) Overstocking of items because they are considered to be "good buys," only to discover that they move slowly and require valuable storage space.

(16) Too many products on the market, additional ones appearing almost daily, result in misdirected merchandising and sales programs.

(17) Some employees exhibit resistance to convenience foods, assuming that they are ordinary edibles that increase profits and cheat the customer.

CONVERSION TO A CONVENIENCE FOOD PROGRAM

It is relatively easy and less complicated to design, erect, and institute an operation from the blueprint stage to final completion than to convert an established conventional operation. When conversion is undertaken, however, major and at times insurmountable problems may arise.

Use of Traditional Equipment

At the inception of a contemplated conversion, the question of utilizing present equipment is usually posed. Traditional forms of equipment are usable, especially when a trial or test program is to be undertaken. Conventional ovens are usable until it becomes necessary to replace them with convection, micro-wave or with some other type of fast heating oven. Pouch-packed food can be heated in vessels containing water.

The Starting Point

A logical starting point, when embarking on a trial program, is to select and feature one convenience food entrée. If the restaurant is service-oriented and menus are employed, the item can be featured as a "clip-on" display. The same entrée should be featured once a week for four weeks. If the customer reaction is favorable, the next step is to select and feature a second item. The two entrées can then be featured on different days. An 8- to 12-week trial period is ample time to collect sufficient operational data, so that a meaningful evaluation can be made. If after the eighth week superficial signs point to success, then two more entrées should be featured, for a total of four.

Of the four main categories of entrées (meat, poultry, casseroles or pies, and fish) the featured selections should be based on the mode and popularity of the accustomed service. For example, if fish is not popular with the clientele, it should not be featured, since it will not be possible to collect enough data to determine the merits of the program.

Test Data Evaluation

The data collected from the trials should supply the pertinent answers regard-ing the feasibility of a conversion. The following questions raise salient points that require evaluation:

(1) Did the customer receive faster service?

(2) Did the tables "turn over" faster? Visual time checks will have to be made for customers who ordered the test entrée.

(3) Is waste reduced?

(4) Is ordering and inventory control of the test entrées less complicated?

(5) Has there been adverse customer criticism?

(6) Has there been favorable customer reaction?

(7) Have any of the kitchen personnel resisted the change?

(8) Have any of the service personnel resisted the change? Were any unflat-tering remarks made to the customers, such as, "Don't order the item since it's factory prepared," etc.?

(9) If resistance did occur, can it be coped with without damage to the employee and customer relationship?

(10) Will the resistance result in a loss of business and image?

(11) Was it easier to "cost-out" the item?

(12) Will sales forecasting prove more useful?

(13) If the entrée required garnishing, seasoning and special plating, were the recommended procedures properly followed?

(14) Were the entrées more uniform or equal in uniformity when compared to items prepared by traditional means?

(15) Would it be possible to reduce labor costs if more convenience entrées were added?

(16) If nationality or ethnic entrées were served, did they attract new customers who would not usually frequent the restaurant?

(17) Did the convenience test entrées meet your quality standards?

(18) Was the purveyor's service adequate?

(19) Did the preparation of the test entrées interfere with normal kitchen procedures?

CATEGORIES OF CONVENIENCE FOODS

Convenience foods are manufactured in every conceivable category. The number of items on the market is endless. Because of the continuous influx of new dishes, product surveys are valid for relatively short periods of time, so that any actual count of the available production becomes dated. The following are the product categories: appetizers, soups, entrées, specialty entrées, vegetables, salads, bread and rolls, desserts and beverages. Examples of convenience products available under each main category:

Appetizers (including snacks, hors d'oeuvres):
Juices, fish, fruit cocktail, chicken and beef liver, patés, shellfish (escargot, mussels) shrimp, stuffed clams and oysters, cheese puffs and whirls, egg roll, stuffed cabbage.

Soups:
Chowders (corn, clam), bisques, purées, minestrone, vegetable, chicken, cream of potato, oyster stew, cream of shrimp, beef, green pea plain, green pea with ham, barley and mushroom, onion, egg drop, won ton.

Entrées:
Seafood, beef, poultry products, lamb, pork, pasta, casseroles, pies, stews.

Specialty Entrées:
Nationality foods such as beef Stroganoff, cheese ravioli, chicken Cacciatore, manicotti, lasagne, pizza, eggplant and veal Parmigiana, veal scallopini, blintzes, tortillas, tamales with chili, chow mein (chicken, shrimp, beef, vegetable), chicken Kiev, chicken Polynesian, chicken Tetrazzini, chicken a la cordon bleu, beef Burgundy, chicken coq au vin, sauerbraten, scallops Florentine, beef enchilada, beef filet de Boeuf Wellington, beef Bourguignonne, pancakes, sausages, egg and egg products, waffles.

Vegetables:
Blanched, potatoes, onions, Spanish and buttered rice, rice Verdi and Pilaf, spinach soufflé, and vegetables Bavarian, Danish, Japanese, Mexican, Spanish, and Chinese, potatoes stuffed with chives, and other potato dishes.

Salads:
Fish, meat, tossed, fruit, and other prepared salads.

Bread and Rolls:

Rolls (all types, such as Danish, cinnamon, Croissants, finger, Parker House, sesame and bagels).

Breads, such as sliced rye, white, garlic, cinnamon, raisin, dark, black, corn, potato.

Muffins, blueberry, corn, bran, nut.

French toast, crumpets.

Desserts:

Puddings, fritters, cake and pies (many varieties).

Many nationality desserts.

Beverages (non-alcoholic):

Soft drinks (post-mix dispensers).

Ice tea from dispensers.

Hot tea (tea bag).

Coffee (freeze-dried and frozen liquid concentrate).

Ades (post-mix and reconstituted from powder mixes).

Juices (from post-mix dispensers).

GARNISHING

The emergence of pre-prepared frozen entrées on a broad scale has revived the importance of garnishing and in addition, has led to innovative methods of food handling, preparation and plating. If an organization is to achieve sustained success in this field, emphasis must be placed on garnishing and plating. These are the two essentials that provide the customer with excitement and satisfaction. In addition, the patron's inner mood is stimulated, which brings about a sense of enjoyment and thus sets the stage for a return visit, and a favorable recommendation to others.

To avoid the stamp of bland and stereotyped food, management must be creative and imaginative. A bit of showmanship and ingenuity will go a long way in attaining an effective, palatable, attractive and quality convenience food service (Fig. 9.6).

The "Garnish Chef"

A relatively new food specialist has materialized in recent years; namely, a person capable of accomplishing the goals of creating an attractive and appealing convenience food service. The person responsible for these functions is referred to as the "garnish chef." Besides supervising and programming methods and schemes for garnishes, he has the duties of preparing sauces, gravies, dressings, the addition of spices, and plans plating patterns. His aims are to present the food in a tasty, attractive and appetizing manner.

Courtesy of American Spice Trade Association

FIG. 9.6. AN EXAMPLE OF ATTRACTIVE PLATING AND
GARNISHING. DISH CONSISTS OF CURRIED CHICKEN AND
RICE WITH GARNISHES

What Are Garnishes?

French chefs define garnishes as all the accompaniments that are served with the main dish or entrée. The French call it *garni*. The noun garniture is also employed, which refers to something that garnishes, an embellishment, or something that decorates.

The American defines garnishes as simple decorations or accessories designed to increase eye appeal, impart attractiveness, and stimulate the appetite. Many products and devices are employed for this purpose: olives, nuts, radishes, tomato slices or wedges, parsley, cucumbers, egg forms, berries, fruit slices, lemon, mushrooms, yogurt, cheeses, paprika, decorative forms of soft cheese, mayonnaise, whipped products, bacon bits, carrots, celery, interesting bread and cracker shapes, and other products which serve a similar function. In addition to edibles, interesting geometric designs and attractive plates can be developed for these purposes.

The French include all the products and devices considered to be garnishes by the Americans, plus everything else that is served with the entrée. These may consist of gravies, sauces, relishes, butters, cheese, potatoes, stuffing, and all vegetables. These items may be served with the entrée or on separate plates. The French name their garnishes either from the locality where they originated or from the chef who devised them. Many dishes are named from the accompanying garnish.

The Scandinavians are considered to be masters of decorative garnishes. The Smörgåsbord or open sandwiches are creative, colorful, and simple. They produce excitement and create an inner feeling of enjoyment.

Since it is necessary to produce a dish that goes beyond simple embellishments, the French method of total garnishing is recommended. For this discussion the subject is separated into three parts, namely: garnishes for decorations, plating and geometric forms, and sauces.

Definition of Entrée.—Entrées generally consist of fish, meat or poultry. However, they can also be composed of dishes like macaroni and cheese or eggplant parmigiana. A main course with no more than one vegetable is still considered an entrée; with two or more vegetables, it becomes a dinner (Tressler, Van Arsdel, and Copley 1968).

Classes of Garnishes

Garnishes fall into three classes: (1) those used solely for decoration; (2) those used for decoration and are edible; (3) and those that form an integral part of the entrée.

Garnishes as Decorations.—Decorative garnishes are employed to attract or enhance eye appeal. The correct and balanced use of color becomes an essential aspect of these adornments. Colors that clash will tend to downgrade the appeal factor. Too much of one color will create an unbalanced display. Follow the scheme employed by artists, by using the primary colors yellow, red and blue. Restrict the display to as few colors as possible. The fewer colors used, the easier it is to obtain color harmony. Every time a new color is added, the risk of creating discord is increased.

Secondary and complementary colors are attractive and blend well. The complement of each shade is directly opposite it on a color wheel (Fig 9.7). Colors that suggest warmth are yellow and red; blue, violet and dark green give a cool effect. Too much white will create a washed-out or bland appearance, whereas too many dark areas result in a somber, dreary mood. If the plate is dark, light colors should be used, and if light, the darker hues. The same idea applies to light or dark entrées. Color tinting or shading can be accomplished by mixing a small amount of a certified food color in juices, syrups or gelatin. Beet, cherry and other liquids can also be used. Tinting produces soft engaging tones.

When selecting decorative type garnishes do not make them too elaborate. Avoid a gaudy display; it will tend to downgrade appeal. Garnishes that are simple and blend into the entrée impart a more natural appearance and effect. Garnish placement in relation to the main dish is important. Try to avoid a

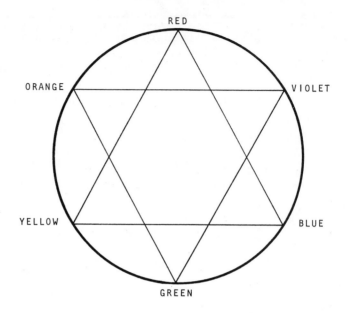

Primary Colors: red, yellow, blue

Secondary Colors: orange, violet, green

FIG. 9.7. PRIMARY AND SECONDARY COLOR WHEEL

"machined" and "wooden-like" appearance, which will create the illusion of blandness and triteness. Try to animate the plate by placing the embellishments lightly and according to some prearranged plan. Garnish placement should become a part of the preparation schedule. Planning should entail a simple drawing of the dish and location of each product. It may be necessary to photograph the finished dish. The picture can then be hung at the garnishing station. Many multi-unit companies use illustrated manuals that contain recipes, methods of preparation, portion sizes and colored photographs of each dish.

Examples of decorative garnishes are: ice forms and ice beds, paprika, watercress, interesting plate shapes, forms of hard sugar icing, plastic cocquille and potato shells, small flower petals, buds, paper doilies, sprigs of various herbs. Avoid using a single sprig of parsley. For primary color decorations try curled lemon peel, a small red pepper, a strip of pimento, mint sprig, a spinach leaf, a small bunch of violet-blue grapes, curly endive, strips of red or green cabbage, dyed raw potato wedges, dyed cauliflower flowerets. Various uniquely shaped bread slices or crackers can also be used as adornments.

Edible and Decorative Garnishes.—These garnishes are used for decorating and can be eaten along with the entrée. An almost unlimited number of products are available for these adornments. Dual-purpose garnishes should possess certain characteristics to make them interesting. These may include: flavor to enhance or subdue the character of the entrée; appealing color, shapes, forms and particle size; and a good texture. Fruits, nuts, spices, meats, fish, herbs, vegetables, relishes, condiments, preserves, gelatins, breads and crackers are examples of these products.

Textured garnishes, if properly used, are highly favored. These include nuts, croutons, coconut, olives (sliced, diced, whole), diced fruit, colored glazed fruit, diced or sliced cheese, bacon bits, raisins, diced dates, cherries.

Integral Garnishes.—These garnishes form an integral part of the entrée. They are used to produce or reduce flavor. These may be sauces, gravies, relishes, condiments, stuffing, glazes, nuts, spices, meat, fish and poultry products. Besides the addition of color or contrast, they should be employed with entrées that exhibit compatible flavor characteristics. Sweet and sour products will blend well with entrées of a similar nature. Those that are overly sour, too sweet, or extremely tart or spicy will cause flavor imbalance.

Shapes and Dimensions.—The shape or form and size of the garnish is important to the success of the overall display. These factors require as much study as the kind of garnish that is to be added. Several small or sliced olives may be more appealing than a large whole one. A lemon slice may not be as attractive as a wedge. Several melon balls may look more appetizing than a melon wedge. A round shape may prove to be more suitable than a rectangle. Julienne and slivered cuts may be beneficial in creating a desired effect.

The dimensions of the embellishment must be studied in its relationship to the entrée. It should not distract or overshadow the main or featured item. Harmony and rhythm will result if the size of the garnish fits the proportions of the entrée. Too much or too little of the product will tend to spoil the desired effect. Accenting is a basic reason for decorative garnishes. If the proportions are wrong, eye appeal is reduced. Wrong proportions result in confusion and poor registration.

Plating

The effects of an attractive garnish will be lost if the dish or plate on which the food is placed is not appropriate. Attractive and interesting plates are accessory garnishes. The correct size of plate is another factor to be considered. It should not be too large, nor too small for the portion.

The selection of dishes should be made with infinite care, at the initial planning stages when the menu is formulated. Regardless of whether the dishes are disposable or permanent, careful study is essential (Fig. 9.9). Because of the high cost, permanent wares are seldom changed to correct mistakes. Disposables, on the other hand, can be changed with each order.

The choice of plates is as important as the decor. Plates should blend into or complement the surroundings. Numerous styles and shapes of dishes are marketed. Novelty dishes can create excitement and eye appeal. These may be odd-

Courtesy of Stouffer Food Division of Litton Industries, Inc.

FIG. 9.8. AN ATTRACTIVE PREARRANGED PATIENT'S DIN-
NER TRAY, WITH FESTIVE TOUCH, AT TUCSON MEDICAL
CENTER, ARIZONA

Courtesy of Gulf States Paper Corporation

FIG. 9.9. ATTRACTIVELY ARRANGED DISPOSABLE DISHES

shaped dishes for desserts, metal ware for entrées, or fish forms for seafood. Many novelty designs are made for children. Service ware, which is a dominant feature of fine European restaurants and *haute cuisine* places in this country, imparts elegance and glamor to a table setting (Fig. 9.10).

Monochrome or one-color dishes are ideally suited for high-contrast entrées, and those items that may cover the full surface of the plate, such as salads, stews, and casseroles. Dishes that are highly colored or have ornate patterns are appropriate for entrées which have the same overall tone, such as a lobster Newburg.

Courtesy of American Spice Trade Association

FIG. 9.10. CHICKEN AND MUSHROOM MARENGO ATTRACTIVELY PLATED

Utensils such as knives, forks and spoons should also be selected with care. If they are too heavy or too light, the effect will tend to downgrade the service. Inexpensive utensils may impart a metallic character to the food.

The Garnishing Station

The volume of the establishment and the number of items listed on the menu are the guides for evaluating the number of garnishing stations necessary for expedient service. For a small to medium-sized operation, one all-purpose station may be sufficient. For a high-volume establishment or one that has many items on the menu, two or more stations may be necessary. These may be separated into hot and cold garnish stations.

Garnish stations should be designed to allow for unobstructed production flow. The area should contain ample shelving, under-the-counter refrigeration, a small sink, trunnion kettle, mixer or blender, bain marie, small pans that fit into counter slots so that their base is refrigerated, and a bulletin board to hold garnishing instructions.

An ideally designed station could be shaped like a crescent or semi-circle (organ console). By standing in the center, the employee can comfortably reach all the garnishing ingredients. A minimum of two shelves is required to hold the containers of herbs, spices and condiments. Spice containers must be covered, and each should have its own measuring spoon to avoid mixing and contamination. A central spice storage closet or locker should be constructed to store all spices and herbs. Only those spices needed for immediate use should be placed in the garnish area (Fig. 9.11).

The lower shelf may contain pans of nuts, sliced fruit, olives, pickles and other garnishes. Items such as fruits, pickles and olives should be kept moist, but not sopping wet. Excess moisture can be removed by blotting on absorbent paper. Salad garnishes, including lettuce, should be kept dry and crisp. Soggy lettuce or leaves with brown edges should not be used.

Depending on the number of sauces and gravies, one or two small trunnion kettles should be sufficient. A small bain marie is required to keep sauces and gravies at their proper temperature. Sauces and gravies should be prepared at frequent intervals to retain their fresh, tasty and zesty character.

Garnish Costs

The costs of all garnishes should be calculated and added to the price of the entrée. Those products that require computation, and at times are forgotten, are: portions of jelly, mustard, spices, herbs, relishes, and other small or minor accompaniments. Start the calculation with the number of portions that can be obtained from a unit measure. If, for example, the product is packed in 1-lb containers, determine the cost per pound and the approximate number of portions each unit will yield. The resulting figure will denote the cost per portion. Total all the garnishing costs and add it to the cost of the entrée. The cost of all

Courtesy of American Spice Trade Association

FIG. 9.11. POACHED FLOUNDER WITH HERBED TOMATO SAUCE, ATTRACTIVELY GARNISHED. PROPERLY COVERED AND LABELED SPICE CANISTERS ARE ALSO SHOWN

garnishes and other accompaniments can also be totalled and figured separately to determine their percentage of the food cost.

Suggested Garnish Applications

The following are selected examples of garnishes that are compatible with a fast convenience food operation:

(1) Appetizers.—Cucumbers (sliced, scalloped), sliced beets, carrots (sliced, diced, slivered, curled), radishes (sliced, whole, flowered), green and red peppers

(sliced, diced), pimento (diced, slivered), olives (green, ripe) stuffed and unstuffed (sliced, whole), anchovies, sardines, smoked salmon (lox), small sweet gherkins, pickled vegetables, various pickles, small cocktail onions, onion (slices and diced), parsley (minced, sprigs), chives (minced or sprigs), slivers of cold luncheon meat, nuts, cheese (bits, chunks, slices), water chestnuts, paprika, stuffed dill pickles, stuffed celery, frozen avocado pulp; fancy toothpicks, doilies.

Canapé garnishes: hard-cooked eggs (chopped, sliced or wedges), olives, cucumbers (sliced, chopped), pickles, pimento, soft cheese such as cream that is spread with a pastry decorator, paprika, chopped onions, nuts, mushrooms, anchovy, beets, hard cheese, herring, liver, bacon bits.

(2) **Soups.**—(a) *Clear soup:* avocado bits or pulp and whipped, minced herbs, parsley, watercress, citrus fruit slices, dusting of nutmeg, finely grated raw vegetables, carrots, celery, diced meat, croutons, chives, toasted sesame flakes, tomato, vermicelli, rice, noodles, mushrooms, thin lemon slices, egg drop and chow mein noodles.

(b) *Thick soup:* sliced frankfurters, sliced hard cooked eggs, dusting of cooked egg yolk, croutons, grated cheese, diced cold meats, chicken, veal, bacon bits, noodles.

(c) *Cream soup* (bisques): ball of whipped cream, almonds, minced herbs and spices, small cream puffs, diced or slivered vegetables, parsley, diced meat, diced chicken, sherry.

(d) *Miscellaneous soups*

Asparagus: paprika.

Bean: bacon bits, sliced frankfurters, sliced lemon, toasted bread cubes, grated cheese, cream sherry, croutons, grated carrots.

Carrot: ripe olive rings, parsley.

Celery: almonds, chives, parsley, browned bacon and onion.

Chowder: macaroni rings, lemon slices, cheese.

Chicken: pimento, carrot bits, green pepper, grated cheese, ham and almonds.

Corn: pimento, carrot bits, green pepper.

Mushroom: bread crumbs, minced olives.

Onion: croutons.

Pea: frankfurters, pimento, carrots, paprika, croutons, bacon bits, noodles, chopped ham, popped corn.

Potato: chives, parsley, paprika.

Tomato: cream, croutons, herbs, almonds, bacon bits, diced or shredded pepper, cucumber, popped corn, cereal flakes.

Vegetable: cheese chunks or grated, beef chunks, meatballs, mushroom, various macaroni products.

(3) **Fish.**—Watercress, parsley, bacon bits, browned butter, various forms of onions, chopped or diced hard cooked eggs, celery slices, lemon slices or wedges,

lemon slices dusted with cooked egg yolk, lemon dusted with parsley, radish forms, sweet and sour cucumber slices (vinegar, sour cream); tomatoes (baked, broiled, raw and sprinkled with herbs, capers, various pickles); various sauces (hollandaise, curry, creole, egg, anchovy); various butter combinations (lemon, parsley, anchovy); citrus fruit slices, chives, olives, raisins, almonds, mushrooms (Fig. 9.12).

Courtesy of American Spice Trade Association

FIG. 9.12. POACHING FISH ROLLS THAT ARE ATTRACTIVELY GARNISHED WITH VARIOUS SPICES AND HERBS

(4) **Meat and Poultry.**—Herbs, pepper slices, cucumbers, jellied cranberry, pimento, fruit slices, mint, mint and other jellies, lemon forms, truffles, mushrooms, carrot forms (raw and cooked); tomatoes (baked, broiled, raw, cored and stuffed); chive butter, shallot butter; peaches and pears (cups up) filled with chutney, chopped dill pickles, relishes, cherries, almonds, minted pears, raisin in ham sauce, decorated ruffled potatoes around a stew, horse radish, small onions.

(5) **Miscellaneous Garnishes.**—

Apples: salads, in waffles, fritters, with meat, diced in stuffing, with duck, broiled slices with meat.

Bamboo shoots: with chicken, in stews, pork, Oriental dishes.

Breakfast cereal flakes: topping for casseroles, in soup, or as a breading.

Cherries (frozen): with chicken, tuna and ham salads, in sauce for meat and meat balls, on fish, pancakes, waffles, French toast, omelets, Waldorf salad, cole slaw, cottage cheese, in poultry stuffing, in Oriental dishes, add to relishes, in sweet and sour recipes.

Chives: in sour cream for baked potatoes, fish, sprinkle on hors d'oeuvres, fish salads, on yams, on onion and cheese soup, on mayonnaise, soufflés, scrambled eggs, cream soups, chive butter for meat.

Fruit butters: with meats, fish, salads.

Horseradish: boiled beef, fish, spare ribs.

Kumquats (boiled or candied): with Oriental dishes, salads, meat, and stuffed with cream cheese.

Mushrooms: sliced or chopped for sauces, soups, stuffing and fish dishes, stew, veal parmesan, spaghetti, salads, sandwiches, in vegetables.

Green Noodles: with Italian veal dishes, as a topping for vegetables, in soup, in casseroles, in salads.

Ripe Olives: shrimp creole, seafood, chicken fricasse, beef stew, spaghetti sauce, chili con carne.

Cling Peaches: with pork, steak (filled with horseradish and sour cream or relish) with fish, with eggs, waffles, in salads, broiled with various fillings.

Minted Pears: pork chops, fresh ham or lamb.

Pineapple: in or with salads, souffles, as tidbits, broiled or sautéed with meat, in Oriental dishes. Adds texture, flavor and aroma.

Prunes: fruit salad, turkey, regular salads, fruit plate, compote, egg garnish, fruit gravies, tuna salad.

Raisins: ham sauce, carrot salad, barbecue sauce, poultry stuffing, syrups for pancakes and waffles.

Sesame (toasted flaked): seasonings, breading mixes, sprinkle on casseroles, mix with nuts for fish.

(6) **Nuts.**—Nuts are an excellent garnish. They can be used whole, cut, broken, ground, raw or roasted. Common nuts can be substituted for one another with the exception of chestnuts, coconuts, and black walnuts. Sweetened coconut, grated or shredded and toasted or untoasted, can be used on poultry, fish, on salads, in sauces and Oriental dishes. Chestnuts have many novel applications. These nuts are starchy and have a texture similar to the potato. Each type of nut will add its own special flavor. Salted nuts should not be used as edible food garnishes. Black walnuts can be used as a primary food flavoring. They should be applied raw, never roasted. To extend nut flavor in foods, use small pieces or slices. Their flavor is enhanced with brown sugar or by adding a small amount of maple syrup or almond flavor. The following are suggested uses for nuts:

Add toasted nuts to creamed or saucy meat dishes or vegetables.

Add nuts to sour cream for meat or baked potatoes.
Add nuts to meat, poultry or to seafood salads.
Add slivered or sliced nuts to tossed vegetable salads.
Add small cream cheese nut balls to jellied salads.
Mix coconut with food color for a topping.
Pistachio nuts are excellent for color contrast and flavor.
(7) **Spices and Herbs.**—Table 9.1 lists the popular spices and herbs for garnishing.

TABLE 9.1

SPICES AND HERBS AS GARNISHES

Spice or Herb	Typical Garnish Applications
Allspice	pickles, relishes
Basil	herb dressings, stuffing, tomato sauces
Bay leaves	pickled meats, salad dressing, sauces
Caraway seeds	cheese, cole slaw, sauerkraut
Celery flakes	potato salad, meat sauces
Celery seed	cole slaw, salad dressing, pickles
Chili powder	cheese, chili, baked fish
Cinnamon	pickles, relishes, pickled meats and seafood; spiced fruit
Cloves	pickles; relishes, ham, spiced fruits
Dill seed	pickles, spiced vegetables, marinated shrimp
Ginger	pickles, relishes, pickled meats
Marjoram	salad dressings, stuffings
Oregano	pizza, Italian sauces, salad dressings
Paprika	salad dressings, sausages, casseroles, cottage cheese, soups, baked fish, salads, cheese dips
Black pepper	pickles, relishes, spiced meats and vegetables, salad dressing
Poppy seed	noodle pudding, cheese
Saffron	Sauces, Spanish-type casseroles, rice
Sage	poultry stuffing, sausages
Sweet pepper flakes	relishes, salads, stewed tomatoes, dressing, sauces
Tarragon	salad dressings, herb vinegar, sauces
Thyme	salad dressings, clam chowder, oyster stew
Tumeric	sauces, pickles, relishes, prepared mustard

Source: American Spice Trade Association.

SAUCES AND GRAVIES

Sauces

Sauces are the specialties of French cuisine and the foundation of the true art of cooking. They are the elixir of the gourmet and the bane of weight watchers. The world's leading chefs are perfectionists in sauce cookery. The saucier chef is second in command in French kitchens.

Compositions of sauces are countless and combinations unlimited. Variations of identically named sauces are many. For example, hollandaise is a generic name for a variety of mixtures representing this category. The same holds true for other commonly accepted sauces. Sauces are like soup: their basic ingredients or stock are fish, poultry or vegetable. However, combinations vary from simple mixtures to complex recipes. Flavor covers a wide range, from mild to strong; the consistency is from thin to thick liquids.

Functions of Sauces.—Sauces are any flavorful soft or liquid dressing, relish or seasoning served as an accompaniment to food. They are used for moistening, flavor control and as a garnish to make the food more appealing. Sauces have a long history. Those with strong flavors were once employed to depress the character of poor quality meats and other food. As a garnish, sauces provide contrast and enliven the appearance. For example, wet-cooked meat which is gray may be covered with a red sauce; pasta with a green or red sauce; and roast meat with a clear brown sauce.

Gravies are defined as the juices that drip from cooking meat, poultry or fish. They are made into sauces by thickening and seasoning, and should impart the flavor of the food with which they are served.

Although one of the functions of sauces is to moisten, the amount placed on a food should be small in relation to the product or entrée. Sauces that are thin and "run" so that they do not adhere to the food are of little value. Thin sauces should be served separately as dips.

The Anatomy of Sauces.—The earliest sauces were probably simple mixtures of juices and pulped foods. When spices and herbs were discovered, they were added by dusting or sprinkling on the food. Highly flavored fruits and herbs were used to mask old meat flavors and spoiled food. With the development of corned and pickled meats, highly seasoned sauces were added to improve the flavor. Unfortunately, sauces are still used to cover up cooking mistakes, on left overs, or on poor-quality products. However, the intent of sauces is not to disguise, but to add appeal and flavor.

A simple sauce, other than water, is a clear salad dressing, consisting of vinegar, oil, salt and pepper. This product serves two functions: seasoning and wetting. This mixture may benefit lettuce, but it does not go well with other foods such as vegetables. This simple sauce has its drawbacks, as it is watery and unstable. Successful sauces should have a smooth, velvety viscous consistency, with all its ingredients in a stable state. To improve upon the texture of a simple sauce, a stablilizer is added, which holds the components together, thus imparting a pleasing mouth feel. To further a sauce's value, various sizes and kinds of solids are added to make them more compatible with food.

Basic Composition of Sauces.—The compositions of sauces are infinite; however, their basic ingredients may be classified under four headings: (1) liquid carrier, (2) fats and oils, (3) thickeners, (4) sweetening and flavoring agents.

Liquid carriers may include water, non-alcoholic and alcoholic (beer, wine) beverages, milk, soup stock, vegetable juices or marinades. Meat sauces are prepared from stock. These are thin-flavored liquids. Their flavor is obtained from poultry, meat, or vegetables. The kinds of commonly used stocks are fish, brown, white and clear.

Fats and oils employed are from meat, poultry, fish or plants.

Thickeners commonly used are starches (corn, waxy maize, potato, flour, gums, or any combination of these). The traditional thickeners are the light and brown *roux*. Roux is a cooked combination of fat, margarine or butter, and flour. Other products that make excellent thickeners are cream, eggs and butter.

Flavoring ingredients are unlimited in numbers and include herbs, spices, salt, vegetables, fruit, mushrooms, and cheese.

Sweeteners most commonly employed are sugar, corn syrup or corn syrup solids and corn sugar.

Basic Sauces.—Classic varieties are the French white and brown sauces, the German white sauce, and mayonnaise. Basic categories are Bechémal or white sauce; Velouté or golden sauce; espagnole or brown; hollandaise or white to yellow sauce.

The Color of Sauces.—Color is an essential property of sauces. Since sauces provide eye appeal, the proper coloring performs the function of an attractive garnish. Sauces obtain their color from plant matter, dairy products and egg yolks. Only the plant material imports a clear, transparent color to a sauce.

Red Sauces.—The color is derived from tomatoes, paprika, or red pimientos. Beets and beet juice are also excellent since they yield brilliant hues. Cranberry products also provide a good red color. Convenience variations include tomato paste, tomato sauce, tomato sauce with okra, and tomato sauce with onion and pepper.

Yellow Sauces.—The yellow sauces derive their color from egg yolk, pineapple, saffron and white wine. Juices from canned chunks, slices or crushed pineapple provide a clear golden sauce.

Green Sauces.—Puréed spinach or parsley are excellent for green coloring. Artichoke pulp, chard, beet greens, and avocado are used for tinting and as colored particles.

Gravies

Gravies are similar to sauces. They are the juices of meats, fish, poultry and vegetables with the addition of spices and herbs. Gravies are an important part of precooked frozen foods. They enhance the appearance, protect them from loss of moisture during freezing and storage, and protect meat fats from oxidative rancidity during storage.

Gravy is best when served hot. A tepid, thick, floury product will downgrade the food's quality.

Effects of Frozen Storage on Sauces, Gravies and Dressings

Sauces, gravies and salad dressings all have characteristic structures that may be damaged during freezing, storage and thawing. The starch in sauces and gravies and the oil and starch in salad dressings are the key ingredients which may contribute to a structural breakdown. Those that are thickened with common cereal flour and starches appear curdled after freezing and thawing. Although heating to serving temperature improves the appearance somewhat, the original character is not entirely restored. Those sauces and gravies prepared with waxy rice or other waxy cereals have the greatest stability. So-called "freeze-resistant" starches have proved to be of value for use in sauces and gravies that are to be frozen. In some products, like frozen meat pot pies, some wheat flour is used to produce the desired flavor, opacity and texture. Freeze-stability is attained by using waxy starch or flour with wheat flour at about a 50:50 ratio.

Some sauces are prepared with a high consistency without the use of starchy thickening agents. Stability is excellent and the assortment of sauces available is substantial. Cocktail and creole sauces are prepared in this manner.

Composition and Applications of Sauces

The literature encompassing sauces, gravies, and marinades is vast and is ably covered in numerous cook books. No attempt is made in the following discussion to duplicate these writings. However, to help build a foundation and understanding of the subject and align it with convenience foods, it is necessary to briefly touch upon and develop the basic elements, composition and applications of a number of popular sauces, gravies and marinades.

White Sauces.—*Béchamel* and *Velouté* are the standard white sauces. Béchamel may consist of a light roux, milk and seasonings. Butter is suggested to produce a delicate flavor. Velouté has the addition of poultry, meat or fish stock, which is added to the roux. There are many variations and interpretations of the basic recipes. These sauces are excellent for vegetables, egg dishes, meat, poultry and serve as the basis for cream soups and soufflés. They also form the base for a number of white sauce combinations.

Cream sauce is Béchamel enriched with cream in place of milk.

Supreme sauce is Velouté enriched with cream in place of milk.

Mornay sauce is made from either of the two basic white sauces. Cheese and a small amount of French mustard are added. The cheese may be grated Swiss or a combination of Parmesan and Swiss. Mornay sauce is excellent on hash, egg dishes, fish, pastas and veal.

Cheese sauce may consist of butter, milk, processed cheese, such as American, with or without flour. The sauce is seasoned with mustard, cayenne, and other spices. This sauce may be used on vegetables, such as, asparagus, broccoli, potatoes and cauliflower.

Poulette sauce may consist of Velouté and meat or fish stock for extra flavor, plus onions, celery, cayenne, egg yolks, and mushrooms. Cream may be added for enrichment. This sauce goes well with cucumbers, and soufflés.

Cardinal sauce is Velouté sauce with fish stock and a shellfish butter mixture. Generally used on shellfish.

Egg sauces are Béchamel or Velouté enriched with egg yolks and cream. Used on fish, poultry, vegetables: excellent for poached or boiled fish and some Italian dishes.

White Mustard sauce may consist of Béchamel with French mustard and cream added. Used on fish. Other variations employing Béchamel or Velouté sauces are: pimiento, celery and onion, parsley, oyster, cheese and tomato, caper, curry, white wine and tarragon sauce, anchovy and horseradish sauces.

Brown Sauces.—Brown sauces are widely used on broiled chicken, roasts, steaks, pork, and for a variety of other dishes. The basic brown sauce consists of brown roux, flour, stock or bouillon, and seasonings. Wine such as Madeira or sherry and Worcestershire sauce are optional ingredients.

Brown mushroom sauce may consist of brown sauce with sautéed mushrooms, tomato paste or purée, seasonings and white wine. This is a popular American sauce and is used on egg dishes, pastas, broiled or sautéed poultry and meat.

Ragout brown sauce may consist of the basic brown mixture with tomato and herbs.

Ragout and tomato sauce is the ragout brown mixture with tomato and herbs.

Madeira sauce contains Madeira wine which is added to the brown sauce. This is a medium-consistency sauce and is excellent for egg dishes, ham, beef slices and veal.

Bordelaise sauce may contain minced onion, thyme, white pepper, bay leaf, garlic, sherry wine and brown sauce. For meat such as steak, hamburgers and egg entrées.

Diable or pepper sauce is a brown sauce with black and cayenne pepper, shallots, butter and herbs. This sauce may be used on broiled chicken, pork and pot roast.

Robert sauce is a popular sauce and may contain brown sauce, onions, butter, white dry wine, French prepared mustard and parsley.

Tomato Sauces.—Tomato sauce is another basic sauce to which other ingredients are added or it can be used alone. Tomato sauce may consist of vegetables (diced carrots, celery, onion), meat (ham or bacon bits), butter, olive oil, flour, stock, tomatoes (paste, canned, purée) and seasonings (thyme, bay leaf, tarragon, garlic, sugar and salt).

Hunter's sauce may contain tomato sauce, dry white wine or brandy, butter, minced onions, mushrooms and seasonings (parsley flakes, thyme and white pepper).

Creole sauce may consist of flour, brown sauce, green pepper, onion, olives and tomatoes (pulped or paste), seasoning (pepper, sugar, cloves, celery). Used on meat loaf, boiled beef, fish, rice, pasta and egg dishes.

Spanish sauce may contain tomatoes, mushrooms, paprika, chili, sugar, Worcestershire sauce, flour, shortening and green pepper, onions and paprika.

Barbecue sauce may consist of tomato purée, red pepper, onion, cloves, chili, allspice, garlic, mustard, vinegar and sugar. For spare ribs, pork chops, meats.

Milanese sauce may consist of tomato sauce, mushrooms, ham, (cut or diced), and Parmesan cheese. Used primarily on pasta dishes.

Hollandaise Sauce.—Basic hollandaise contains egg yolk, butter and lemon. This sauce or variations of it are gaining favor in America. It is used on vegetables and fish (poached, steamed or boiled) and eggs Benedict.

Mock hollandaise sauce contains egg yolks, butter, lemon juice or vinegar, milk and flour.

Mandarin sauce is a combination of green pepper, chutney, sesame seeds and oil, which are added to hollandaise sauce.

Béarnaise sauce may be hollandaise sauce mixed with chervil leaves, parsley flakes, instant minced onions, tarragon leaves, and white and red pepper. Another version may contain hollandaise sauce, tarragon, vinegar, sherry or white wine and salt. Béarnaise sauce is used on steak, fish, chicken, and egg dishes.

Hollandaise herb sauce is a mixture of hollandaise sauce, chives, tarragon, minced parsley and shallots. Used on boiled and poached fish.

Other Sauces.—*Raisin sauce* contains raisins, brown and granulated sugar, seasonings (cloves, cinnamon, mustard, vinegar) pineapple or lemon juice and butter. Used on ham, cold meat and tongue.

Cumberland sauce contains currant jelly, orange and lemon peel, egg yolk, vinegar, dry mustard, seasonings (salt, pepper) and sugar; port wine and raisins are optional. Used in place of raisin sauce.

Sweet and sour sauce contains lemon juice, salt, pepper, crushed pineapple, honey, soy sauce, red wine vinegar, sour cream and raisins. For use on fish and poultry.

Cold Sauces.—This category of sauces consists of mayonnaise, salad dressing and cooked salad dressing. Many varieties of each are used. Most of the popular cold sauces are obtainable in the ready-to-use form.

Mayonnaise is a thick, creamy emulsion consisting of vinegar or lemon juice, salad oil, egg yolk, and seasoning, such as mustard, salt and water. Variations of the basic mayonnaise formulation exist and must be labeled accordingly with such terms as whipped or salad dressing.

Salad dressing such as the French version, may contain wine vinegar, oil, herbs, salt, pepper, mustard. This dressing is also referred to as "vinaigrette." Sugar, paprika, pickle relish, cheese, horseradish and a host of other products may be added to the basic dressing.

Cooked salad dressing contains sugar, salt, mustard, flour, whole egg or egg yolk, milk, vinegar or lemon juice and butter. This dressing can be stored in a refrigerator, and has excellent storage stability if placed in a closed vessel.

Remoulade dressing consists of mayonnaise, mustard, pickles, capers, parsley, chives, tarragon and onion. Used for fish.

Tartar sauce is a mixture of mayonnaise, various relishes or pickles, onion, capers, and herbs.

Thousand Island dressing is a mixture of mayonnaise, chili sauce, green pepper, chopped stuffed olives and cream.

Russian dressing may contain mayonnaise and chili sauce.

Other variations of cold sauces are blue cheese, Roquefort, Cheddar, and Green Goddess dressings.

EFFICIENCY COMPONENTS FOR SAUCES

There are numerous sauce and gravy components on the market that require little effort to convert into tasty and useful products. These components encompass a variety of gravy and sauce bases and a large selection of mixes. The bases and mixes are available as dehydrated, freeze-dried, and canned.

It was previously shown that stock plays an important role in the development of gravies and sauces. Stock is the liquid or extract resulting from cooking meat, poultry, fish or vegetables with water and various seasonings. There are four primary stocks: brown, white, fish and poultry. The consistency of the stock may vary from thin to concentrated. Consommés, broth or bouillon are examples of thin-consistency stocks. These are used as bases for soups, gravies and sauces. Stocks that are used for bases have been strained, clarified or concentrated. Following are a number of widely used bases and mixes:

(1) Brown base for a number of brown sauces.

(2) Espagnole base for gravies and sauces such as ragout.

(3) Mushroom base for brown mushroom sauces.

(4) Ham base for pea soup, lentil soup, creole sauce and tomato dishes.

(5) White base for white sauces.

(6) Chicken base for soups and gravies and to add chicken flavor.

(7) Onion base, to add onion flavor, for soups, dips.

(8) Turtle soup base, for soup by addition of turtle meat, chicken or veal and sherry wine.

(9) Lobster base for lobster bisque, sauce Newburg and other lobster dishes.

(10) Marinade bases for use as a marinade by brushing on the food.

(11) Spaghetti sauce mix (dehydrated or freeze-dried): add the product to water and tomato purée and allow to simmer for 30 min. Can be enhanced by the addition of meat, mushrooms and cheese.

(12) Creole sauce mix (dehydrated or freeze dried); mix with water and tomatoes and simmer for 30 min.

Examples of Sauces Prepared from Efficiency Components

(1) *Tomato sauce:* condensed tomato soup, butter, boiling water or brown stock.

(2) *Tomato and cheese sauce:* condensed tomato soup, seasoning and processed American cheese.

(3) *Creole sauce:* tomato sauce, seasonings, olives, pickle relish, green pepper, celery, onions.

(4) *Onion sauce:* onion soup, thickeners, cheese and seasonings. Should be reduced by heating for 5 min.

(5) *A la King sauce:* mushroom soup, green pepper, brown butter, and milk. Reduce by heating and add strips of pimiento.

(6) *Mushroom sauce:* mushroom soup, butter, flour, Worcestershire sauce. Reduce by heating.

(7) *Hollandaise sauce:* mayonnaise, lemon juice or vinegar, milk, flour, salt and butter. Or mayonnaise, sour cream, prepared mustard, and lemon juice. Both need to be reduced slightly.

(8) *Smitane sauce:* chicken stock or broth, sour cream, butter, shallots and onions (freeze-dried), pepper, salt and some white wine.

(9) *Onion sauce (quick):* onions (freeze-dried, minced or chopped), Tabasco, olive oil and salt.

(10) *Barbecue sauce:* brown or beef base, minced freeze-dried onions, wine vinegar, brown sugar, Worcestershire sauce, prepared mustard, Tabasco, and water. Reduce by simmering for 30 min.

(11) *Sweet-sour:* Onion soup base, chopped sweet pickles or sweet relish, prepared mustard, lemon juice, pineapple juice and diced pineapple.

CONVENIENCE SAUCES AND GRAVIES

Many sauces and gravies are commercially prepared and frozen. These products are quick-frozen and cover a wide assortment of popular sauces and gravies. They are easily thawed and heated. The advantages that these products offer are: fresh flavor, elimination of a large and sundry inventory of ingredients, and reduction of labor. These frozen sauces and gravies may need the addition of some spices, herbs or other products such as wine or cheese to increase the appeal factor. The following is a partial listing of these frozen products: hollandaise, Bernaise, Bordelaise, Madeira, smitane, supreme, Eugenie, Hongroise, Mornay, cheese, and mushroom.

An interesting assortment of prepared sauces and gravies that are packed in cans are being produced. Many of these require little or no preparation, except heating. Some may have to be diluted: others may need the addition of seasoning or a garnish. The following is a partial list of sauces and gravies available in cans: A la King, barbecue, brown, various cheese sauces, chili, hollandaise, Italian, marinara, mushroom, mustard, Newburg, pepper, pizza, various spaghetti sauces, Stroganoff, supreme, sweet and sour, white cream sauce (enriched Béchamel) white sauce, and Worcestershire sauce.

Following are a number of canned gravy bases and mixes: beef gravy base, beef gravy mix, beef au jus mix, Swiss steak gravy mix, chicken gravy base and mix, ham base and mix, onion base and mix, and turkey base and mix.

The items listed at the end of this paragraph are representative examples of dry (dehydrated or freeze-dried) sauce and gravy mixes. These products may be packaged in air and moistureproof film and contain about 8 oz of mix per package. Reconstitution is performed by adding the contents of the package to a specified amount of water, then heating slowly and stirring. If the original recipe calls for wine, it is added to the sauce as a wine concentrate. The items are: A la King, barbecue, Bordelaise, brown gravy mix, various cheese sauces, chicken, ham, hollandaise, Mornay, Newburg, pizza, spaghetti sauces, Stroganoff, tomato, turkey, white sauce roux, and white sauce supreme.

Salad dressings and cold sauces are available in a wide selection of items that are packaged in cans, jars or as dry mixes. These products include the most popular varieties such as: mayonnaise, salad dressing, French, Italian, Thousand Island, Russian, tartar sauce, cole slaw dressing, horseradish, Blue and Cheddar cheese, and Green Goddess dressings.

It is advisable to read and follow the manufacturer's instructions for re-constituting, heating and other specific recommendations which may help to produce a quality gravy or sauce. When purchasing prepared sauces and gravies those that exhibit low-to-medium spice flavors and aromas should be selected. It is much easier to enhance and build up seasoning characteristics than to attempt to tone them down. In addition, the extra seasonings that may be required can create a tailored sauce or gravy with an outstanding and distinctive character.

Seasoning Various Convenience Sauces*

To further implement the previous discussion with regard to adding season-ings to convenience sauces, bases or mixes, the following examples are used for illustration:

(1) *Mild barbecue sauce*

onion salt	1/4 cup
instant garlic powder	1 tbsp
powdered mustard	1 tsp
paprika	1 tsp
ground black pepper	1/2 tsp

These seasonings are added to 2 qt of unseasoned barbecue sauce.

(2) *Béarnaise sauce*

chervil leaves	2 tbsp
parsley flakes	2 tbsp
instant minced onion	2 tbsp
tarragon leaves	2 tsp
ground white pepper	1 tsp
ground red pepper	1/8 tsp

These seasonings are added to 2 qt of hollandaise sauce.

(3) *Curry sauce*

instant minced onion	1/2 cup
curry powder	3 tsp

*Source: American Spice Trade Association.

garlic powder	1 tbsp
ground thyme	1/2 tsp
ground white pepper	1/4 tsp

These seasonings are stirred into 1 gal cream sauce.

(4) *Poulette sauce*

instant minced onion	1/2 cup
chervil leaves	1/3 cup
parsley flakes	1/4 cup
ground nutmeg	1/2 tsp

Stir these ingredients into 3 qt of Supreme sauce.

(5) *Red wine sauce*

instant minced onion	1/3 cup
parsley flakes	2 tbsp
ground white pepper	1½ tsp
garlic salt	1 tsp
marjoram leaves	1 tsp
bay leaf	1 leaf

Stir into 1 pt of French or Italian red wine and 1 gal of brown sauce.

(6) *Hunter sauce*

instant minced onion	1/2 cup
parsley flakes	1/2 cup
thyme leaves	1 tsp
ground white pepper	1/2 tsp

Mix with 2 qt of brown mushroom sauce.

BUTTER SAUCES

Butter sauces take the "commonplace" out of ordinary dishes. They impart distinctive flavors to vegetables, fish, chops or steaks and poultry. Many pre-prepared frozen pouch-packed vegetables contain a variety of butter sauces to enhance the flavor.

Butter sauces are relatively easy to prepare. By starting with fresh unsalted butter, the spices and other ingredients can either be worked into softened butter, which then melts on the hot food, or it can be added to the melted product. In the latter case, when pouring the seasoned butter over the food care must be taken to stir constantly and to spoon out the seasoning with the butter, since herb spices sink to the bottom of the liquid. These sauces may be prepared in advance and refrigerated. They also may be frozen for 4 to 6 weeks.

Butter sauce bases are butters that are prepared by melting and clarifying. Clarifying consists of heating the butter until it melts. The clear yellow liquid that forms on top is skimmed off and used. The heating time determines the final color, such as tan to light brown, or deep brown. The former is known as brown butter, and the latter as black butter. To these are added a wide variety of products. The following are examples of popular butter sauces and their uses:

(1) *Maitre d'Hotel butter sauce:* parsley flakes, onion salt. Used on steaks, omelets, vegetables and fish.

(2) *Shallot butter sauce:* red wine, pepper, freeze-dried shallot powder, for steaks, hamburgers, chicken, vegetables.

(3) *Mustard butter sauce:* powdered mustard, seasonings for vegetables, egg dishes, ham and pork.

(4) *Garlic butter:* powdered garlic mixed into butter. Used on vegetables, meat, Italian bread, pasta, and fish.

(5) *Bercy butter sauce:* shallots, meat glaze, white wine, seasonings and lemon juice. Used on steak.

(6) *Herb or tarragon butter:* parsley, tarragon, lemon juice, seasonings. Used on broiled or grilled meat, vegetables and poultry.

(7) *Dill butter:* dill, instant minced onion, mustard, allspice, pepper. Used on fish, chicken, vegetables and veal.

In addition a variety of cheeses may be mixed with butter, such as smoky, Romano, blue, and Cheddar. Many other additions may also be employed to create butter sauces with distinctive flavors. These are: anchovy, almonds, hard-cooked eggs, olives, tomato, horseradish, curry, cinnamon, chili, and thyme.

Courtesy of American Spice Trade Association
FIG. 9.13. PROPER SPOONING OF SAUCY CLOVE SAUCE ON A SMOKED PORK TENDERLOIN

Maintaining the Quality of Sauces

Crust formations are avoided by keeping sauces covered until used. Crusts should be removed by skimming. It is not advisable to stir the crust into the sauce as this will produce lumps.

Lumpy, thin or thick sauces can be corrected. If they are too thick, heat them or bring to a simmer and add more liquid, such as stock, milk or water. These may have to be reseasoned to correct dilution. If the sauces are too thin, add a quantity of thickener, such as egg yolk or flour, and stir into the body. If the sauce is lumpy strain to remove the solid particles or lumps, or heat, or put into a blender at low speed.

Store sauces by placing them in covered containers. Prior to storing in the refrigerator, they should be cooled to room temperature.

Reheating can be done in a trunion kettle, bain marie, or double boiler. During heating, sauces and gravies should be stirred to avoid scorching.

For quality results prepare only enough sauces and gravies for short periods (Fig. 9.13).

MISCELLANEOUS ENHANCEMENT FOODS

Cheese

One of the oldest of ready-to-eat foods known to mankind is cheese. Cheeses are among the most versatile of all edibles. They impart charm to a meal, appeal to the appetite, and provide the food service operator with solid merchandising effects. There are more than 400 varieties of natural cheese. However, only a relatively small number is known to the general public. Cheeses are employed with soup, soufflés, sauces, desserts, with or in eggs, meat dishes, pasta, fondue, croquettes, fish, casseroles, sandwiches, and as garnishes.

Selecting cheese is largely a matter of personal preference tempered by the local popularity of the item. Some areas prefer strong cheese, whereas others favor mild varieties. The categories of cheeses are: *natural,* such as Blue, Cheddar, Swiss and Limburger; *pasteurized process cheese* such as American; *pasteurized process cheese food.* The last mentioned is a blend of cheeses that have been pasteurized and may include other ingredients, such as fruits, vegetables, meats, or spices; pasteurized process cheese spread which is soft and spreadable at room temperature; coldpack or club cheese, and coldpack cheese food.

Description and Applications of Some Popular Natural Cheeses.—

(1) *Bel Paese:* mild, sweet flavor, light, creamy yellow interior. Uses: appetizers, sandwiches, desserts, snacks.

(2) *Blue:* tangy, piquant flavor, semisoft; white interior marbled or streaked. Uses: appetizers, salads, dressings, desserts, and snacks.

(3) *Brick:* mild to moderately sharp flavor. Uses: appetizers, sandwiches, desserts, and snacks.

(4) *Camembert:* distinctive mild to tangy flavor, soft, smooth texture. Uses: appetizers, desserts, and snacks.

(5) *Cheddar:* mild to very sharp flavor; smooth texture, firm to crumbly. Uses: appetizers, main dishes, sauces, soups, sandwiches, salads, desserts, and snacks.

(6) *Cream:* delicate, slightly acid flavor, soft, smooth texture, white. Uses: appetizers, salads, sauces, sandwiches, desserts, snacks.

(7) *Edam:* mellow, nut-like, salty flavor, firm, rubbery texture. Uses: appetizers, salads, sandwiches, sauces, desserts, and snacks.

(8) *Gorgonzola:* tangy, spicy and a bit peppery, semisoft. Uses: appetizers, salads, desserts, and snacks.

(9) *Gouda:* mellow, nut-like, mealy. Uses: appetizers, salads, sandwiches, sauces, desserts, and snacks.

(10) *Mozzarella:* delicate, mild flavor, creamy white, slightly firm. Uses: main dishes such as pizza or lasagne, sandwiches, and snacks.

(11) *Parmesan:* sharp, distinctive flavor, very hard, granular texture. Uses: grated for seasoning.

(12) *Provolone:* mellow to sharp flavor, smoky and salty, firm. Uses: appetizers, main dishes, sandwiches, desserts, and snacks.

(13) *Ricotta:* mild, sweet, nut-like flavor; soft, moist texture. Uses: salads, pastas, and desserts.

(14) *Romano:* very sharp, piquant flavor, very hard and granular. Uses: seasoning and grating.

(15) *Roquefort:* sharp, peppery, piquant flavor, semi-soft. Uses: appetizers, salads, dressings, desserts and snacks.

(16) *Swiss* (also called Emmentaler): mild, sweet, nut-like flavor, firm, elastic body with large round eyes. Uses: sandwiches, salads, fondue, snacks and grated in soup.

Cheese Cookery.—Successful cheese cookery depends on brief heating at a low temperature. High temperatures and over-cooking make the cheese tough and stringy, and cause the fat to separate.

Cheese blends more readily with other ingredients and melts more quickly if shredded or diced. When preparing cheese sauce, stir in the shredded cheese after the white sauce is completely heated or cooked. When making a cheese omelet, add the shredded cheese after the omelet is cooked, just before folding. Casserole dishes containing cheese should be baked at low-to-moderate temperatures. To prevent cheese toppings from toughening or hardening during baking, cover them with crumbs or add the cheese just a few minutes before removing the food from the oven.

Convenience foods, such as casseroles, macaroni, broccoli, seafoods, and salads, are enhanced with cheese or with the addition of some extra cheese. Mushroom cheese sauce is easily prepared from condensed canned cream of mushroom soup, milk, shredded Cheddar cheese, Worcestershire sauce and paprika. An easy, tasty cheese sauce is quickly prepared from evaporated milk, process Cheddar, finely diced, dry mustard, curry powder and marjoram. Try different varieties in place of the more commonly used cheeses.

Cheeses keep best when refrigerated. Soft cheeses are highly perishable. Hard cheeses, such as Cheddar or Swiss, will keep several months, if tightly wrapped. Cheeses with strong odors should be stored in tightly covered containers to avoid odor contamination with other foods. Cheese that has dried out and becomes hard may be grated.

Freezing is not recommended for most cheeses because they become crumbly and mealy when frozen. Small pieces (1 lb or less) of the following varieties can be frozen satisfactorily: Brick, Cheddar, Edam, Gouda, Swiss, Provolone, Mozzarella, and Camembert. Small quantities of Blue, Roquefort and Gorgonzola can be frozen for salads or dressings, or other uses where a crumbly texture is acceptable. Wrap cheeses tightly, freeze quickly, at 0°F. or below, and store no more than 6 months.

Dehydrated cheese, such as Cheddar and Parmesan are available for a number of applications. Rehydration consists of adding water, milk, wines or other liquids, and the cheeses may be cooked or prepared and used cold.

A large assortment of cheese mixes are available. These are packed in plastic 1-lb tubes. They include many popular cheeses, such as Cheddar, Blue, Swiss, and Gruyère. These are mixed with such products as nuts, caraway, pepper, various wines, bacon bits, smoked items and herbs.

Wines

The scope of this book limits the discussion of wine cookery. The use of wine for both drinking and cooking has increased during the last decade. The character of numerous convenience foods can be improved by the addition of wine. The primary rule associated with wine cookery is never use cheap "cooking wine." It is the flavor of a wine that makes a dish memorable, not the alcoholic content, which evaporates during cooking. Cognac, Armagnac and other brandies may be used in a variety of dishes, from sauces to soups to desserts. A good brandy should always be used. Only a small amount is necessary to produce delicate subtle effects.

By the application of "trial and error" methods, the most desirable wine and the amount needed will be found for a specific dish. Before adding wine to thick sauces, it may be necessary to reduce its volume by pre-heating. Where liquid volume is not a factor, the wine may be mixed into the sauce or gravy.

As a guide the following types of wines are suggested: for soup, use dry sherry, Sauterne, or Madeira. White vermouth blends favorably with onion soup; for red meat, use dry red, or for white meat (veal) use a dry white wine; for fish, use dry white wine; for poultry, use full-bodied white or red wine. Madeira blends well with beef and some poultry.

Strengths of wine vary. Read the label for its alcoholic content. For example, two tablespoons of sherry is equivalent to about one-half cup of dry red wine.

Foods which are poached, boiled or stewed in wine are superior in flavor and tenderness. Foods cooked in wine freeze and heat better. Wine also tends to smooth out and blend the flavor of spices and herbs and to fix them in the frozen product. Wines used for sauces should be added within the last minutes of cooking so that the wine flavor remains in the sauce, not in the product.

Lemons

Lemon is a highly regarded citrus fruit. It enjoys wide popularity as an additive and has a number of diversified applications. The juice is the most unique and useful of all the citrus fruits. In the culinary arts, it has broad employment as a condiment. As a thirst-quenching beverage, its popularity is derived from its high acidity and tangy flavor. These characteristics also make it popular in cocktails, blended juices and in hot and iced tea. It is also an excellent source of vitamin C.

Because of the high acidity, flavor, and antioxidant action of lemon juice, its use as a specialty condiment is strongly favored. It is added to mayonnaise, canned tomato juice, breakfast prunes, pickling, sauces, soufflés, marinades, puddings, pies, cake, meat, fish, poultry, soup and vegetables. It is compatible with most seafood and shellfish. The natural balance of its chemical and physical properties makes it highly desirable as a food adjunct and flavor enhancer. Some form of lemon can be found in most households and food service establishments in the Western world.

Lemon juice is available in many forms, such as: juice from the whole fresh fruit, dehydrated, freeze-dried, frozen, and preserved in bottles. When fresh whole lemon is used as a garnish, it should not be sliced too far in advance of serving. Sliced lemon, when exposed to the atmosphere, will turn brown as a result of enzymatic action, shrink, and form a hard, unappealing surface. If a lemon is cut in advance, it should be placed in a covered dry container and stored in the refrigerator. It will tend to lose its vitamin C content by oxidation when exposed to air for more than a few minutes.

For quick flavor enhancement, use lemon juice on convenience entrées such as casseroles. A small amount sprinkled or brushed on the surface is sufficient. Use lemon juice in some pre-prepared sauces; the optimum amount can be determined by experimentation. The flavor of many vegetables can be distinctly improved with lemon, e.g., green beans, spinach, broccoli, and cauliflower.

Imitation Bacon Pieces

Imitation bacon pieces, chips or slivers, although not a spice, are useful for garnishes and flavoring. This product is made from vegetable protein to which a bacon or hickory smoked flavor is added. These items are all vegetable and contain no meat or natural meat flavor. They require no refrigeration and may be stored in the spice closet.

Many applications are claimed for its use. As a garnish, bacon pieces may be used on potatoes, green salads and vegetables, omelets, casseroles, scrambled eggs, in sandwiches, on curries, on soup, on rice.

Bacon pieces may be added to soufflés, sandwich fillings, dips and canapés, in eggs, some baked goods, in baked vegetables, in sauces just prior to serving, in stews, or wherever the particular flavor will enhance a dish.

Mushrooms

Mushrooms have joined the vanguard of popularity and are widely used by food service installations. Consumption has doubled over the last ten years. Mushrooms rank high as an epicurean delicacy and portray an image of elegance to many people. They are a versatile accompaniment for such foods as appetizers, soups, sauces, meats, fowl, seafood, cheese, egg dishes and vegetables. Mushrooms, broiled or sautéed, are superb on toast or as a vegetable.

Cultivated mushrooms, either white or beige, are available fresh, canned, frozen or dried. In most recipes these forms are interchangeable.

Fresh mushrooms are shipped under refrigeration and should be kept cold until used. Before preparation, they should be rinsed briefly in cold water. They need not be peeled. Mushrooms may be used raw in salads and garnishes. The fresh variety is sold in baskets which contain 3 to 9 lb net. Mushrooms range in size from 3/4 to about 3 in. in diameter. The large mushrooms are used for stuffing, whereas the smaller ones are used chopped or sliced. Sautéeing requires 3 to 5 min.

Canned mushrooms require no preparation other than heating for a short time. If they are to be sautéed, the liquid should be drained and saved for use in soups or sauces. This form is packed in 8- and 16-oz cans and No. 10 tins.

Frozen mushrooms need neither washing, peeling nor thawing. They are handled in the same manner as the fresh pack; however, the cooking time is longer because of their frozen state. This variety is packed in $1\frac{1}{2}$-lb plastic bags, and in 20- and 45-lb cases.

Dehydrated mushrooms require reconstitution before use. Soak in water for about 1/2 to 3/4 hr. After reconstitution they can be used like the frozen type.

To prevent mushrooms from darkening during cooking, add lemon juice. Slice by cutting from the round side down through the stems, or remove the stems and use the caps, saving the stems for other uses. Browning mushrooms before using them will make their flavor more distinctive.

Mushrooms are compatible with an endless assortment of foods and dishes. The following are selected examples:

Soup: cream of tomato, chowders, vegetable, creamed chicken, barley, bisques.

Vegetables: peas, onions, green beans, stewed tomatoes, eggplant, carrots, rice.

Entrées: veal Parmesan, pastas, meat and fish casseroles, poultry and meat pies, stews, fricassee, Creoles, egg dishes, croquettes, fritters, and soufflés. Many nationality dishes contain mushrooms, such as French, Italian, Spanish and Oriental.

Salads: vegetable salad, German potato salad, ham salad and spreads, fish salads, chopped egg and with cream cheese.

ADAPTATION OF CONVENIENCE FOODS

If pre-prepared frozen foods are to be profitable, successfully merchandized, and readily accepted by the clientele, procedural programs may have to be instituted to modify and embellish them with special and distinctive flavors. It was pointed out that appealing garnishes, sauces and seasonings can often make the difference between a highly desirable program and one doomed to failure. In this segment of the discussion examples are given of expedient methods of accomplishing this essential goal.

A question that is sometimes asked at this juncture is why further work must be performed on these products, since they are supposed to be fully prepared, and are made ready for serving by the simple application of heat. Many convenience foods may be heated and served without further or intermediate preparation. However, a number of processors are offering prepared items which border on the bland side, in order to reach and satisfy the "average" taste acceptance of the consuming public. Another reason is the shift or change in the character of some seasonings that results from freezing or canning.

Additional seasonings are also considered an advantage to those restaurants that must meet the taste demands of their customers. This situation may be the result of ethnic, nationality or local food preferences. Others are of the opinion that a certain amount of blandness is beneficial, leaving the option of the amount of seasoning to the individual operator or his customers. The latter opinion is shared by a host of food service personnel, who realize that the public is becoming increasingly aware of quality and flavor characteristics so that some measure of enhancement is necessary to meet this trend. In addition, a degree of sophistication has entered the food service scene; the public is looking forward to and enjoying nationality, ethnic and specialty dishes.

To cater to these demands, operators are adapting and transforming numerous basic convenience foods into tasty and appetizing dishes. For example, pre-prepared frozen meat loaf with brown gravy may be converted into a number of distinctive-tasting entrées by adding simple mixtures of spices, herbs, dehydrated vegetable seasonings, sauces, and other compatible products. Pre-prepared frozen beef slices, chunks or tips may be transformed into a variety of nationality dishes, such as Russian, Italian, Mexican, Hungarian and Oriental. An added advantage is a reduction in the amount of inventory and a saving of valuable freezer storage space.

Amendments to Original Specifications May Be Necessary.—The adaptation or tailoring of convenience foods into specialty dishes should be planned well in advance of purchasing. Amendments to the various specifications given in Chapter 7 may be necessary. The following points are suggested: (1) pre-prepared frozen foods should not be heavily spiced, so that fresh and distinctive seasonings may be added accordingly; (2) they should not be completely garnished so that fresh, crisp and attractive embellishments may be added as desired.

Some spices should be added early in the cooking process to give them ample time to mature to a desirable blending and delicate suspension. Whole spices require longer periods of time to produce their ultimate flavor, while ground spices require less time. Certain spices are more compatible if added near the end of the heating period or immediately thereafter. Seasoning salts are usually added at the very end of the cooking period, or after the food is removed from the stove or oven.

Seasonings, Key to Tasty Convenience Foods

The key to tasty and appetizing convenience foods is the seasonings added to them. These products work wonders with convenience foods and are convenient products in themselves. Spices, herbs, aromatic seeds, spice blends, add instant flavor to any dish in which they are used.

Proper seasoning is an art. With a little patience this art is easy to learn and adapt. The best flavor is one so smooth and well blended that individual traits are difficult to detect. There are no hard-and-fast rules for the use of seasoning; however three basic practices should be followed: (1) underseason, rather than overseason, because it is difficult to reduce the seasoning level without injuring the product; (2) experiment with various seasonings and become familiar with the seasonings that are available; (3) use only fresh, high-quality seasonings. Spices should be stored in a cool, dry location away from bright light and placed in tightly closed containers. Containers should be dated when purchased and replaced after six months.

Definitions: *Spice:*—The word spice covers six categories: true spices, herbs, seeds, dehydrated vegetable seasonings, spice salts, and spice blends.

True Spices.—These are products of tropical plants. They may be from the bark, roots, buds, flowers, fruits or other parts of the plant. Examples are pepper, cloves, nutmeg, ginger and cinnamon.

Herbs.—These are leaves of plants, such as sage, mint, marjoram, thyme, and oregano.

Seeds.—These come from plants, such as celery, mustard, dill, anise, cardamon and caraway.

Dehydrated Vegetable Seasonings.—These are vegetables—celery, garlic, onion, shallots, and parsley with more than 90% of the water removed. Rehydration in water brings back their flavor for instant use.

Spice Blends.—These are spices, herbs, seeds and dehydrated vegetable seasonings that are ground and mixed according to formula. These products are among the fastest-growing seasonings in the food service industry. Blends, such as barbecue spice, chili powder, curry powder, apple pie spice, Italian seasoning, poultry seasoning, hamburger spice, fish spice and pork spice are being marketed.

Spice Salts.—These are combinations of a dehydrated vegetable, such as onion, garlic, celery and table salt. Table salt and monosodium glutamate (MSG) are not spices.

Spice Groups According to Flavor.—Spices can be grouped according to their flavor and compatibility with certain foods. Although these groups suggest some uses, the desirability of each use is a matter of preference.

Sweet Spices.—These spices go well with pastries, fruit dishes, nuts, and ham. This group include allspice, cardamom, cinnamon, cloves, coriander, ginger, nutmeg, mace, poppy and sesame seeds (Fig. 9.14).

Protein Spices.—These are employed with meat, fowl, fish, egg, and bean dishes. They include red pepper, celery, chili powder, curry powder, marjoram, sage, mustard, poultry seasoning, thyme and rosemary.

Salad Herbs.—These seasonings blend well with salads and vegetable dishes. Basil, caraway, celery, parsley and tarragon are examples in this group.

General Use Spices.—The following are useful in so many ways that they belong to several groups. Among them are dehydrated onion and garlic, oregano, mace, marjoram, paprika and black pepper.

Methods of Sensory Evaluation for Spices.—In Chapter 7, Quality Control, methods of sensory evaluation were described. These procedures can be applied to seasonings and their resulting effects on food.

Examine the spices visually. Observe their distinctive color and shape. Next smell them for their aroma-producing characteristics. Some spices are not

Courtesy of American Spice Trade Association

FIG. 9.14. SPICING MELON BALLS WITH NUTMEG AND CINNAMON

TABLE 9.2

SPICES FOR CONVENIENCE FOODS

Spice	Application
Allspice	Whole: pickling, meats, gravies, boiling fish. Ground: baking, puddings, relishes, fruit preserves. Try adding a dash to tomato sauce.
Basil	An important seasoning in tomato paste and tomato dishes. Use in cooked peas, squash and snap beans. Famed for use in turtle soup. Sprinkle chopped basil leaves over lamb chops before cooking.
Bay leaves	For pickling, stews, sauces and soups. Excellent for fish or chowder. Good with meats, such as fricassee of kidney, heart or oxtail. Add bay leaf, with whole peppercorns, to tomato sauce for boiled cod.
Caraway	Widely used in baking, especially rye bread. Good in sauerkraut, new cabbage, noodles and soft cheese spreads. Sprinkle canned asparagus with caraway before heating. Sprinkle over French-fried potatoes; on pork, liver, or kidneys before cooking.
Cardamom	Whole (in pod): used in Mixed Pickling Spice. Seed (removed from pod): flavors demitasse. Ground: flavors Danish pastry, bun breads, coffee cakes. Improves flavor of grape jelly. Sprinkle ground cardamom on iced melon for breakfast or dessert.
Celery	Excellent in pickling, salads, fish, salad dressings, and vegetables. For a different flavor, add celery seed to braised lettuce (about 1/2 tsp to a head of lettuce). Excellent in tomato juice cocktail.
Celery flakes	Soups, stews, sauces, stuffings.
Chives	Excellent as garnish for hot and cold dishes; superb topping for soups, salads, dairy dishes, meat, fish and egg dishes, and are compatible with all green vegetables. Popular in sour cream dressing for baked potatoes.
Cinnamon	Whole: pickling, preserving, flavoring puddings, stewed fruits. Serve with clove-stuck lemon slices in hot tea. Used in hot wine drinks. Ground: baked goods, often in combination with allspice, nutmeg and cloves. The principal mincemeat spice. Combine with mashed sweet potatoes and with sugar for cinnamon toast. Dust on fried bananas.
Cloves	Whole: for pork and ham roasts, pickling of fruits, spiced sweet syrups. Ground: baked goods, chocolate puddings, stews, vegetables. For a tastier meat stew add a small onion studded with 2 or 3 whole cloves.
Coriander	Whole: in mixed pickles, gingerbread batter, cookies, cakes, biscuits, poultry stuffings, mixed green salads. Ground: in sausage making, to flavor buns. Rub ground coriander on fresh pork before roasting.
Cumin	An important ingredient in curry and chili powder. Good in soups, cheese, meat pies, stuffed eggs. For canapés, mix chutney with snappy cheese and garnish with cumin seed.

TABLE 9.2 (Continued)

Spice	Application
Dill seed	Used for pickling, in cooking sauerkraut, salads, soups, fish and meat sauces, gravies, spiced vinegars, green apple pie. Add dill seed on potato salad, cooked macaroni or when cooking sauerkraut.
Dill weed	Dill weed is particularly suited to uncooked mixtures, such as salads, sour cream sauces and mayonnaise. It is delicious in baked potatoes, sandwich fillings, white sauce mixes, buttered green beans and fish butter sauces.
Fennel	Popular in sweet pickles and Italian sausage. Used in boiled fish, pastries, candies and liqueurs. Add a dash to apple pie for an unusually good flavor.
Ginger	Whole: chutneys, conserves, pickling. Stew with dried fruits, applesauce. Ground: gingerbread, cakes, pumpkin pie, Indian pudding, canned fruits, pot roasts and other meats. Rub chicken inside and out with mixture of ginger and butter before roasting.
Mace	Whole (called "Blade"): excellent in fish sauces, pickling, preserving. Add a chopped blade to gingerbread batter. Good in stewed cherries. Ground: essential in fine pound cakes, contributes a golden tone and exotic flavor to all yellow cakes. Valuable in all chocolate dishes. Use 1/4 tsp ground mace to 1 pint of ready whipped cream.
Marjoram	Delicious combined with other herbs in stews, soups, sausage, poultry seasonings. Good in fish and sauce recipes. Sprinkle over lamb while cooking for an excellent flavor touch.
Mint flakes	Flavoring soups, stews, beverages, jellies, fish, sauces.
Mixed vegetable flakes	Seasoning soups, stews, sauces, stuffings.
Mustard	Whole: garnish salads, pickled meats, fish and hamburgers. Powdered: meats, sauces, gravies. Add 1/2 tsp powdered mustard for each 2 cups of cheese sauce for macaroni.
Nutmeg	Whole: to be grated as needed. Ground: baked goods, sauces, puddings. Topping for eggnog, custards, whipped cream. Good on cauliflower, spinach. Sprinkle on fried bananas, on bananas and berries with cream. Excellent spice for flavoring doughnuts. A pinch of nutmeg adds flavor to the crust for meat pie.
Oregano	Any tomato dish tastes twice as good with a pinch of this herb; 1/4 or 1/2 tsp can be sprinkled sparingly over pork, lamb, veal and chicken. Add it to omelets, cheese dishes, soups, tossed salads, cream sauce for quartered, hard-cooked eggs. Give zest to vegetables with a pinch of oregano in snap beans, spinach, creamed white onions, Zucchini.
Paprika	Used as colorful red garnish for any pale foods. Important ingredient in chicken paprika and Hungarian goulash. Used on fish, shellfish, salad dressings, vegetables, meats, gravies, canapés. For an excellent canapé mix paprika with cream cheese and celery seed and serve on crackers.
Parsley flakes	Seasoning and garnish. Flavor soups, salads, meat, fish, sauces, and vegetable dishes. For spiced potato cakes made from left-

TABLE 9.2 (Continued)

Spice	Application
	over mashed potatoes, or try adding to reheated mashed potatoes, some parsley flakes, onion salt and paprika.
Pepper (black and white)	Adds a spicy tang to almost all foods. A must in the kitchen and on the table. Whole (black and white): in pickling, soups and meats. Ground (black and white): meats, sauces, gravies, many vegetables, soups, salads, eggs. Dash fresh black pepper in tossed green salad. White pepper particularly useful in light-colored sauces, soups, and vegetables where dark specks are not wanted.
Red pepper (Cayenne)	Whole: pickles, relishes, hot sauces. Crushed: sauces, pickles, highly spiced meats, a prime ingredient of many Italian specialty dishes, including certain sausages. Ground: with discretion in meats, sauces, fish, egg dishes. A touch of ground red pepper (or cayenne) plus 1/4 tsp paprika added to 2 or 3 tbsp butter makes excellent sauce for vegetables.
Rosemary	In lamb dishes, in soups and stews. Sprinkle on beef before roasting. Flavors fish and meat stocks. Add a dash of rosemary to boiled potatoes in the early stages of cooking.
Saffron	In baked goods. Most highly esteemed in "Arroz Con Pollo," the rice-chicken dish of Spain. To add golden color and delicious flavor to rice, boil pinch of saffron in water for a moment before adding rice.
Sage	Particularly good with pork and pork products. Used in sausages, meat stuffings, baked fish and poultry. Excellent in salad greens.
Savory	Combined with other herbs, makes an excellent flavoring for meats, meat dressings, chicken, fish sauces. A pinch of savory gives a lift to scrambled eggs.
Sesame	A rich toasted-nut flavor when baked on rolls, breads and buns. Principal ingredient in Middle-Eastern candy, halvah. Add to lightly cooked cold spinach which has been blended with soy sauce.
Sweet pepper flakes	A convenient way of adding green or red pepper flavor to sauces, salads, vegetables, casseroles, when a fine diced pepper is called for.
Tarragon	In sauces, salads, chicken, meats, egg and tomato dishes. The important flavoring of tarragon vinegar. Just before taking broiled chicken out of oven, season and sprinkle with finely minced tarragon and serve with pan gravy.
Thyme	In stews, soups and poultry stuffings. Excellent in clam and fish chowders, sauces, croquettes, chipped beef, fricassees. Thyme and fresh tomatoes go together like hand in glove. Sprinkle thyme over sliced tomatoes in bed of lettuce, use vinegar and olive oil dressing, with salt and pepper.
Turmeric	Flavoring and coloring in prepared mustard, and is used in combination with mustards as flavoring for meats, dressings, and salads. Used in pickles, chow-chow and other relishes. Try a little turmeric in creamed eggs, fish, seafood.

Source: American Spice Trade Association.

aromatic, but others definitely are. Try to remember and classify the aromas. Spices, such as ground cinnamon, pepper, nutmeg or clove have pronounced odors.

The next step is to taste the spice. Only a minute quantity is required. Rinse the mouth thoroughly between taste tests. Try to keep the sample on the tongue until the flavor develops. This test is important as it denotes the flavor potential of each and the flavoring power that exists.

The final test is to determine the effects on actual foods. Use a bland food such as eggs. Mix 6 eggs with 2 tbsp of milk and 1/4 tsp of salt. Divide and pour the mixture into 6 soup bowls; stir 1/8 tsp of a different spice into each bowl and then scramble the eggs, one batch at a time. Taste each finished dish and study its flavoring characteristics. Repeat, using different strengths of spices.

The results of these tests should reveal that when spices are used in small quantities, the flavor of the food is improved, but is not always recognizable. Spices give "background" flavor, or an "undertone" character to food.

A spice in larger quantities may dominate the food in which it is used. This is frequently desired for such dishes as chili, curry or pizza. Since the pungency of each spice differs, and its effect on food varies, it is not possible to formulate strict rules for the amount to use. In the following section examples of seasonings are suggested without denoting a specific quantity of each. It is recommended that 1/4 tsp of each spice per pound of meat or pint of sauce or soup be tried. For instant garlic powder or red pepper, the quantity should be reduced to 1/8 tsp. Tables 9.2 and 9.3 list the popular seasonings and suggested applications of each.

CONVENIENCE SOUPS

Soups are among the earliest of convenience packaged foods. They have been marketed for generations in both the canned and dried mixed forms, and are readily identified with contemporary American living. The newer additions to the family are frozen soups. Soups have increased in both popularity and in number of varieties during the last decade. During this period a trend has developed away from thin soups, such as the consommés, to the heavier, heartier types like bean, chowder, pea, minestrone and potato.

Prepared soups are excellent examples of convenience items, since they require a minimum of handling. They also generate a healthy margin of profit. Although most prepared soups may be served without intermediate preparation, many novel and specialty variations are easily made. These have a high appeal factor and are creating interest with the public.

Canned Soup

Canned soup continues to be widely accepted in spite of the inroads made by the frozen varieties. The No. 3 tall can with a liquid capacity of about 48 oz is the preferred size. Most canned soups are condensed (double strength) so that

TABLE 9.3

SEASONING BLENDS

Blend	Description and Suggested Use

Many mixtures, or blends of spices have been developed by spice manufacturers to make the art of seasoning a quick and easy task. In some cases a specific blend may be unique with the company that produces it; in others, the blend may be one that has been adopted by most spice packers. The following are the blends that are now sold by most spice firms and thus would be available to restaurants throughout the country.

Barbecue spice — A ground blend of many spices such as chili peppers, cumin, garlic, cloves, paprika, salt and sugar. Designed to be the basic seasoning for a barbecue sauce, but good also in salad dressing, meat casserole, hashed brown potatoes, eggs and cheese dishes.

Chili powder — A ground blend of chili peppers, oregano, cumin seed, garlic, salt and sometimes such spices as cloves, red pepper and allspice. Basic seasoning for Mexican-style cooking, including chili con carne. Good in shellfish and oyster cocktail sauces, boiled and scrambled eggs, gravy and stew seasoning. Try it in ground meat or hamburgers.

Cinnamon sugar — There are few if any times in cooking and baking when cinnamon isn't accompanied by sugar, and this skillful blend of the two thus becomes a very convenient product. It is especially useful for cinnamon toast and as a quick topping for many other sweet goods.

Crab Boil or Shrimp Spice — These products are similar or identical (depending on the manufacturer), both being mixtures of several whole spices that are to be added to the water when boiling seafood. Typically, the mixtures include whole peppercorns, bay leaves, red peppers, mustard seeds, ginger and other spices in whole form.

Curry powder — A ground blend of as many as 16 to 20 spices, designed to give the characteristic flavor of Indian curry cookery. Ginger, turmeric, fenugreek seed, cloves, coriander, cumin seed, black pepper and red pepper are typical, others being used according to the manufacturer's individual formula. Used in curry sauces, for curry eggs, vegetables, fish and meat. Try a dash in French dressing, scalloped tomatoes, clam and fish chowders and split pea soup.

Herb seasoning — A savory blend of herbs, particularly suited to salad dressings. Actually, the blend varies somewhat according to the brand but the end uses are essentially the same. Note that the term "herb" specifically refers to the milder-flavored leafy products (marjoram, oregano, basil, chervil) as opposed to the stronger-flavored tropical spices (pepper, cloves, cinnamon).

Italian seasoning — Italian dishes have become so popular in this country that cooks asked for a simple way to achieve the characteristic flavoring of this cuisine. While no one blend could accomplish this completely, it is well known that such seasonings as oregano, basil, red pepper and rosemary are certainly typical of many Italian creations, particularly the popular pastas and pizza. Italian seasoning characteristically contains these and possibly garlic powder and others. Uses: all Italian dishes, salads, dressings, hamburgers, seafood, tomato soup.

Mixed pickling spice — A mixture of several whole spices, usually including mustard seed, bay leaves, black and white peppercorns, dill seed, red peppers, ginger, cinnamon, mace, allspice, coriander seed. Useful for pick-

TABLE 9.3 (Continued)

Blend	Description and Suggested Use
	ling and marinating meats and to season vegetables, relishes, and sauces. Also good in stews and soups.
Poultry seasoning	A ground blend of sage, thyme, marjoram, and savory and sometimes rosemary and other spices. For poultry, veal, pork and fish stuffings. Good with paprika for meat loaf. For a delightful combination, add to biscuit dough to serve with poultry.
Seafood seasoning	A ground blend of approximately the same spices as used in Crab Boil and Shrimp Spice with the addition of salt. Especially good in seafood sauces because the ground seasoning blends into the sauce completely.
Seasoned or flavor salt	This product goes by different names, according to the brand, but the idea is essentially the same. It is a mixture of spices, herbs and salt designed as an all-purpose seasoning. Many restaurants now place it next to the pepper on the table; others use it in preparation. It is especially suited to meats, vegetables, sauces and dairy foods.

Source: American Spice Trade Association.

they require dilution by an equivalent quantity of liquid added before heating. The yield when diluted is 12 8-oz or 15 6-oz portions. Special garnishes, spices, herbs and seasoning blends may be added to improve the flavor and appearance.

Ready-to-serve soups are available, which do not require dilution and may be consumed directly after heating. These soups are widely dispensed from vending machines.

Frozen Soups

An interesting assortment of frozen soups is marketed. These are usually packed in 48-oz cans. Soups packed in plastic pouches are available, each pouch containing one 6-oz portion.

Freezing of certain kinds of soup preserves their natural flavor. Soup such as tomato can be subjected to the canning process without marked change in flavor or consistency. However, canning has undesirable effects on soups, such as oyster stew, clam chowder, fish chowder, onion, cream of shrimp, cream of corn, cream of potato, green split pea and snapper. Nationality soups, such as egg drop, won ton, onion and minestrone are available frozen.

Many of the frozen cream soups and bisques are enriched with pure cream and butter. These ingredients produce a thick, rich velvety texture. Manufacturer's instructions are explicit, and must be followed for quality results. Some instructions suggest that the soup be thawed prior to heating, while others recommend a combined thawing and heating procedure. In addition, some processors suggest dilution with a certain quantity of water or milk; others recommend that their products be served without dilution (see Fig. 9.15).

Boil-in-the-pouch products need not be thawed, but can be placed in a vessel of boiling water for about 5 min.

Courtesy of Stouffer Food Division of Litton Industries, Inc.

FIG. 9.15. FROZEN SOUP, PARTIALLY THAWED, BEING TRANSFERRED
TO SOUP POTS

Dry-mix Soups

Dehydrated or dry-mix soups require careful reconstitution. Directions must be followed to ensure satisfactory results. Ample time should be allowed for heating; 10 to 12 minutes are usually required for a satisfactory reconstitution.

Characteristics of Quality Prepared Soups

Convenience soups should meet a number of sensory characteristics that are essential for quality and overall acceptance when compared with their freshly prepared counterpart. The dominant flavor and aroma should be clearly detectable. For example, if the soup is tomato, a noticeable flavor of tomato should be present.

After-tastes, off-flavors and aromas, and faulty textures will tend to diminish quality. Too much starch or flour will produce a pasty texture and insipid taste. Too much salt or seasonings will affect the quality. Soggy, mushy ingredients will also reduce acceptance. If the soup contains meat or fish, these should be tender, and not chewy. Soups such as bisques, chowders or purées should not be too watery. Solid content should be readily detected and vegetables should be firm.

Examples of Flavor Improvement and Specialty Combinations

The flavor, quality and eye appeal of soup may be improved by the use of a number of devices. These include the mixing of one kind of soup with another compatible variety (pea and tomato); by the addition of spices, herbs, wine, cheese, and attractive, tasty garnishes. The following examples are based on the use of soup packed in 48-oz. containers. Quantities of suggested additives are omitted, as the final flavor range should be determined by prior testing.

Canned Split Pea Soup
   (1) Whip in chili powder and instant garlic.
   (2) Whip in onion flakes, celery flakes, instant minced garlic and black pepper.
   (3) Combine with tomato soup and add a quantity of sweet cream.
   (4) Season with onion and celery salt.
   (5) Whip in ground mace, cloves and savory. When heated sprinkle on onion salt.

Tomato Soup
   (1) Whip in ground cloves, white pepper, allspice and basil leaves.
   (2) Whip in mixed vegetable flakes.
   (3) Sprinkle caraway seeds over the hot soup prior to serving.
   (4) Add crumbled oregano or basil for an interesting flavor variation.
   (5) Whip in instant minced onion, chives, Worcestershire sauce and add one can of cream of corn soup.
   (6) Combine with pepper pot soup.
   (7) Combine with chicken noodle soup, milk, chives, parsley.

Cream of Mushroom
   (1) Whip in instant minced onion, ground nutmeg, and garnish with paprika.
   (2) Combine with chicken noodle soup, add water or milk and a small amount of poultry seasoning.
   (3) Combine with cream of corn soup.

Chicken Soup
   (1) Whip in instant garlic powder, celery seed and instant onion powder.
   (2) Combine with tomato soup, rice, freeze-dried chopped onions, and dried celery.
   (3) Combine with celery soup.

Vegetable Soup
   (1) Whip in instant onion and garlic powder, ground allspice, and bay leaf.
   (2) Combine with chicken soup, and add chopped parsley.
   (3) Add milk, pepper, salt, parsley, butter and flour for thickening.
   (4) Combine with pea soup and add milk.

Bisques
   (1) Combine clam chowder, chicken gumbo and enrich with cream.
   (2) Combine, tomato soup, frozen lobster meat, and enrich with cream. Season with paprika, onion and celery flakes, salt and pepper.

CONVENIENCE BREAKFAST FOODS

Convenience breakfast foods currently marketed cover a range of products which will complement a majority of menu applications and volume requirements. The so called "light" breakfast consisting of juice, dry cereal, toast or a sweet roll and coffee is considered to be the forerunner of the convenience food concept.

The present assortment of convenience breakfast products are designed to fill out the menu so that most contingency situations can be met. Breakfasts for some establishments pose a number of problems, such as slow service due to confusion in the kitchen or in the preparation area. This situation is the result of erratic work loads and the number of varied orders that require individual preparation and service. The introduction of pre-prepared breakfast foods has helped to ease the service problem and has also provided the restaurant with the opportunity to increase the number of breakfast items offered for sale. A disadvantage associated with some of these products is the higher unit cost per portion than those comparable items cooked on location.

The following is a partial list of convenience breakfast foods: frozen juices, instant juice crystals, pre-portioned fruit juices, frozen fruit, fully pre-cooked bacon and ham slices, pre-cooked link and patty sausages, frozen whole eggs, dried whole eggs, assortments of frozen omelet mixes, frozen potato products, including hashed brown, frozen crepe, frozen creamed chip beef, frozen waffles, frozen French toast, toaster-heated waffles and French toast, waffle and pancake powdered mixes, frozen muffins, biscuits, pastries and rolls.

Convenience Breakfast Meats

Bacon.—Cooked bacon slices that may be frozen or refrigerated are conveniently packaged and easy to prepare. The advantages are: uniform slices, a reduction in waste, ease of preparation, and versatility, in that the bacon is adaptable to other uses.

Preparation is by simple heating in a broiler, oven, microwave oven or on a griddle. Microwave heating is accomplished in about 15 to 20 sec, heating in a broiler in about 3 to 4 min, and on a griddle in about 2 min. The heating time is dependent on the degree of doneness desired.

Sausage Links and Patties.—These products offer the same advantages as the pre-cooked bacon. Heating time is about the same as for bacon and depends on the degree of doneness. Sausages heated in a microwave oven may require browning in a broiler.

Convenience Egg Forms

Dried Whole Eggs.—Dried whole eggs may be used in place of shell eggs only in thoroughly cooked dishes such as scrambled eggs, casseroles and soufflés. Cooking is best when done in either conventional or convection ovens. Water or a 50–50 mixture of water and milk can be used for reconstitution. The measured amount of dried egg is sprinkled over an equivalent amount of liquid. It is then blended by whipping or with a mixer.

After reconstitution, the liquid eggs should be poured into a pan to a maximum height of 1 in. In addition to baking, the egg liquid mixture can be steamed. Overheating should be avoided, as it may result in a chewy, rubbery textured product.

Frozen Omelet Mixes.—These items are packed in various sizes, such as half gallon, quarts, or a 4-oz portion-pack carton. Frozen omelet mixes possess several interesting advantages, such as uniformity, reduction in waste, reduction in labor, and positive inventory control. A wide selection of omelet mixes is available, such as ham, western, eastern, mushroom, onion, cheese and plain. The eggs are homogenized before freezing. The plain omelet mix may be filled with jelly, chopped beef, or herbs. Prior to preparation these products must be thawed. Heating may be performed in the conventional manner. In addition to breakfast applications the omelets may be used for lunch entrées. The plain omelet can be transformed into a Spanish or Creole specialty. Fillings like crabmeat, minced clams, marinara, sautéed chicken livers, and potatoes and bacon bits are suggestions for interesting dishes. In all cases the basic rule to follow is to cook eggs at a low temperature to avoid a tough texture.

Frozen omelet mixes can be employed for shirred and baked egg dishes. Cheese, sausage and various vegetables may be added to the plain omelet mix and baked at 350°F for about 15 min or until the proper degree of doneness is reached. Pre-prepared and frozen scrambled eggs and beef patties or bacon are obtainable packed in 24 individual portions per case.

Crepes, Pancakes, Waffles and French Toast

Crepes.—These are frozen thin, round pancakes that may be used for either breakfast or dessert dishes. They can form the base for such dishes as crepes suzettes, German and Swedish pancakes. Before preparation, they should be thawed so that they are pliable. They may be heated flat or rolled. Many novel fillings can be used, such as fruit fillings, jams, preserves, onion and cheese mixtures, cherry sauce and other sweet sauces.

Pancakes.—Pancakes are available as powdered mixes, liquid frozen batter, and pre-prepared frozen. The latter should be thawed before heating in a microwave oven, convection oven or on a griddle. Powdered pancake mixes are easy to handle. The amount of water required is about equal to the weight of the mix. Two-thirds of the water is placed in a bowl and the mix is added slowly and mixed with a wire whip. After blending, the remainder of the water is added. The batter is portioned and then placed on a pre-heated griddle (390°–400°F) for about 1 min per side. Five pounds of powdered mix will produce about 80 to 90 2-oz pancakes. These mixes may also be used for a batter dip or a breading material. Manufacturer's instructions vary and must be followed for quality results.

Waffles and French Toast.—Both waffles and French toast have been available to the retail trade for many years. They are presently packed in institutional sizes. These products may be heated in toasters, in ovens, or on a griddle. Cost per unit portion is substantially higher than those products which are freshly prepared. However, they are useful for mass institutional production and for low volume restaurants to fill an occasional order. Frozen waffles and French toast need not be thawed before heating. They should be thawed, however, if toppings are to be incorporated into the body of the product.

VERSATILE BASIC PRE-PREPARED FROZEN FOODS

Basic pre-prepared frozen foods may be used as the starting point to fashion a wide selection of dishes. Many standard and specialty dishes are possible by manipulating such basic products as beef slices, beef chunks or tips; chicken breasts, chunks and parts; meat loaf and meat balls; turkey products, veal slices and steaks; and prepared items like chow mein. These products and others are marketed bulk packed in useful steam table pans or in pouches. They are prepared plain, with sauces, gravy or au jus.

The employment of basic pre-prepared frozen products presents a number of interesting advantages: (1) many dishes may be created from a basic ingredient; (2) storage space is reduced; (3) inventory and purchasing are eased, since the number of items is decreased; (4) incorporated accompaniments such as vegetables, sauces and other ingredients will possess a fresh character and can be added for individual appeal; (5) procedures are relatively simple so that the preparations can be incorporated into a smooth flowing system.

Beef Products.—Prior to the conversion, sauces and gravies should be removed and set aside. After thawing, sauces and gravies can be spooned off and used as the foundation in preparing the final embellishments. If they are not used up, they may be refrigerated or refrozen for the future.

The following are several suggestions for the adaptation of beef chunks, tips and slices:

(1) Convert to a goulash by the addition of a sauce containing paprika, tomato sauce, instant onion, ground red pepper and sweet pepper flakes.

(2) Prepare a beef Stroganoff by adding sour cream, mushrooms, chopped onions, sherry wine and dry mustard.

(3) Teriyaki may be created by the addition of soy sauce, sugar, ginger and powdered garlic. After the sauce is added, marination is required prior to final heating.

(4) Ready-to-cook braised beef tips with mushroom gravy can be converted into the following dishes: beef and Spanish rice, beef and kidney beans or chili con carne, beef and buttered noodles, beef stew with the addition of cooked diced potatoes, peas, carrots and onions.

(5) Beef tips to which a traditional Madeira wine sauce is added.

(6) Beef chunks can be used as a filling for beef pot pies, or they can be served with noodles, dumplings or spaetzle.

(7) Braised beef slices can be transformed into a flavorful Swiss steak combination by adding a beef and tomato gravy, chili sauce, cornstarch, instant diced and sliced onions.

(8) Other suggestions include beef Bourguignonne, beef Burgundy with red wine, Yankee pot roast, peppered beef, sweet and sour beef, beef kabob.

Meat Loaf and Meat Balls.—These products are useful foundations for a number of popular dishes. Meat loaf and meat balls are marketed pre-prepared plain or with sauces and gravies.

The following dishes can be prepared from these products: meat balls Polynesian by adding sweet and sour sauce, pineapple, green pepper and pimiento.

Other variations are feasible by adding horseradish dressing, chili, oregano, onion flakes, chili and garlic powder; curry, celery flakes and toasted sesame seeds, tarragon; a herb mixture containing chives, parsley, minced onion and tarragon; tomato purée and basil, and variations of barbecue sauces. Other dishes are Swedish meat balls, meat balls Stroganoff, spaghetti sauce and meat balls, meat balls in tomato sauce for a hero sandwich.

Chicken Breasts, Chunks and Parts.—These products can be used for a variety of delightful, interesting and tasty dishes, such as Polynesian chicken, curry chicken, chicken Cacciatore, coq au vin, chicken pilaf, chicken Bengal, chicken fricassee, chicken a la king, chicken Tetrazzini, chicken stew, chicken and noodles au gratin, chicken breasts with wine sauce made from condensed mushroom soup, paprika and sauterne wine; chicken salad.

Turkey Breasts, Chunks and Parts.—Turkey products, like chicken, are processed into a number of forms, such as rolls, patties, diced meat, slices, breasts, and parts like thighs, wings, and drumsticks. These pre-prepared forms can be transformed into dishes such as turkey Tetrazzini, turkey Milanese, turkey a la king, turkey salad, sliced turkey and giblet gravy, turkey Parmesan, and turkey with dressing.

Chow Mein.—Basic vegetable chow mein consisting of water chestnuts, sugar, chicken or beef stock, bean sprouts, sweet red pepper, bamboo shoots, onions, soy sauce, celery, green pepper and spices may be used to create several interesting Oriental dishes. Products like shrimp, pork, chicken, turkey and beef may be added to fashion a number of popular Chinese dishes with exotic names like Subgum, Cantonese, Hsia Min and Chu Jow Chow Mein.

Veal and Other Basic Foods.—Veal slices and chunks may be used for scallopini, Parmesan, veal and peppers, veal cordon bleu, veal and rice curried, veal paprika, veal stew with red wine, and veal in Creole sauce.

Other meats like pork or ham may be treated in a similar manner to form a variety of standard and specialty dishes.

NATIONALITY AND ETHNIC DISHES

International or nationality and ethnic foods have developed into a major segment of the vast convenience food service industry. Popularity has now reached the level where processors are rapidly adding new products and improving existing recipes.

Nationality dishes are packed in all forms—canned, frozen, bulk and portion packs. At the present time Mexican, Italian, and Chinese foods are leading the roster of international products, followed by French, Russian, German, Polynesian, Spanish, Hungarian, Irish, English, Jewish-style and Kosher foods. The order in which these foods are given does not represent the volume or popularity. The popularity of ethnic foods changes from one locality to another. New York, Miami, and Los Angeles, for example, are major markets for Jewish-style and Chinese food. Mexican foods excel in Houston and Los Angeles, while Italian dishes have wide acceptance in New York, Boston, and Detroit. Pizza is the most popular of all nationality foods.

General Characteristics

Nationality frozen food, for the most part, shares one common denominator with its foreign counterpart—the name of the dish. Although many of the foods currently available are based on authentic recipes, they are actually formulated to meet the average American taste requirements and are intentionally underspiced. For example, pre-prepared frozen Mexican foods are not overly or "fiery" spiced. The final applications of spices and other interesting additions are reserved to the discretion of the individual food service establishment.

The overall acceptance of nationality foods is generated by the glamor and romance associated with eating products from faraway places. This feeling stems in part from the hordes of American travellers that have visited foreign countries in recent years. In addition, many restaurants have welcomed a change to exotic dishes, since they have helped to convey an exciting atmosphere and have also created a new and distinctive reputation for the establishment. Operators also find that nationality foods can be easily merchandised, that they generate a high profit, and since they are pre-prepared, they do not require the services of expensive chefs. The younger generation has also shown a flair for these foods. Many of the leading nationality dishes, such as pizza, tacos and lasagne, are served in schools and other areas frequented by youth.

The boundless assortments of pre-prepared and semi-prepared nationality foods are staggering. Every menu segment is represented, from appetizers to desserts and beverages. The field of foreign foods is only briefly explored here, and a number of popular dishes are described.

Certain pre-prepared frozen ethnic foods that represent a number of national backgrounds are meeting with country-wide acceptance. These are: poultry Tetrazzini, lasagne, beef and chili enchiladas, chicken and Rock Cornish hen breast a la Kiev and Cordon Bleu, beef Stroganoff, veal Parmigiana, veal scallopini, Italian spaghetti, pizza, sauerbraten, chicken Cacciatore, and coq au vin.

Mexican Foods

Mexican foods are prepared from several basic products: the corn base of which a tortilla or corn pancake is an example; frijoles or bean dish; and chili or Mexican peppers. The latter should not be confused with chili powder which is a blend of spices consisting of chili peppers, oregano, cumin seed, garlic, cloves, red pepper and allspice. This is a basic seasoning for Mexican cooking, including chili con carne.

Mexican cooking has usually been associated with the addition of "hot" spices. This may be the case with several of the traditional Mexican dishes. However, the wide range of recipes do not call for an overabundance of spices.

Following is a list of convenience foods prepared in the traditional Mexican manner, but with a spice level acceptable to the American taste: Enchiladas, Chili Rellnos, Tacos, Tamale Pies, Refritos, Guacamole and Burritos.

The Tacos Fad.—Tacos, the Mexican sandwich, are widely consumed in the southwestern part of the United States. They are served in fast food outlets, specialty shops, schools and institutions. The shell of the tacos is a deep-fried corn tortilla, which is used to hold a filling consisting of seasoned browned ground beef. Other fillings are employed, such as pork, poultry and seasoned chopped vegetables.

Pre-prepared tacos shells are available that require a simple heating operation after they are filled. Heating is done in an oven preset at 400°F for 5 to 10 min. Garnishes are added when the tacos is served, either as a side dish or placed on top of the product. Ripe olives, chopped onions and tomatoes, and sliced avocado and sour cream may also be used as garnishes.

Spanish or Mexican rice, mashed cooked beans and chili beans make a tasty combination with tacos.

Guacamole.—Guacamole is a popular Mexican appetizer prepared from a mixture of spices consisting of onion and garlic salt, chili powder, and lemon juice. The spice mixture is added to diced tomatoes and mashed avocados.

Enchiladas.—Enchiladas differ from tacos in that they are served on a dish and eaten with a fork. The fillings are rolled into the tortilla, which is then covered with chili sauce and garnished with cheese. Fillings vary from beef and spicy sauce to chopped onion, spices and cheese. Parmesan or Cheddar cheese may be used for garnishes. Seasonings may contain Tabasco sauce, ground chili and minced onion. Enchiladas are available pre-prepared frozen and are packed in steam-table size pans for volume feeding operations.

Refritos.—Refritos are refried beans. Pinto beans are widely used for this dish. The beans are seasoned with minced onion and garlic, and dried ground chili peppers. The beans are mashed, seasoned and then sautéed or fried. This popular dish is also packed in steam-table pans.

Tamales.—Tamales are made as pies, or the filling is wrapped in a soft corn masa which is a mixture of ground corn. Seasoned meats and beef chili may be used for fillings. Tamale pies are prepared by spreading a thick cornmeal dough in a shallow pan. A filling consisting of pepper, chili powder, chopped parsley, tomatoes, shortening, minced onions and ground beef is placed over the cornmeal, and it is then topped with a corn-meal layer. The top is garnished with a a sharp cheese and the dish is baked until brown.

Italian Dishes

The increasing interest in Italian cuisine has motivated manufacturers of convenience foods to create and market numerous products incorporating Italian recipes. Authentic Italian food varies with the locality or province. Tomato products and garlic are heavily employed in the central and southern portions of Italy, but Roman and north Italian cooking use less. White sauces delicately treated with spices, herbs, and light wine are favored in these areas. Minestrone soup, for example, covers a wide range of recipes depending on the province in which it originated. Basic Italian minestrone soup usually contains vegetables, pasta, meat and legumes, to which a grated cheese is added.

Leading Italian convenience dishes favored in the United States are pizza, poultry and seafood Tetrazzini, lasagne, spaghetti in Italian sauce with meatballs, spaghetti and clam sauce, chicken Cacciatore, manicotti, ravioli, veal and eggplant Parmesan, veal scallopini, poultry Milanese, ziti, Italian salad dressings, Italian sauces (marinara and mushroom), and minestrone. Many kinds of pasta are also obtainable frozen, including egg noodles, green noodles, rigatoni, cavatelli, and gnocchi. Italian style macaroni and cheese with wine is also marketed.

Italian Seasonings.—Italian seasonings are characteristic. They use as a base such spices and herbs as oregano, basil, red pepper, rosemary and garlic powder. Blended variations are marketed which may be used to create many Italian recipes.

A typical pizza sauce may contain crushed red pepper, ground thyme, fennel seed, ground sage, ground oregano, ground basil, parsley flakes, ground black pepper, garlic powder and minced onions. These ingredients are blended into tomato paste, Italian-style plum tomatoes and olive oil. Pizza dough is a modified biscuit flour mix which provides a tender crust, provided a minimum of mixing is used. Prepared pizza freezes well and has good storage capabilities.

Seasonings for lasagne may be celery flakes, instant minced garlic and onion, oregano leaves, black pepper and basil leaves.

A typical minestrone seasoning consists of garlic and onion powder, celery flakes, sweet pepper flakes, basil leaves and black pepper. A rapid method of preparing this soup is to add the seasoning mixture to vegetable soup or a combination of vegetable and bean soup.

Beef or veal scallopini with a wine mushroom sauce is quickly prepared from frozen pre-cooked meat slices to which a mixture of olive oil, minced garlic and onion, mushrooms, pepper and salt are added. The combination is sautéed, during which time the red wine is added.

Pizza.—Pizza heads the list of nationality dishes. These are made with many flavors and garnishes, such as sausage, cheese, sausage and cheese, peppers and beef, mushroom, and meatball. The large round pizza with a thin crust are most popular, while those made with a thick crust, square and rectangular, are less in demand. Frozen pizza is easily reheated either in an oven or broiler (Fig. 9.16).

Lasagne.—Another Italian dish which has wide appeal is lasagne. A basic recipe consists of one of the several cheeses, (Parmesan, Ricotta and Mozzerella), tomato sauce, ground pork, beef or chicken, olive oil, and seasonings like celery flakes, garlic, onion, oregano, black pepper and basil leaves. The pasta used is made in strips 1 in. wide.

Courtesy of American Spice Trade Association

FIG. 9.16. SPICES, MUSHROOMS AND OTHER INGREDIENTS USED TO EMBELLISH A SUPER PIZZA

Ravioli.—Another important frozen Italian food is Ravioli, produced with assorted fillings, like cheese, mushroom, and beef. Sauces are varied and may include tomato purée, onion, garlic, celery flakes, parsley, basil and oregano. They are packed in oven-ready pans.

Other Italian Frozen Dishes.—Other Italian frozen dishes which are obtainable are veal and peppers, stuffed peppers Italian style, scallops Florentine, and zucchini with tomatoes.

Chinese Foods

Pre-prepared Chinese foods appeared in the retail market long before many other nationality products. These products were packed in cans and consisted chiefly of chow mein and chop suey dishes. The phenomenal growth of all types of foreign foods has placed Chinese products in the lime-light of popularity. Many of the foods which are available not only provide a festive touch to a menu, but they are easily prepared and served. Compared to other nationality foods, Chinese dishes are relatively inexpensive and return an interesting margin of profit.

American-style Chinese dishes are usually concocted for the domestic palate, which seems to be the case for the vast majority of nationality foods. Authentic Chinese cooking is based on several regional themes, such as Cantonese cooking, Honan recipes and the classic Fukien cuisine. Cantonese dishes are generally prepared by sautéing, grilling and roasting, whereas Honan specialties favor sweet and sour recipes. Fukien cooking can be characterized as leaning more to the American tastes, as it comprises an assortment of notable Chinese dishes.

The choice of pre-prepared Chinese foods is impressive. They are favored at all levels of the food service industry. The following are a number of readily obtainable convenience Chinese foods:

(1) Fried rice with smoked pork, beef or without meat. These dishes may be served as entrées or in place of potato or a vegetable.

(2) Chow mein is marketed as all vegetable, chicken, shrimp, pork or beef.

(3) Egg rolls are obtainable in many sizes and with a variety of fillings, like shrimp, meat and shrimp, and meat. These products may be used as accompaniments, appetizers or as hot hors d'oeuvres.

(4) Sweet and sour beef or pork that contains Oriental vegetables and chunks of meat. Those products designated as either Chinese or Polynesian are similar in many respects. For example, breaded chicken or shrimp, in a sweet and sour sauce, containing pineapple and topped with cut or sliced almonds are featured as either Chinese or Polynesian.

(5) Frozen Chinese soups are obtainable as egg drop, Chinese noodle and won ton.

(6) An assortment of Chinese products are packed in No. 10 cans, e.g., fried and dried noodles; sliced, diced and stripped bamboo shoots; whole and sliced water chestnuts; Oriental mixed vegetables; chow mein; and sauces.

(7) Pre-prepared spare ribs in a sweet and sour sauce with pineapple tidbits added are available. This product may contain the following additional items: soy sauce, chili sauce, pimiento, diced green pepper, water chestnuts, sweet pickle juice, ginger, garlic cloves, and passion fruit nectar.

Frozen Chinese dishes are available in half and full sized steam table pans and in boilable pouches. Egg rolls are packed bulk, 12, 24, 48, 100 or 200 units per case.

Creating Chinese Dishes with Basic Prepared Ingredients.—Prepared Chinese foods may require enhancing and a change in texture. An objectionable characteristic of some prepared Chinese foods is the soggy or mushy texture. This condition may be corrected by the addition of crisp and firm freshly cooked or heated garnishes or ingredients. For example, shrimp, meats, mushroom, sliced almonds, sliced or diced fresh green or red pepper, and pineapple chunks may be placed on top of a portion of chow mein just before serving. Other products, such as pea pods, bamboo shoots, and water chestnuts, may also be added, if they can provide the desirable textural qualities. Seasonings like powdered mustard, ground ginger, cinnamon, cloves, and fennel may be added to enhance the flavor.

In addition, a number of classic Chinese dishes may be prepared from basic cooked meats, poultry, fish and shellfish. The following are selected examples:

(1) *Steak Kew:* Prepared cooked tenderloin is lightly marinated in a red

wine and soy sauce, and then lightly sautéed with mushrooms and Chinese vegetables.

(2) *Beef in Oriental oyster sauce:* Slices of beef and mushrooms are enriched with prepared Oriental oyster sauce.

(3) *Sweet and pungent beef, poultry or pork:* Cubes or chunks of frozen raw beef, poultry or pork are breaded and deep-fried and then served in a sweet and sour sauce with pineapple garnish.

(4) *Almond Gai Ding:* Diced cooked chicken is blended with bamboo shoots, mushrooms, water chestnuts and other vegetables and served in a rich soy sauce.

(5) *Moo Goo Gai Pan:* Sliced cooked chicken is blended with celery, bamboo shoots, mushrooms and hearts of Chinese vegetables.

(6) *Lobster Cantonese:* Chopped lobster meat is blended in a meat and egg sauce and accented with garlic and shallots.

(7) *Shrimp Soong:* Cooked whole shrimp is blended with Chinese vegetables and mixed with toasted vermicelli.

(8) *Wor Bar Sub Gum:* Cooked cubed lobster, pork, chicken and shrimp are simmered in an Oriental prepared oyster sauce and served on a bed of Chinese vegetables.

French Dishes

Will it be boeuf Bourguignonne, quiche Lorraine, boeuf à la mode, sole Mornay, poulet Chasseur, coquilles St. Jacques, potage Saint Germain, soupe a l'Oignon or escargots? These are but a partial list of numerous pre-prepared frozen French dishes available to the food service industry. Because of the large assortment of these foods, restaurants are availing themselves of the opportunity to specialize in a French cuisine without the need for highly trained chefs. Many of the pre-prepared French dishes are formulated from authentic recipes. Only those recipes that have wide appeal and are easy to process were chosen for commercial distribution.

Convenience French dishes are made to fit each segment of a menu. Pre-prepared French appetizers, for instance, are quiche Lorraine, crab or lobster quiche, coquille Saint Jacques, escargots, pâté de foie gras, and crepes filled with various meats, poultry or cheese.

Authentic frozen soups are potage Saint Germain, soupe a l'Oignon or Vichyssoise.

Entrées are varied and consist of poulet Chasseur, boeuf Bourguignon, boeuf à la mode, ragout of boeuf, sole Mornay, poulet Jardiniere à la crème, and Coq au Vin.

Dressings and sauces are obtainable that provide a touch of authenticity to vegetables and salads. Many of these items are manufactured in the United States, but some are imported from France.

French style pre-prepared foods are handled, prepared, garnished and served in the same general manner as other convenience products. Manufacturers' instructions must be followed for quality results. Included with most products is a set of suggestions for garnishing and other accompaniments considered to be compatible in flavor and appèarance.

French-type desserts available include chocolate mousse, crepes, miniature pastries, custards, tarts and cream puffs. The following breads and rolls are obtainable: croissants, brioche, and la baquette (a long, slender loaf of bread with a crunchy crust). More than 100 varieties of French cheese are exported to the United States. Cheese like Camembert is exported frozen. The cheese is frozen at its peak of perfection to assure perfect ripeness. Other cheeses are canned and keep for months under refrigeration.

Glossary of Some Convenience French Dishes.—(1) *Boeuf à la Mode:* Cubes of tender beef are simmered with vegetables in a white wine sauce. Seasonings such as whole cloves, parsley flakes, bay leaf, thyme leaves and whole black pepper are added.

(2) *Boeuf Bourguignonne:* A beef stew with vegetables in a Burgundy wine sauce with various seasonings.

(3) *Coq au Vin:* Chicken cooked in a red wine sauce with mushroom, bacon and onions.

(4) *Poulet Chasseur:* Chicken, hunter style, spiced, with tomatoes, shallots, garlic, basil or tarragon, and white wine.

(5) *Coquilles St. Jacques:* Scallops prepared in butter and served with parsley butter or cream sauce in a scallop shell.

(6) *Ragout:* A stew with a rich gravy.

(7) *Quiche Lorraine:* Eggs, diced bacon or ham, heavy cream, nutmeg, pepper, minced onions, white pepper and ground nutmeg. These ingredients are placed in a pastry shell and baked.

(8) *Potage Saint Germain:* Green split pea soup, served with crumbled bacon, ham slivers, cheese, or croutons.

(9) *Sole Mornay:* Flat or rolled fillets of sole covered with a cheese sauce and garnished with mashed potatoes.

(10) *Soupe à l'Oignon:* French onion soup consisting of meat broth strongly flavored with onion, slices of cooked onions, and served with grated Parmesan cheese.

(11) *Vichyssoise:* A cream soup of puréed potatoes, chicken stock and leeks. This soup is generally served cold and garnished with chives.

Other Leading Nationality Dishes

Several Russian dishes are gaining wide acceptance. These are beef stroganoff and chicken à la Kiev. Beef stroganoff consists of simmered and seared slices of beef tenderloin, rich sour cream, beef gravy and mushrooms. This dish is also obtainable with meat balls. Chicken à la Kiev contains chicken breasts (boneless and skinless) stuffed with a finger of seasoned butter, egg-dipped, and breaded for deep frying. Germany is represented with sauerbraten and potato dumplings, Sweden with its meat balls, Hungary with beef goulash, and Japan with several prepared dishes such as teriyaki.

OTHER CONVENIENCE DISHES

A vast segment of the convenience food market remains for discussion. These include combination dishes such as casseroles, pies and stews, meat, poultry, and fish products. These groups of pre-prepared and frozen foods follow the same handling patterns as those previously described. The crucial problem confronting food service buyers is to assort and evaluate the numbers of convenience foods so that meaningful selections can be made. Scores of similar-named items are marketed by a long list of manufacturers. This situation poses an exercise in differentiating and assorting the various sales claims of the processor and in determining which food offers optimum capabilities, value and consumer acceptance. Methods of quality evaluation have been demonstrated in Chapters 7 and 8.

Testing Programs

The Food Service Department of the University of Massachusetts decided to embark on an extensive convenience foods evaluation survey as the first step towards adopting its own program. Their objective was to evaluate pre-prepared foods that would equal or better the quality of those prepared conventionally. Eight hundred products were tested, of which about 350 were entrées. Of these, 50 entrées were judged as acceptable to the school's standards. The results of the tests emphasized two important facts regarding brand-named products: (1) it cannot be assumed that foods sold under known brands are all quality products; and (2) poor quality was found from all producers (Stoneham, 1971).

The maze of new products constantly offered to the food service industry may require additional evaluation stemming from the rigors of freezing, storage and subsequent heating. These evaluations center around the time-temperature effects on frozen food stability. Presently there is little public information on the stability of frozen prepared foods. The variation in raw materials and formulations is infinite, and such variables affect stability (Olson, 1971).

Products such as custards, and cooked egg whites are changed by freezing and reheating. Turkey and fatty fish dishes show marked deterioration during frozen storage. Creamed soups, gravies, and poultry casseroles and pies can withstand freezing, storage and heating, provided that formulations are altered to withstand these conditions.

Factors of Product Evaluation

In Chapter 7, Quality Control, parameters for determining quality were discussed. These included flavor, texture, color, nutrition, ease of convenience and an economic evaluation. Pre-prepared foods should be selected for their natural color traits, pleasing texture, and appealing balanced flavor. Accompaniments such as gravy and sauces must be smooth, and compatible with foods that they are placed on. Existing Government standards that regulate the amount of meat and poultry required in pre-prepared dishes may require implementation. Lists are presented in Chapter 7 that show the various percentages of meat and poultry in pre-prepared dishes. However, no mention is made of the grade and cut of meat or poultry nor the quality and composition of other ingredients, as long as they are wholesome. The final quality will also depend on the method and type of heating equipment and whether a workable relationship exits between the proposed food and the heating device.

Finally, an evaluation may have to be made of a packer's recipe. Each processor has his own ideas as to the formulation and the desires of the trade. For example, the following are the listed product ingredients on the labels of two brands of Sloppy Joes: Brand A—braised lean chopped beef, spices, sweet pickles, peppers, vinegar, and barbecue sauce. Brand B—beef, water, relish, chili sauce, onions, flour, vinegar, paprika, corn starch, sugar, salt, pepper, and garlic. The packer of Brand B also gives the following information: The beef is USDA Grade-Choice; percentages of the main ingredients are given as 45% beef, 8% relish, and 8% chili sauce. Brand B lists guidelines for heating, serving and garnishing, whereas Brand A does not provide this information.

Both packers neglected to state the effects of prolonged storage on the final quality. This information should be requested from the processor. If the processor states that an item may be stored in a freezer at $-18°F$ for a 1-yr period, you may also have to know the length of storage at $-10°F$ or $0°F$ if your freezer cannot maintain the lower or recommended temperature. In addition, you must understand and decipher packing codes. This information will aid in stock rotation and will give an indication of the length of optimum storage time remaining.

Processors' Guidelines.—One important factor that has been continually stressed in this book is to follow the preparation instructions issued by the manufacturers (Fig. 9.17). It is assumed that all products have been properly tested in the processors' kitchens and instructional guidelines written as a result of his program. If the instructions are not clear, or a step is missing, the manufacturer or his agent should be notified. After their procedures are understood the data should be recorded and disseminated to others. Instruction cards, clearly marked, which list each step of the procedure should be drawn up and posted at the appropriate station. However, prior to a full production run, several trials of the processor's instructions should be made. These directives are merely guidelines, and since a number of production variables may be encountered, trials are recommended for quality results.

Some manufacturers are more diligent in their efforts to assure that their products meet with full satisfaction. For example, one processor of pre-prepared frozen foods (Anon. 1971I) has issued comprehensive instructions for

EXCHANGES: Each serving (
ounces (by volume) will supply
2 meat exchanges (less 5 grams
fat) and 1 bread exchange.

TABLE OF ANALYSIS	Per 100 gram.	Each 6 oz. serving
Carbohydrates (gms)	9.4	15
Protein (gms)	10	16
Fat (gms)	3	5
Available Calories (mg)	108	173
Sodium (mg)	20	32

COOKED MEAT CONTENT = 31%

FROZEN
SAUCE, GROUND
BEEF & MACARONI

FOR MODIFIED DIETS: SODIUM CONTROLLED, FAT CONTROLLED,
SOFT, BLAND, DIABETIC DIETS.

INGREDIENTS: Tomato sauce (water, tomato paste, tapioca starch, wheat flour, artificial color), cooked ground beef, macaroni.

NET WT. 5 LBS.

14 — 6 oz. servings by volume.
14 — 5.6 oz. servings by weight.

HEATING INSTRUCTIONS
Minimum recommended serving temperature 160° F.
Remove label. Pierce center of cover.

CONVENTIONAL OVEN
Preheat oven to 450° F.
Heat 55 to 70 minutes.

CONVECTION OVEN
Preheat oven to 450° F.
Heat for 30 to 45 minutes.

INFRA RED OVEN
Set temperature control at #6 or #7.
Place tray in oven. Heat for 30 to 45 minutes.

PRESSURE STEAMER
Low pressure 4 # to 7 #.
55 to 65 minutes.
High pressure 15 #.
30 to 45 minutes.

MEDI-DIET T.M.

DISTRIBUTED BY NATIONAL HOSPITAL FOODS, INC. 540 FRONTAGE RD., NORTHFIELD, ILL. 60093
SPECIALISTS IN PREPARED ENTREES FOR MODIFIED DIETS
A SUBSIDIARY OF WILSON-SINCLAIR CO.

Courtesy of National Hospital Foods, Inc.

FIG. 9.17. HEATING AND SERVING INSTRUCTIONS PROPERLY DISPLAYED, ARE SHOWN AT RIGHT SIDE OF PRODUCT LABEL; THESE INSTRUCTIONS ARE CONCISE AND MEET MOST HEATING OPERATIONS

each of his products. Included in these are guidelines for heating the food by various means, and a question sheet for the operator's use. Each set of questions pertains to a different method of heating. Time and temperature data are entered in the blank space provided for each question, when determined. In addition, the processor includes a sheet that shows the effects of holding time on the heated food. The results are interesting and helpful, since it provides the operator with a guide for maximum holding time on a steam table and what happens to the product if it is held too long. Instructions are also given for serving the products, and the garnishes and other accompaniments that are best suited for them.

Pre-prepared Combination Dishes

Pre-prepared combination dishes are an important segment of the convenience food market. These products form the backbone or nucleus of fast food concepts. They were among the first items to meet with success during the infancy of the frozen food industry. Presently this segment is extensive and includes such dishes as: stews, macaroni and cheese, macaroni and beef, creamed chicken, tuna noodle casserole, crab and lobster Newburg, chicken and noodles au gratin, veal and peppers, chicken fricasse, various casseroles, spaghetti and meat balls, braised lamb and curry, pot roasts, Swiss steak, chicken and beef turnovers, and pot pies.

Over the years many combination dishes introduced did not measure up to consumer expectations. Because of this dissatisfaction, consumers whose initial encounter with convenience foods was disappointing were reluctant to try other products.

Combination dishes should be served in interesting shapes, properly garnished, correctly seasoned so that a balanced flavor is achieved; and they should possess contrasting natural color. The aroma should be tantalizing and fresh. The food should be served hot, but over-cooking must be avoided. Over-cooked combination dishes are perhaps a major area for consumer dissatisfaction. Over-cooking and holding may darken or discolor an otherwise natural looking product. Changes in texture may also occur, so that the food becomes tough, soft, rubbery, or mushy. Crusts should be flaky, and the food should not be watery, dry or mealy. The meat, poultry or fish should not be tough or chewy. Vegetables should have a sparkling, natural color, and should be tender, not mushy.

Packaging.—Pre-prepared combination foods are marketed in cans, and frozen in steam-table pans, boilable pouches, or in single-portion pans. An array of canned foods is represented. These are packed in individual portions (for vending) and in intermediate sizes up to the No. 10 can. Canned prepared products are not new; however, innovations in processing and canning have helped develop many choice entrées. The outstanding advantage of canned items is easy storage. Canned entrées may be combined with fresh or frozen foods to increase their appeal and reinforce the flavor. Examples of canned entrées are: corned beef hash, beef stew, chow mein and chop suey, stuffed peppers and cabbage, ravioli, noodles in combination with a variety of products, sloppy Joe mixtures, chili con carne, assorted prepared rice dishes, and many beef and chicken combinations. Pre-prepared sandwich fillings are packed in cans and include, salad components (celery, peppers), tuna, chicken, ham and shrimp salads.

A Cross Section of the Meat, Poultry and Seafood Market

The following is a representative list of pre-prepared and frozen foods, which together with other products discussed in the text form the composite convenience market:

Meat Dishes

Beef, Burgundy	Meat loaf
Beef, corned	Meat patties
Beef, liver	Pork chops, plain or stuffed
Beef, peppered	Pork loin in gravy
Beef, roast and slices	Pork sliced in gravy
Beef, in gravy	Steak, salisbury in various sauces
Beef, short-ribs	Steak, cubed
Beef, tips	Steak, tips
Ham in raisin sauce	Steak, Swiss
Ham and pork loaf	Veal, slices
Lamb in broth	Veal, patties
Meat balls in various gravies and sauces.	Veal, patties breaded

Poultry Dishes
Poultry, chicken, squab, stuffed and roasted
Poultry breasts, in various sauces
Turkey, sliced with gravy or dressing
Fried chicken, in barbecue sauce
Fried chicken livers

Seafood Dishes

Codfish, baked	Lobster, in various sauces
Crab in various sauces	Perch fillets
Crab-cake patties	Scallops
Fish sticks	Shrimp, in various sauces
Haddock, in lemon butter sauce	Sole, in lemon butter sauce
Halibut, in various sauces	

Vegetables

The consumption of vegetables has increased during the last few years. This rise in sales is attributed to the public's acceptance of vegetables prepared with sauces and specialty combinations. Another factor that has contributed to this interesting growth are the simple recipes being disseminated which can transform a bland-tasting green vegetable into a product that is flavorful and appealing. Before the latter half of the last decade the consumption of green vegetables declined. At the food service level only a few varieties of vegetables were served because of public apathy towards them. Reasons given for this situation stemmed from vegetables that were poorly prepared, over-cooked and watery. The vegetables that commanded wide acceptance during this period were potato products, green beans, onions and rice. Frozen potatoes, the first to be introduced, soared in popularity. Because of this meteoric acceptance they formed the foundation for the vast frozen food industry.

Prepared Vegetables.—Those vegetables that have gained public support have been converted into appetizing dishes by the addition of sauces, herbs, spices, cheese and interesting garnishes.

Sauces such as butter mixtures, hollandaise, cheese, herb, wine, white, Creole and tomato are incorporated into the vegetables. These and other products like souffléed foods are flash-frozen, and are obtainable in various size pans or pouch-packed.

Garnishes consisting of mushrooms, nuts and cheese have also aided in the creation of tasty vegetables. Simple spice or herb combinations have also induced appeal. Vegetable combinations encompassing items like corn and lima beans; carrots, peas, onions and mushrooms; green beans, carrots, dill and seasonings; beets with orange sauce; zucchini, onions and tomatoes, and other mixtures are being readily ordered. Vegetables prepared from nationality recipes are also finding favor with the dining public. Regional types, such as okra, yams, blackeye peas, chopped collard, kale, mustard and turnip greens, are finding their way into a number of widely used combinations. The change in the public attitude toward vegetables because of this increased palatability can be traced to the influence of foreign cooking. Vegetables were among the major foods consumed by Europeans. These were either home-grown or locally produced, and were less expensive than meat. Many recipes were formulated to create dishes of lasting appeal. Some were truly inventive. Many vegetable dishes created by the French have been modified and followed in America.

Notable Italian dishes employ a number of green vegetables, such as spinach and zucchini. Dairy and dietary restaurants specialize in vegetable dishes that are prepared and formed into shapes resembling meat loaf, patties, cutlets, casseroles and stews.

Green Beans.—Green beans are widely consumed and their appeal may be enhanced in numerous ways. To illustrate methods of transforming or altering the flavor and texture of vegetables, green beans are used as an example.

(1) Certain seasonings tend to subdue the beany flavor and add a delicate tone. Tarragon, sage, pepper and onion powder, basil leaf, dill, mint, mustard seed, oregano, savory, or thyme may be used to impart a distinctive character.

(2) A Parmesan cheese dish can be created by adding a mixture of freeze-dried sliced onions, pimiento, garlic powder, paprika and grated Parmesan cheese to either canned or frozen green beans.

(3) Varieties of butter sauces are excellent with green beans.

(4) A mixture containing toasted sesame seeds, ginger, melted butter, and black pepper is added to the juice of canned green beans, producing a delicious combination.

(5) Bacon bits and reconstituted freeze-dried brown onions will add appeal to bland-tasting green beans.

(6) A simple au gratin dish may be prepared by adding grated cheese to a cream soup (mushroom). This is mixed with the green beans and placed in a pan, after which it is sprinkled with grated cheese and baked.

(7) A No. 10 can of green beans may be flavored with onion powder, white pepper and ground mace.

(8) Nuts such as pecans can be heated with butter and seasoned with salt and pepper. This is then spooned on top of a portion of green beans prior to serving.

A Survey of Some Available Prepared Vegetables.—

(1) Brussels sprouts au gratin, containing Cheddar cheese sauce and seasonings.

(2) Peas in an enriched herbed butter sauce.

(3) Creamed spinach containing chopped spinach in a mild Cheddar cheese sauce with seasonings added.

(4) Spinach soufflé consisting of chopped spinach and eggs in a seasoned cream sauce.

(5) Corn soufflé, a mixture of corn, milk, eggs, flour, pepper, monsodium glutamate, butter and sugar.

(6) Green beans containing sliced almonds in a butter sauce.

(7) Glazed carrots consisting of sliced carrots, orange rind and orange juice, brown sugar, butter and pepper.

(8) Rice combinations containing peas and mushrooms in a chicken flavored sauce with pimiento and paprika added. Other rice dishes are herbed and curried, Creole, Spanish and Oriental.

(9) Other prepared vegetables are: asparagus in hollandaise sauce, French beans with mushrooms, baby lima beans in butter sauce, corn and peas with tomatoes, onions in cream sauce, peas and onions, peas with celery, peas and potatoes in cream sauce; Bavarian, Danish, Japanese, Mexican and Spanish vegetables, mashed turnips, candied sweet potatoes, Hawaiian style sweet potatoes, fried eggplant sticks, eggplant and zucchini Parmesan; pinto beans and ham, and blackeye peas and ham.

Methods of Heating.—Pouched packed vegetables may be heated in a microwave oven, provided that the instructions are followed which are outlined in Chapter 5, Microwave Cookery, or in a pan of boiling water.

Those products that are packed in steam table pans may be heated in a pressure steam cooker according to instructions suggested by the processor.

Courtesy of Sani Serv

FIG. 9.18. FOOD WARMER FOR A HOLDING STATION, THAT IS HEATED BY TWO 250 WATT INFRARED HEAT LAMPS

For volume preparation these vegetables dishes may be heated in a convection oven preheated to a temperature of 390°-410°F. Depending on the product, heating from the frozen state will require about 35 min, and when thawed about 20 min.

Serving temperatures should range between 140° to 160°F for optimum appeal.

BIBLIOGRAPHY

ANON. 1966. Cheese in Family Meals. Home and Garden Bull. *112*, United States Department of Agriculture. Washington, D.C.

ANON. 1967. Quantity Food Preparation Guide, OE-82015. United States Department of Health, Education, and Welfare. Washington, D.C.

ANON. 1970A. From conventional to convenience. Institutional Distribution 6, No. 8, 54–56.

ANON. 1970B. Primer For Gourmet Cooking Groups. Foods From France Information Center, New York, N.Y.

ANON. 1970C. Sauces and Gravies, Technical Bull. *129*. The Hubinger Co., Keokuk, Iowa.

ANON. 1970D. Vegetables in family meals. Home and Garden Bull. *105*, United States Department of Agriculture, Washington, D.C.

ANON. 1970E. Gracious Dining. Idle Wild Farm, Pomfret Center, Conn.

ANON. 1970F. A Glossary of French Foods and Cookery. Foods From France Information Center, New York, N.Y.

ANON. 1971A. The Food Service Market for Frozen Foods. National Frozen Food Association, Inc., Hershey, Pa.

ANON. 1971B. Convenience Foods. Cooking for Profit. *40*, No. 5, 20–22.

ANON. 1971C. Cherrific Sales Boosters. National Red Cherry Institute, East Lansing, Mich.

ANON. 1971D. Cling Peach Recipes. Cling Peach Advisory Board, San Francisco, Calif.

ANON. 1971E. Convenience Foods for the Food Service Market. Dell Food Specialties Co., Beloit, Wis.

ANON. 1971F. Saber Club Cheese Bull. *1*, No. 1., New York, N.Y.

ANON. 1971G. Mushrooms, Pride of the Menu. American Mushroom Institute, Kennett Square, Pa.

ANON. 1971H. Vegetables back in spotlight. Frozen Food Age *20*, No. 2, 7–26.

ANON. 1971I. New Kettle Cooking Entrees. Uncle Ben's Inc., Houston, Texas.

CARLISLE, H., and HALL, R. L. 1969. Be an Artful Seasoner With Spices and Herbs. United States Department of Agriculture Yearbook, 249–252.

ENDRES, J. 1971. Some technical aspects of frozen entrees. Activities Report of Research and Development Associates for Military Food and Packaging Systems, Inc., Natick, Mass. *23*, No. 2, 57–60.

KERR, R. G. 1964. Fish Cookery For One Hundred. United States Department of the Interior, Washington D.C.

LOWENBURG, M. E. 1970. Socio-cultural basis of food habits. Food Technol. *24*, 751–756.

MARTIN, S. 1971. Boom in frozen snack products. Quick Frozen Foods *34*. No. 1, 49–51.

MONTAGNE, P. 1961. Larousse Gastronomique. Crown Publishers, New York.

MCGEARY, B. K., SMITH, M. E. 1969. Nuts, a Shell Game That Pays off in Good Eating. United States Department of Agriculture Yearbook, 196–204.

OLSON, R. L. 1971. Inventory control as affected by stability of frozen foods. Activities Report of the Research and Development Associates for Military Food and Packaging Systems, Inc., Natick, Mass. *23*, No. 2, 98–103.

PRESTBO, J. A. 1970. The vanishing chef: restaurants serve more frozen dishes. The Wall Street Journal *85*, No. 53, 1 and 33.

ROGERS, J. L. 1969. Production of Pre-Cooked Frozen Foods for Mass Catering. Food Trade Press, Ltd. London.

RIETZ, C. A., and WANDERSTOCK, J. J. 1965. A Guide to the Selection, Combination, and Cooking of Foods, Vol 2. Avi Publishing Co., Westport, Conn.

SANSTADT, H. 1971. Canned entrées are better than ever. Cooking for Profit *40*, No. 250, 28–32.

SCHERTZ, E. P., and BRODY, A. L., 1970. Convenience Foods. Report for Iowa Development Commission. Arthur D. Little, Inc., Cambridge, Mass.

STONEHAM, J. M. 1971. Phasing in convenience foods through extensive testing. Activities Report of Research and Development Associates for Military Food and Packaging Systems, Inc., Natick, Mass. *23*, No. 1, 87–92.

TRESSLER, D. K., VAN ARSDEL, W. B., and COPLEY, M. J. 1968. The Freezing Preservation of Foods, 4th Edition, Vol. 4. Avi Publishing Co. Westport, Conn.

CHAPTER 10

Convenience Desserts and Beverages

CONVENIENCE DESSERTS

Convenience desserts are the most successful and readily accepted area of the ready-to-serve food arena. Numerous convenience desserts like ice cream are taken for granted because they have been a part of the American scene for generations. The same applies to fresh baked products that are sold by local bakeries or in supermarkets. However, this chapter is devoted to frozen baked products and to other forms of desserts of recent origin.

The growth of the pre-prepared frozen dessert market has been phenomenal. High-quality products are readily obtainable. This situation is primarily due to advances made in baking technology, freezing techniques, and the development of new equipment for the food establishment to simplify heating and serving. In addition, consumer demands have accelerated as a result of wider assortments of interesting and appealing products. Desserts are naturally "mouth-watering" items, and if they are tasty, attractive and imaginative, they tend to generate high demand. The profit margin is excellent, far exceeding other food items.

Categories of Convenience Desserts

The following are the primary categories of convenience desserts: puddings, fruit, pastry, pies, cakes, pancakes, and frozen combinations that include ice cream, soft-serve, ice milk, sherbet, water or fruit ice, and frozen dairy confections.

Baked products include pastry, pie, cake, bread, rolls, buns and quick breads. These products are obtainable in the following forms: ready-to-serve, partially baked, ready-to-serve frozen, prepared frozen, canned prepared, and prepared mixes.

(1) *Ready-to-serve products* have been baked and are ready to be served. Breads, sweet rolls, doughnuts, pastries, and cookies are examples of these.

(2) *Partially-baked products* are "half baked." Baking must be completed on the premises before serving. Available forms are loaves of bread, rolls, and buns.

(3) *Ready-to-serve frozen products* are fully prepared products ready to serve after thawing. If desired, these products can be heated before serving. Cakes, pastries, some pies, rolls, and buns are sold in this manner.

(4) *Prepared frozen products* have not been baked prior to freezing. They require baking before serving. Breads, pies, and rolls are available in this fashion.

(5) *Canned prepared products* must be completely baked before serving. Cookies, biscuits, and rolls are in this group.

(6) *Prepared mixes* are convenient preparations containing basic ingredients

330

like flour, shortening, sugar, and leavening. Ingredients such as water, milk, or eggs may have to be added. Pie crusts, cakes, and roll mixes are obtainable in this form.

The Pre-prepared Frozen Convenience Dessert Market

The available number of pre-prepared frozen convenience desserts is infinite. The two categories that enjoy the widest popularity are pies and ice cream. Among the pies, apple continues as America's favorite, followed by cherry and blueberry. The following is a representative selection of pies available in the pre-prepared frozen classification. These are not listed in order of popularity.

apple	lemon cream
apple crumb	mince
deep dish apple, cherry and blueberry	Neopolitan cream
banana cream	peach
blueberry	pecan
boysenberry	pineapple
cherry	pumpkin
chocolate cream	raisin
coconut cream	rhubarb
coconut custard	strawberry cream
lemon meringue	strawberry

The most popular cream pie is chocolate, followed by banana, Neopolitan and lemon.

In addition a variety of tarts and turnovers are marketed. Cakes and pastries are available that provide the operator with a large selection of products. These include:

apple Danish cake
banana cake
cheese cakes, including blueberry, cherry, pineapple, strawberry and Danish
chocolate cakes, including fudge layer, nut, swirl, German and chip
devil's food cake
coconut cake
almond crunch
pound cakes, including almond and raisin
orange cake
strawberry shortcake
Danish pastries
coffee cake, such as plain, cinnamon and pecan
coffee rings, including almond and caramel pecan rolls
brownies
cream puffs
eclairs
strudel, such as cheese, apple, blueberry and pineapple

Miscellaneous Products:
cinnamon loaf
cornsticks
crepes
croissants
crumpets
French toast
muffins, like bran, blueberry and corn
pancakes
waffles

Storage Life

Freezing is an ideal method of prolonging the shelf life of most baked products. Bread, if quick frozen and held at 0°F, will remain fresh for many months. When thawed, the bread will have a freshness equivalent to that of a product held for two days at 70°F. Cakes and cookies will retain their palatability for at least 6 months at 0°F, and longer at lower temperatures. Proper thawing conditions, such as a low-moisture atmosphere, are essential to prevent rapid staling. Although almost all kinds of cakes can be frozen and thawed without notable change, the following defects as a result of prolonged storage may occur: loss of volume, abnormal softness or compressibility, crumbliness and tenderness. (Tressler, Van Arsdel and Copley 1968).

The following are examples of storage life of products held at 0°F:

angel cake, 4 mo	pound cake, 9 mo
cheese cake, 12 mo	sponge cake (egg yolk), 2 mo
chocolate cake, 6 mo	sponge cake (whole egg), 6 mo
cookies, 12 mo	turnovers, 12 mo
fruit cake, 12 mo	yellow cake, 9 mo
fruit pies, 12 mo	

Cake

The assortment of cake available to food service establishments has increased since the advent of freezing preservation. The varieties of cake were limited for restaurants located too far from large cities having commercial bakeries to provide them with interesting selections. Many feeding places were forced to install baking facilities because of the limited supply of baked products. Since most cake freezes well, this picture has changed, so that products covering a broad description are readily available. Another advantage has been an upsurge in popularity due to the larger selections and better quality. A number of commercial bakers are presently producing excellent frozen baked goods. For example, frozen baked products from the Kitchens of Sara Lee, Deerfield, Illinois and Creative Bakers, Inc., Brooklyn, N.Y. and others, are scoring a remarkably high average of consistent quality products.

In addition to the quality factor, other advantages are offered that make frozen cake goods interesting to handle. These are: the elimination of waste because of staleness, a large assortment to vary the dessert menu, and a high profit margin. Storage is easy and damage due to poor storage practices is reduced because of rigid cartons used for packing. Versatile and eye-appealing creations are possible with basic cakes, such as sponge and sheet varieties. These can be decorated, sliced and sandwiched with ice cream, garnished with different toppings (nuts, whipped cream), or made into a strawberry type of short cake.

Quality Parameters.—A number of factors are responsible for determining the quality of cakes. They are:

(1) The cake should have a uniform shape and be free of cracks and sags.

(2) The color of the cake should be uniform. A light-colored cake should have a uniform golden brown hue on all sides.

(3) The crust should be thin and tender.

(4) The bottom should show no evidence of burning.

(5) The crumb should be medium with a fine even grain. It should be moist and smooth but not tacky or soggy.

(6) Unless the type of cake calls for a dominant flavor, the flavor should be balanced with no foreign or off-traits (oily, starchy).

(7) If icing is present, it should not be separated from the cake or show any unevenness, nor should it run when thawed or pull away from the cake when cut.

(8) The top of the cake should show no discolor, which may have been caused by moisture as a result of intermittent thawing.

Handling Hints.—Unfrosted cakes can be thawed in the freezer wrapping. If a cake is frosted, it should be removed from the carton and the wrapping removed to prevent stickiness and injury to the frosting.

Unused cake should not be refrozen. It can be stored in a refrigerator for a short time.

Handling instructions provided by the processor should be read and followed.

Pies

Pies are the leading American dessert. Varieties and quality are limitless. Pies of the same name, like apple, are produced in an infinite number of versions with a wide assortment of crusts, fillings and toppings.

Pies are consumed at all hours of the day and night, at the end of a meal or as an in-between the meal snack. They are merchandised in numerous fashions, and are sold in all levels of food service establishments, including stands, vending machines, snack bars and international posh restaurants. Pies enjoy a dual role of distinction, as they are popular for festive occasions like Thanksgiving, and at other times as well. The peak amount of pie is consumed during the fall of the year. During the autumn, fruit pies are preferred to other varieties. It is almost possible to date the time of the year or the season by the kind of pie filling that is used. For instance, rhubarb is a spring pie, strawberry pie denotes early summer, cherry and berry pies are midsummer favorites, fresh apple pie appears during the late summer, and pumpkin denotes the harvest or fall season. However, with the advent of successfully frozen pies, the general assortment is available the entire year.

Types of Pies.—Double crust fruit pies are the most widely consumed. Apple is the favorite, followed by cherry and blueberry. Depending on locality, ingredients such as cinnamon, nutmeg, mace, or ginger are frequently added to enhance the flavor of the filling or crust. Cheeses like sharp or mild Cheddar are used as tasty garnishes. Ice cream and sweet sauces are also widely used. Colorful combinations of fruit fillings are used that add a festive touch to the pie menu. These combinations may consist of two, three or four fruits, including prune, apricot and plum. These pies are generally open-faced, or they may contain a latticed, criss-crossed crust, so that the color shows through. Another favorite is deep dish pie that accents the fruit. This is a bottom crust pie and is usually served hot and garnished with cheese, ice cream or a sweet sauce. Single crust products share a large segment of the market. These include custard, cheese, ice cream, meringue and chiffon pies.

Tarts or miniature pies enjoy wide acceptance. These are open faced pies made from either a flaky or pastry crust. Tarts made from pastry crusts usually contain a cream filling placed between the topping and the bottom crust. Tarts are ideal for creative touches and unique decorations. Frozen tart shells are available that can be used for novel merchandising effects.

Turnovers, which are small pies, consist of fillings completely encased in a flaky crust. Cherry and apple are popular varieties. Turnovers are produced in several shapes that include half moons, triangles or rectangles. Portion sizes are 2, 3, or 4 oz. These products may be deep-fried, oven-heated or eaten cold.

Characteristics of a Quality Pie.—A pie consists of two main sections and an optional section. The two main sections are the crust and filling. The optional section may be the compatible accompaniment in the form of garnishes, decorations, and toppings.

The ideal crust should be crisp, tender and fragile, and should not shrink during baking. It should break short and should not be pasty or soggy. Its color should be golden with mottled brown running through it. It should exhibit a clear aroma with a fresh-baked character. The taste should be clear and free from foreign flavors such as oil or burned particles.

The filling must be clear, brilliant and not viscous. It may ooze without being watery. It should not be gelatinous, gummy or stiff. The flavor of the main ingredient, if fruit, should be true and dominant, without being overpowering. The filling must also be free from foreign flavors and off-tastes.

The percentage of the main ingredient should be sufficient to fill the pie cavity when baked and to provide each portion a full and equal measure.[1]

Frozen Pies.—Frozen pies are available either fully baked or with unbaked

---

[1] The Food and Drug Administration has under consideration Standards of Identity and Quality for frozen cherry pie.

crusts. Fully baked pies need no further preparation other than thawing to room temperature before serving.

Frozen pies with unbaked crusts are excellent when prepared according to instructions provided by the processor. The filling and fruit of the frozen pies are already finished. During the baking operation, both the crust and filling have identical time cycles, so that they are finished together. The dual completion is only possible if the pies are baked from the frozen state. Conventional or convection ovens are suited for this type of baking.

The Lloyd J. Harriss Company of Saugatuck, Michigan, bakers of quality frozen pies, has provided the following information for the handling, baking and serving of these products.

(1) Cut a number of 1½ in. slits, or prick the top crust with the tines of a fork. This allows steam to escape while baking. For custard and pumpkin pies, the protective wax sheet should be removed.

(2) An aluminum cookie sheet should be placed on the lowest rack of the oven. The pies are then positioned on the metal sheet. Fruit pies are baked in a pre-heated oven at 425°F from 45 to 55 min until a golden brown color appears on the outer surface of the crust. Custards and pumpkins require 55 to 65 min.

(3) After baking, the pies should be air-cooled to room temperature before serving. For ideal refreshment, pie should never be served too hot or too cold.

(4) Berry pies will tend to boil quicker than other fruits. To overcome this problem, the pie may be baked for a shorter time and at a higher temperature (additional 25°F).

(5) Custard and pumpkin pies often require an additional 10 to 15 min baking time. This facilitates the reduction of moisture and "sets" the pie filling. If these pies are removed prior to the completion of the "setting process," the filling may "run" and poor flavor may also result.

(6) The oven should not be overloaded. This may cause a heat loss which may prevent the oven from attaining the proper baking temperature during the baking cycle. Experimentation with the oven is necessary to determine its optimum working capacity.

Pie Defects and Probable Causes.—(1) *Raw pie:* May be caused by a pie that is too cold. Pie temperature prior to baking should be zero to +5°F. Lower temperatures will result in slow heating, unless compensation is made to extend the baking cycle.

(2) *Raw or soggy bottoms:* May be caused by an oven that is too cool, insufficient bottom heat, dirty oven floor, pie bottom dough too rich, or bottom rolled too thin.

(3) *Burned pies:* May be caused by improper temperatures, usually the result of a faulty oven thermostat; or the pie was partially thawed and it cooked too rapidly.

(4) *Burned bottoms:* May be caused by excessive bottom heat of the oven or an uneven distribution of heat.

(5) *Blisters on crust:* Crust not stippled or docked and too much egg-wash.

(6) *Filling runs out during baking:* Pies were filled too much, pies were not properly sealed, oven was too cool, too much sugar in the filling, and filling was too thin.

(7) *Shrinkage of crust:* Oven too cool.

Pie and Tart Shells.—Pie and tart shells are available unbaked and frozen. They are versatile items and may be used for a base for many kinds of novel fillings. Depending on the processor's instructions, the shells require about 10 min baking in a pre-heated oven set at 400°F. Formation of a golden brown color is usually a good indication that the shell is completely baked. If a filling requires heating, the shells should be partially baked to compensate for this condition.

Pie shells are ideal for cream, pecan, cheese, custard and pumpkin fillings. Graham cracker shells are obtainable, which may also be used for cheese fillings.

Many fillings are adaptable for use in tart and pie shells. Tart shells make an excellent and attractive device to hold puddings, berries and other fruit. Pre-prepared and canned puddings like vanilla, custard, chocolate or lemon can be dressed up in a tart shell.

Vanilla pudding makes a fine combination with peach slices and raspberries, topped with ice cream or whipped cream. Chocolate pudding becomes a specialty when served in a tart shell, then topped with whole nuts and whipped cream. Custard served in a tart shell and topped with crushed pineapple is easy to prepare and tasty. Whipped products, such as prune, date, or strawberry, are attractive and novel when served in a tart shell. Possibilities are endless and most may be served as the specialty of the day. Since they are easy and quick to prepare, tart shell desserts will fit into mass volume feeding programs.

Puddings

Puddings are marketed in cans that are comparable to those which are prepared on the premises. Because of the ease in handling, reduction in waste and simplified storage, these canned desserts have gained many adherents. They are sold in 3½ to 4½-oz portion packs or in larger cans for volume food service. Technological developments in formulation and processing paved the way for high-quality canned puddings.

Canned puddings are available in all the popular varieties, such as chocolate, butterscotch, lemon, tapioca, vanilla, banana, and rice. Numerous attractive combinations are possible which lend appeal to these desserts. Special dishes should be used, such as parfait glasses, for enhancement. Garnishes like nuts, chocolate sprinkles, whipped topping, coconut, dates, sweet sauces, crushed pineapple and peaches, make interesting and tasty accompaniments.

Cakes From Mixes That Need No Baking.—The Ruxford Laboratories of Newark, New Jersey, have developed cake mixes that can be formed into quality baked products without baking. These mixes are being marketed to the food service industry under the trade name of No-Bake-Cake-Mixes. Because of their convenience and ease of preparation, these products are gaining favorable acceptance.

The mixes contain only natural ingredients to which hot water is added as the initial preparation step. One quart of hot water is added to 9 lb of the mix. The water is wire-whipped into the powder for about 1/2 min. After mixing, the composite mass is then poured into metal forms or cake pans. The mixture has a leavening system which is promptly activated by the hot water. Leavening is completed within 1/2 hr, at which time the product may be topped. Several hours of resting time is required for the cake to form into an acceptable texture. The mixes are sold in various popular flavors. The finished cake has a general shelf life of several days at room temperature (70°F).

Standards of Identity for Bakery Products and Frozen Desserts

Standards of Identity have been promulgated by the FDA for bakery and frozen desserts. Bakery products are covered in part 17 and frozen desserts in part 19.

Standards of Identity are provided for the following bakery products:

(1) Bread, white bread, and rolls, white rolls, or buns, and white buns
(2) Enriched bread and enriched rolls
(3) Milk bread and milk rolls or buns
(4) Raisin bread and raisin rolls or raisin buns
(5) Whole wheat bread, graham bread, entire wheat bread, and whole wheat rolls, graham rolls, entire wheat rolls, or whole wheat buns, graham buns, and entire wheat buns.

Standards of Identity are provided for the following frozen desserts: ice cream, frozen custard, French ice cream, French custard ice cream, ice milk, fruit sherbets, water ices, non fruit sherbets, and non fruit water ices.

Baked Products from Frozen Dough

Baked products that are produced from frozen dough and are finished on the premises have taken a prominent step forward over the last ten years. A multitude of bakery items can be easily prepared with the use of frozen dough.

Bread and rolls, over the years, have become highly abused menu items. Among the faults resulting from these improper handling practices are bread and rolls that are unappealing, soggy, doughy, underbaked, stale and sour. Numerous feeding establishments have built a fine reputation by serving interesting and appetizing assortments of baked items. Restaurants located in some American cities, such as San Francisco, Chicago, New York, Miami, New Orleans and Boston, are expected to provide quality baked products, as one way to retain their clientele. Specialty items like brioche, pecan rolls, croissants, popovers, corn sticks, salt sticks, and many kinds of breads are served as part of the daily menu. With the advent of frozen dough on a commercial scale, food service establishments were provided with the means of upgrading their bread and roll service. Small bread loaves baked on the premises and made in different sizes, shapes and styles have met with national acceptance. The consumer seems captivated with the idea of slicing his own fragrant, fresh and hot bread at the table. This concept was introduced over a decade ago by Bridgeford Foods Corporation, Anaheim, Calif.

Baking on the Premises.—Frozen yeast prepared dough baking is adaptable to all sizes of feeding establishments. Production is suitable for most fast food preparation systems. Thawing refrigerators or cabinets, convection or conventional ovens and finished product holding chests will accommodate this form of preparation.

Preparation is not complicated. However, for quality results, handling instructions provided by the processor should be followed. Generally the frozen dough should be thawed well in advance of preparation. The frozen dough is separated into individual loaves before they are placed in buttered pans. They are then allowed to thaw overnight in a refrigerator. If forced thawing is required, the frozen dough may be placed in a warm atmosphere (85° to 140°F) for a 45 to 90 min period. When thawed, the dough is placed in a proofing area or cabinet until it has risen to the desired size. Some dough may expand 3 to 4 times its original size. Proofed dough does not have to be baked immediately but may be stored in a refrigerator at 38°F for up to 12 hr. Depending on the type and condition of the oven, baking time will average 20–30 min at about 350°F.

Frozen doughs are available from which a large assortment of baked products may be prepared. The following are selected examples of these products: white, rye, Vienna, pumpernickel, and Italian style bread. Raisin, cinnamon, nut and date may be prepared from yellow bread dough. In addition, various coffee cake and Danish cake doughs may be purchased. Quick breads may be made easily and quickly from basic frozen dough. Assortments of muffins, including bran, corn, blueberry, and biscuits are examples of these products.

Crepes

Crepes were briefly discussed in Chapter 9. As convenience desserts they are gaining in popularity because they add charm and a touch of haute cuisine to a menu. These products are obtainable frozen, as dry mixes, or pre-prepared frozen. The latter require no further preparation other than heating. Crepes should not be prepared too far in advance, as they have a tendency to dry out and may become rubbery.

Many novel and creative ingredients and fillings can be served with crepes. In addition to crepe suzettes, there are crepes Jubilee. This is a glamorous and simply prepared dessert. Two or three balls of ice cream are put on the crepe, which is placed flat on a dish. A sauce, containing canned cling peach slices, dark sweet cherries, peach preserves and liqueur is spooned over the ice cream. Crepes Finlandia is another interesting dessert containing a hot lingonberry sauce and peach slices. The crepes are folded and a liqueur like Grand Marnier followed by Kirsch are spooned over the top and ignited.

CONVENIENCE BEVERAGES

All non-alcoholic hot and cold beverages can be served from some type of semi-automatic or fully automatic dispensing equipment, or directly from the original container, such as bottled sodas, milk or fruit juice. The development of dispensing equipment started prior to and after World War II. Milk and cream dispensers were designed during the early 1930's. Vending equipment, post-mix soda units, hot chocolate and tea serving units, and juice dispensers are all products of the post-war era.

The following beverages are served in most food service establishments: coffee, tea, soft drinks, ades, juices, milk and milk products, and hot chocolate. Serving equipment is available for these products in many styles, sizes and capacities. *The Food Beverage Service Handbook,* (Thorner and Herzberg 1970) provides in depth all the pertinent information concerning hot and cold beverages. Specific details are given for each beverage and their handling and service within a feeding establishment. Sanitation, quality control techniques, the effects of water on beverages, and spoilage problems are fully discussed. In this section, a brief resumé of beverage dispensing associated with fast food operations is outlined.

Coffee

A fast food service operation should not be burdened with conventional methods of coffee brewing. The development and commercial applications of freeze-dried and frozen liquid concentrated coffee, both of which can be successfully dispensed by machine, puts the brewing operation in line with other modes of quick-service techniques. Brews resulting from freeze-dried and frozen liquid concentrate coffee are uniform, and possess the quality and palatibility factors necessary to meet the taste standards of the average coffee drinker.

Many of the evils associated with conventional coffee brewing which have resulted in poor quality coffee are eliminated. Improper urn sanitation, incorrect or sloppy brewing practices, staling, and off-tastes because of prolonged holding are eliminated. Poor sanitation has led the list of factors contributing to off-tasting coffee, which was followed by poor brewing techniques.

Frozen Coffee Concentrate.—The Minute Maid Coffee System offered by the Minute Maid Division of The Coca-Cola Company has developed a novel and practical system for the brewing of coffee automatically. Feeding organizations ranging in size from a luncheonette to a large state university have found that this system is beneficial for their coffee service.

This system uses a frozen coffee concentrate that is packed in cans. A precision, trouble-free, dispenser was developed as part of the program. The dispenser is extremely flexible. It is completely self-contained, as it heats the water to the proper temperature, accurately proportions the hot water and coffee concentrate, and then mixes and dispenses the product on demand. The unit delivers a single cup or a serving bowl of coffee, as required. Another advantage is the elimination of costly and constant sanitation, as this equipment has provisions for cleaning the feedlines automatically.

    Freeze-dried Coffee.—Freeze-dried coffee properly made has all the quality characteristics of the fresh brewed product. Dispensing equipment has been developed that produces a flavorful and full-bodied brew in seconds. Figure 10.1 shows this dispenser, which is manufactured by Columware, Inc., Lynwood, California. The jar of freeze-dried coffee is placed upside down on top of the machine. The original jar acts as the reservoir. The crown of coffee beans shown in the picture is only provided for decoration. The crown is removable and acts to hide the jar of freeze-dried coffee. The unit covers about 2 sq ft of counter space, yet it has the capacity to brew up to 600 cups an hour. Provisions are made to draw the hot water for tea or other purposes. This unit is

Courtesy of Columware, Inc.

FIG. 10.1. A POSTMIX FREEZE-DRIED COFFEE DISPENSER

unique in that it has only two moving parts. It may also be used to dispense soup or tea by changing canisters. In addition it is self-cleaning, and the measure per cup of freeze-dried coffee may be adjusted as desired. A major advantage is the elimination of stale coffee, as the shelf life of freeze-dried coffee is long; the product will not deteriorate as long as it is kept air-tight.

Tea

Present methods of preparing and serving hot or iced tea are compatible with fast food service. The tea bag was originally designed to facilitate tea brewing. It is still considered adequate for fast food techniques. The iced tea dispenser (Fig. 10.2) manufactured by Columware, Inc. has been marketed for many years. If the manufacturer's instructions are followed, it will dispense a high quality product. For volume service, soluble tea may be used and prepared in

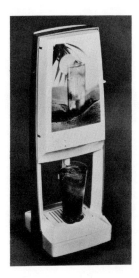

Courtesy of Columware, Inc.

FIG. 10.2. AN ICED TEA DISPENSER

quantity. These products will dissolve in cold water. For this purpose soluble tea is available in two sizes: a 3/4-oz packet will make 1 gal of tea, whereas a 6 3/4-oz jar or packet will produce 9 gal of the brew.

Fully prepared liquid teas are being marketed. These items are sweetened and may be purchased with or without lemon. They are sold as concentrated syrups and may be dispensed in post-mix dispensers, or in ready-to-drink 12 oz cans for vending machines.

Other Beverages

Other beverages, e.g., dairy drinks, juices, ades, sodas, and hot chocolate, can all be dispensed from semi-automatic or automatic equipment. Most of the equipment used for this purpose has been on the market for many years. Bever-

Courtesy of The Bastian-Blessing Company

FIG. 10.3. AN EXCELALL ROTOFLO BEVERAGE DISPENSER
FOR JUICES AND ADES

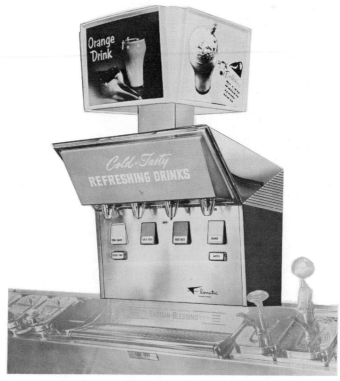

Courtesy of The Bastian-Blessing Company

FIG. 10.4. A POSTMIX SODA DISPENSER

age dispensers of one type or another can be found in nearly all food service establishments.

Dairy beverages are dispensed from bulk containers or served in individual cartons. Coffee whiteners (dairy or nondairy types) are dispensed from plunger-activated units or from portion control packets.

Dispensing of fruit and vegetable juices consists of two basic methods: premix and postmix. Premix are those methods that involve serving the juice directly from the container or mixing the ingredients prior to service, such as reconstitution of concentrates or powders into batches for volume feeding. Figure 10.3 shows a dispenser used for serving juices and ades. This is a refrigerated visual merchandiser. Units of this type are designed to maintain aeration of the product to a minimum. Excessive aeration can result in off-tasting, flat beverages.

Soft drinks, e.g., carbonated or still sodas, are dispensed as: (1) premix, which are used for: (a) bottles; (b) cans; (c) vending: cans, bottles, individual cup service; (d) still drink dispensers; (e) concentrates; (f) powders; and (2) postmix, which includes (a) in-store dispensers, vending machines, liquid

Courtesy of Columware, Inc.

FIG. 10.5. A POSTMIX HOT CHOCOLATE DISPENSER

Courtesy of Sani-Serv

FIG. 10.6. A HEAVY DUTY COUNTERTOP SHAKE MAKER

powder; and (b) fountain, draft arm dispensers. Figure 10.4 shows a postmix soda dispenser.

Hot chocolate and cocoa beverages are dispensed as follows: (1) bottled, (2) canned, (3) container, pints or quarts, and (4) batch, for volume feeding. Postmix dispensing is used for (1) automatic syrup or powder (Fig. 10.5), and (2) manual syrup or powder.

Beverages like shakes are easily dispensed from equipment shown in Fig. 10.6.

BIBLIOGRAPHY

ANON. 1970. The nicest thing that ever happened to people who make and serve coffee. The Coca-Cola Company, Atlanta, Ga.

ANON. 1971A. Cling Peach Food Service Recipes. Cling Peach Advisory Board, San Francisco, Calif.

ANON. 1971B. The Engineered Bake-off System. Despatch Oven Company, Minneapolis, Minn.

ANON. 1971C. Secrets of Perfect Pie Serving. Lloyd J. Harriss, Saugatuck, Mich.

ANON. 1971D. Canned puddings. Food Service *33*, No. 9, 29–33.

ANON. 1971E. There's big dough ahead for frozen breadstuff. Quick Frozen Foods *34*, No. 3, 72–74.

ANON. 1971F. Unusual breads are menu boosters. Hotel and Motel Management *186*, No. 5, 34–36.

BLAIR, E. C. 1970. Convenience desserts. Volume Feeding *35*, No. 3, 27–35.

DEMUS, T. A. 1969. Baking Treats Ad Infinitum. United States Department of Agriculture Yearbook, 213–225.

DESROSIER, N. W. 1970. The Technology of Food Preservation, 3rd Edition. Avi Publishing Co., Westport, Conn.

SANSTADT, H. 1971. In cake merchandising, easy does it! Cooking for Profit *40*, No. 247, 23–29.

SULTAN, W. J. 1965. Practical Baking, 2nd Edition. Avi Publishing Co., Westport, Conn.

THORNER, M. E., and HERZBERG, R. J. 1970. Food Beverage Service Handbook. Avi Publishing Co., Westport, Conn.

TRESSLER, D. K., VAN ARSDEL, W. B., and COPLEY, M. J. 1968. The Freezing Preservation of Foods, 4th Edition, Vol. 4, Avi Publishing Co., Westport, Conn.

Index